Introduction to Professional Counseling

COUNSELING AND PROFESSIONAL IDENTITY IN THE 21ST CENTURY

Richard Parsons and Naijian Zhang, Series Editors

Becoming a Skilled Counselor, Richard Parsons and Naijian Zhang

Research Methods for Counseling, Robert Wright

Group Work: An Introduction for Helping Professionals, Robert Conyne

Introduction to Professional Counseling, Varunee Faii Sangganjanavanich and Cynthia A. Reynolds

Becoming a Multiculturally Competent Counselor, Changming Duan and Chris Brown

Counseling Individuals Through the Lifespan, Daniel Wai Chung Wong, Kim Hall, Cheryl Justice, and Lucy Wong Hernandez

Career Development and Counseling: Theory and Practice in a Multicultural World, Mei Tang and Jane Goodman

Counseling Assessment and Evaluation: Fundamentals of Applied Practice, Joshua C. Watson and Brandé Flamez

Ethical Decision Making for the 21st Century Counselor, Donna S. Sheperis, Michael Kocet, and Stacy Henning

Counselor as Consultant, David Scott, Chadwick Royal, and Daniel Kissinger

Counseling Theory: Guiding Reflective Practice, Richard Parsons and Naijian Zhang

Introduction to Professional Counseling

Varunee Faii Sangganjanavanich
The University of Akron

Cynthia A. Reynolds
The University of Akron

Los Angeles | London | New Delhi
Singapore | Washington DC

Los Angeles | London | New Delhi
Singapore | Washington DC

FOR INFORMATION

SAGE Publications, Inc.
2455 Teller Road
Thousand Oaks, California 91320
E-mail: order@sagepub.com

SAGE Publications Ltd.
1 Oliver's Yard
55 City Road
London EC1Y 1SP
United Kingdom

SAGE Publications India Pvt. Ltd.
B 1/I 1 Mohan Cooperative Industrial Area
Mathura Road, New Delhi 110 044
India

SAGE Publications Asia-Pacific Pte. Ltd.
3 Church Street
#10–04 Samsung Hub
Singapore 049483

Acquisitions Editor: Kassie Graves
Editorial Assistant: Elizabeth Luizzi
Production Editor: Stephanie Palermini
Copy Editor: Cate Huisman
Typesetter: Hurix Systems Pvt. Ltd.
Proofreader: Penelope Sippel
Indexer: Kathy Paparchontis
Cover Designer: Candice Harman
Marketing Manager: Shari Countryman

Library of Congress Cataloging-in-Publication Data

Introduction to professional counseling / [edited by] Varunee Faii Sangganjanavanich, The University of Akron, Cynthia Reynolds, The University of Akron.

pages cm. – (Counseling and professional identity in the 21st century)

Includes bibliographical references and index.

ISBN 978-1-4522-4070-1 (pbk.) –
ISBN 978-1-4833-1158-6 (web pdf) 1. Counseling psychology. I. Sangganjanavanich, Varunee Faii.

BF636.6.I58 2015
361'.06—dc23

2013032287

14 15 16 17 18 10 9 8 7 6 5 4 3 2 1

Brief Contents

Detailed Contents

Editors' Preface

Introduction to the Series
Counseling and Professional Identity in the 21st Century

If you are holding this text in anticipation of starting your journey toward becoming a professional counselor, then welcome. You are about to begin a journey that will challenge, reward, and even sometimes frustrate you, but it is one that, if successful, will result in you becoming a part of an awesome, highly responsible, and extremely gratifying profession. The text you hold in your hands, *Introduction to Professional Counseling,* is more than a graduate text book. It is an encapsulation of what it is to be a counselor and to be part of the profession of counseling. *Introduction to Professional Counseling* not only paints a picture of the richness of our profession and the opportunities for those within it, but it does so in a way that engages your heart as well as your head.

As is obvious, one text, one learning experience, will not be sufficient for the successful formation of your professional identity and practice. Becoming and being a counselor will be a lifelong process—a process that we hope to facilitate through the presentation of this text and the creation of our series: *Counseling and Professional Identity in the 21st Century.*

Counseling and Professional Identity in the 21st Century is a new, fresh, and pedagogically sound series of texts targeting counselors in training. This series is *not* simply a compilation of isolated books matching those that are already in the market. Rather each book, with its targeted knowledge and skills, will be presented as but a part of a larger whole. The focus and content of each text serves as a single lens through which counselors can view their clients, engage in their practice, and articulate their own professional identity.

Counseling and Professional Identity in the 21st Century is unique not just in the fact that it packages a series of traditional texts, but that it provides an *integrated*

Table EP.1 CACREP 2009 Standards Addressed

	1. PROFESSIONAL ORIENTATION AND ETHICAL PRACTICE	5. HELPING RELATIONSHIPS	7. ASSESSMENT	8. RESEARCH AND PROGRAM
Chapter 1		5a 5b 5g		
Chapter 2				
Chapter 3		5b 5c		
Chapter 4		5c		
Chapter 5		5c		
Chapter 6		5c 5d		8e
Chapter 7		5g	7b	
Chapter 8	1a 1d 1e	5g		8e
Chapter 9	1a 1b 1f 1g 1h 1i	5a 5c 5d 5g		
Chapter 10		5b 5c 5d		
Chapter 11		5b 5c 5d		
Chapter 12		5b 5c 5d		

curriculum targeting the formation of the readers' professional identity and efficient, ethical practice. Each book within the series is structured to facilitate the ongoing professional formation of the reader. The materials found within each text are organized in order to move readers to higher levels of cognitive, affective, and psychomotor functioning, resulting in their assimilation of the materials presented into both their professional identity and their approach to professional practice. While each text targets a specific set of core competencies (cognates and skills)—competencies identified by the Council for Accreditation of Counseling & Related Educational Programs (CACREP) as essential to the practice of counseling (see Table EP-1), each book in the series will emphasize one of the following:

a. the assimilation of concepts and constructs provided across the texts found within the series, thus fostering the reader's ongoing development as a competent professional;

b. the blending of contemporary theory with current research and empirical support;

c. a focus on the development of procedural knowledge, with each text employing case illustrations and guided practice exercises to facilitate the reader's ability to translate the theory and research discussed into professional decision making and application;

d. the emphasis on the need for and means of demonstrating accountability; and

e. the fostering of the reader's professional identity and with it the assimilation of the ethics and standards of practice guiding the counseling profession.

We are proud to have served as coeditors of this series, feeling sure that each book within it will serve as a significant resource to you and your development as a professional counselor. Let your journey begin!

Richard Parsons, PhD

Naijian Zhang, PhD

Chapter 1

Overview of Professional Counseling

Varunee Faii Sangganjanavanich

Welcome to professional counseling! You have already begun your journey to become a professional counselor. You may feel upbeat in beginning your exciting journey that encompasses your personal and professional goals. You may have dreams and fantasies about your life a few years from now working as a professional counselor in a desirable work setting. What do you hope to see when looking back at your experience during your graduate training? Some of us who are professional counselors remember how overwhelming it was to learn about the profession, but we found that a comprehensive introduction to professional counseling was critical and worthwhile.

Throughout your graduate program in counseling, you will gain plenty of information and experience intended to prepare you to function as a professional counselor. In this chapter, you will be introduced to professional counseling, including its definition and identity. You will learn about the importance of self of the counselor, the therapeutic relationship, and major theoretical approaches in the counseling context. You will also learn about the counseling process and basic skills used in counseling. Reflection exercises and case illustrations will enhance your learning about professional counseling, professional identity, and therapeutic relationship as well as counseling process.

You will find that this chapter provides a brief overview of professional counseling. Later in this textbook, you will be able to obtain more comprehensive information regarding the history of the counseling profession (Chapter 2), counseling professional associations and accrediting agencies (Chapter 10), and credentials of professional counselors (Chapter 11). The information will further facilitate your understanding of the roots, development, and current issues of the counseling profession from macro-level perspectives (e.g., organizations, state laws, policies) and will help strengthen your professional counselor identity. In addition, to start paving your path to become a professional counselor, you can start exploring roles and functions of professional counselors (Chapter 3) and begin to think about your career options, such as types of professional counselors and settings in which they work (Chapter 4). In the appendix, you will also find ways to navigate your graduate program in counseling and make your training experience worthwhile. This is the time to begin your adventurous journey!

LEARNING OBJECTIVES

After reading the information and engaging in the reflection exercises provided in this chapter, you will be able to

1. Describe the professional counseling definition and professional identity of counselors,

2. Identify the characteristics of counselors and counselors in the therapeutic relationship and process, and

3. Discuss major counseling theoretical approaches.

PROFESSIONAL COUNSELING

Many disciplines, whether closely related to the counseling profession (e.g., social work) or not (e.g., finance, nutrition and dietetics), utilize *counseling* to describe the nature of their work. At times, the utilization of this term can be confusing to the general public and consumers. It is a guarantee that once in your lifetime as a professional counselor, you will be asked, "What is counseling?" You may also be asked, "Is counseling the same as psychotherapy?" Do you have an idea how to respond to these questions and to describe *professional counseling?*

There are ongoing debates about the similarities and differences between counseling and psychotherapy. You may find that many counseling scholars and counselors use both terms interchangeably. Historically, *psychotherapy* was differentiated as a form of helping that focused on serious problems of an intrapsychic nature with treatment delivered by a trained professional (Frank, 1988).

Traditionally, professionals have differentiated between the two terms using the following criteria:

- Length of treatment (psychotherapy is long term; counseling is short term),
- Seriousness of presenting issues (psychotherapy is for more serious issues; counseling is for less serious issues),
- Physical location of treatment (psychotherapy is offered in an inpatient setting; counseling is offered in an outpatient setting),
- Focus of treatment (psychotherapy focuses on past issues; counseling focuses on present issues),
- Type of presenting issues (psychotherapy is for long-term personality disorders—mental illness; counseling is for developmental issues of everyday existence—mental health), and
- Outcomes (psychotherapy offers insight; counseling facilitates action).

In practice, these historic and traditional differences have blurred and are no longer justified. As a result, counseling practitioners and consumers often use both terms interchangeably. However, as the practice of professional counseling has become an identifiable profession with educational requirements, training standards, an ethical code, and codification in state legislation and regulations, professional counseling has become a well-defined field with the number of licensed professionals surpassing numbers of practitioners of both psychology and social work (US Department of Labor, 2012).

Definition

What is counseling? Why do we need to know its definition? Professional counseling has an evolving definition. Over a decade ago, the American Counseling Association (ACA) the primary association in the United States representing professional counselors, defined professional counseling as "the application of mental health, psychological, or human development principles, through cognitive, affective, behavioral, or systemic interventions, strategies that address wellness, personal growth, or career development, as well as pathology" (Gladding, 2004, p. 6).

More recently, ACA established a task force, "20/20: A Vision for the Future of Counseling," to reconceptualize the definition of professional counseling. Currently, *professional counselor* refers to "a professional relationship that empowers diverse individuals, families, and groups to accomplish mental health, wellness, education, and career goals" (ACA, 2010). This definition simplifies the nature of the counseling relationship, roles of professional counselors, consumers of professional counseling services, and practicing areas of professional counselors.

Counseling: A Unified Profession

Vision 20/20 was a task force developed by ACA leaders (Kaplan & Gladding, 2011) to strengthen the profession through a clearer mission statement for professional advocacy nationally and in statehouses around the country in a time of diminishing resources. Thirty-two organizations participated in the 20/20 process, including ACA divisions, regions, and interest groups, but not all 32 had voting delegates in attendance. Based on the recommendation of the 20/20 taskforce, Kaplan and Gladding (2011) described seven areas that are critical to promote the mission of professional counseling:

- Strengthening identity
- Presenting ourselves as one profession
- Improving public perception/recognition and advocating for professional issues

---

Exercise 1.1

QUESTIONS TO PONDER

Directions: Answer questions below. If you would like, you may definitely discuss your answers with your peers.

First, let's write down your answer to the following questions:

1. What will be the future definition of professional counseling in the next 10 years?

2. What specialty areas of practice are yet to emerge?

3. How will future changes affect the professional identity of counselors?

Next, once you have pondered some answers, let's begin thinking about the following:

4. What does it mean to be a professional counselor?

5. What are common attributes of professional counselors?

6. How does this identity impact you as a professional counselor at the local, state, and federal level?

- Creating licensure portability
- Expanding and promoting the research base of professional counseling
- Focusing on students and prospective students
- Promoting client welfare and advocacy (p. 369)

With the evolution of professional counseling definitions over 30 years, the definition of professional counseling will likely shift in the future. You, as a professional counselor, will witness the next definition as part of advocating for a unified profession and diverse specialties. Later in this textbook, in Chapter 12, you will learn more about the importance of advocacy for professional counseling and how it directly and indirectly impacts you and your work as a professional counselor.

The definition of professional counseling is evolving. Over the past decade, the definition has evolved from focusing on an individual's development and mental health issues to focusing on an individual's empowerment and wellness. Although its definition has changed over time, one thing still remains significant in the professional counseling relationship—a counselor. In the next section, you will be introduced to the importance of self of the counselor in the therapeutic context.

SELF OF THE COUNSELOR

The counselor is an instrument in the therapeutic process. Many prominent counseling theorists (e.g., Virginia Satir, Carl Rogers) emphasized the importance of self of the counselor. Satir (1987) stated, "Therapy is a deeply intimate and vulnerable experience, requiring sensitivity to one's own state of being as well as to that of the other. It is the meeting of the deepest self of the therapist with the deepest self of the patient or client" (p. 17). Because the self of the counselor is believed to be a vital part of promoting the client's optimal growth and development, Rogers (1961) suggested that, for therapy to be effective, the counselor needs to provide three conditions of growth: unconditional positive regard, congruence, and empathy with the client. Building on Rogers's conditions of growth, recent research studies found that, in order to achieve favorable therapeutic outcome, counselors should be empathic, warm, supportive, and hopeful when working with their clients (Lambert & Barley, 2001). These characteristics of counselors allow clients to feel understood, accepted, empowered, and encouraged. Gladding (2004) further recommended that "counselors should possess personal qualities of maturity, empathy, and warmth" (p. 34) in order to help clients to feel comfortable and to allow clients to share their stories without feeling judged by the counselor. However, you may have heard a story about or may have even experienced an ineffective counselor who does not seem to listen to the client and often expresses anger or frustration toward her or his client. This situation can emerge for various reasons, including a lack of understanding of counseling and its process, poor training, or life stressors on the counselor. Those reasons, except personality, are likely to be corrected and improved via education, training, and supervision.

In contrast, if the counselor expresses anger or frustration toward her client caused by personality issues (e.g., tantrums, egocentricity) or negative motivations (e.g., loneliness, assertion of power and control) of the counselor, this issue needs to be further examined. The personhood of counselors is one of the most essential factors for facilitating the client's growth and development; therefore, self-examination and reflection are indeed important to the development and growth of counselors. Self-examination and reflection can facilitate the counselors' understanding of their motivations, desires, and actions related to becoming professional counselors. To help you get started on your self-reflection as a professional counselor, Exercise 1.2 provides questions that may stimulate your thoughts, feelings, and self-dialogue about becoming a professional counselor.

Exercise 1.2

MY MOTIVATION TO BECOME A COUNSELOR

Directions: Carefully reflect upon and honestly complete the statements below about your motivation(s) to become a professional counselor. If you would like, you may definitely discuss your answers with your loved ones, friends, peers, instructors, and/ or supervisors.

1. I have known that I wanted to be a counselor since_____.

2. I would like to be a counselor because I want to_____.

3. Being a counselor gives me (a)_____,
   (b) _____, and (c)_____.

4. My family, friends, or loved ones agree that I should pursue a career as a counselor, because they see_____ in me.

5. If I can't be a counselor, I would _____ because _____.

6. When I face life's difficulties, I tend to blame_____ because _____.

7. If I could choose clients, I would definitely choose to work with people who (a)_____, (b)_____, and (c)_____.

8. Following up on #7, I like working with people who have these characteristics because_____.

9. When I become a counselor, my clients will describe me as (a)_____, (b)_____, and (c)_____.

In addition to examining your thoughts and reflecting on your feelings associated with becoming a professional counselor, a reflection on the self of the counselor involves the examination of your values and beliefs. Personal beliefs and values play an important role in the work of professional counselors with clients. For example, you may find it difficult to work with clients who are unmotivated and less ambitious, because these characteristics conflict with your personal belief system that people should be motivated, high achieving, and highly ambitious. It is essential that you examine and confront your personal motivations, beliefs, and values in order to be an effective counselor who is able to recognize and filter your personal motivations, beliefs, and values when working with clients who are different from you. In the next section, you will learn about the therapeutic relationship and how important your role is as a professional counselor in the therapeutic context.

THE THERAPEUTIC RELATIONSHIP

You, by now, have grasped how important it is for professional counselors to be aware of self and their motivations in entering the counseling profession as well as their personal values and beliefs. This awareness is important, because professional counselors use themselves as a *therapeutic tool* to help their clients achieve optimal growth and well-being. In this section, you will learn about the therapeutic factors, process, and necessary skills in counseling.

As mentioned earlier, modern research studies (e.g., Lambert & Barley, 2001) have suggested that counselors should possess the four characteristics: empathy, warmth, supportiveness, and hope, in order to facilitate favorable therapeutic outcomes. These four characteristics contribute to the development of a collaborative therapeutic relationship in which the client and counselor work together to facilitate changes in the client. Needless to say, such a relationship occurs when both parties, the client and counselor, are in agreement on how counseling should be. It is important, however, to note that counselors are responsible for initiating a warm and accepting therapeutic environment that allows the clients to be willing to confront their issues, assume responsibilities, and ultimately reach resolutions to their problems.

Therapeutic Factors

Regardless of the theoretical approaches employed, professional counselors are required to build a collaborative therapeutic relationship with clients in order to facilitate the clients' self-exploration and to help them achieve their optimal well-being. Frank and Frank (1991) described common factors as active ingredients or core elements that are infused in every therapeutic approach. Lambert (1992) identified those common factors as extratherapeutic factors (client's factors), therapeutic relationship factors, hope and expectancy, and therapeutic models and techniques. Extratherapeutic factors refer to the client's factors, such as willingness to change. Therapeutic relationship factors refer to the characteristics of the counselor such as warmth, empathy, and acceptance. Hope and expectancy refer to the client's perception that her or his presenting issues will be alleviated or that therapy will have an even better outcome. Therapeutic models and techniques refer to theoretical approaches and strategies that counselors employ in treatment and intervention. According to reviews of their outcome studies in counseling and psychotherapy, Lambert and Barley (2001) concluded that these common factors (i.e., characteristics of the counselor, nature of the therapeutic relationship) accounted for 30% of a client's overall improvement in treatment.

As mentioned in earlier sections, professional counselors and clients play an important role in the therapeutic process and outcome. You now understand the importance of professional counselors possessing warmth, empathy, and acceptance in order to develop a meaningful therapeutic relationship and to facilitate change in their clients. Professional counselors need to be able to show the clients these qualities throughout the therapeutic process.

Therapeutic Process

Counselors in training often find themselves nervous or anxious when they first see the clients. Questions such as "What should I do in the counseling room?" "What do I do first?" or "Can I take my lecture notes with me in the room so I know what to do?" generally come up during their first clinical experience. This need-to-know behavior is considered normal, as the counselor needs to understand the stages of the counseling process and how they unfold. Because counseling is a combination of art and science, the therapeutic process cannot be *prescribed* as a step-by-step model, as it largely depends on the theoretical approaches and work settings of the counselor. Nonetheless, there are common stages of the counseling process that provide you a framework when working with clients regardless of your theoretical orientation or work settings. Six stages in the counseling process include establishing the relationship, assessment, treatment planning, intervention, evaluation, and termination.

Stage I: Establishing the relationship

As previously mentioned, the relationship is central in the counseling process and is an essential factor that leads to successful therapeutic outcomes. You can imagine how difficult it must be to share very personal details about or undesirable qualities of yourself to a complete stranger. All human beings, including your clients, want to feel respected and accepted, although one knows that her or his actions are not exactly acceptable (e.g., stealing, having an affair). Counseling is a process in which clients can discuss those thoughts and feelings with the counselor, who genuinely accepts them just as they are and cares about their well-being. Therefore, counselors should create an inviting therapeutic environment that invites the clients to share their struggles and suffering without feeling judged. To create such an environment, counselors need to demonstrate their warmth, acceptance, and empathy to their clients. Later in this chapter, you will learn how professional counselors can create this welcoming environment by using counseling skills.

Stage II: Assessment

The purpose of the assessment, sometimes called the initial interview or intake assessment, is to evaluate the relevant factors that contribute to the client's presenting issues (Corey & Corey, 2007) such as interpersonal relationships, financial situations, medical conditions, and family history. The counselors may conduct an initial assessment based on their theoretical orientation or work protocols (e.g., asking the client's history of substance use in an addictions counseling facility), which generally inform the focus of the assessment (e.g., past versus present conditions). Professional counselors utilize many forms of assessment, including having an informal conversation with the client, using a set of structured questions, conducting a behavioral observation to determine the client's behavioral and emotional state, and using empirically validated assessments or instruments to assess behavioral and emotional issues of the client. Often, in clinical mental health settings (e.g., hospital, behavioral health clinic), professional counselors are required to diagnose the client with a form of mental disorder by using standardized diagnostic criteria (e.g., the *Diagnostic and Statistical Manual of Mental Disorders,* or DSM). The diagnosis then serves as a starting point for the treatment, as it informs the counselor about the nature of the disorder and its symptoms (e.g., development, progression) and treatment planning (e.g., intervention strategies, amount of time and resources involved).

Stage III: Treatment planning

The treatment planning stage is a collaborative effort between the client and the counselor to generate therapeutic goals and ways to achieve them. It is important that clients be actively involved in treatment planning, because they are the ones who will carry out the treatment plan. When planning the treatment with a client, professional counselors should consider the following factors. First, treatment plan should be tailored to the client's unique needs and presenting issues (e.g., not every client who presents with depressive symptoms will have the same goals, interventions, and amount of time spent in counseling). Second, the treatment plan should reflect optimistic, realistic, and attainable goals that the client is able to achieve. Third, the plan should be concrete and measureable (e.g., behaviorally specific actions) in order to determine whether treatment goals have been accomplished at the end of counseling. Last, the plan should be flexible, so that the counselor and client can adjust or modify it as needed.

Stage IV: Intervention

Professional counselors often use therapeutic interventions (often called techniques) that derive from their theoretical orientation or model in counseling. Therapeutic interventions align not only with the counselor's theoretical approach but also with the treatment goals. That is, professional counselors use interventions to help clients accomplish set goals (e.g., increase self-esteem, decrease depressed mood) that promote their mental health and well-being. Interventions are used to help clients gain insight or take action. While insight presents some value, actions are important to clients, as actions facilitate changes within and outside of the therapeutic context (Corey & Corey, 2007). Considering the use of therapeutic interventions, it is important that professional counselors utilize interventions that are known or suggested, based on research and/or literature, to be effective with the client's presenting issues to ensure ethical practice (ACA, 2005).

Stage V: Evaluation

Once they have implemented therapeutic interventions, professional counselors are responsible for evaluating the therapeutic process and outcomes to determine whether those interventions served the treatment goals. Methods of evaluation include formative and summative evaluation. Formative evaluation refers to an evaluative method that occurs throughout counseling in order to periodically assess the client's progress toward therapeutic goals. Summative evaluation, on the other hand, refers to an evaluative method that occurs toward the end of the counseling process to determine whether the therapeutic goals have been accomplished. Formative evaluation has its focus on the counseling process, whereas summative evaluation has its focus on the counseling outcome (Dougherty, 2008). Regardless of the method of evaluation, there are many strategies that professional counselors can utilize to evaluate the therapeutic process and outcome, including having informal conversations with clients to assess their perceptions of change, observing behavioral and emotional changes in clients, and using empirically validated assessments or instruments to quantify changes that occurred while clients were in counseling. It is important for you to understand that professional counselors can utilize more than one evaluation method as appropriate in order to have a better picture and more well-rounded perspective on the therapeutic process and outcome, which ultimately inform adjustment or improvement in the counseling process and, often, the counselors themselves.

Stage VI: Termination

Once the client achieves a satisfactory therapeutic outcome, it is time for termination, where the client can generalize what she or he learned in counseling to other life contexts such as family, community, and work. Ideally, termination happens when the counselor and the client mutually agree that the client has achieved the treatment goals, and it provides a sense of closure for both parties. Professional counselors need to prepare clients for termination by fostering their independence, encouraging them to take charge of their own lives, helping them identify problems they have overcome throughout the counseling process, helping them plan for future situations and actions, and helping them setting up long-term goals. To help you better understand the counseling process, Case Illustration 1.1 provides you an example of how professional counselors work through the six stages of the counseling process.

Throughout the therapeutic process, professional counselors work collaboratively with clients to achieve therapeutic goals. As you can imagine, achieving therapeutic goals is not an easy process for either the client or the counselor. Many believe that goal achievement is possible when the client and counselor are able to work collaboratively with each other to achieve the same goals and have a strong *therapeutic alliance,* which will be described in the next section.

CASE ILLUSTRATION 1.1

SIX STAGES OF THE COUNSELING PROCESS

Directions: The case illustration below describes six stages in the counseling process, including establishing the relationship, assessment, treatment planning, intervention, evaluation, and termination.

Aaron was referred to you, a professional counselor, due to social phobia (a form of anxiety disorder characterized by extreme shyness and heightened self-consciousness in particular social situations).

Stage I: Establishing the relationship.

Aaron presents in the first counseling session with little to no verbal and eye contact. Aaron admits to you that "it is really embarrassing to me that I can't even talk to you. I know it is silly, but I'm so scared to talk to you." You provide many empathetic responses to Aaron and reassure him that counseling is a place for him to discuss his concerns and generate possibilities. You tell Aaron that you admire his courage in recognizing the issue and coming to counseling. At the end of the initial session, you observe that Aaron seems more relaxed, and he starts to make more eye contact when speaking to you.

Stage II: Assessment

Aaron notes that he blushes when knowing he is about to enter social situations (e.g., going to a graduation party). Aaron also expresses that he feels nausea when he starts to feel anxious. Aaron reports that he has difficulty making friends at school. After asking a series of structured questions to determine the severity of his symptoms by using the DSM, you also administer a standardized social anxiety scale to Aaron. His scores demonstrate high level of anxiety.

Stage III: Treatment Planning

You and Aaron establish treatment goals together. Goals include decreasing anxiety-related symptoms in social situations, and increasing social skills. Both you and Aaron believe these goals are realistic and attainable, and Aaron is willing to commit to them.

Stage IV: Intervention

You introduce Aaron to multiple forms of relaxation techniques; including breathing exercises, meditation, and stress management; suggested by several research studies to be effective methods in dealing with anxiety disorders, including social phobia (social anxiety). You also utilize role-playing, a therapeutic technique that is specific to treating social anxiety, to help Aaron practice his social skills and gain comfort when relating to others.

Stage V: Evaluation

At the midpoint of the counseling process, you ask Aaron for his input regarding the relaxation techniques and role-playing that you have utilized. Aaron mentions that he feels more comfortable utilizing those skills in the counseling session but is not yet ready to try them out with others in actual social situations. You and Aaron then readjust the length of counseling and integrate other interventions to help Aaron feel more comfortable in actual social situations. Toward the end of the counseling process, you again administer the same standardized social anxiety test to Aaron in order to compare the results with his scores from when he first entered counseling. His recent scores demonstrate a mild level of anxiety. In addition, Aaron reports that he is able to enter a party and talk to people without blushing or feeling nauseous, although he reports that making eye contact is still somewhat difficult for him.

Stage VI: Termination

You and Aaron agree that the treatment goals have been accomplished. You explore Aaron's perceptions of counseling and the things he learned along the way. Aaron states he feels prepared for social situations and is able to relate to others more than he could on his first day in counseling. Aaron tells you his future plans for how he would like to further improve himself.

Therapeutic Alliance

Therapeutic alliance, often called working alliance, is defined as "a collaborative process whereby both client and therapist agree on shared therapeutic goals; collaborate on tasks designed to bring about successful outcomes; and establish a relationship based on trust, acceptance, and competence" (Teyber, 2006, p. 43). Therapeutic alliance comprises three important components of the relationship: counseling relationship, collaborative goals, and trust, which can bring about changes and help clients to achieve their goals. Needless to say, therapeutic alliance is critical to the treatment outcome. When the client and counselor have a bond, shared agenda, and goal, the client is likely to reach her or his goal (Gelso & Carter, 1994). This collaborative relationship not only facilitates change during the counseling session and by the end of the treatment also helps clients feel empowered with a sense of confidence in their ability to cope with their future issues.

You may wonder how you, as a professional counselor, can create a warm, accepting, and supportive therapeutic environment and relationship as well as build a strong therapeutic alliance with your clients throughout the counseling process. As you move further through your graduate training in counseling, you will learn the necessary skills that professional counselors use to build a therapeutic relationship with clients, to facilitate the counseling process, and to foster a working alliance. As a part of the requirements of counselor training and preparation, you will be required to practice and implement these skills during your clinical training— practicum and internship—where you will be spending a majority of your time working with actual clients under faculty supervision. For the purpose of this chapter, you will be introduced to the basic counseling skills, called *microskills*.

Microskills

Microskills are the foundational skills of effective helping relationships. Professional counselors employ these skills to create the necessary conditions from which positive changes can occur. Through empathic understanding in a non-judgmental, accepting, and safe environment, individuals can grow and change in a positive direction. To create such a therapeutic environment, professional counselors are trained to appropriately use their microskills when working with clients. Microskills include the following:

- Attending—communicate to the client that you are attending to her story through nonverbal (e.g., head nodding, eye contact) and verbal (e.g., uh-huh, yes) acknowledgment.
- Listening—pay attention to the client's story to accurately capture his thoughts and emotions.
- Silence—pause after the client's statement to help her elaborate more on the story and/or to provide a brief moment for the client to reflect on her story.
- Restatement—rephrase the client's primary statement or response to let him know that you are listening and paying attention.
- Reflection of feelings—reflect the expression, emotions, and/or feelings associated with a particular event or story that the client tells you.
- Summarizing—capture the content (both thoughts and emotions) or identify themes or patterns associated with the client's story in order to keep the therapeutic conversation focused and to promote clarification.
- Probing—ask open-ended questions to facilitate the client's understanding and exploration of her story.

To help you better grasp how professional counselors utilize microskills in the counseling sessions, you can engage in the following activity. Case Illustration 1.2 contains what the client, Tamika, says to a counselor, you, during the first session.

CASE ILLUSTRATION 1.2

TAMIKA

Directions: Please read the client's story below, and practice using microskills (attending, listening, restatement, reflection of feelings, summarizing, and probing).

Tamika was referred to counseling due to the symptoms of depression. During the first session, Tamika told you she felt depressed all the time. Tamika mentioned she could not sleep, would wake up in the middle of the night to cry, and could not eat very much. As a result of that, Tamika had a hard time waking up in the morning to go to work. Tamika also noted that she was no longer able to enjoy things she used to like, such as exercising and going out with a group of friends.

Tamika told you that these symptoms began when she learned that her husband had an affair. Tamika said she was shocked, because her husband was very close to her and her children. Tamika expressed, "I had no idea he was having an affair. It never occurred to me that my husband, my one and only love, would do something like this to me." Concerning her depressive symptoms, Tamika stated, "I am so afraid that I have to feel like this for the rest of my life."

Once you read and practice using microskills in Case Illustration 1.2, you can look at Table 1.1 which provides a summary and examples of microskills. So, let's practice!

It is important to understand that microskills do not pertain to a specific counseling theoretical approach. Rather, microskills are meant for counselors, regardless of their theoretical orientation, to use as foundational skills to facilitate the counseling process and to foster the therapeutic relationship with the clients. Although counseling researchers have suggested that common factors such as empathy and a therapeutic relationship are important (Lambert, 1992, says they account for 30% of treatment effectiveness), in reality, professional counselors implement theoretical frameworks as their approaches to treatment and intervention (which Lambert described as accounting for 15% of treatment effectiveness). As a part of your counseling training, you will be introduced to theoretical frameworks and philosophies that guide the work of professional counselors. In the next section, you will learn major counseling theoretical approaches that professional counselors implement when working with clients.

Table 1.1 Microskills

Microskills	Description	Example
Attending	Communicate to the client that you are attending to her story through nonverbal and verbal acknowledgment.	Nonverbal (e.g., head nodding, eye contact) and verbal (e.g., uh-huh, yes) acknowledgment.
Listening	Pay attention to the client's story to accurately capture his thoughts and emotions.	Indicate that you understand that the client's experience (e.g., symptoms of depression) is associated with a recent situation (e.g., husband has an affair).
Silence	Pause after the client's statement to help her elaborate more on the story and/or to provide a brief moment for the client to reflect on her story.	Use silence after the client mentions her feelings of hurt and betrayal.
Restatement	Rephrase the client's primary statement or response to let him know that you are listening and paying attention.	"You said it was difficult for you to get up and go to work everyday."
Reflection of feelings	Reflect the expression, emotions, and/or feelings associated with the particular event or story that the client tells you.	"You feel hurt and betrayed when you learn that your husband is having an affair."
Summarizing	Capture the content (both thoughts and emotions) or identify themes or patterns associated with the client's story in order to keep the therapeutic conversation focused and to promote clarification.	"You said that you felt depressed and betrayed when you found out about his recent affair. It is hard for you to get up in the morning, and you do not find yourself enjoying your favorite activities. As you mentioned, you did not see this coming and fear that these feelings will last forever."
Probing	Ask open-ended questions to facilitate the client's understanding and exploration of the story.	"How do these symptoms of depression and feelings of hopelessness affect your life?"

THEORETICAL APPROACHES

Why do we need theory when working with clients? Can we work with clients without using any theory? These are two important questions to answer. Professional counselors use theoretical approaches as a guiding framework when working with clients. Your theoretical orientation serves as your compass that helps you navigate therapeutic directions, including case conceptualization, treatment plans, and interventions. Without your compass, you and your clients may feel that counseling lacks direction, and it may be difficult for your clients to achieve therapeutic goals.

The theoretical approaches of professional counseling have included a number of important historic movements within the psychology and mental health fields, including the psychodynamic, humanistic–existential, behavioral, and multicultural movements. Each has made a critical contribution to what you now think of as professional counseling. Each theoretical approach has a different focus, such as events (e.g., past, present, future), interactions (e.g., intrapsychic or interpsychic), or goals (e.g., insight or action). The different focus of each theory makes it unique and distinct it from others.

Just as you will learn therapeutic skills in your counseling training, you will learn a great deal regarding different therapeutic approaches. In this chapter, a brief summary of major theoretical approaches used in counseling is presented to you in order to provide a basic understanding and main focus of different approaches. You will also be provided with ways that you can use to begin to find your theoretical orientation.

Psychodynamic Approach

The psychodynamic approach is based on the work of world-renowned medically trained physicians—Sigmund Freud (1856–1939), an Austrian neurologist; Carl Gustav Jung (1875–1961), a Swiss psychiatrist; Alfred Adler (1870–1937), an Austrian physician trained in ophthalmology; and many others (e.g., Karen Horney, Anna Freud). Freud is credited with being the father of psychodynamic therapy, and he developed the concepts of the unconscious mind, libido, transference, and defense mechanisms. Freud created *talk therapy,* or psychoanalysis, a method for treating mental illness via dialogues between the client and psychoanalyst. Freud had his clients spend a great amount of time in therapy to examine and analyze their childhood experiences, because he believed these experiences shape the client's personality and are linked to the client's presenting issues.

Similar to Freud, Jung believed in the unconscious mind and psychoanalysis as a mean to access the unconscious—unexamined psychological materials. Jung and Freud were contemporaries and worked together for six years (1907–1913). They, however, split over the role of the unconscious, libido, and religion. Unlike Freud, Jung believed that spirituality played an important role in one's personality development, and not every human being was motivated by sex drive. Jung invented the concepts of extraversion and introversion, archetypes, and the collective unconscious, which are important concepts that have informed the practice of counseling. The popular personality inventory, the Myers-Briggs Type Indicator, was developed based on his theory of personality types.

Alfred Adler was also a contemporary of Freud and Jung and was one of the original five members who founded the Wednesday Psychological Society, so called because this group of prominent physicians met each Wednesday in Vienna (Freud, Adler, Wilhelm Stekel, Max Kahane, and Rudolf Reitler) (Rose, 1998). Adler developed a new model of psychotherapy—individual psychology—based on psychodynamic concepts proposed by Freud. Adler was opposed to negative views of human beings. He believed that family constellation, internal logic, and social engagement influence the personality development of individuals. His contributions have included an understanding of the importance of family unit/environment as well as one's perception of self and the social interests that shape one's personality development. His theory provided a shift from a purely psychodynamic psychotherapy (i.e., examining one's intrapsychic process) to more humanistic psychotherapy (i.e., exploring one's interpersonal process).

Humanistic–Existential Approach

Unlike the psychodynamic approach, the humanistic approach focuses on the relationship between the client and counselor. After being trained in psychoanalysis, humanistic–existential theorists are opposed to pessimistic ideas and negative views of human beings. They believe that individuals are self-directed and strive toward positive direction, self-actualization, and integration. Humanist–existentialist therapists believe that there is an inborn tendency for individuals to reach their full human potential if they are provided an environment that is conducive to such growth that includes empathy and a caring, nonjudgmental attitude. They take a phenomenological perspective that stresses the subjective experience of the client and emphasizes the fact that every human being is unique. To facilitate this self-directed path of human beings, counselors need to provide an accepting, safe, and meaningful therapeutic experience.

The most important figure in the humanistic–existential approach was Carl Rogers (1902–1987), an American psychologist. His person-centered therapy (originally nondirective or client-centered therapy) was instrumental in shaping the way that professional counseling is practiced today. His contributions included the concept of unconditional positive regard, empathy, and congruence or genuineness—necessary conditions for the therapy and counselor to have. In 1987, he was nominated for the Nobel Peace Prize for his work to bring government leaders from all over the world together in encounter groups to foster communication between people of differing political beliefs who were in conflict with each other.

Similar to Rogers, Rollo May (1909–1994) and Viktor Frankl (1905–1997) believed that the therapeutic relationship between the client and counselor is central. May and Frankl also considered the significance of how individuals make meaning in their lives. They, along with Irvin Yalom (1931–present), a contemporary existential theorist, focused their attention on the client's anxiety toward freedom, isolation, meaning, and death. It is important to note that humanistic–existential counselors do not try to *fix* or change the client's feelings but instead try to help clients make meaning out of their lives. These counselors facilitate movement to what is usually called *self-actualization* of their human potential.

CASE ILLUSTRATION 1.3

JENNIFER

Directions: Please read the client information, answer the following questions, and discuss your answer with a small group of your peers.

Client Information

Jennifer is a 40-year-old, stay-at-home mother who has four children. Jennifer has been married to her husband, who provides an upper-class lifestyle for her, for 10 years. Her husband has a nice job that brings home a lot of income, but his job requires him to be away a couple of days a week. The couple owns multiple properties and lives in a nice neighborhood. Jennifer spends a lot of time and effort building a perfect family, and she makes sure people know that her family is perfect (e.g., sending cards with a picture of her family/children smiling, hosting parties to show her place, going on expensive vacations).

Jennifer grew up in a middle-class family. Her mother is a religious stay-at-home housewife and mother who is now helping Jennifer raise her children, and Jennifer is very close to her mother. Her father is emotionally absent; he is a recovering alcoholic with whom she has a good relationship. Jennifer had a good relationship with her brother until, recently, he mentioned that Jennifer acts like she is better than others and forgets where she comes from. Her brother describes Jennifer as "materialistic."

Jennifer devotes her life to becoming a good wife and mother. She enjoys an upper-class lifestyle and believes that she is a successful person compared to her parents and brother. However, Jennifer reports that she is never happy. For example, she just had a new baby boy (fourth child), but she had wished for a baby girl, so that she could have two boys and two girls. Jennifer states, "I never really truly feel happy. I try my best in everything, but I'm always three steps behind other people." Jennifer is considered to be one of the people who "keep up with the Joneses."

Jennifer has a hard time admitting that she is a perfectionist and a competitive person. In the counseling sessions, you often hear Jennifer talk about her vision of perfection, including perfect schools for her children, extracurricular activities that make her children be the best, and having a new home that is bigger and better than her current one. You also hear Jennifer express concerns about one of her children acting out and being difficult, about casual arguments with her husband, and about her relationship with her brother.

Jennifer wants to feel "true happiness," so her life can be perfect.

Questions:

1. Which approach do you choose, between psychodynamic and humanistic–existential, as your theoretical framework when working with Jennifer? Please identify your rationale for your choice.

2. How will you integrate the microskills in the chosen therapeutic approach and your work with Jennifer?

Behavioral Approach

Behavioral and cognitive behavioral therapies developed from the work of the more strict behaviorists, who were heavily influenced by positivism, like B. F. Skinner, Hans Eysenck, and Joseph Wolpe, as well as their cognitive–behavioral kin, Albert Ellis, William Glasser, and Aaron Beck. From the 1920s to 1950s, the behaviorists and their concepts of classic conditioning, operant conditioning, and social learning came to the forefront of the mental health fields. Later, in the 1950s, Albert Ellis developed what came to be known as rational emotive behavioral therapy, Aaron Beck developed cognitive therapy, and William Glasser developed reality therapy.

In contrast with the insight-based approach of the earlier psychodynamic therapies or the newer relational approach of humanistic therapies, these cognitive–behavioral therapists believed psychological distress emerges from one's thought and belief—cognitive distortion or irrational belief. Reflecting this belief, counseling focused on changing a person's thoughts and beliefs in order to facilitate behavioral changes. One of the significant contributions of behavioral and cognitive behavioral approaches is to highlight the importance of therapeutic outcomes, now called empirically supported treatment or evidence-based treatment. These outcome-based therapies later influenced the development of newer therapeutic approaches, such as acceptance commitment therapy (ACT) by Steven Hayes and dialectical behavior therapy (DBT) by Marsha Linehan.

Multicultural Approach

Paul Pedersen (1999), the grandparent of this approach, called multiculturalism "the fourth force in counseling," following the contributions of the first three—psychodynamic, humanist–existentialist, and behaviorist. In this approach, the role of culture broadly defined is critical to the understanding of the individual and applies to all counseling relationships. Culture was narrowly defined as race and ethnicity early in the development of this approach, but later more broadly as including ethnographic variables (e.g., race, ethnicity, religion, history, and common ancestry), demographic variables (e.g., age, gender, gender identity, sexual orientation, geographic location of residence), status variables (e.g., social, economic, and educational), and affiliation variables (both formal and informal).

This tradition grew out of the work in the late 1970s through 1990s of Paul Pedersen, Harry Triandis, Courtland Lee, Derald Wing Sue, Patricia Arredondo, Manuel Casas, Joseph Ponterotto, and others. Sue, Arredondo, and McDavis (1992) published their multicultural counseling competencies in 1992 simultaneously in the ACA's flagship journal, *Journal of Counseling and Development,* and the Association for Multicultural Counseling and Development's journal, *Journal for Multicultural Counseling and Development.* The multicultural approach to counseling addresses the importance of providing treatment and interventions that pertain to the unique needs of diverse populations and are relevant to the client's cultural reference. Later in this textbook, in Chapter 6, you will learn more about multicultural counseling competencies and how you, as a future counselor, can develop such competencies.

Finding Your Theoretical Orientation

Halbur and Halbur (2011) suggested 10 strategies that can assist you in selecting a theoretical orientation. Those strategies include finding yourself, examining

---

Exercise 1.3

MULTICULTURAL ISSUES IN THE COUNSELING PROFESSION

Directions: As a future professional counselor, please answer the following questions:

An increase of diversity in the US population forces the counseling profession to respond to cultural issues that have emerged between clients and counselors. The ACA *Code of Ethics* (2005) requires professional counselors to attend to the client's cultural worldview when engaging in the therapeutic relationship. It is also important that professional counselors practice multicultural counseling, as it is an ethical practice considered by the profession at large.

1. In your opinion, what should multicultural counseling look like?

2. How can professional counselors become multiculturally competent?

3. What is your vision of, or what are your ideas about, multicultural counseling practice in the next five years?

---

your values, looking at your preferences, utilizing your personality, capturing your uniqueness, allowing others to inspire you and your learning, reading original works of the theorists, practicing, studying with masters, and broadening your experiences. For example, you may take a look at your personal values, such as how you view human beings (e.g., people are good or bad by nature), and compare your view with different theoretical orientations by reading original writings of those theorists who have the same view that you do. You may find you select and deselect some theoretical orientation through this process.

It is important to note that, in reality, many professional counselors and mental health professionals practice an integrative approach to counseling. An integrative approach refers to "a perspective based on concepts and techniques drawn from various theoretical approaches" (Corey & Corey, 2007, p. 145). This approach allows counselors to utilize frameworks and interventions from more than one theory to better suit the client's need and to compensate for the limitations of one theory with the benefits of other(s). As mentioned earlier, you will learn about different therapeutic approaches as you progress through your graduate training in counseling, as theoretical frameworks are central to professional counseling. Professional counselors implement these frameworks to guide their therapeutic treatment and interventions when working with clients.

KEYSTONES

You have already begun your exciting journey of becoming a professional counselor. This chapter provides an overview of the counseling profession. You were introduced to the definition of professional counselor and identity of professional counselors. You gained an understanding of the importance of the self of the counselor, the therapeutic relationship, counseling process, basic counseling skills, and major theoretical approaches in the counseling context. The items below capture the concepts discussed in this chapter.

- The current definition of professional counseling is "a professional relationship that empowers diverse individuals, families, and groups to accomplish mental health, wellness, education, and career goals" (ACA, 2012).
- It is important that you, as a professional counselor, examine and reflect upon your personal motivation, values, and beliefs in order to better understand yourself in the therapeutic process.
- To achieve favorable therapeutic outcomes, counselors should be empathic, warm, supportive, and hopeful with their clients (Lambert & Barley, 2001). These characteristics of counselors allow clients to feel understood, accepted, empowered, and encouraged.
- There are common stages of the counseling process that provide you a framework when working with clients regardless of your theoretical orientation or work settings. Six stages in the counseling process include establishing the relationship, assessment, treatment planning, intervention, evaluation, and termination.
- Microskills include attending, listening, restatement, reflection of feelings, summarizing, and probing. These skills are the foundational skills in counseling regardless of the counselor's theoretical orientation.
- Major theoretical approaches in counseling include the psychodynamic, humanistic–existential, behavioral, and multicultural. Each approach possesses its uniqueness.

ADDITIONAL RESOURCES

Corey, G. (2013). *Theory and practice of counseling and psychotherapy* (9th ed.). Belmont, CA: Thomson Brooks/Cole.

Norcross, J. C. (2011). *Psychotherapy relationships that work* (2nd ed.). New York, NY: Oxford University Press.

Rogers, C. (1975). Empathy: An unappreciated way of being. *Counseling Psychologist, 21,* 95–103.

Yalom, I. (2003). *The gift of therapy: An open letter to a new generation of therapists and their patients.* New York, NY: Perennial Currents.

REFERENCES

American Counseling Association (ACA). (2005). *ACA Code of ethics*. Alexandria, VA: Author.

American Counseling Association (ACA). (2010). *20/20—A vision for the future of counseling*. Retrieved from http://counseling.org/20–20/definition.aspx

Corey, M. S., & Corey, G. (2007). *Becoming a helper* (5th ed.). Pacific Grove, CA: Thomson/Brooks/Cole.

Dougherty, M. A. (2008). *Psychological consultation and collaboration in school and community settings* (5th ed.). Pacific Grove, CA: Brooks and Cole.

Frank, J. (1988). What is psychotherapy? In S. Bloch (Ed.), *An introduction to the psychotherapies* (pp. 1–2). Oxford, UK: Oxford University Press.

Frank, J. D., & Frank, J. B. (1991). *Persuasion and healing: A comparative study of psychotherapy*. Baltimore, MD: Johns Hopkins University Press.

Gelso, C .J. & Carter, J. (1994). Components of the psychotherapy relationship: Their interaction and unfolding during treatment. *Journal of Counseling Psychology, 41,* 296–306.

Gladding, S. T. (2004). *Counseling: A comprehensive profession* (5th ed.). Upper Saddle River, NJ: Prentice-Hall.

Halbur, D. A., & Halbur, K. V. (2011). *Developing your theoretical orientation in counseling* and psychotherapy (2nd ed.). Boston, MA: Allyn & Bacon.

Kaplan, D. M., & Gladding, S. T. (2011). A vision for the future of counseling: The 20/20 principles for unifying and strengthening the profession. *Journal of Counseling & Development, 89,* 367–372. doi: 10.1002/j.1556–6678.2011.tb00101.x

Lambert, M. J. (1992). Psychotherapy outcome research: Implications for integrative and eclectic therapists. In J. C. Norcross & M. R. Goldfried (Eds.), *Handbook of psychotherapy integration* (pp. 94–129). New York, NY: Basic Books.

Lambert, M. J., & Barley, D. E. (2001). Research summary on the therapeutic relationship and psychotherapy outcome. *Psychotherapy: Theory, Research, Practice, Training, 38*(4), 357–361. doi: 10.1037/0033–3204.38.4.357

Pedersen, P. (1999). *Multiculturalism as a fourth force*. Philadelphia, PA: Brunner/Mazel.

Rogers, C. R. (1961). *On becoming a person*. Boston, MA: Houghton Mifflin Company.

Rose, L. (1998). Freud and fetishism: Previously unpublished minutes of the Vienna Psychoanalytic Society. *Psychoanalytic Quarterly, 57,* 147–166.

Satir, V. (1987). The therapist story. *Journal of Psychotherapy and the Family, 3*(1), 17–25. doi: 10.1300/J287v03n01_04

Sue, D. W., Arredondo, P., & McDavis, R. J. (1992). Multicultural counseling competencies and standards: A call to the profession. *Journal of Multicultural Counseling and Development, 20,* 64–88. doi: 10.1002/j.2161–1912.1992.tb00563.x

Teyber, E. (2006). *Interpersonal process in psychotherapy: An integrative model* (5th ed.). Belmont, CA: Thomson Brooks/Cole.

US Department of Labor. (2012). *Occupational outlook handbook* (2012–2013 ed.). Washington, DC: Author.

Chapter 2

History and Philosophy of the Counseling Profession

MARK POPE

Counseling is about helping. From the little boy who is being bullied in the school playground by an older, bigger classmate, to the couple who are having great difficulty in dealing with their inability to conceive a child, to the 75-year-old man who sits by the window of his apartment wondering if anyone will come visit him today, to the single mother of four who has just lost her job, to the teenage girl who has just found out that she is pregnant, to the 20-something young man who has just realized that he is in the wrong gendered body, to the 50-year-old who drinks several cocktails every night because he is so stressed by his work and unable to sleep, to the family of four who are living on $16,000 a year, who consistently don't have enough food, and parents who go hungry in order to ensure that their children have enough, and who "dumpster dive" for their next meal. Counseling is about helping people in each of these situations (and so many more).

The roots of counseling lie in the traditional practices of indigenous healers around the globe, including *qigong* and acupuncture (Chen, 2003), shamanism (Moodley, 2005), animism from Africa (Vontress, 1991), *Bhutavidya* (Rao, 1986), native healing in the United States (Garrett & Garrett, 1996), ayurvedic practice (Ramachandra Rao, 1990), meditation (Suzuki, 1960), and so much more. Entire books have been written on this (Ehrenwald, 1976; Moodley & West, 2005; Sheikh & Sheikh, 1989) and many of these traditional methods are still practiced even today in different parts of our planet.

Counseling, as a profession, is only 100 years or so old, but helping those who are troubled by the problems of everyday life is much older. As Paul Pedersen, one of the elders of the multicultural counseling movement, stated, "The functions of counseling have been practiced for thousands of years and are not merely an invention of the last century or two" (Pedersen, 2005, p. xi). In this chapter, the term *counseling* will be used in its broadest sense. In this view, counseling includes and is, therefore, also synonymous with *psychotherapy* and even the generic terms *caregiving* and *helping*. You will learn historical perspectives and values of the counseling profession. You will also be introduced to current trends and issues in the counseling profession. Reflection exercises including case studies will enhance your learning about the development of the profession.

LEARNING OBJECTIVES

After completing the reading and reflection exercises provided in this chapter, you will be able to

1. Identify the founder of professional counseling,

2. Understand the historical events that led to the founding of professional counseling,

3. Identify the primary association representing professional counselors,

4. Identify the four founding associations of the primary association representing professional counselors,

5. Identify what the common values of professional counseling are, and

6. Understand the contemporary professional issues in the field.

CASE ILLUSTRATION 2.1

PROFESSIONAL COUNSELOR?

Pat is a 23-year-old woman who lives in the suburbs of a major American city. She had just completed college with a degree in human services but was unsure of what to do next in terms of finding a job. She liked her high school counselor and thought that counseling might be a good job; however, she does not want to work in school, and "kids are not her thing." She went to a career counselor at a local community college who gave her an instrument called the Values Scale that helped her identify her top five values as altruism, creativity, social interaction, variety, and autonomy.

- Would she be a good candidate for a career as a professional counselor? Please provide your rationale.
- What should she be doing to explore her career option as a professional counselor? Please identify ways of exploration or strategies that she may employ.

THE HISTORY OF PROFESSIONAL COUNSELING

In the late 1800s and early 1900s in the United States, counseling as a profession was born. Several historians of professional counseling have placed the date as 1913 (Aubrey, 1977; Pope, 2000) and have attributed that founding to a small group of disaffected social workers who realized that case management, the traditional focus of that field, was simply not enough. People also needed a place to consider the barriers they faced and to gain knowledge about themselves so that they could learn to apply their internal, personal resources to these problems of everyday life.

Roots of the Profession of Counseling

That break from the profession of social work has been personified historically by the work of Frank Parsons, who is credited as the founder of the field of professional counseling (Aubrey, 1977; Brewer, 1942; Davis, 1969; Pope & Sveinsdottir, 2005; Whiteley, 1984). Parsons and his colleagues at the Breadwinner's Institute of the Vocation Bureau of the Boston Civic Service House, a Jane Addams styled settlement house that arose to help individuals and their families who were migrating from rural areas to resettle in urban centers, found that they had to do more than just case management. They found that the process of helping also meant helping people look at themselves through a process they called *vocational guidance,* what we now term *career counseling* (Brewer, 1942).

Career counseling arose from the need to help people who were having financial, employment, and personal problems as a result of this major societal transition—the transition from an agrarian society to an industrial one at the end of the 1800s and beginning of the 1900s. Career counseling arose in response to and as an immediate outcome of this transition and with it came the foundation for a broader, new profession—*professional counseling.* Pope (2000) characterized this transition in this way:

The societal upheaval giving birth to career counseling was characterized by the loss of jobs in the agricultural sector, increasing demands for workers in heavy industry, the loss of "permanent" jobs on the family farm to new emerging technologies such as tractors, the increasing urbanization of the USA, and the concomitant calls for services to meet this internal migration pattern, all in order to retool for the new industrial economy. (p. 195)

Although societal transition and social insecurity can give birth to a new profession, it takes much more than such upheaval to sustain it over time. The other social factors that served to maintain this new field included the support of the Progressive social reform movement, the rise of psychological testing as a scientific endeavor, and the emergence of laws that were supportive of vocational guidance and that were receiving much societal support (Pope, 2000). These critical factors helped strengthen the development of professional counseling and made professional counselors become more pervasive in various settings, including the military, colleges, and schools.

From 1920 to 1960, the focus for and growth of the new profession of counseling were educational institutions—K–12 schools as well as colleges and universities (Aubrey, 1977; Pope, 2000). With the end of World War I and the passage of the Smith–Hughes Act, another transition began, and, with the economic depression of the 1930s, these social and legislative processes put the focus of American society squarely on educational counseling and served to solidify the role of counseling (previously called *guidance*) in the schools (Pope, 2000). "The union of education, of social work, and of psychometrics in the vocational guidance of youth and adults was now somewhat more complete [in the 1930s]" (Super, 1955, p. 4). Elementary and secondary education received an influx of students as a result of both increased needs for literacy to cope with increasing demands of industrialization and the increase in numbers of school-aged children as a direct result of the boom in pregnancies following the end of World War I (Schwebel, 1984).

In the 1940s, 1950s, and 1960s, the federal government focused on the training of professional counselors as a direct result of and response to a new social transition engendered by two major events that set the tone for all subsequent worldwide actions: World War II and the Union of Soviet Socialist Republics' (USSR's) successful launching of rockets that orbited the Earth and even landed on the moon (the Sputnik and Lunik programs). For example, the Counseling and Guidance Training Institutes were established under the National Defense Education Act (NDEA) to provide improved training for counselors who were to identify and encourage science and math majors for college education. This was a boom period for the training of counselors, and almost 14,000 counselors received training in these NDEA institutes (Borow, 1964). This training was created as a mechanism to support the passage of the National Defense Education Act in 1957, a direct response to the successful launching of Sputnik and the desperation of American government officials at the loss of this supposed American superiority in technology.

Around the same time, many important counseling organizations were formed to respond to the growing needs of the US populations. A unification committee was formed and began meeting in 1950. The four main groups behind the unification movement were the National Vocational Guidance Association (NVGA), the National Association of Guidance and Counselor Trainers (NAGCT, now the Association for Counselor Education and Supervision), the Student Personnel Association for Teacher Education (SPATE, now the Association for Humanistic Counseling), and the American College Personnel Association (ACPA). These four professional associations became the first four divisions of the American Counseling Association (ACA), and its formation was followed by that of the American School Counselor Association in 1953.

The unification committee made its report at the 1951 NVGA convention, and a new professional association with a new name was born—the Personnel and Guidance Association (PGA). In 1952, that name was changed to the American Personnel and Guidance Association (APGA), and the first officers of APGA included President Robert Shaffer, President-Elect Donald Super, and Treasurer Frank Fletcher, all three of whom were also leaders in NVGA (Pope, 2009). The APGA became the American Association for Counseling and Development (AACD) in 1983 and then the American Counseling Association (ACA) in 1992, responding to pressure from a variety of changes in society as well as a change membership (Pope, 2009). Table 2.1 lists the divisions that currently are affiliated with ACA.

While most attention of this organization focused on the identification of individuals who had strong potential to rescue America, many societal problems caused by the economic depression after World War II (e.g., unemployment, financial insecurities, family issues) started to emerge and impact the public's mental health and well-being. There was a growing realization that mental health was also a critical issue in health and that attending to physical health issues was not simply enough, as the results of both world wars were proving. In the decade following World War I (1921–1931), Glass (1973) reported that "suicide was the leading cause of death in military personnel" (p. 9) and noted the corresponding rise in the incidence of all mental health issues among veterans. These numbers continue to rise, and in 1946 Congress established the National Institute of Mental Health (NIMH). The mission of NIMH was to transform the understanding and treatment of mental illnesses through both basic and clinical research, in order to assist with prevention, recovery, and cures.

Table 2.1 Current Divisions of the American Counseling Association

AAC—Association for Assessment in Counseling (name changed in 1992), formerly Association for Measurement and Evaluation in Counseling and Development (name changed in 1984), formerly Association for Measurement and Evaluation in Guidance (1965).

AADA—Association for Adult Development and Aging (1986).

ACC—Association for Creativity in Counseling (2004).

ACCA—American College Counseling Association (1991).

ACEG—Association for Counselors and Educators in Government (name changed in 1994), formerly Military Educators and Counselors Association (1984).

ACES—Association for Counselor Education and Supervision, formerly the National Association of Guidance and Counselor Trainers (1952).

ACPA—American College Personnel Association, but disaffiliated in 1992 to once again become a standalone association (1952).

AHC—Association for Humanistic Counseling (name changed in 2010), formerly Counseling Association for Humanistic Education and Development (name changed in 1999), formerly Association for Humanistic Education and Development (name changed in 1974), formerly Student Personnel Association for Teacher Education (1952).

ALGBTIC—Association for Lesbian, Gay, Bisexual, and Transgender Issues in Counseling (name changed in 2007), formerly the Association far Gay, Lesbian, and Bisexual Issues in Counseling (1996).

AMCD—Association for Multicultural Counseling and Development (name changed in 1985), formerly Association for Non-White Concerns in Personnel and Guidance (1972).

AMHCA—American Mental Health Counselors Association (1978).

ARCA—American Rehabilitation Counseling Association (1958).

ASCA—American School Counselor Association (1953).

ASERVIC—Association for Spiritual. Ethical, and Religious Values in Counseling (name changed in 1993), formerly Association for Religious and Value Issues in Counseling (name changed in 1977), formerly National Catholic Guidance Conference (1974).

ASGW—Association for Specialists in Group Work (1973).

CSJ—Counselors for Social Justice (1999).

IAAOC—International Association of Addictions and Offender Counselors (name changed in 1990), formerly Public Offender Counselor Association (1972).

IAMFC—International Association of Marriage and Family Counselors (1989).

NCDA—National Career Development Association (name changed in 1985), formerly National Vocational Guidance Association (1952).

NECA—National Employment Counseling Association (name changed in 1992), formerly National Employment Counselors Association, formerly part of NVGA (1966).

In the mid- to late 1950s, the Vocational Rehabilitation Act (VRA, 1954), the Mental Health Study Act (1955), and the National Defense Education Act (NDEA, 1958) were all enacted into law. Each had an important impact on professional counseling. The VRA recognized the needs of people with disabilities and became law as a result of the particular needs of World War II veterans. It also mandated the development of rehabilitation counselors and authorized funds for their training. The NDEA was passed as a direct result of the USSR's successes in space and focused on improving science and math performance by students in the public schools. Guidance counseling was seen as a critical component of such a program and would encourage students to explore their career interests, abilities, and opportunities. Grants were given to schools to provide guidance activities and to institutions of higher education to improve the training of guidance counselors in the schools. The Mental Health Study Act established the Joint Commission on Mental Illness and Health, which initiated studies that eventually led to the passage of the Community Mental Health Centers Act and the establishment of more than 2,000 mental health centers across the country that would provide direct counseling services to people in each community.

Enhancing the Professionalization of Professional Counseling

The late 1970s, however, were characterized by a declining economic system rather than by the growth and prosperity of the early 1960s. This began a new transition in the 1980s—from an industrial age to an information and technology age (Pope, 2000). This new transition spawned another host of problems, such as loss of jobs in the industrial sectors of our economy, increasing demands from employers for technological skills, loss of "permanent" jobs to contract labor, loss of job security, and marginalization of organized labor, all in order to retool for the information and technology economy (Pope, 2000).

During this new period, the emergence of the private-practice professional counselor was the direct result of the beginnings of national acceptance of counseling as an important service to provide to a citizenry in such transitions. This practitioner, whose livelihood depended on continuous marketing of counseling services, provided the vitality for the expansion and growth of the professional practice of counseling during this period as well as for the credentialing of such practitioners (Pope, 2000).

Professions are defined by and really legitimized in the eyes of the public by standards for training enforced by an accreditation body, an ethical code promulgated and enforced by a professional association, voluntary certification coordinated by a certifying organization, and a license to practice issued and enforced by a state government (Pope, 2000). To further legitimize the practice of professional counselors, in 1976, the Commonwealth of Virginia became the first state to license professional counselors to provide counselor services under the state laws. During this time, ACA was instrumental in establishing professional and ethical standards for the counseling profession and it has made considerable strides in accreditation, licensure, and national certification. ACA established the Council for Accreditation of Counseling and Related Educational Programs (CACREP) in 1981 to provide a national accreditation body for counselor training programs, the National Board for Certified Counselors (NBCC) in 1982 to provide a national certification body, the American Counseling Association Insurance Trust (ACAIT) in 1991 to provide high-quality and low-cost professional liability insurance for members, and the American Counseling Association Foundation (ACAF) in 1998 to provide support for the profession. It also developed a model licensing law that has been used in the licensing of professional counselors and mental health counselors in all 50 states and the District of Columbia.

The rise in the use of technology in business and industry in the United States led to the passage of two very important federal laws during this stage: the Omnibus Trade and Competitiveness Act (1988) and the Carl D. Perkins Vocational Education Act (1984). The Omnibus Trade Act included provisions to assist persons to enter into, or advance in, high-technology occupations, or to meet the technological needs of other industries or businesses, as well as to provide pre-employment skills training, school-to-work transition programs, and school–business partnerships.

The Carl D. Perkins Vocational Education Act was signed into law in October 1984. The Perkins Act replaced the Vocational Education Act of 1963, which had been amended in 1968 and 1976, and extended the federal authorization for vocational education programs through fiscal year 1989. It was notable for strengthening programs for underserved populations, which it listed as "disadvantaged individuals, handicapped individuals, adults requiring training/retraining, Indians, limited English-proficient students, participants in programs to eliminate sex bias in vocational education, native Hawaiians, single parents/homemakers, criminal offenders, and unemployed or workers threatened by unemployment" (Appling & Irwin, 1988, p. 9). The Perkins Act has been amended continuously by the federal government, but even today it continues to be the vehicle for counseling authorization in the schools.

From Poverty to Cultural Diversity

At the end of the 1980s and beginning of the 1990s, the field of counseling had found itself being extended in a variety of new directions, with culture broadly defined as the new rope that tied professional counseling together. The rapid growth of professional counseling and demands for professional counselors reflected societal concerns in various areas. One extension was into lower socioeconomic classes, who were being required to go to work because of new governmental policies like the Greater Avenues to Independence (GAIN), the Job Training Partnership Act (JTPA), Welfare to Work (WtW, 1997), and the Workforce Initiative Act of 1998. WtW was the harshest of these laws, as it set five years as the limit on how long any person in the United States could receive economic support through a federally administered economic support program called Temporary Assistance for Needy Families, which replaced the federal program called Aid to Families with Dependent Children. The idea was to get those who had experienced or had characteristics associated with long-term welfare dependence into lasting unsubsidized jobs—to get them in jobs first (called a *work first* service strategy) and then to train them postemployment (which never happened). The role of counseling professionals was to assist in this process wherever they could, which varied from state to state and from local agency to local agency. The focus of federal implementation monies was to help those who were most likely to have the greatest problems, such as individuals with disabilities, individuals who required substance abuse treatment, victims of domestic violence, individuals with limited English proficiency, and noncustodial parents. With the focus on work first in the legislation, there was no provision for assessment and training as a precursor to finding a job that would then be more likely to be maintained over the lifetime of the individual.

There was also renewed interest in and support for previously neglected populations in the US society, such as individuals with disabilities. In 1990, the Americans with Disabilities Act was established to protect the right to employment of persons who were physically or mentally challenged. Not only did it prohibit job discrimination against people with disabilities, but also it mandated that individuals with disabilities have the same access to goods, services, facilities, and accommodations afforded to all others. This law had far-reaching consequences for professional counselors in all settings.

An important health insurance law was also enacted during this time, the Mental Health Insurance Parity Act (MHIPA, 1996). MHIPA was supported by a coalition of mental health professional associations working together, including the ACA, American Psychological Association, American Psychiatric Association, and National Association of Social Workers. This law prevented health insurance plans that provided mental health services from discriminating between physical and mental health services in payments or financial maximums. This was important not only for professional counselors who were in independent practice but also for any community-based agency that provided mental health services.

In mid- to late 1990s, there was an increasing technological sophistication that has led to instant communication by phone, by document transmission using fax machines, and via the Internet to anywhere in the world. Personal communication devices such as cell phones made it possible to contact a person wherever he or she was. Extensions of these changes for the professional counselor were the provision of services by phone and over the Internet. This is only the beginning of this trend, as these technological advances continue to drive the worldwide dissemination of information and innovations in the delivery of counseling services.

The Health Insurance Portability and Accountability Act (HIPAA, 1996) was enacted as a direct result of technological changes. HIPAA was enacted to promote "administrative simplification" in the administration of healthcare benefits by establishing national standards for the electronic transmission of health information, for the use and disclosure of personally identifiable health information, and for the security of information. What HIPAA did in reality was revolutionize the manner in which electronic records are maintained or transmitted, by requiring any healthcare entity to inform clients of this law and to have proof that they have done this.

Bringing Licensing to Closure

The counseling profession has continued to grow since the mid-1900s. The profession has a long history of responding to the public's needs in career, education, and mental health services. Professional counselors have become increasingly visible, and all US states recognize services provided by professional counselors as legitimate through professional licensures. As mentioned, in 1976, the Commonwealth of Virginia was the first state to license professional counselors,

---

Exercise 2.1

USING TECHNOLOGY IN COUNSELING

Directions: As individuals utilize multiple forms of technology in everyday life, professional counselors employ current technology to serve their clients. As mentioned in the chapter, professional counselors have used Internet chat and videoconference as primary means to provide face-to-face counseling sessions to clients.

Please find a few study partners and/or classmates to discuss the following questions:

- What are other forms of technology that professional counselors can implement to serve clients?
- What are benefits and limitations of those forms of technology identified above?
- What are your thoughts concerning the use of social media in counseling?

and in 2009 California became the last state in the United States to do this. This final licensing law was the culmination of 30 years of work by professional counselors in California and all around the United States. It was a big deal, because it meant that professional counselors were now licensed in all 50 states and the District of Columbia, and that was important for a whole host of issues, but especially for meeting the minimum qualification for providing services to any national entity, including the Department of Defense through TRICARE or the Veterans Administration.

Professional counseling is one of the youngest mental health professions, and to be officially recognized to provide services to national organizations or institutions, counseling groups want to have coverage nationwide. Since states control the licensing and therefore the practice of professions within their borders, having licensed practitioners in every state (and DC) is critical to being allowed to provide and being paid to provide services. In 2009, with the addition of California to the ranks of states allowing licensed professional counselors to practice, the entire counseling profession had arrived.

As presented in this section, the history of professional counseling in the United States is rich and tied to the changing social issues of the times. From the abolition of child labor laws in the early 1900s to the high-stakes testing and accountability in the schools of the early 2000s, from the early vocational guidance movement to the modern movement to protect the privacy rights of Americans, professional counseling has been a part of all of this. Today's counseling profession is a product of these changes.

VALUES OF THE COUNSELING PROFESSION

Values are about what we find to be important in our lives or, in this case, in a profession, and that inform our decisions and behaviors. The common values of a profession are exhibited in its code of ethics. The ACA was founded in 1952 and, understanding the value of an ethics code for any group of professionals, formed its first ethics committee in 1953. After much study and discussion, the first code of ethics for the ACA was finally published in 1961. It has been regularly revisited and revised since then, because ethical issues, like culture, are dynamic and evolve and change within the sociocultural context of society.

Professions are defined by what they value, and the creation of a formal code of ethics is standard practice to inform new members of the profession; to unify, advise, and protect existing members; to help resolve ethical issues; to protect those who are served by the profession; and to help establish, maintain, and distinguish a professional association and its members from other such associations.

Ethical and Professional Counseling Practice

Professional counseling's values are fully displayed in this statement from the preamble to the *ACA Code of Ethics* (2005):

> Professional values are an important way of living out an ethical commitment. Values inform principles. Inherently held values that guide our behaviors or exceed prescribed behaviors are deeply ingrained in the counselor and developed out of personal dedication, rather than the mandatory requirement of an external organization. (p. 1)

Also from that preamble is a statement of the common values that professional counselors are expected to have:

> ACA members are dedicated to the enhancement of human development throughout the life span. Association members recognize diversity and embrace a cross-cultural approach in support of the worth, dignity, potential, and uniqueness of people within their social and cultural contexts. (p. 1)

Further, each of the eight sections of the Code of Ethics is introduced by a statement of values—values that show and explain why professional counselors are dedicated to helping others and to the growth and development of human beings on our planet.

In still an altruistic yet more commercial way, a code of ethics is also designed to signal the public, the consumer of counseling services, that our first value is to do no harm to those we serve. Without that, we (nor really any profession) could not exist. Clients have a right to enter a counseling relationship with very specific expectations about the counselor's professionalism and values. At such a basic level, our values must be about protecting client privacy and confidentiality, seeking supervision and consultation as necessary, not discriminating against a client in the provision of services, and not engaging in sexual or detrimental social relationships with clients. Our values also are clear that a counselor must act if there is a concern about client safety or harm to others, which is also both an ethical and a legal mandate.

Reported Values of Counselors

Many have written about what the specific values of professional counselors are or should be. In one comprehensive study, Consoli, Kim, and Meyer (2008) reviewed the empirical literature on the values held by counselors. They found that there was "an important degree of commonality in the values held by counselors" (p. 183) and that counselors' values fit into four major categories: personal, inter-personal, social, and environmental. They also found, however, that the general

THE CASE OF THE ANXIOUS ARTIST

Barack was a 22-year-old African American man who was having a problem with his mother. His mother, who had never herself graduated from college, wanted him to go to college, but he had been working as a graphic artist at a local marketing company for the last four years, since he graduated from high school. Trying to appease her, he said that he would go for career counseling, but, as he began to look for a counselor, he was unsure of what listing to look under in the Yellow Pages online website or in the United Way Directory that he had gotten on the United Way website. As he began looking on the Internet, he began to feel anxious about this, started breathing rapidly, and had to stop using the computer. The next day it was all so bad that he was not able to go to work because of the anxiety. This persisted for a week and he was unable to get to work.

- Where do you start with this client?
- What strengths does this client possess?
- What anticipated challenges do you see for yourself as his counselor?
- What outside resources or people might you mobilize or integrate?
- What about working with this client—would he be a good fit for you?
- What do you see as a possible concern for you personally with a client such as this?

counselor values profile was complex. For example, they reported that "counselors agree about not only endorsing certain values, but also de-emphasizing others. In addition, while endorsing a given value (e.g., independence), counselors also tend to embrace another, likely moderating value (e.g., interdependence)" (p. 183).

In their review, Consoli et al. (2008) found that

- Personal values included autonomy, independence, personal responsibility, interdependence, coping ability, flexibility, self-esteem, self-expression, acceptance of conflict and ambiguity, demonstration of self-control, and construction of purpose and meaning in life.
- Interpersonal values included intimacy, friendship, cooperation, benevolence, the right to disagree, receipt of support and interpersonal recognition, and devaluation of vertical or strictly hierarchical interpersonal arrangements.

Counselors also valued mutual consent in relationships, such as in a sexual relationship, and devalued over-controlled sexuality and traditional morality.

- Social values included a de-emphasis on social power, social influence, control, or authority over others, and on dominance, and a devaluation of social conformity, such as in doing what is accepted and proper, and being a conformist.
- Environmental or contextual values included harmony or unity in the relationship between person and nature, and devaluation of alternatives such as control over or subjugation to nature.

It is important to note that Consoli et al.'s (2008) critique of the literature on counselors' values was that these reported values were at times counterposed to the values of ethnic minority clients. For example, counselors generally valued personal autonomy and independence and rejected hierarchical relationships, while individuals from ethnic minority groups in the United States value interdependence and collectivism, which respects hierarchical relationships, although this was less of an issue with ethnic minority individuals who were more acculturated into the dominant US culture.

CURRENT TRENDS AND ISSUES IN THE COUNSELING PROFESSION

At the end of its first 100 years as a profession, like any dynamic profession, professional counseling continues to change and grow. This section presents highlights of various trends and issues in our profession. It includes issues such as new ways of looking at dual relationships; ADHD and repressed memories; HIPAA and how it is changing confidentiality and recordkeeping; the development of distance counseling; evidence-based practice; the Affordable Care Act, Medicare, TRICARE, and the Veterans Administration; and other social issues that are impacting professional counseling.

New Ways of Looking at Dual Relationships

In the 2005 revision of the ACA Code of Ethics, a new concept emerged on dual relationships. Prior to this revision, all relationships between the counselor and the client outside of the counseling session were frowned upon and discouraged, but this approach failed to address the reality of counselor–client relationships in rural communities and in small cultural groups where counselor and client may see and interact regularly outside of the professional relationship. Through discussions in the ethics literature and the ACA Ethics Revision Task Force, a new approach to this thorny issue arose, conceptualized as beneficial or detrimental dual relationships (Cottone, 2010).

ADHD and Repressed Memories

At the beginning of the 21st century, debates were ongoing on the merits of the ADHD (attention deficit with hyperactivity disorder) diagnosis in adults as well as the repressed memories issue, where primarily women claimed that they had been sexually abused or mistreated as children, with the memories of this emerging during their counseling treatment.

The debate on the ADHD diagnosis when used with adults is aided by research that supports a genetic component for ADHD along with a positive response to behavioral/pharmacological interventions. There are others, however, who argue that ADHD, as a diagnosis, is nothing more than a fad that supports poor behavior in those with the diagnosis as well as the pharmacological industry, which makes huge profits off of the popularity of the ADHD diagnosis.

Repressed memories as a phenomenon emerged in the 1990s. The debate appeared in the general population, the justice system, and the mental health professions regarding the accuracy of memories that surfaced during treatment sometimes 20 years after the alleged behavior occurred. Research on the nature of memory has been critical to this issue, but no definitive studies have been reported in the literature as to the reliability of such memories.

HIPAA: Changing Confidentiality and Record Keeping

As was previously noted in this chapter, HIPAA was passed in 1996, but the regulations to enforce the act were not approved until 2003. These regulations covered such healthcare procedures as electronic storage and transmission of client records, confidentiality, and clients' access to their healthcare records. Issues of who these regulations apply to and how they affect the independent practice of counseling are yet to be fully resolved.

The Development of Distance Counseling

Distance counseling is a counseling approach that has developed from advances in technology and the needs of more individuals for professional counseling services. Technology-assisted methods may include telecounseling (counseling via telephone) as well as the use of secure e-mail communication, Internet chat, videoconferencing, or computerized stand-alone software programs as the medium for providing counseling services. There is now a professional association representing distance counselors—the American Distance Counseling Association—as well as a professional certification, the Distance Credentialed Counselor, administered by the Center for Credentialing and Education, an affiliate of the National Board for Certified Counselors.

There are a number of issues that are specific to this mode of counseling services delivery, including issues of confidentiality, privacy, informing clients about the privacy issues involved in e-mail and other web-based communication so they can provide informed consent about treatment, discovering clients' identity, making proper assessment of client suitability for electronic counseling, application of reporting laws, and how to approach crisis interventions. One of the most important issues is the practice of counseling across state lines, due to the fact that all professional licensing laws in the United States are administered by the states.

Medicare, TRICARE, and the Veterans Administration

The recognition of professional counselors as providers of mental health services under Medicare, TRICARE (healthcare system for families of members of the US armed forces), and in Veterans Administration (VA) healthcare facilities continues to make substantial progress. Since the 1990s, bipartisan legislation has been regularly introduced in the US Senate to establish Medicare reimbursement of licensed professional counselors and marriage and family therapists. Such legislation would cover only medically necessary outpatient mental health services and would reimburse licensed professional counselors and marriage and family therapists at the same reimbursement rates and under the same terms and conditions as clinical social workers.

For many years, licensed professional counselors have been the only mental health service professionals required to operate under physician referral and supervision within the TRICARE program. Congress included language in the National Defense Authorization Act for fiscal year 2011, which was signed into law by President Barack Obama, directing the Department of Defense to adopt regulations to allow counselors to practice independently.

In 2010, the VA issued an occupational standard for "licensed professional mental health counselors" (LPMHCs). The standard established LPMHCs at the same GS series levels of pay and responsibility as clinical social workers. The VA, however, restricted eligibility for LPMHC positions to counselors with a master's degree in mental health counseling or a related field from a program accredited by CACREP. ACA joined the American Mental Health Counselors Association (AMHCA) and the National Board for Certified Counselors (NBCC) in asking the VA to allow alternate eligibility for counselors from non-CACREP programs, but the VA declined, as doing so would grant an exemption for counseling from similar requirements placed on other master's level mental health professions.

Evidence-Based Counseling Practice

The counseling profession has moved toward evidence-based practice (EBP) or empirically supported treatment, which has its origin in the medical professions. EBP was developed in answer to the question, "How do we know that what we do works?" That is, treatment should account for the increase or decrease of the client's presenting symptoms and promote the client's well-being. EBP suggests that clinical decisions should be based on valid and reliable findings from well-designed research studies. For the past decades, many counseling treatment modalities (e.g., acceptance commitment therapy, cognitive behavioral therapy, dialectical behavioral therapy) have developed their treatment methods to be evidence based for specific mental and emotional disorders through well-established research studies in randomized settings. Although the counseling profession has moved toward EBP for the past decades, there are still growing needs for EBP across different specialties (e.g., addictions counseling) with diverse client populations, especially those who are historically underserved.

The Affordable Care Act

The Patient Protection and Affordable Care Act, commonly referred to as the Affordable Care Act, was created in 2010 to protect clients' rights for public and especially private health insurance systems (ACA, 2012). The Affordable Care Act provides new coverage options that help clients make informed choices about their health, including mental health and counseling services. This law is relatively new, and it is important that professional counselors understand how it impacts them as mental healthcare providers and their service to clients.

Other Social Issues That Are Impacting Professional Counseling

As has been seen earlier in this chapter, social issues have a long history of effects on the counseling profession, and they also have effects on both professional counselors and their clients. In the late 1990s and early 2000s, the ACA and its divisions developed a number of important documents that both provided guidance to practitioners in providing services to clients who may come from cultures dissimilar to their own and reinforced its commitment to social justice and cultural diversity. These documents included the Association for Multicultural Counseling and Development's *Multicultural Counseling Competencies;* the Association for Lesbian, Gay, Bisexual, and Transgender Issues in Counseling's *Competencies for Counseling Lesbian, Gay, Bisexual, Queer, Questioning, Intersex, and Ally Individuals* and *Competencies for Counseling Transgender Clients;* and the ACA's *Advocacy Competencies.* (All of these documents may be found online at www.counseling.org/Resources.)

Exercise 2.2

PROFESSIONAL COUNSELING 20 YEARS FROM NOW

Directions: From the information given in the chapter, you learned the history and current trends of the 100-year-old counseling profession. Try to imagine the counseling profession 20 years from now.

Please find a few study partners and/or classmates with whom to discuss the following questions:

1. How will the definition of professional counseling change? Please describe the new definition.

2. How will professional counselors describe themselves differently? Please describe.

3. How will professional counseling licensure change? Please describe the licensure changes.

4. What do you expect to be professional issues 20 years from now? Please list at least three.

KEYSTONES

Counseling, as a profession, is only approximately 100 years old, but helping those who are troubled by the problems of everyday life is much older. The roots of counseling lie in the traditional practices of indigenous healers around the globe. The practice of counseling has become an identifiable profession with educational requirements, training standards, a written ethical code, and codification in state legislation and regulations. Professional counseling has become a well-defined field, and the number of licensed professional counselors has surpassed the number of counseling-related mental health practitioners, including psychologists and social workers.

To help you grasp the concept of how professional counseling developed, below is a chronological summary of the history of professional counseling:

- In the late 1800s and early 1900s in the United States, counseling as a profession was born. Several historians of professional counseling have placed the date at 1913.

- Frank Parsons is credited as being the founder of the field of professional counseling (Aubrey, 1977; Brewer, 1942; Davis, 1969; Pope & Sveinsdottir, 2005; Whiteley, 1984). Parsons began the Breadwinner's Institute of the Vocation Bureau of the Boston Civic Service House, a Jane Addams styled settlement house.

- Foundation is further attributed to a small group of disaffected social workers who realized that case management, the traditional focus of that field, was simply not enough. They also needed to help people look at themselves through a process they called vocational guidance, what we now term career counseling, which arose from the need to help people who were having financial, employment, and personal problems as a result of the major societal transition from an agrarian society to an industrial one at the end of the 1800s and beginning of the 1900s (Brewer, 1942). Career counseling arose in response to and as an immediate outcome of this social transition, and with it came the foundation for a broader, new profession—professional counseling.

- In 1913, the National Vocational Guidance Association (now the National Career Development Association) was founded in Grand Rapids, Michigan, at the Third National Conference on Vocational Guidance (Brewer, 1942; Pope, 2009). The NVGA/NCDA went on in 1952 to be one of the four founding divisions of the American Personnel and Guidance Association, now the American Counseling Association, the preeminent association of professional counselors in the United States.

- From 1920 to 1960, the growth of the new profession of counseling was focused on educational institutions, in K–12 schools as well as colleges and universities (Aubrey, 1977; Pope, 2000). Educational counseling emerged from the work of humanitarian, progressive social reformers in the schools.

- In the 1940s, 1950s, and 1960s, the development of counseling was characterized by the focus of societal resources on colleges and universities and the training of professional counselors as a direct result of and response to a new social transition engendered by two major events that set the tone for all subsequent worldwide actions: World War II, and the USSR's successful launching of rockets that orbited the Earth and even landed on the moon (the Sputnik and Lunik programs) (Pope, 2000).

- The USSR successfully launched the first space probe, Sputnik I, in 1957, and then followed that by landing a rocket, Lunik II, on the moon in 1959. This impelled federal legislators to begin to address problems in science and math education all across the United States. The National Defense Education Act of 1957 was a direct response to the successful launching of Sputnik. This was a boom period for the training of counselors, and almost 14,000 counselors received training in NDEA institutes (Borow, 1964).

- At this same time, there was a growing realization that mental health was also a critical issue in health, and that simply attending to physical health issues was not enough, as the results of both world wars were proving. In 1946, Congress established the National Institute of Mental Health (NIMH).
- In the late 1970s, the emergence of the private-practice professional counselor was the direct result of the beginnings of national acceptance of counseling as an important service to provide to a citizenry in such transitions. These practitioners, whose livelihood depended on continuous marketing of counseling services, provided the vitality for the expansion and growth of the professional practice of counseling during this period as well as for the credentialing of such practitioners (Pope, 2000). In 1976, Virginia became the first state to license professional counselors.
- At the end of the 1980s and the beginning of the 1990s, counseling found itself being extended in a variety of new directions, with culture broadly defined as the new rope that tied professional counseling together.

At the milestone 100-year anniversary of this dynamic profession, professional counseling continues to change and grow. Highlights of various trends and issues in our profession include the rise of social constructivism and brief solution-focused therapy as new models; new ways of looking at dual relationships; ADHD and repressed memories; HIPAA and how it is changing confidentiality and recordkeeping; the development of distance counseling; Medicare, TRICARE, and the Veterans Administration; and social issues that are impacting professional counseling. Distance counseling is a counseling approach that has developed from advances in technology and the needs of more individuals, especially in rural or more remote geographic locations, for professional counseling services. Technology-assisted methods may include telecounseling (counseling via telephone) as well as the use of secure e-mail communication, Internet chat, videoconferencing, or a computerized stand-alone software program as the medium for providing counseling services.

ADDITIONAL RESOURCES

Brewer, J. M. (1919). *The vocational guidance movement.* New York: Macmillan.

McDaniels, C. O. (1964). *The history and development of the American Personnel and Guidance Association 1952–1963.* Unpublished doctoral dissertation, The University of Virginia, Richmond, VA.

Pope, M. (2006). *Professional counseling 101: Building a strong professional identity.* Alexandria, VA: American Counseling Association.

Sue, D. W., Arredondo, P., & McDavis, R. J. (1992). Multicultural counseling competencies and standards: A call to the profession. *Journal of Counseling & Development, 70,* 477–486. doi: 10.1002/j.1556–6676.1992.tb01642.x

REFERENCES

American Counseling Association (ACA). (2005). *ACA code of ethics.* Retrieved from http://www .counseling. org/Resources/

American Counseling Association (ACA). (2012). The Affordable Care Act: What counselors should know. Retrieved from http://www.counseling.org/docs/public-policy-faqs-and-documents/what-counselors-should-know-about-the-affordable-care-act-%2812–12%29. pdf?sfvrsn=4

Appling, R. N., & Irwin, P. M. (1988, November 1). *Federal vocational education legislation: Recurring issues during the last quarter century.* A Congressional Research Service Report. Washington, DC: Library of Congress.

Aubrey, R. F. (1977). Historical development of guidance and counseling and implications for the future. *Personnel and Guidance Journal, 55,* 288–295. doi: 10.1002/j.2164–4918. 1977. tb04991.x

Borow, H. (1964). Notable events in the history of vocational guidance. In H. Borow (Ed.), *Man in a world at work* (pp. 45–64). Washington, DC: Houghton Mifflin.

Brewer, J. M. (1942). *History of vocational guidance.* New York, NY: Harper & Brothers.

Chen, N. N. (2003). *Breathing spaces: Qigong, psychiatry, and healing in China.* New York, NY: Columbia University Press.

Consoli, A. J., Kim, B. S. K., & Meyer, D. M. (2008). Counselors' values profile: Implications for counseling ethnic minority clients. *Counseling and Values, 52,* 181–197. doi: 10.1002/j.2161–007X.2008.tb00103.x

Cottone, R. R. (2010). Roles and relationships with clients in rehabilitation counseling: Beyond the concept of dual relationships. *Rehabilitation Counseling Bulletin, 53,* 243–248. doi: 10.1177/0034355210368565

Davis, H. V. (1969). *Frank Parsons: Prophet, innovator, counselor.* Carbondale: University of Southern Illinois Press.

Ehrenwald, J. (Ed.). (1976). *The history of psychotherapy: From healing magic to encounter.* New York: Jason Aronson.

Garrett, J. T., & Garrett, M. T. (1996). *Medicine of the Cherokee: The way of right relationship.* Santa Fe, NM: Bear & Company.

Glass, A. J. (1973). Army psychiatry before World War II. In *Neuropsychiatry in World War II* (vol. 1, ch. 1). Washington, DC: US Army Office of the Surgeon General. Available at http://history .amedd. army. mil/booksdocs/wwii/NeuropsychiatryinWWIIVolI/chapter1. htm

Moodley, R. (2005). Shamanic performances. In R. Moodley & W. West (Eds.), *Integrating traditional healing practices into counseling and psychotherapy* (pp. 2–14). Thousand Oaks, CA: Sage.

Moodley, R., & West, W. (Eds.). (2005). *Integrating traditional healing practices into counseling and psychotherapy.* Thousand Oaks, CA: Sage.

Parsons, F. (1909). *Choosing a vocation.* Boston, MA: Houghton Mifflin.

Pedersen, P. B. (2005). Series editor's foreword. In R. Moodley & W. West (Eds.), *Integrating traditional healing practices into counseling and psychotherapy* (pp. xi–xii). Thousand Oaks, CA: Sage.

Pope, M. (1997, June). *Career counseling comes out: The revolution in schooling in America.* A lecture presented for the Centre for Educational Research, University of Hong Kong, Hong Kong.

Pope, M. (2000). A brief history of career counseling in the United States. *Career Development Quarterly, 48,* 194–211.

Pope, M. (2009). Jesse Buttrick Davis (1871–1955): Pioneer of vocational guidance in the schools. *Career Development Quarterly, 57,* 248–258.

Pope, M., & Sveinsdottir, M. (2005). Frank, we hardly knew ye: The very personal side of Frank Parsons. *Journal of Counseling & Development, 83,* 105–115. doi: 10.001002/j.1556–6678.2005.tb00585.x

Ramachandra Rao, S. K. (1990). *Mental health in ayurveda: Source book of charaka & sushrutas-amhita* (National Institute of Mental Health and Neuro Sciences). Bangalore, India: Nimhans.

Rao, A. V. (1986). Indian and Western psychiatry: A comparison. In J. L. Cox (Ed.), *Transcultural psychiatry* (pp. 291–305). London: Croom Helm.

Schwebel, M. (1984). From past to present: Counseling psychology's socially prescribed role. In J. M. Whiteley, N. Kagan, L. W. Harmon, B. R. Fretz, & F. Tanney (Eds.), *The coming decade in counseling psychology* (pp. 25–49). Schenectady, NY: Character Research Press.

Sheikh, A. A., & Sheikh, K. S. (Eds.). (1989). *Eastern and Western approaches to healing: Ancient wisdom and modern knowledge.* New York, NY: John Wiley & Sons.

Super, D. E. (1955). Transition: From vocational guidance to counseling psychology. *Journal of Counseling Psychology, 2,* 3–9. doi: 10.1037/h0041630

Suzuki, D. T. (1960). Lectures on Zen Buddhism. In D. T. Suzuki, E. Fromm, & D. Martino (Eds.), *Zen Buddhism and psychoanalysis* (pp. 1–76). New York, NY: Harper & Row.

Vontress, C. E. (1991). Traditional healing in Africa: Implications for cross-cultural counseling. *Journal of Counseling & Development, 70,* 242–249. doi: 10.1002/j.1556–6676.1991.tb01590.x

Whiteley, J. (1984). *Counseling psychology: A historical perspective.* Schenectady, NY: Character Research Press.

Chapter 3

Professional Roles, Functions, and Consultation With Other Professionals

STEPHEN V. FLYNN

VARUNEE FAII SANGGANJANAVANICH

Counseling professionals execute a number of professional roles and functions within the mental health marketplace. We, as professional counselors, develop and enhance our roles through education, training, and experience that start early on in our graduate training programs. Some foundational roles include those of individual counselor, group counselor, consultant, and researcher. These roles are multifaceted, and you can find yourself juggling many functions within each role. For example, a group counselor must function as a screener of group members, group facilitator, and critical incident reporter. Understanding the transcendence of the professional counseling through various roles and functions can help describe and cultivate your counselor professional identity. Further, distinguishing the counseling profession from other allied mental health professions is essential to the establishment of a unifying professional identity.

In this chapter, you will be provided an overview of professional counseling and related mental health professions, including a brief history as well as similarities and differences in terms of professional identity, roles, and functions of each profession. We further highlight the uniqueness of the counseling profession and roles and functions of professional counselors. We later describe professional collaboration between professional counselors and professionals in various mental health and educational settings in order to serve diverse client populations. Reflection exercises and case studies will enhance your learning about the professional identity, roles, functions, and collaboration of professional counselors.

LEARNING OBJECTIVES

After reading this chapter and participating in the reflective exercises provided, you will be able to

1. Describe the professional identity, roles, and functions of professional counselors;

2. Compare the professional identity, roles, and functions of professional counselors to other mental health professionals; and

3. Discuss ways that professional counselors consult with other professionals in various settings.

PROFESSIONAL COUNSELING: ISSUES WITH DIFFERENTIATION AND CONNECTION

There have been seemingly endless discussions surrounding the uniqueness of and overlap between professional roles and functions within and among various mental health professions. West, Hosie, and Mackey (1987) described similarities in roles, professional expectations, and tasks across various mental health professions. Some common areas of overlap between professional counseling and other mental health professions include crisis management, individual counseling, group counseling, assessment, diagnosis, multiculturalism, and the general use of the term *counseling* as a service provided to the clients (Vacc & Loesch, 2000).

It is important for you to understand that, in reality, various professions coexist in the field of mental health, performing similar services. The overlapping services provided by these professions (e.g., counseling, social work, applied psychology, and marriage and family therapy) can create confusion and blurring of professional boundaries and identities as well as problems with parity in regard to status, access, and earnings. For example, the term *counseling* is shared by all mental health professions, including professional counseling, social work, psychology, and marriage and family therapy. The general use of the term *counseling* as a process that all mental health practitioners utilize places the counseling profession in a less-than-ideal situation. Namely, the overuse of the term can prevent the counseling profession from differentiating itself from other mental health professions. Reclaiming the word *counseling* as a particular service offered by professional counselors is important to the differentiation of the counseling profession. Although many efforts are put forth to differentiate professional counselors from other mental health professionals (e.g., psychologists, social workers), role confusion, overlap in professional services, and poorly differentiated professional identities persist.

Role Confusion

Many have maintained the belief that the very future and survival of the counseling profession depends on the achievement of a unique professional identity (Calley & Hawley, 2008; Ritchie, 1994; Smith, 2001). Foundationally, the creation of a professional identity is important, because it helps professional counselors to understand who they are, what they do, and what they should avoid doing. For example, when engaged in providing treatment to clients, you, as a professional counselor, are required to understand their roles and responsibilities as defined by the profession and state licensure boards and to follow the codes of ethics set by the professional counseling organizations (e.g., American Counseling Association). Moreover, a professional identity aids counselors with making meaning of the work they do through creating a shared sense of belonging and community (Friedman & Kaslow, 1986; Heck, 1990).

According to Remley and Herlihy (2007), the counseling profession has a difficult time distinguishing itself from other professions. Several reasons professional counselors face difficulties creating a unique space for themselves in the mental health world include (a) likeness in theories and techniques across mental health professions, (b) education and training delivered in programs accredited by different accreditation bodies (or none at all), and (c) the common goal of helping clients through therapeutic services across various mental health professions (Emerson, 2010). A final issue that has continued to cause dissonance amongst counselors is the confusing and at times contradictory standards promoted within sister mental health professions (e.g., social work, marriage and family therapy, and applied psychology) (Gale & Austin, 2003; Vacc & Loesch, 2000). For example, all of the aforementioned professions have ethical standards addressing intimacy with former clientele; however, many of them are slightly different in regard to prescribed years. Specifically, the American Counseling Association (ACA, 2005) prescribes a five-year period following the last professional contact; the American Association of Marriage and Family Therapy (AAMFT, 2012) and American Psychological Association (APA, 2002) both prescribe two years after the termination of professional services; and the National Association for Social Work (NASW, 1999) mandates that social workers never engage in romantic activities with former clients.

To make matters more confusing, there are mixed messages regarding ethical issues within the ACA (2005) *Code of Ethics* itself. For example, according to the code section on the counseling relationship (Section A Introduction), counselors are required to donate, "a portion of their professional activity to services for which there is little or no financial return" (ACA, 2005, p. 4). However, a few pages later in the section on the counseling relationship (A. 10.b. Establishing Fees), the code states, "In the event that the established fee structure is inappropriate for a client, counselors assist clients in attempting to find comparable services of acceptable cost" (p. 6). Thus, a different meaning can be interpreted depending on which ethical code is observed.

Distinction and Extinction

The counseling profession must carve out a unique identity for itself or risk falling into professional irrelevance. Particularly, you, as a professional counselor, must have a strong counselor identity to distinguish yourself from other related mental health professionals. Similar to other professions, the counseling profession must have an identity that provides a distinct reflection of the services rendered by its practitioners. To respond to the issue of differentiation, as an initial effort, the ACA and the American Association of State Counseling Boards (AASCB) have employed a collaborative effort, entitled *20/20—A Vision for the Future of Counseling* (ACA, 2010). This effort has made the strengthening of counselor identity a top priority (Kaplan, 2006) by highlighting the importance of a unified counseling profession among counselors with different specialty areas (e.g., addictions counselors, career

---

Exercise 3.1

PROFESSIONAL ETHICAL CODE COMPARE AND CONTRAST

Directions: Find the websites for the American Counseling Association, American Association of Marriage and Family Therapy, American Psychological Association, and National Association of Social Workers. Within each website you will find a direct link to the respective profession's code of ethics. Review all four ethical codes in their entirety. As you are reviewing each professional code of ethics, compare and contrast all major and minor aspects of the various ethical considerations. As you are reviewing the various ethical guidelines, consider which professional organization has the most rigorous set of mandates, and pay attention to the unique aspects of each code of ethics.

counselors, clinical mental health counselors, marriage and family counselors, and school counselors). As a consequence of this effort, on October 28, 2010, the ACA Governing Council approved the following definition of counseling: "Counseling is a professional relationship that empowers diverse individuals, families, and groups to accomplish mental health, wellness, education, and career goals (n.d.)" This definition signified an important step in the distinction of the counseling profession (ACA, 2010).

The counseling profession has made initial steps toward the creation of a unique identity; however, the issues associated with professional overlap, lack of uniform licensure standards, lack of parity in insurance reimbursement, underdeveloped research identity, and not being compensated in a manner commensurate with training serve as barriers to the goal of professional distinction (Hendricks, 2008; Hill, 2004; Lambie, 2007; Nelson & Jackson, 2003; Osborn, 2004; Weinrach, Thomas, & Chan, 2001; Wilkerson & Bellini, 2006). Although it may appear that the aforementioned issues are separate, they are interconnected. For example, if counseling researchers produce empirical evidence supporting a unique counseling technique, professional counselors could reap the benefits of specializing in an empirically supported treatment (e.g., effectively alleviating a mental health issue, increasing positive reputation in the community and appropriate fiscal compensation). As a result of this new treatment, professional counselors would put forth an effort to enhance the profession's issues involving parity and professional identity. While these professional issues seem somewhat linear to ameliorate, the personal issues that permeate the counseling profession prove more difficult to solve.

Unfortunately, many dedicated counseling professionals find themselves burned out due to giving of themselves in a primarily altruistic manner and not creating effective boundaries. Common issues involving counselor burnout and impairment include overriding unselfish concern, ignoring one's stress level, frustration, job dissatisfaction, stress-related health problems, lowered work productivity, inability to cope with occupational stress, interpersonal conflict, apathy, burnout, poor boundaries, feeling pulled in too many directions, vicarious trauma, and role ambiguity (Hill, 2004; Lambie, 2007; Myers, 2003; Myers et al., 2002; Nelson & Southern, 2008; Trippany, White Kress, & Wilcoxon, 2004). Interestingly, role ambiguity, caused by a lack of understanding of appropriate professional role expectations, is one of the reasons contributing to counselor burnout. Therefore, it is important for professional counselors to understand similarities and differences between the counseling profession and other mental health disciplines in order to effectively manage role ambiguity.

In the next section, you will be introduced to a brief review of various applied mental health services, to the history of professional organizations, and to the essence of services rendered in professional counseling, applied psychology, social work, and marriage and family therapy. Following this review is a brief section that compares and contrasts the characteristics of professional counseling with those of other applied mental health professions. It is important to note that we provide only an overview of the major issues and events of the professional counseling and related mental health professions in this chapter. Some of the information presented in this chapter may be similar to what you previously read in Chapter 2. This is to provide a context for professional identity and the development of professional counselors when compared to other related professionals. You will find more about different counselor credentials later, in Chapter 11, and about advocacy for professional counseling in Chapter 12.

PROFESSIONAL COUNSELING AND RELATED MENTAL HEALTH PROFESSIONS

The process of counseling can be traced back to the Enlightenment Era. Ancient priests from Egypt, Mesopotamia, and Persia would recite incantations said to be healing in nature (Hackney & Cormier, 2009). Historically, scholars (e.g., Beesley, 2004) describe the first contemporary counselors emerging in the late 1800s. These were in the form of school personnel (usually primary and secondary teachers) who performed the role of counselor in helping students not only with their academic concerns but also with personal issues, such as emotional difficulties and behavioral problems. In 1952, the American Personnel and Guidance Association (APGA) was formed. The APGA was the result of the merger of the National Vocational Guidance Association (NVGA), the National Association of Guidance and Counselor Trainers (NAGCT), the Student Personnel Association for Teacher Education (SPATE), and the American College Personnel Association (ACPA). More than 30 years later, the APGA changed its name to the American Association of Counseling and Development (AACD). AACD remained the name until 1992, when the AACD adopted a new name and became the current ACA.

In late 1950s, the demand for counseling professionals significantly increased due to the USSR's 1957 launch of the Sputnik satellite. The increase in Russian technological advancements encouraged the US Congress to pass the National Defense Education Act of 1958 (NDEA), which provided support for guidance programs in schools and training for guidance counselors (Bradley & Cox, 2001). The funding for increased use of counseling professionals was essentially educational reform, so the United States could maintain its status as frontrunner in global technological advancement.

Since 2010, counseling has been redefined as the application of mental health, psychological, or human development principles through cognitive, affective, behavioral, or systematic intervention strategies that address wellness, personal growth, or career development, as well as psychopathology (ACA, 2010). According to Emerson's (2010) review of literature on counselor professional identity, counseling philosophy comprises four components: wellness, developmental perspective, prevention, and empowerment. Counseling can be further defined by examining the chartered divisions within ACA. As of 2012, ACA had 19 chartered divisions. (See Chapter 10 for a comprehensive list of ACA divisions.) These chartered divisions provide a map of the various roles and functions professional counselors can maintain. For example, the Association for Specialists in Group Work (ASGW) is one of the ACA chartered divisions. The ASGW is dedicated to the promotion of best practices in, research on, and training of group workers. Professional counselors who belong to this division are interested in group counseling topics and often have specializations in group work.

Applied Psychology

The history of psychology dates back to the ancient times. Ancient philosophers such as Aristotle proffered various psychological notions (e.g., the golden mean, virtuosity, and eudaimonia); however, at this point psychology was considered a branch of philosophy. Antecedents to contemporary applied psychology were the fields of mesmerism, phrenology, and hypnosis. However, it was not until the efforts and theories and of G. Stanley Hall, William James, and Sigmund Freud that psychology became an independent and unique arena for scientific inquiry. (See Hothersall, 2003, for a comprehensive review.) In 1892, Hall (1844–1924) became the first president of the American Psychological Association (APA), and the first APA meeting was held in December of the same year.

Psychology became increasingly in demand following World War II (WWII). This was partly due to the returning servicemen needing an increase in applied psychological service to cope with psychological issues such as adjustment, reintegration to the community, and trauma. During this time, the APA rapidly grew due to its mergers with the American Association of Applied Psychology (AAAP) and the Society for the Psychological Study of Social Issues (SPSSI). The AAAP had been the dominant organization in the United States for individuals with applied psychological interests. The SPSSI was an organization that focused scientific inquiry on social and policy issues within the United States. Other consequences of WWII included the GI Bill, the opening of the Veterans Administration clinical psychology training program, and the emergence of the National Institutes of Mental Health. All of the aforementioned occurrences took place during what is colloquially thought of as the "golden age of psychology" (Hunt, 2007).

According to the APA, *psychology* can be defined as

the study of the mind and behavior. The discipline [of psychology] embraces all aspects of the human experience from the functions of the brain to the actions of nations, from child development to care for the aged. In every conceivable setting from scientific research centers to mental health care services, the understanding of behavior is the enterprise of psychologists. (www.apa.org/support/about/apa/psychology.aspx#answer)

Based on this definition, you now understand that the profession of applied psychology centers primarily on understanding and treating psychological pathology (i.e., abnormality or disease). Day-to-day applied psychologists are involved in diagnosis of personality and personality reorganization. Applied psychology is usually subdivided into school, counseling, clinical, industrial, and community psychology (Vacc & Loesch, 2000). The profession of psychology can be further defined by examining the various divisions within APA. APA currently has 56 chartered divisions, including the following:

- Adult Development and Aging
- American Psychology-Law Society
- American Society for the Advancement of Pharmacotherapy
- Applied Experimental and Engineering Psychology
- Behavior Analysis
- Behavioral Neuroscience and Comparative Psychology
- Clinical Neuropsychology
- Developmental Psychology
- Educational Psychology
- Evaluation, Measurement, and Statistics
- Exercise and Sport Psychology
- Experimental Psychology
- Health Psychology
- Intellectual and Developmental Disabilities
- International Psychology
- Media Psychology
- Psychoanalysis
- Psychologists in Independent Practice
- Psychologists in Public Service
- Psychopharmacology and Substance Abuse
- Psychotherapy
- Rehabilitation Psychology

- School Psychology
- Society for Child and Family Policy and Practice
- Society for Community Research and Action: Division of Community Psychology
- Society for Consumer Psychology
- Society for Environmental, Population and Conservation Psychology
- Society for Family Psychology
- Society for General Psychology
- Society for Humanistic Psychology
- Society for Industrial and Organizational Psychology
- Society for Military Psychology
- Society for Personality and Social Psychology
- Society for the History of Psychology
- Society for the Psychological Study of Ethnic Minority Issues
- Society for the Psychological Study of Lesbian, Gay, Bisexual and Transgender Issues
- Society for the Psychological Study of Men and Masculinity
- Society for the Psychological Study of Social Issues
- Society for the Psychology of Aesthetics, Creativity and the Arts
- Society for the Psychology of Religion and Spirituality
- Society for the Psychology of Women
- Society for the Study of Peace, Conflict and Violence: Peace Psychology Division
- Society for the Teaching of Psychology
- Society for Theoretical and Philosophical Psychology
- Society of Addiction Psychology
- Society of Clinical Child and Adolescent Psychology
- Society of Clinical Psychology
- Society of Consulting Psychology
- Society of Counseling Psychology
- Society of Group Psychology and Group Psychotherapy
- Society of Pediatric Psychology
- Society of Psychological Hypnosis
- State, Provincial and Territorial Psychological Association Affairs
- Trauma Psychology

Social Work

Similar to psychology and counseling, social work goes back to ancient times. Many ancient civilizations engaged in acts of charity for the needy. For example, the ancient Greeks created a system of charity, because they recognized the

Exercise 3.2

ACA AND APA CHARTERED DIVISIONS

Directions: Review the presented chartered divisions within the ACA and the APA. Write down the names of two divisions within ACA and two additional divisions from APA that you currently have interest in. Type out these four divisions' names, brainstorm the reasons you are interested in each particular division, and write these reasons under each name. Next, review what you brainstormed, and carefully note which of the four divisions produced the most interest and, in particular, which produced the most salient interests. Do a web search for the ACA/APA divisions that were most salient, and review the particular website of each. Identify member benefits and when/where the next division meeting will be, and determine the requirements for becoming a member. Finally, consider attending the next conference and/or joining the various divisions.

people in need were vital to the communities in which they lived. The ancient Greek aristocrats demonstrated their charity through public philanthropy (e.g., paying for public sporting events) (Zanker, 1998). Contemporary American social work has its roots in the mass migration of the 19th century. The resultant crowding of various eastern American cities created a variety of social problems and health care needs. To help with these problems, the first professional social workers were trained in Massachusetts General Hospital in 1905 by Dr. Richard Clarke Cabot.

The National Association of Social Workers (NASW) was established in 1955 as the leading professional organization for social workers. The emergence of the NASW was the result of the mergers of the American Association of Social Workers (AASW), the American Association of Psychiatric Social Workers (AAPSW), the American Association of Group Workers (AAGW), the Association for the Study of Community Organization (ASCO), the American Association of Medical Social Workers (AAMSW), the National Association of School Social Workers (NASSW), and the Social Work Research Group (SWRG). Although, Nathan Cohen (1902–2001) served as the first president of the NASW, the merger of the seven organizations was the vision of social reform leader Joseph P. Anderson (1910–1979). (See Popple & Leighninger, 2010, for a comprehensive review of the history of social work in the United States.)

Although definitions of social work often vary among state or territorial jurisdictions, the International Federation of Social Workers (IFSW) has defined the social work profession as

> The social work profession promotes social change, problem solving in human relationships and the empowerment and liberation of people to enhance well-being. Utilizing theories of human behavior and social systems, social work intervenes at the points where people interact with their environments. Principles of human rights and social justice are fundamental to social work. (http://ifsw .org/resources/definition-of-social-work/)

The profession of social worker focuses on community problems that may cause psychopathology (e.g., family system issues, unemployment, and poverty). Understanding multifaceted social systems and delivering socially oriented services are highlighted, usually in the context of the medical model. Social workers are concerned with (a) social advocacy, (b) clinical practice within hospitals and agencies, and (c) consultation with community organizations, families, and individuals (Vacc & Loesch, 2000).

Marriage and Family Therapy

You may understand, based on your professional conversations and reading materials, that marriage and family therapy (MFT) is one of counseling specializations. (See Chapter 4 for more details.) Although that information is accurate, counseling and MFT have different roots. The roots of MFT start around the late 1800s and early 1900s. The early efforts can be categorized in the following groups: social work, marriage and family life education, and marriage counseling. The time period acknowledged as the formal beginning of the family therapy movement is the decade following WWII (Goldenberg & Goldenberg, 2004). After initial efforts to help with the sudden reuniting of families following WWII, more formal marriage and family theories/pioneers began to emerge. As a result of these efforts, counseling and psychological interventions became acceptable to people from a larger range of education and socioeconomic backgrounds. In 1929, physicians Abraham and Hanna Stone opened the first formal marriage and family center, known as the Marriage Consultation Center, in New York. Many other marriage and family centers started to emerge throughout the 1930s, the most notable being Emily Mudd's Marriage Council of Philadelphia (Gurman & Messer 2003). In 1937, Nathan Ackerman became chief psychiatrist of the Child Guidance Clinic at the Menninger Clinic in Topeka, Kansas; it is he who is credited with developing the concept of family psychology. Ackerman was also the first to initiate a debate on family therapy at a meeting of the American Orthopsychiatric Association (1955), with the intention of opening lines of communication in this new branch of psychiatry (Hecker & Wetchler, 2003).

During the early years there was some talk about the connection and implications of mathematics and engineering constructs to the comprehension of human communication. The Macy Foundation conferences were the arena where much talk on these matters began. The emerging field of science and its many implications for the field formulated the foundation of cybernetics theory that eventually helped conceptualize the family as a social system (Goldenberg & Goldenberg, 2004). In the 1950s, Palo Alto, California, produced many MFT pioneers (e.g., Gregory Bateson, Don Jackson, Jay Haley, and Virginia Satir). It was during this period that Gregory Bateson and Don Jackson headed two important projects. Bateson, an anthropologist, and Haley, his student, applied the concept of cybernetics to communication patterns in living organisms, with an emphasis in the area of paradoxes. At the same time, psychiatrist Don Jackson, with the help of Virginia Satir, founded the Mental Research Institute (MRI). Jackson and Satir focused more on family therapy than Bateson did; Bateson was opposed to therapeutic interventions of any kind. These two projects combined to form a force that continues to influence the field of MFT today (Hecker & Wetchler, 2003).

With the emergence of professional organizations, the field of MFT further demonstrated its legitimacy. The National Council of Family Relations (NCFR) was founded in 1938, and the American Association of Marriage Counselors (AAMC) was founded in 1945. These two prominent professional organizations helped establish the field of MFT through the creation of standards for marriage and family counseling and identifying marriage therapy and family therapy as distinct fields. In the 1970s, the AAMC renamed itself the American Association of Marriage and Family Therapy (AAMFT), and during the renaming process expanded the goals and membership criteria (Goldenberg & Goldenberg, 2004).

Although definitions of MFT therapy vary among state and territorial jurisdictions, we found the Ohio Counselor, Social Worker, and Marriage and Family Therapist Board (CSWMFT) provided a concise definition of the MFT process. According to Ohio licensure law as drafted by CSWMFT, the essence of MFT is "the diagnosis, evaluation, assessment, counseling, management and treatment of mental and emotional disorders, whether cognitive, affective, or behavioral, within the context of marriage and family systems, through the professional application of marriage and family therapies and techniques" (http://codes.ohio.gov/orc/4757.01). In practice, marriage and family therapists primarily help with relationships and interaction from a systemic perspective. Thus, the practice of MFT requires special conceptualization and procedures that are different from individually oriented therapies. It is the specific expertise in interpersonal relationships, interaction, and systems theory that qualifies a professional as a marriage and family therapist (AAMFT, 2007). Marriage and family therapists believe that all couples who willingly commit themselves to each other, and their children, have a right to expect equal support and benefits in civil society. Thus, these therapists affirm the right of all committed couples and their families to legally equal benefits, protection, and responsibility (AAMFT, 2005).

Compare and Contrast

While there are unique histories, organizations, and definitions associated with each mental health profession, there are many similarities among professional counseling, applied psychology, social work, and marriage and family therapy. Virtually all major elements of each mental health profession have overlap and distinctiveness (e.g., theories, skills, ethical tenets, and educational standards). Although overlap in theory and skill are somewhat obvious (e.g., the study of cognitive behavioral theory and therapy), specific educational standards may be less evident. One example of a capstone educational issue is the study of the family unit and development in all mental health professions. Not only do all professions require graduate education on the family unit and development, but the AAMFT

Exercise 3.3

ARE YOU IN THE RIGHT PROFESSION?

Directions: Review the roots, tenets, history, political climate, and founding organizations of each profession. Consider the historical similarities between and differences among the different organizations. As you're reflecting on these factors, write down the elements of each profession that you find interesting, exciting, and inspiring. Next, write down the elements of each profession that you find uninteresting, boring, and uninspiring. As you reflect on these various factors, consider which profession seems to be most in line with your interests and inspiration. Next, visit O*NET Online (www.onetonline.org) and go to the function entitled "find occupations." Here, type in the particular profession(s) you have interest and passion in. You will be taken to a page that describes various pragmatic facts about the profession you have chosen, including (but not limited to) national and statewide average salary, common functions of the profession, and personal traits that might aid you should you consider a career in that particular profession.

and NASW have designated the study of the family unit and its development as a central aspect of their professional mission.

Similarly, both APA and ACA have professional divisions dedicated to promoting the study of the family unit (e.g., International Association of Marriage and Family Counselors [belongs to ACA] and Society for Family Psychology [belongs to APA]). Despite the apparent overlap among all mental health professions, the major differences play out when considering the macro values instilled in a profession's practitioners (e.g., social workers deeply value context). For example, if confronted with a depressed client, a professional counselor may approach treatment using an individually oriented theory (e.g., cognitive behavior therapy), while a marriage and family therapist might utilize a systemic approach (e.g., strategic family therapy) to address the depression. A social worker may view the depression primarily as a result of a variety of contextual/social factors (e.g., poverty and geographical location), while a psychologist could see the depression as stemming from an intrapsychic conflict or a disease.

A significant area of overlap is between the entire counseling profession and APA's Division 17: Society of Counseling Psychology. The common use of the word *counseling* in both *professional counseling* and APA's Division 17 indicate the possibility of an overlap. Further, the literature has repeatedly indicated the reality of a professional overlap between these two fields (e.g., Bernard, 2006; Gale & Austin, 2003; Steenbarger, 1991). Common areas of overlap include but are not limited to conceiving of counseling as a service to clients, education (e.g., diagnosis, assessment, theories of counseling), training in a variety of counseling formats (e.g., individual, group, family, and couple), similarity in ethical codes, similarity in chartered divisions (e.g., Society for Humanistic Psychology [APA] and Counseling Association for Humanistic Education and Development [ACA]), and training to work with a spectrum of issues ranging from preventative mental health care to personality disorders.

Despite the overlaps between professional counseling and counseling psychology, there are major differences between the two professions that help you differentiate them from each other. First, in terms of state licensure, a minimum required education to be licensed as a professional counselor is a master's degree, while a minimum required education to be licensed as a psychologist is a doctoral degree in psychology. Second, it is important to note that, for professional counselors, the term *counselor* varies from one state to another. While some state licensure boards (e.g., those of Colorado and Pennsylvania) use the term *licensed professional counselor,* many state licensure board use different terms, including *licensed professional clinical counselor* (e.g., Ohio) and *licensed mental health counselor* (e.g., Florida). However, counseling-psychologist licensure boards across the United States utilize a unified term, *licensed psychologist,* for their licensees. Third, in terms of education and training, counselor education programs are accredited through CACREP; counseling psychology programs are accredited through APA. Last, in terms of professional identity and organization, ACA is the central professional organization for professional counselors, and APA is the main professional organization for counseling psychologists. Although ACA and APA are two separate organizations, both serve the same purpose: to create a professional community and to promote professional identity among members. However, ACA and APA produce different professional journals and have different chartered divisions and ethical codes.

Unique Contributions of the Counseling Profession

Based on the compare and contrast listed above, there are many similarities between professional counseling and other mental health professions. Therefore, the creation of an integrated and unique professional identity has been a salient issue within the counseling profession, and you may face this issue at some point in your career as a professional counselor. According to Weinrach, Thomas, and Chan (2001), professional identity is "the possession of a core set of values, beliefs, and assumptions about the unique characteristics of one's selected profession that differentiates it from other professions" (p. 168). Scholars (Calley & Hawley, 2008; Smith, 2001) have described the lack of a unified identity within professional counseling as detrimental to the future of the profession. Myers, Sweeney, and White's

---

Exercise 3.4

SIMILARITIES AND DIFFERENCES: WHAT IS THE POINT?

Directions: Consider all of the similarities between the counseling profession and the counseling psychology profession. Next, ask yourself two questions: (1) What is different about these two professions? and (2) What are the similarities between these two professions? As you reflect on the differences and similarities between the counseling profession and the counseling psychology profession, we invite you to consider the point of clearly delineated boundaries between various professions. Specifically, we invite you to ask yourself why it is important to think about the similarities and differences between various professions.

(2002) theoretical article entitled, "Advocacy for Counseling and Counselors: A Professional Imperative," postulated that counselors were criticized for an inability to distinguish themselves from members of other professions. Advocacy efforts proposed by Myers et al. (2002) and other recent researchers (e.g., Emerson, 2010; Mellin, Hunt, & Nichols, 2011) have built on a body of work that has attempted to describe the unique aspects of the counseling profession and create a unifying professional identity.

In this body of work, the counseling profession has been described as humanistic, prevention oriented, steeped in human development, holistic in nature, and incorporating a wellness/strength-based philosophy. According to Nelson and Southern's (2008) thought piece entitled "Reaffirming Our Roots," the core values of Carl Rogers and strength-based interventions are the foundation of the counseling profession. Hansen (2003) echoed this, indicating that the identity of the counseling profession is rooted in humanism and human development. Classic research described counseling as oriented in health, based in developmental education, inclusive, relational, and holistic (Swickert, 1997). Similarly, Kelly (1995) described counselors as valuing holistic-humanistic empowerment in relation to personal development and interpersonal/social concerns. Myers (1992) added wellness as a salient philosophy to counselors' professional identity. Along the same lines, West, Osborn, and Bubenzer (2003) espoused one of the most inclusive descriptions of counseling professional identity. Specifically, they described counselors as possessing a philosophical orientation to reflect a strong identification with prevention, human development over the lifespan, and interventions designed not only to remediate but also to enhance the length and quality of life for all persons.

These definitions and descriptions of counseling create a distinct professional identity. It is safe to conclude that professional counselors view the world through a humanistic and developmental philosophical lens and that they believe in prevention-oriented and strength-based approaches that incorporate holistic and wellness-oriented theory and techniques.

Although all professions, including professional counseling, make ongoing efforts to differentiate themselves from others, in reality, counseling professionals and closely related mental health professionals work collaboratively with each other. For example, school counselors work with school psychologists and teachers on a daily basis in order to provide comprehensive service to students in school settings. Therefore, it is important for you to understand how professional counselors will work with these professionals, regardless of the professional setting. In the next section, you will learn how professional counselors work with other professionals in various settings.

CASE ILLUSTRATION 3.1

PRACTICE WHAT WE PREACH

Peter recently graduated from his counseling program and took a job he was offered as a professional school counselor at an urban high school. Because of his youthful ambition, Peter immediately established an extracurricular program at his high school designed to develop interpersonal and leadership skills. As the school year continued, Peter found himself taking on additional tasks he hadn't expected. He began coordinating all of the standardized testing at his school, began writing IEPs as requested by his principal, and even picked up an additional 30 new students on his caseload. Feeling as though he was being asked to do too many things, Peter began to resent his principal, his colleagues, and his job. As a result, his students suffered.

Peter found himself feeling angry and disappointed in his job, which negatively affected his professional functioning. Specifically, Peter began arriving late to work, missing meetings, feeling distracted during counseling sessions, and, at times, relieving his stress with the excessive use of alcohol. Peter recalled that during graduate school he learned that professional counselors value preventative care, wellness, and holistic-oriented healing modalities. Peter thought to himself, "I'm a professional counselor; maybe I should practice what I preach." Following this thought, Peter called a local counselor and scheduled an appointment to work on assertiveness and alcohol use (preventative care). In addition, Peter reflected about how he used to feel more focused and energetic when he maintained a healthy diet and participated in weekly yoga sessions. Consequently, Peter signed up for yoga in his local community center and began monitoring what foods he ate (holistic wellness).

After four weeks of counseling, Peter was able to establish appropriate boundaries with his coworkers and significantly cut back on his alcohol use. In addition, through eating a well-balanced diet and practicing yoga, Peter felt more energetic, focused, and therapeutic.

PROFESSIONAL CONSULTATION AND COLLABORATION

Professional counselors play a significant role in the personal wellness, careers, and education of diverse client populations. We, as professional counselors, perform our roles and functions in various settings, such as community and educational institutions. Professional counselors work alongside other professionals, such as social workers, psychologists, doctors, and teachers, to help enhance the overall quality of service to clients. In this respect professional counselors become an integral part of a multidisciplinary team.

Consultation and collaboration are two of the ways that professional counselors can work with other professionals to enhance the quality of service provided to clients. You may wonder about the differences between them. Dougherty (2005) defined *consultation* as "a helping relationship in which human service professionals work with individuals and/or groups in a variety of settings (such as agencies, schools, and businesses) to help them work more effectively" (p. 1). *Collaboration* is similar, however, collaboration involves a process in which two or more parties working together to assist another individual or group toward some desired outcome (Allen, 1994). Effective consultation occurs when professionals have an understanding of the differences and similarities between the professions they are working with. This understanding helps in creating effective boundaries and a shared vision, with mutual respect for the ally professionals. Consultation and collaboration can be cost effective for a company; that is, it is relatively inexpensive for a company to hire a few individuals with expertise to enhance a systemwide issue. For example, if a business is having an issue with poor health amongst employees, counseling professionals with expertise in the area of wellness could stand to make a significant profit for assessing the wellness of the employees, suggesting potential approaches to improving it, and working with organizational managers to create strategies to enhance the well-being of employees. Therefore, consultation and collaboration can be (and often are) reciprocally beneficial for both the provider and receiver of the professional service.

Although consultation and collaboration may be activities that many professional counselors aspire to take part in, recent evidence suggests that professional counselors do not receive adequate training in consultation (Sangganjanavanich & Lenz, 2012). You may find that, in your graduate program, you learn a great deal about counseling both in theory (e.g., theory course) and practice (e.g., practicum or internship). You, however, may find that consultation is being taught in one didactic course (without giving you an opportunity to work under supervised experience) or, in the worse case, consultation is only a part of an introductory course. In an effort to promote the importance of consultation in the counseling profession, we describe consulting roles in two work settings: community and educational settings.

Community Settings

The main goal of an organizational consultant is to improve the effectiveness of an organization (for-profit or nonprofit) through data collection, problem identification, and assessment of organizational wellness. The consultant often functions as an expert who possesses information or skills that the consultee needs, and she transmits that knowledge in her role as an advisor, educator, trainer, or technical expert. The consultant's function is to provide the information and/or the training that best matches the consultee's interests and needs. The major trends in organizational consulting are linked to several societal factors: the impact of living and working in an information society, the ever-increasing pace of change in all aspects of life, the growing awareness that change requires systemic thinking, the realization that change can be successfully accomplished only through social influences (e.g., reliance on computer hardware and software), and increasing internationalization and diversity within organizations (Dougherty, 2008). (This last item reflects the effects of organizational culture and diversity on the consultant's suggestions and expertise.)

The main goal of mental health consultation is to work with human service personnel and/or administrators to help them understand work-related problems, such as challenging cases and systemwide problems within mental health programs. The consultant functions primarily as an expert in assessing the situation, diagnosing the client, and making recommendations for the consultee's use in the case. Specifically, the consultant builds a relationship with the consultee; assesses the client's difficulty by gathering information from the client and other sources; assesses the consultee's strengths, weaknesses, and work setting by visiting the consultee at work; and files a written report, usually a letter or a case record, which should be reviewed in a meeting with the consultee. A few contemporary trends within mental health consultation include the use of internal resources, training of nonprofessionals, and the utilization of group consultation. There is currently a move toward collaboration, that is, toward having consultants take some direct responsibility for implementing at least part of the plan to help the client (as opposed to the consultee having complete responsibility for the outcome of the consultation). This process has been entitled *reciprocal consultation*.

A second trend is the use of nonprofessionals (e.g., parents, volunteers, and paraprofessionals) within the consultation process. Mental health consultants can aid these consultees in working with other individuals and systems with the same methods (e.g., therapeutic interventions and communication skills) they utilize with mental health professionals. Finally, group consultation is gaining positive attention in mental health consultation. This has been deemed as cost effective and described as a superior method, reaching more professionals in a single consultation experience than can be reached in individual consultation. For example, if you were to consult with an entire organization on methods for counseling families and couples, you would reach more professionals in a shorter period of time. Also, the dialogue engaged in during this group experience would have the effect of enhancing the entire system's understanding around a particular issue (e.g., family defensiveness, prevention of parentification) (Dougherty, 2008).

Educational Settings

School-based consultation involves direct (e.g., implementing interventions and providing trainings) and indirect (e.g., case conceptualization and system-wide assessment) services to change a student's behavior or the behavior of the adults involved with students. School counselors, school social workers, and school psychologists are the professionals who most often provide school-based consultation. Federal initiatives such as the No Child Left Behind Act, children's eligibility for special services, and the school reform movement have spawned educational changes, including year-round schooling, increased oversight, educational accountability, and new scholastic standards (Dougherty, 2005). These changes have, in part, increased the demand for school consultation and have changed the scope of practice for school oriented consultation providers. Contemporary trends within the role of school-consultant role include increasingly being asked to offer services to the family of prekindergarten children, creating a positive environment within schools adjusting to various educational reform movements, and combating teacher turnover through creating teacher support groups (Dougherty, 2008).

CASE ILLUSTRATION 3.2

INDIRECT AND DIRECT CONSULTATION IN SCHOOLS

As the only school counselor employed at your elementary school, you are approached by many teachers for help with students. Currently, Mr. Rogers, who teaches the third grade, is having trouble managing the behavior of one of his students in the classroom. Knowing that you have expertise in the areas of psychology and child development, he comes to you for help devising employable strategies that might effectively mitigate his issues. You set aside a time to sit down with Mr. Rogers to discuss his concerns, and he expresses to you that Wyatt never stays in his seat and that he's constantly calling out of turn or without raising his hand—and these are just the mild outbursts. You agree with Mr. Rogers that something should be done to help Wyatt behave more appropriately in the classroom and consequently improve his school performance.

Before collaborating on strategies, both you and Mr. Rogers set aside time to observe Wyatt in other classrooms to see if these issues manifest similarly in Wyatt's other classes. While sitting in and observing one of Mr. Rogers's class periods, you notice that just before Wyatt calls out, he starts tapping his toes rapidly on the floor. You also notice that when Wyatt receives praise for raising his hand, he is more likely to do so next time he has an answer.

You decided it will be best to consult in two ways. The first is by working directly with Wyatt; you decide to bring him in for individual counseling sessions where you can work on helping him recognize the warning signs his body gives when he's about to call out or misbehave (e.g., toe tapping), and you can teach him techniques he can use to calm himself down (e.g., breathing, mental imagery, and self-talk). The second is by working with Mr. Rogers; you can indirectly support Wyatt by helping Mr. Rogers recognize Wyatt's warning signs before an outburst occurs and help Wyatt build his awareness of these signals. You can also help Mr. Rogers develop a variety of strategies to praise and reward Wyatt for his positive behaviors (e.g., token economy, response cost, or behavioral contract).

Little has been written on consultation in postsecondary schools; however, evidence suggests an increased need for consultation at the postsecondary level. Specifically, in a national survey of 272 counseling center directors, 91% reported an increasing trend of severe psychological issues in college (Gallagher, 2001). In addition, Gallagher reported that postsecondary administrators view consultation as one of the top five counseling center activities. The central role for consultation within a postsecondary setting is to provide education, training, and services to enhance the functioning of faculty and staff. Some contemporary examples of college consulting include consulting with faculty on various intrapersonal and interpersonal issues (e.g., ethically and multiculturally appropriate pedagogy practices), consulting with residence life staff on contextual and multicultural issues (e.g., the burning of sage and sweet grass in dormitory rooms), and enhancing staff team functioning (e.g., clear communication amongst dining service staff) (Ellington, Kochenour, & Weitzman, 2000; Flynn, Duncan, & Jorgensen, 2012; Hipple & Ramsey, 1985; Westbrook et al., 1993).

KEYSTONES

Within this chapter, professional roles, functions, and consultation/collaboration were discussed. First, how does professional counseling effectively differentiate itself from other applied mental health professions? Within this chapter much of the content and exercises promote an understanding of the unique professional identity and roles associated with counseling. Second, professional counselors can use this chapter as a roadmap for understanding the historical background, identity, roles, functions, and professional organizations of the various applied mental health fields. Specifically, this section attempts to clarify allied colleagues' professional identities, which should be helpful when entering into a collaborative role with a mental health professional from an allied profession. Last, we reviewed the role of consultant within both community and educational settings and discussed contemporary issues that professional counselors are currently working on within both of the aforementioned settings. Below are a few specific informational points for consideration.

- Professional counselors have a unique identity in the mental health marketplace, and counseling professionals can choose from a wide variety of roles and behaviors within the profession.
- Understanding the unique history, professional organization, and purpose/ definition of allied mental health professions provides a road map to understanding counseling's unique professional identity and areas of professional overlap as well as the various strengths possessed by each profession.
- Through education, professional training, reading widely, supervision, and mentorship, counseling professionals can achieve the necessary skills to become consultants or entrepreneurs in a given area. Often these areas of interest align with a CACREP curriculum, one of ACA's chartered divisions, or with the counselor's professional identity.

ADDITIONAL RESOURCES

Book

Lippitt, G., & Lippitt, R. (1986). *The consulting process in action* (2nd ed.). La Jolla, CA: University Associates.

Websites

American Association for Marriage and Family Therapy: http://www.aamft.org
American Counseling Association: http://www.counseling.org
Association for Counselor Education and Supervision: http://www.acesonline.net/
Chi Sigma Iota: http://www.csi-net.org/
Council for Accreditation of Counseling and Related Educational Programs: http://www.cacrep.org/ template/index.cfm

REFERENCES

Allen, J. (1994). Presidential perspective. *The ASCA Counselor, 31.*

American Association of Marriage and Family Therapy (AAMFT). (2005). *AAMFT position on couples and families.* Retrieved from http://www.aamft.org/iMIS15/AAMFT/MFT_Resources/MFT_Resources/Content/Resources/Position_On_Couples.aspx

American Association of Marriage and Family Therapy (AAMFT). (2007). *Approved supervision designation: Standards and responsibilities handbook.* Washington, DC: Author.

American Counseling Association (ACA). (2005). *ACA code of ethics.* Alexandria, VA: Author.

American Counseling Association (ACA). (2010). *20/20—A vision for the future of counseling.* Retrieved from http://counseling.org/20–20/definition.aspx

American Psychological Association (APA). (2002). Ethical principles of psychologists and code of conduct. *American Psychologist, 57,* 1060–1073.

Beesley, D. (2004). Teachers' perceptions of school counselor effectiveness: Collaborating for student success. *Education, 125,* 259–270.

Bradley, R. W., & Cox, J. A. (2001). Counseling: Evolution of the profession. In D. C. Locke, J. E. Myers, & E. L. Herr (Eds.), *The handbook of counseling* (pp. 641–652). Thousand Oaks, CA: Sage.

Calley, N. G., & Hawley, L. D. (2008). The professional identity of counselor educators. *The Clinical Supervisor, 27,* 3–16.

Dougherty, M. A. (2005). *Psychological consultation and collaboration in school and community settings* (4th ed.). Pacific Grove, CA: Brooks/Cole.

Dougherty, M. A. (2008). *Psychological consultation and collaboration in school and community settings* (5th ed.). Pacific Grove, CA: Brooks/Cole.

Ellington, K. T., Kochenour, E. O., & Weitzman, L. M. (2000). University counseling center consultation: Developing a faculty outreach program. *Consulting Psychology Journal: Practice and Research, 51,* 31–56.

Emerson, C. H. (2010). *Counselor professional identity: Construction and validation of the counselor professional identity measure.* In The University of North Carolina at Greensboro, ProQuest Dissertations and Theses, 287. Retrieved from http://search.proquest.com/docview/366911552?accountid=3778

Flynn, S. V., Duncan, K. J., & Jorgenson, M. F. (2012). An emergent phenomenon of American Indian post-secondary transition and retention. *Journal of Counseling and Development, 90,* 437–449.

Friedman, D. K., & Kaslow, N. (1986). The development of professional identity in psychotherapists: Six stages in the supervision process. In F. W. Kaslow (Ed.), *Supervision* (pp. 29–50). New York, NY: Haworth Press.

Gale, A. U., & Austin, B. D. (2003). Professionalism challenges to professional counselors' collective identity. *Journal of Counseling and Development, 81,* 3–10.

Gallagher, R. P. (2001). *National survey of college counseling center directors 2001.* Washington, DC: International Association of Counseling Services.

Goldenberg, I., & Goldenberg, H. (2004). *Family therapy: An overview* (6th ed.) Pacific Grove, CA: Brooks/Cole.

Gurman, S. A., & Messer, B. S. (2003). *Essential psychotherapies* (2nd ed.). New York, NY: Guilford Press.

Hackney, H., & Cormier, S. (2009). *The professional counselor: A process guide to helping* (6th ed.). Upper Saddle River, NJ: Pearson.

Hansen, J. T. (2003). Including diagnostic training in counseling curricula: Implications for professional identity development. *Counselor Education and Supervision, 43,* 96–107.

Heck, E. J. (1990). Identity achievement or diffusion: A response to Van Hesteren and Ivey. *Journal of Counseling and Development, 68,* 532–533.

Hecker, L. L., & Wetchler, L. J. (2003). *an introduction to marriage and family therapy.* Binghamton, NY: Haworth Clinical Practice Press.

Hendricks, B. C. (2008). Introduction: Who are we? The role of ethics in shaping counselor identity. *The Family Journal, 16,* 258–260. doi: 10.1177/1066480708317725

Hill, R. N. (2004). The challenges experienced by pretenured faculty members in counselor education: A wellness perspective. *Counselor Education and Supervision, 44,* 135–146.

Hipple, J., & Ramsey, A. (1985). Consultation through quality circles. *Journal of College Student Personnel, 26,* 556–558.

Hothersall, D. (2003). *History of psychology* (4th ed.). New York, NY: McGraw-Hill.

Hunt, M. (2007). *The story of psychology.* New York, NY: MacMillan

Kaplan, D. (2006). The top four myths that surround counselor identity. *Counseling Today, 48,* 40.

Kelly, E. W., Jr. (1995). Counselor values: A national survey. *Journal of Counseling & Development, 73,* 648–653.

Lambie, G. W. (2007). The contribution of ego development level to burnout in school counselors: Implications for professional school counseling. *Journal of Counseling and Development, 85,* 82–88.

Mellin, E. A., Hunt, B., & Nichols, L. M. (2011). Counselor professional identity: Findings and implications for counseling and interprofessional collaboration. *Journal of Counseling & Development, 89*(2), 140–147.

Myers, J. E. (1992). Wellness, prevention, development: The cornerstone of the profession. *Journal of Counseling and Development, 71,* 136–139.

Myers, J. E. (2003). Coping with caregiving stress: A wellness-oriented, strengths-based approach for family counseling. *The Family Journal, 11,* 153–161. doi: 10.1177/1066480702250162

Myers, J. E., & Sweeney, T. J. (2008). Wellness counseling: The evidence base for practice. *Journal of Counseling and Development, 86,* 482–493.

Myers, J. E., Sweeney, T. J., & White, V. E. (2002). Advocacy for counseling and counselors: A professional imperative. *Journal of Counseling & Development, 80*(4), 394–402.

Nelson, K. W., & Jackson, S. A. (2003). Professional counselor identity development: A qualitative study of Hispanic student interns. *Counselor Education and Supervision, 43,* 2–14.

Nelson, K. W., & Southern, S. (2008). Reaffirming our roots. *The Family Journal, 16,* 105. doi: 10.1177/1066480708314526

Osborn, C. J. (2004). Seven salutary suggestions for counselor stamina. *Journal of Counseling and Development, 82,* 319–328.

Popple, R. P., & Leighninger, L. (2010). Social work, social welfare and American society (8th ed.). Upper Saddle River, NJ: Prentice-Hall.

Remley, T., & Herlihy, B. (2007). *Ethical, legal, and professional issues in counseling* (2nd ed. updated). Upper Saddle River, NJ: Prentice-Hall.

Ritchie, M. H. (1994). Should we be training licensed psychologists? *ACES Spectrum, 55*(1), 15.

Sangganjanavanich, V. F., & Lenz, A. S. (2012). The experiential consultation training model. *Counselor Education and Supervision, 51*(4), 296–307. doi: 10.1002/j.1556–6978.2012.00022.x

Smith, H. B. (2001). Professional identity for counselors. In D. C. Locke, J. E. Myers, & E. L. Herr (Eds.), *The Handbook of Counseling* (pp. 569–579). Thousand Oaks, CA: Sage.

Steenbarger, B. N. (1991). Root metaphors and parables: A comment on Van Hesteren and Ivey. *Journal of Counseling and Development, 69,* 380–381.

Swickert, M. L. (1997). Perceptions regarding the professional identity of counselor education doctoral graduates in private practice: A qualitative study. *Counselor Education and Supervision, 36,* 332–340.

Trippany, R. L., White Kress, V. E., & Wilcoxon, A. S. (2004). Preventing vicarious trauma: What counselors should know when working with trauma survivors. *Journal of Counseling and Development, 82,* 31–37.

Vacc, N. A., & Loesch, L. C. (2000). *Professional orientation to counseling* (3rd ed.). Florence, KY: Brunner-Routledge.

Weinrach, S. G., Thomas, K. R., & Chan, F. (2001). The professional identity of contributors to the Journal of Counseling and Development: Does it matter? *Journal of Counseling and Development, 79,* 166–170.

West, J. D., Hosie, T. W., & Mackey, J. A. (1987). Employment and roles of counselors in mental health agencies. *Journal of Counseling and Development, 66,* 135–138.

West, J. D., Osborn, C. J., & Bubenzer, D. L. (2003). Dimensions of leadership in the counseling profession. In J. D. West, C. J. Osborn, & D. L. Bubenzer (Eds.), *Leaders & legacies: Contributions to the profession of counseling* (pp. 3–23). New York, NY: Brunner-Routledge.

Westbrook, F. D., Kandell, J. J., Kirkland, S. E., Phillips, P. E., Regan, A. M., Medvene, A., & Oslin, Y. D. (1993). University campus consultation: Opportunities and limitations. *Journal of Counseling and Development, 71,* 684–688.

Wilkerson, K., & Bellini, J. (2006). Intrapersonal and organizational factors associated with burnout among school counselors. *Journal of Counseling and Development, 84,* 440–450.

Zanker, G. (1998). Beyond reciprocity: The Akhilleus-Priam scene in *Iliad* 24. In C. Gill, N. Postlethwaite, & R. Seaford (Eds.), *Reciprocity in ancient Greece* (pp. 73–92). Oxford, UK: Clarendon Press.

Chapter 4

Professional Settings and Career Choices

CHRISTOPHER SCHMIDT

W hen talking about professional counselors, you may think about a counselor who works with children in school, one who works with an adult client in a drug and alcohol treatment program, or one who works with a group of women surviving intimate partner violence. The fact is, you are right. There are many types of professional counselors. Each type adopts and performs different roles according to her area of expertise, work setting, and/or interest. For example, you may develop a specific interest in family counseling with families adjusting to a child's recent mental health diagnosis, whereas a student-peer of yours might develop a specific interest in geriatric counseling. Each type of professional counselor possesses unique characteristics, skill sets, and bases of knowledge. The diversity of roles and settings within the profession afford counselors with a plethora of choices from which to shape their career paths.

Although there are differences, counselors still share a core set of skills and knowledge. In 2009, the American Counseling Association (ACA), along with its divisions and related organizations (e.g., American College Counseling Association, International Association of Marriage and Family Counselors, National Career Development Association), initiated the project *20/20: A Vision for the Future of Counseling* and proposed *Principles for Unifying and Strengthening the Profession* (ACA, 2010a). The intent of this multiyear undertaking was to clarify and develop a cohesive counseling identity that could be easily presented to clients, counseling students, and the general public. Professional counselors were clearly defined as those who establish "a professional relationship that empowers diverse individuals, families, and groups to accomplish mental health, wellness, education, and career goals" (ACA, 2010a). Additionally, the foundational principles in the document can be used for continued unity among professionals as well as for the advancement of the profession moving toward the year 2020 (Kaplan & Gladding, 2011). The first of these principles addresses the project's intent to foster the development of a common professional identity among counselors regardless of their special areas of practice (Kaplan & Gladding).

In addition to recognizing the necessity of promoting a common professional identity among counselors, it is crucial to understand differences among professional counselors who have unique foci on their service delivery to clients in various settings. For example, a professional counselor in a school functions differently than a professional counselor in a mental health agency. Each role requires a specific skill set, base of knowledge, and counseling approach. Information presented in this chapter will help you identify some of the unique characteristics of professional counselors in various settings. The chapter focuses on the seven types of counselor specialty areas that relate directly to the master's programs or specialty areas currently accredited by the Council for the Accreditation of Counseling and Related Programs (CACREP). You will be first introduced to the varied settings in which individuals in each area tend to work. You will also be provided with information on general duties and job descriptions within the settings. The next sections explore the types of interventions various counselors employ and the various professionals with whom counselors tend to collaborate in each setting. These sections conclude with descriptions of each type of a counselor's specialty area and further information about training, certification, licensure, and employment projections. The latter half of the chapter reviews areas of career exploration helpful for counselors in training; these include the importance of self-knowledge, knowledge of the counseling world of work, and steps toward accessing these bases of knowledge. Reflection exercises including case studies will enhance your learning about the importance of deliberate personal examination of your *self* within this profession and the intricacies of the various counseling specialty areas.

LEARNING OBJECTIVES

After reading this chapter and completing the activities, you will be able to

- Describe the process of counselor development, roles of counselors in varying fields, models of different types of counseling, basic requirements for licensure, and aspects of the self and the world of work important for career exploration;

- Identify each specialty area, professional organizations, certifications and licenses, collaborative opportunities, important counselor identity factors, and steps to consider in making career choices;
- Discuss the impact of both intrapsychic and external experiences on counselor professional development and the core competencies of various professional settings as well as the variability within each; and
- Recognize steps to take in identifying your own biases and values and choosing a field of interest, and the risks and benefits of working in each field.

Reflection Exercise 4.1

MINDFUL AWARENESS

Being mindful is the intentional practice of becoming aware of this very moment and all that it includes. People often mistake becoming more mindful as not feeling or experiencing anything but happy thoughts—whereas true mindfulness does not minimize or mitigate emotions such as anger, frustration, helplessness, or confusion—sentiments that might be particularly present for counselors in training. Instead, mindfulness allows us to become *aware*, not to become *perfect*; to bring our attention to whatever it is that we are experiencing, name it, sit with it, and recognize that it is a piece of our experience that ultimately must be released without judgment and used to better understand the world, our clients, and ultimately ourselves. A simple way to begin to increase our mindfulness, increase our awareness of the events and emotions that make up our day, and increase our understanding of ourselves as people and professionals is to use our senses.

Assume a comfortable position, and—closing your eyes, if you are comfortable with that—begin breathing in through your nose and out through your mouth. Slowly bring your attention to your senses. Inhaling, what is it that you smell? Sit with it, exhale, and release it. Inhaling, what is it that you taste? Sit with it, exhale, and release it. Inhaling, what is it that you hear inside your own mind and in the world around you? Sit with it, exhale, and release it. Inhaling, what is it that you see in your mind's eye? Sit with it, exhale, and release it. Inhaling, what is it that you feel emotionally, physically, spiritually? Sit with it, exhale, and release it. Breathing in through your nose and out through your mouth, slowly bring attention back to your breathing, ease your eyes open, and remind yourself that every moment of every day can be attended to with that same mindfulness. Breathe in each moment, sit with it, exhale, and release it insightfully—withholding judgment and accepting it for exactly what it is meant to be.

PATHS OF PROFESSIONAL COUNSELORS

Three characteristics are important benchmarks in the development of a counselor: counselor identity, counselor self-efficacy, and counselor cognitive complexity. *Identity* refers to our conceptualization of who we are as a counselor and it serves as a reference point for our roles and decisions within the profession (Brott & Myers, 1999). This identity develops as we integrate our attitudes toward professional responsibilities, ethical standards, professional membership, and personal learning styles (Auxier, Hughes, & Kline, 2003). Folkes-Skinner, Elliott, and Wheeler (2010) remind us that the process of counselor training involves significant shifts in identity, self-knowledge, and confidence. *Self-efficacy* relates to confidence and describes one's beliefs about his or her level of ability to practice different aspects of counseling (Kozina, Grabovari, De Stefano, & Drapeau, 2010). Research outcomes have continued to show the benefits of higher levels of *cognitive complexity* on the counseling process. More cognitively complex counselors are better able to (a) identify and integrate multiple ambiguous pieces of information to better understand the client's needs, the relational dynamics, and the treatment implications (Welfare & Borders, 2010); (b) remain objective (Borders, 1989); (c) form complex clinical hypotheses (Holloway & Wolleat, 1980); and (d) avoid stereotyping (Spengler & Strohmer, 1994); and they have increased confidence as well (Fong, Borders, Ethington, & Pitts, 1997). In these three areas, our deliberate focus on the act of *becoming* will assist in the refinement of our professional objectives and the development of our skills and ability to conceptualize client cases, and ultimately our focus will increase our effectiveness with the population with whom we decide to work.

Experiences (i.e., work, education, relationships) and professional training play a significant role in the development of these characteristics. Although doubt remains around the assumption that specific therapeutic training translates to successful therapy (Beutler et al., 2004; Lambert & Ogles, 2004; Ronnestad & Ladany, 2006), students report the importance of training for a number of reasons: interactions with experienced professionals, supportive supervision (De Stefano et al., 2007; Howard, Inman, & Altman, 2006; Orlinsky & Ronnestad, 2005; Schmidt & Adkins, 2011), the support and encouragement of peers (Howard et al., 2006; Schmidt & Adkins, 2011), and the development of a theoretical knowledge.

Much has been written about the developmental process of *becoming* a counselor, but the work of Skovholt and Ronnestad (1992, 2003) gives us a clear model to help us understand this process of evolution. The six phases of therapist/counselor development are outlined in Figure 4.1.

Figure 4.1   Phases of Therapist/Counselor Development

Phase	Description
The Lay Helper	Pretraining period characterized by overinvolvement, boundary problems, and giving advice based on one's own experiences
The Beginning Student	Period of questioning and self-doubt, reliance on supervisors, utilization of simpler counseling/therapy methods
The Advanced Student	Typically highly cautious and thorough; subscribing to high performance standards; differentiating, accepting, or rejecting models
The Novice Professional	Intense and engaging work while beginning on one's own; period of disillusionment with training and exploration of other models
The Experienced Professional	Phase characterized by creating a therapy/counseling role that is congruent with one's self and trusting one's professional judgments
The Senior Professional	"Leaders" in the field with high work satisfaction and a continued commitment to grow professionally

Adapted from Ronnestad and Skovholt (2003).

COUNSELING SPECIALTY AREAS AND SETTINGS

In general, the settings in which you choose to *practice* counseling align with your professional goals and personal values or interests. Your prior experiences certainly play a role in this decision-making process, yet choosing the best environment can be an overwhelming process (Cunningham, 2010). Professional counselors come from a variety of work backgrounds, with careers in education and health care making up the majority (King, 2007). In 2008, counselors held about 665,500 positions in the United States; 41% were vocational and school counselors, 17% were mental health counselors, 13% were substance abuse and behavioral disorder counselors, and 4% were marriage and family counselors (Bureau of Labor Statistics, 2012). It is important to note that each specialty area contains multiple potential positions, each with its own variations in work-related tasks. Reflection Exercise 4.2 will help you begin locating some of the settings and populations to which you are drawn. In the following sections, you will have an opportunity to review basic elements of the counseling subspecialties and the settings in which they are practiced, so that you might begin to reflect on (a) an area of particular interest and (b) an area in which you believe you might be most effective.

Reflection Exercise 4.2

FINDING A FIT: A REFLECTION EXERCISE FOR THE DISCERNING COUNSELOR IN TRAINING

Reflection questions to ask yourself as you discern the best environment for you as a future counselor.

When I think about myself as a counselor,

- ✓ Do I see myself working in a school?
- ✓ Do I see myself working with adults?
- ✓ Do I see myself working with children?
- ✓ Do I see myself working with individuals such as criminals, juvenile delinquents, or abusers?
- ✓ Do I see myself working with groups or families?
- ✓ Do I see myself enjoying working with couples who are facing difficulties or struggling to agree?
- ✓ Do I see myself working with individuals struggling with physical ailments, disabilities, or nutritional needs?
- ✓ Do I see myself in the corporate world?
- ✓ Do I see myself training individuals or working with CEOs on employee productivity?
- ✓ Do I see myself on a college campus?
- ✓ Do I see myself feeling passionate about residential issues of college students?
- ✓ Do I see myself working with individuals struggling with substance abuse?
- ✓ Do I see myself assisting individuals in finding a career that fits their skills, personality, interests, and values?
- ✓ Do I see myself in a hospital setting?
- ✓ Do I require an externally imposed structure on my schedule?
- ✓ Do I prefer to make my own schedule?
- ✓ Do I work best with a team of people?
- ✓ Do I see myself able to navigate the world of paperwork and insurance billing?
- ✓ Do I fit best at a small company where I will likely have to wear many hats and assume different roles?
- ✓ Do I find energy in challenges and obstacles presented by clients mandated to treatment?
- ✓ Do I see myself able to separate from the trauma presented in crisis counseling situations, preserve self-care, and avoid compassion fatigue?

Addictions Counseling

When you think about addictions, what comes to mind? You may think about people who have drinking problems, who consume too many prescription drugs, or who demonstrate compulsive behaviors in other areas such as hypersexual behaviors, Internet overuse, pathological gambling, and workaholism. Hypersexuality refers to the behavior of an individual who has particular urges that occur very frequently or become out of the individual's control. In the case of problematic computer use, the individual's use is so excessive that her normal daily functioning is interfered with. While compulsive Internet behaviors or compulsive sexual behaviors may appear closely related to those of substance use, they are not considered disorders in the most recent edition (the fifth) of the *Diagnostic and Statistical Manual of Mental Disorders,* known as DSM-V (American Psychiatric Association, 2013; DSM-V). The DSM-V did add a new category called "Addictive Disorders," but gambling disorder is the only condition listed. We are learning more about behaviors that have addictive characteristics, but the vast majority of addictive behaviors have to do with substances. Substance use disorders are one of the most prevalent public health issues in the United States (Chandler, Balkin, & Perepiczka, 2011), and therefore, counseling positions working with this population represent the vast majority of positions within the addictions field.

The category "Substance Use Disorder" addresses use of each substance as a separate disorder (e.g., alcohol use disorder, stimulant use disorder); however, each disorder is measured on a continuum from mild to severe, and almost all substance use is diagnosed using the same criteria. The disorder can be either physical or psychological and is diagnosed when two or more of the eleven criteria are met (e.g., tolerance, withdrawal symptoms, persistent desire to stop, time spent trying to acquire, unsuccessful efforts to cut down, failing to fulfill obligations, using in hazardous situations, continuing use despite persistent social and interpersonal problems influenced by the substance). "Substance Induced Disorder" refers to problems caused by substance addiction, such as intoxication, withdrawal, and a list of substance induced mental disorders. Between 20% and 50% of hospital admissions are related to substance use, and about 1 in 10 adults have problems with alcohol. Substance disorders do not discriminate by age, religion, income, ethnicity, geography, or profession (Stevens & Smith, 2001). Considering the nature and extent of the problem in our society, there is a great need for well-trained counselors (Whitter et al., 2006) to provide research-based interventions in multiple settings.

Given the prevalence of substance use disorders and the varying types of individuals impacted, multiple interventions and settings are utilized. Primarily, these include substance abuse treatment facilities and a range of community mental health centers. Additionally, there are numerous other settings where addictions counselors might play a role: hospitals, correctional institutions, private practice, and community improvement programs (James & Simons, 2011). The prevailing model for working with individuals with substance use disorders is the Minnesota model of chemical dependency treatment (Winters, Stinchfield, Opland, Weller, & Latimer, 2000). The theoretical perspective of the model aligns with the disease concept of dependency, the 12-step approach, and multiple forms of psychotherapy and psychoeducation (Winters et al., 2000). The process involves different stages of care: detoxification, residential treatment, outpatient treatment, and aftercare involvement.

While the need for services is great, working with this population certainly has its challenges. There is a high rate of relapse within the population (Festinger, Rubenstein, Marlowe, & Platt, 2001; Hubbard, Flynn, Craddock, & Fletcher, 2001) and high rates of psychiatric comorbidity (McGovern, Xie, Segal, Siembab, & Drake, 2006), referred to previously as a *dual diagnosis* and presently as a *co-occurring disorder*. Dependent on the setting and the stage of the change process (Prochaska & Norcross, 2003) the individual is in, multiple intervention techniques are utilized: group, individual, and family counseling; assessment; mentoring; medical intervention; and psychoeducation (Brooks & McHenry, 2009). Addictions counselors collaborate on cases with other kinds of counselors (e.g., a couple and family counselor), physicians and nurses, psychiatrists, social workers, clergy, nutritionists, and others (McLellan et al., 1998). Treatment models such as the Minnesota model advocate a treatment team approach in which other professionals work in unison with counselors to assist the change process. Familiarity with the expertise of other professionals and effectiveness at collaborative engagement enhance the chances for client recovery (James & Simons, 2011). A great amount of research determining the most effective forms of treatment has been completed over the past 20 years, yet there has been and there remains concern about the dissemination of these findings into application in the field (Rawson, Marinelli-Casey, & Ling, 2002), and many treatment programs offer interventions that have very little empirical support (Thomas, Wallack, Lee, McCarty, & Swift, 2003).

Opportunities to work in the field of addictions continue to increase, with a projected rate of growth of 21% between 2008 and 2018; this is a higher than average trend (Bureau of Labor Statistics, 2012). At the same time, the annual rate of voluntary staff turnover within the addictions field is quite high, with recent research showing it to be at 33.2% for counselors and 23.4% for clinical supervisors (Eby, Burk, & Maher, 2010). The certification and licensure process and requirements for working in the addictions field can be very complicated and therefore confusing (Morgen, Miller, & Stretch, 2012). Many states have unique credentialing requirements separate from those for a licensed professional counselor, which can vary from a certification requiring only a bachelor's degree to a certification requiring a graduate counseling degree. Therefore, there are multiple titles used among different states (e.g., licensed chemical dependency counselor, licensed substance abuse counselor). To understand common requirements for an addictions certification or license, it is helpful to review the requirements for the Master Addictions Counselor (MAC). The MAC was developed jointly through the National Board for Certified Counselors (NBCC) and the International Association of Addictions and Offender Counseling (IAAOC). Individuals achieve the MAC designation by holding the NCC credential, documenting at least 12 semester hours of graduate coursework in addictions (or 500 continuing education hours in addictions), completing three years of supervised experience as an addictions counselor, and receiving a passing score on the *Examination for Master Addictions Counselors* (EMAC). The addictions field offers a variety of positions and settings to choose from and can prove to offer both valuable and meaningful work. Chances are, no matter which setting you choose, you will work with addiction to some extent. Case Illustration 4.1 offers you a small glimpse into an addictions scenario and encourages you to ask a few questions of yourself related to it.

CASE ILLUSTRATION 4.1

MARY ANNE

Mary Anne is a 47-year-old woman who has recently admitted herself to an inpatient facility for addictions. She is the mother of three small girls ages 2, 4, and 6. Mary Anne shares with you that she desperately wants to get clean and sober for her family and is ready to do it with your help. Her intentions appear sincere, and you feel committed and hopeful based on her authenticity and enthusiasm that she will succeed in treatment. Mary Anne collaborates with you on some realistic goals for her time in treatment, and she begins to get to work both in session and outside of session. You begin researching creative interventions to utilize in session, reflecting on what you believe will speak to her and be most effective given her situation. You check in about her family and try to help her keep focused on them as her goal.

After a weekend away from the facility, you return to work the following Monday and are informed that Mary Anne has checked herself out and relapsed. She drove under the influence and was arrested over the weekend for DUI and endangering the welfare of her children, who were with her in the car.

Describe the emotions you feel upon reading this case. If Mary Anne were to return to your care, how would you proceed with her? If Mary Anne never returns to treatment, how do you make sense of your efforts with her? Are there feelings of betrayal, frustration, or hopelessness? What about working with this client would be a good fit for you? What do you see as a possible concern for you personally with a client such as this?

Career Counseling

The historical roots of the counseling profession are embedded in the field of career counseling; Frank Parson's book *Choosing a Vocation* (1909) distinguished the field of counseling as separate from other helping professions (Savickas, 2011). Today, this counseling subspecialty remains focused on helping people in "making [the] greatest decision" (Parsons, 1909, p. 5) of their lives (Hartung, 2010). The work of a career counselor is rarely limited to solely assisting an individual in locating a particular career path due to the fact that one's occupation can impact multiple areas of his or her life: physical, mental, social, and emotional. Therefore, definitions of career counseling encompass a process that is not only a specialty area, but also a core element of all counseling (Gladding & Newsome, 2010).

Career counselors also have multiple settings in which they can provide services. University career centers, private practice, business settings, government agencies, job placement and training centers, and the armed forces represent some of the possibilities. While the fundamental elements of career counseling and development revolve around assessments and interventions (Hartung, 2010), the last 100 years of practice have exhibited a tremendous amount of well-researched theoretical perspectives, assessment instruments, and intervention strategies. These developments are utilized through multiple processes, including career education, the provision of career information, career intervention, career development facilitation, and career coaching. The intentions behind these methods are to help clients evaluate their interests, abilities, skills, and values in order to help them identify suitable occupational paths and then assist them in developing skills to seek out, apply for, and transition into positions. Career counselors also work with individuals who experience career concerns, career transitions, unemployment, and underemployment. Case Illustration 4.2 provides some context for the types of issues a career counselor works with.

A wide variety of assessments exist to assist counselors and clients through this process. Career counselors could find themselves in collaboration with individual or family therapists, employers, and occupational therapists. It is also important to note that computer technology and the Internet have had a greater impact on career counseling than any other counseling specialty due to computer-assisted guidance systems, and practitioners need to possess knowledge of and familiarity with these technologies (Kottler & Shepard, 2011).

Among many other important functions, the National Career Development Association (NCDA), the oldest division within the American Counseling Association, defines the standards and the competencies for the career development and counseling specialty area. Certification and licensing requirements for career counselors vary by setting and location but all require a graduate degree.

CASE ILLUSTRATION 4.2

CRISIS AND TRANSITION

Given the rates of unemployment and the devastation and anxiety that many families face, you have begun to have numerous clients who are presenting with career concerns. Recently, a 51-year-old man came to your office stating that he had no direction or purpose and felt like a failure as a man, since he could no longer provide for his wife and children. As of six months ago, he was laid off from work, and he has been unsuccessfully trying to find new work. He reports to you that he had worked at his last job since he was 18, had been there the last 33 years of his life, and felt like he didn't even know where to look or how to start all over. He reports that he is overwhelmed, feels hopeless, and wonders at times who he is anymore.

Where do you start with this client? What strengths does this client possess? What anticipated challenges do you see for yourself as his counselor? What outside resources or people might you mobilize or integrate? What about working with this client would be a good fit for you? What do you see as a possible concern for you personally with a client such as this?

While a career counselor working in private practice may be required to hold a license as a professional counselor, those working at a university career center might not. The NCDA offers members special levels of achievement depending on their level of knowledge and experience in the field: master career counselor (MCC), master career development professional (MCDP), and fellow. The opportunities for positions in career counseling are higher than average and are expected to grow by 14% between 2008 and 2018 (Bureau of Labor Statistics, 2012).

Clinical Mental Health Counseling

Clinical mental health counseling (CMHC) is the most encompassing counseling specialization due to the variety of settings in which practitioners function and the array of services they provide. It was not until 2009 that CACREP brought *community counseling* and *mental health counseling* together to form the specialization of CMHC; while the title might have been recently adopted, CMHC is firmly connected to the historical roots of the counseling profession as well as other helping professions (Cannon & Cooper, 2009). Largely due to President Kennedy's Community Mental Health Centers Act (1963), opportunities for those interested in providing multisystemic preventative services within community settings expanded (Scileppi, Teed, & Torres, 2000); currently, mental health counseling is considered one of the core mental health professions in the United States (Colangelo, 2009).

Early in the growth of the field, mental health counseling was defined as "an interdisciplinary multifaceted, holistic process of (1) the promotion of healthy lifestyles, (2) identification of individual stressors and personal levels of functioning, and (3) preservation or restoration of mental health" (Seiler & Messina, 1979, p. 6). Lewis, Lewis, Daniels, and D'Andrea (2003) defined this counseling specialization as "a comprehensive helping framework of intervention strategies and services that promotes the personal development and well-being of all individuals and communities" (p. 6). This definition highlights the broad reaches of this specialization and emphasizes the focus on both the individual and the community. Hence, CMHCs are found in numerous settings, some of which include private practice, hospitals, residential care facilities, employee assistance programs, addiction related treatment centers, and school and university settings. CMHCs work with individuals, families, groups, and communities in promoting mental health and treating the entire spectrum of diagnoses (Neimeyer, Taylor, Wear, & Buyukgoze-Kavas, 2011). They are involved with assessment and diagnosis, psychotherapy, treatment planning, psychoeducation, and crisis management. Ultimately, they offer both direct and indirect services to clients and communities (Lewis et al., 2003). Most important, the field has retained its core identity (e.g., developmental, strengths-based, holistic) while effectively responding to changes and needs within the current health care system (Pistole, 2001). While the types of situations a CMHC encounters will obviously vary, the Case Illustration 4.3 provides an example.

Because CMHCs function in such a variety of roles and settings, they tend to collaborate with the entire spectrum of those in the helping fields: human service workers, psychiatrists, school counselors, social workers, and nurses. Their ability to not only provide evidence-based therapeutic interventions, but also successfully connect clients to the larger set of social systems is critical. Considering the knowledge and experience necessary to effectively provide these services, licensure and certification requirements are fairly extensive. All 50 states now offer licensure, which requires a master's degree, a specified number of supervised clinical hours beyond the receipt of a degree, and the passage of a state qualifying exam. (For state specific requirements, see ACA, 2010b.) The job outlook for CMHCs is strong. The occupational trend points toward a significantly higher than average increase (24%) in projected job opportunities between 2008 and 2018 (Bureau of Labor Statistics, 2012). Due to the range of roles that CMHCs play, there is not a formal certificate or degree for every specialization; therefore, time in the field is the best way to tailor skills and garner the training needed for working with a particular population.

CASE ILLUSTRATION 4.3

JAMES

Your client, James, is a 27-year-old white male who was diagnosed with schizophrenia at 24. He was teaching high school history before the onset of his schizophrenia, but he has been living on disability for the past two years. He tells you that he and his psychiatrist have finally found a combination of medications that works to curb his symptoms. However, he is now feeling depressed about the years he has lost to his illness. Your client also has concerns about integrating back into the working world; while he would love to teach again, he fears he is not ready and may lose the hard-earned benefits he relies on.

Where do you start with this client? What strengths does this client possess? What anticipated challenges do you see for yourself as his counselor? What outside resources or people might you mobilize or integrate? What about working with this client would be a good fit for you? What do you see as a possible concern for you personally with a client such as this?

College and Student Affairs Counseling

The 2009 CACREP standards brought together two previously accredited programs under one title due to the significant overlap between the two programs' educational requirements. Since the early 1980s, the need for services within this population has increased alongside the significance of college student issues; therefore, the complexity and demanding nature of the work has also increased (Archer & Cooper, 1998; Watson & Schwitzer, 2011). Many counselors thrive on college campuses due to the variety of roles they can play, the energy of the young adult population, the vast and developing knowledge base required to inform their practice (Smith et al., 2007; Watson & Schwitzer, 2011), and the opportunity to work with a population in the midst of multiple developmental changes. The ultimate goal of utilizing counseling in this environment is to help "students work through psychological and emotional issues that may affect their academic success and personal development" (Dungy, 2003, p. 345).

Counselors within this specialty work in a variety of higher education and student affairs settings, including a college counseling center, housing and residential life, student union management, career services, multicultural support services, and other campus leadership activities (CACREP, 2012). Professionals gain preparation for this work through the core counseling background as well as additional studies in the culture, organization, and administrative structure of higher education, policy-making, and college student development. Review Case Illustration 4.4 for an example of working with this population, and then reflect on some of the questions posed.

Particular to college counseling centers, the dramatic increase in recognized mental health problems on campuses around the country further enhances the importance of these services. It has been said that these counseling centers are essentially becoming community agencies housed within educational institutions (Rudd, 2004). A survey of directors of these centers found that 91% reported an increase in the number of students with severe psychological problems. Within the 37.4% of student–clients having a severe psychological problem, the directors reported that 31.2% of those students could be treated successfully through their

CASE ILLUSTRATION 4.4

ANTHONY'S TRANSITION

Anthony is a college senior, and he dropped into the wellness center at the university that you work at as a counselor. He reports that despite the fact that all of his friends are enjoying the thrill of finishing college and all that comes with that, he feels increasingly anxious and disconnected from his family and peers, and at times has been unable to sit through class or attend his team practices. Anthony states that he experiences consistent and persistent worry about his future. Where will he go after graduation? What will he do for employment? Will he return home to live? How will he afford housing? He has concerns about keeping up relationships made at school and a long list of other concerns. Anthony's speech is a bit rapid, he appears warm and uncomfortable in his seat, and he checks his watch a number of times during the session. After the initial intake session is completed, he agrees to return and work with you for six to eight sessions over the next few weeks.

What is your approach with this client? What concerns do you address first? Are there safety concerns for this client? How do you decipher between normative stress related to a life transition, such as college graduation, and anxiety? What would be three possible treatment goals? What about working with this client would be a good fit for you? What do you see as a possible concern for you personally with a client such as this?

counseling center (Gallagher, 2010). Common issues presented in the college setting include mood disorders, anxiety disorders, and substance use disorders (Hunt & Eisenberg, 2010). Counselors also work with students on a wide range of other issues, including but not limited to self-injury, eating disorders, immediate crises, career planning and decision making, and wellness planning. The counselors in this setting spend the majority of their time involved in one-on-one counseling; the remainder of their time is spent in other forms of direct service (e.g., group counseling, workshops) and additional tasks (e.g., meetings, supervision, completing clinical notes) (Gallagher, 2010).

Psychologists (who hold a PhD or PsyD degree) staff many college counseling centers but certainly not all of them. Beyond holding a state-identified professional counseling license (i.e., licensed professional counselor), there are currently no additional licensing requirements for a college counselor, and the opportunities for positions within this counseling subspecialty are expected to increase 14% between 2008 and 2018 (Bureau of Labor Statistics, 2012).

Marriage, Couple, and Family Counseling

The marriage, couple, and family counselor, widely and previously referred to as the marriage and family therapist (MFT), primarily functions from a qualitatively different theoretical perspective than counselors in the other subspecialties discussed in this chapter. While their core masters' degree coursework is similar, MFT students complete additional coursework specific to this form of counseling and its theoretical foundations. The main differentiating variable between individual counseling and family counseling is how the counselor views the problem at hand. The historical *intrapsychic* paradigm, including the work of Freud, Adler, Ellis, May, Jung, and others, holds the belief that the *problem* exists within the individual, and therefore the individual is the object of the therapeutic intervention. The *interpsychic* paradigm holds that the *problem* is not necessarily located within the individual, but rather is located within the larger systemic context of interactions between people (Goldenberg & Goldenberg, 2012; Nichols & Schwartz, 2007). For instance, where an individual counselor may see client issues in a linear fashion (cause-effect), the family counselor views the issues as involving reciprocal causality, in which each element or person involved is both contributing to and a result of the issues at hand. Additionally, where an individual counselor might see a problem as located within an individual (the client), the family counselor seeks to place the problem in a larger context and determine how interactions between people contribute to it and can be part of the solution. This paradigmatic shift in treatment focus cannot be understated, because it informs all aspects of the MFT counseling process.

The MFT field developed during the 1940s and 1950s, but its time of greatest expansion occurred in the 1970s (Gladding & Newsome, 2010). Since 1970, there has been a 50-fold increase in the number of practicing MFTs (Miller, Todahl, & Platt, 2010). Currently, there are hundreds of master's-level training programs across the country. Graduates of these programs practice marriage and family therapy in many different settings, including private practice, correctional institutions, substance abuse facilities, mental health agencies, and hospitals, to name a few.

In practice, the MFT applies this systemic/interpsychic perspective through the choice of theoretical approach and techniques stemming from that approach in order to teach, gather information, enhance communication, discover underlying systemic problems, alter behaviors, encourage the sharing of emotions, discuss problematic behaviors within the system, and develop posttreatment recommendations. The MFT collaborates with the family or couple to understand the implicit purpose of the *symptom* that brought them into counseling and how it developed and persists; the counselor and family work to positively alter behaviors and cognitions related to family development, and prevent future problems. Case Illustration 4.5 gives some context. Think about how you might begin integrating the points shared above with this couple. Often, if outside a private practice or small clinic,

CASE ILLUSTRATION 4.5

A COUPLE'S CHALLENGE

Anita, 58, and Davis, 56, come into your office for their first appointment. Anita claims that her husband Davis still has not forgiven her for an emotional affair she had with a coworker a few years ago. According to Anita, Davis initially was very angry, and although now he says he forgives her, he never wants to spend time with her. Anita says angrily she does not know how long she has to be punished for her behavior and doesn't know what to do any more. Throughout the session, Davis is very distant; he responds very little to your questions and looks out the window. The couple does not want to consider a divorce, and they cite their religious beliefs as their main reason. In fact, when you brought up divorce, Davis spoke up for the first time without prompting, stating "absolutely not."

What are the immediate emotions you feel after reading this case? How do you think you might choose to engage the couple in the next few sessions? Do you have biases or preconceived notions that you need to reflect on as you prepare to see this couple again? With religion being an important part of this discussion, how do you think you would address and discuss that topic? How can you facilitate the strengthening of this relationship?

the MFT must be able to work as part of an interdisciplinary team, which could include a primary physician, a dietitian, a nurse practitioner, a psychiatrist, an individual counselor, school personnel, and other health care specialists (Patterson, Williams, Edwards, Chamow, & Grauf-Grounds, 2009).

The American Association for Marriage and Family Therapy (AAMFT) is the largest professional association within this field, and it has established the accreditation requirements for graduate programs in marriage and family therapy at all levels (master's, doctoral, and postgraduate) as well as standards for clinical supervision, professional ethics, and clinical practice. Currently, all 50 states regulate the profession through a licensing procedure similar in many ways to the licensed professional counselor licensure. While not the same in all states, the designation LMFT (licensed marriage and family therapist) is used to identify those who have achieved licensure appropriate to a scope of practice in couple and family counseling. The growth in job opportunities is higher than average, with an estimated 14% increase between 2008 and 2018 (Bureau of Labor Statistics, 2012). It is an exciting field that continues to grow, and research points toward its numerous benefits due to the fact that it is logical, fast, satisfactory, and economical (Gladding & Newsome, 2010).

School Counseling

School counselors are primarily employed in elementary (kindergarten through sixth grade) and secondary (seventh through twelfth grade) school settings (Martin, 2002). Counselors working within this subspecialty practice in all types of educational environments (public, private, parochial, alternative, charter, cyber, and vocational–technical schools) assisting students with a range of academic, personal, social, and vocational issues (Elijah, 2011). School counselors facilitate student growth by engaging in preventative and developmental counseling through the use of classroom guidance sessions as well as individual and group work (Perera-Diltz & Mason, 2008). School counselors are not permitted to diagnose a student with a mental health disorder and generally do not provide extensive one-on-one counseling services (Evans, Van Velsor, & Schumacher, 2002); they do, however, make clinical judgments and make referrals to community agencies or private practitioners so that students can access longer-term and more intensive counseling services. In addition, school counselors often assist with student testing and assessment (Sink & Stroh, 2003) and serve as home-school-community liaisons (Johnson, 2000). School counselors play an important role in crisis or critical incidents within the school, such as suicidal ideation (Perera-Diltz & Mason). For example, the school counselor should be a leader and important member of a school's crisis response team, and should play a role in the emergency response design or plan. During an incident, the counselor may be providing individual or group counseling, engaging community resources to assist in the response effort, referring victims of a critical incident to other health care providers, and/or communicating with parents and staff (ASCA, 2007).

In addition to consulting with parents, school counselors may collaborate with a variety of professionals, including school administrators, teachers, medical personnel, and school support staff such as social workers, school psychologists, school nurses, and student resource officers (Gibbons, Diambra, & Buchanan, 2010). For instance, further inquiry into a child's decline in grades might reveal the fact that his or her family has recently become involved with an in-home family counselor who is now also acting as the family's case manager. With approved informed consent, you may begin to consult and collaborate with the in-home counselor on the child's progress. Another example, and reflective questions related to it can be found in Case Illustration 4.6.

CASE ILLUSTRATION 4.6

ALYSIA'S PRESSURE

You are a high school guidance counselor, and two female students come into your office. One student, Tariah, claims she has brought in her friend Alysia, a junior, because Tariah is very worried about Alysia. Tariah explains that Alysia has shared thoughts of hurting herself. Alysia recently took the SATs and scored much lower than she hoped to. Alysia cries while explaining that her parents do not have money for a tutor, and that she needs to get these scores so she can get into her goal school, which is one of the most elite schools in the country. Alysia's parents, who are Jamaican immigrants, put a lot of pressure on Alysia to do well in school and take advantage of the hard-earned opportunities they provide for her. Alysia feels she has shamed them and wishes she would disappear, so her parents can focus more on her younger sister, who shows much more promise.

What are your thoughts and feelings about this scenario? What do you feel your role is as the school counselor? What additional resources might be helpful for Alysia? What do you see as a possible concern for you personally with a student such as this?

Historically, alongside assisting the positive development of numerous young people, practicing school counselors have faced a number of challenges in their work. The American School Counselor Association (ASCA) recommends that counseling programs maintain a student-to-counselor ratio of 250 students to one counselor. However, in the field, the actual ratio is much higher, approximately 459 students for every one counselor. Larger caseloads than what is recommended create challenges with regard to the delivery of services. In addition, ambiguous role definition can engender confusion between school counselors and their constituent groups (Paisley & McMahon, 2001). In the past, school counselors have been delegated myriad noncounseling tasks as a result of ill-defined job duties. Last, some school counselors are working with increasingly diverse student populations (Borders, 2002), yet unfortunately, lack of knowledge of culturally appropriate interventions plagues many school counselors. Despite the inherent challenges, for over a decade professional school counselors have refined, clearly outlined, and implemented a unifying model for a comprehensive school counseling program as described in *The ASCA National Model: A Framework for School Counseling Programs* (ASCA, 2012). This model can be utilized in any school and is based on four components: foundation, management, delivery, and accountability. The foundation outlines the goals and vision for school counseling programs. Management provides information on the appropriate tools for implementing and assessing programs. A primary focus of the ASCA national model is on delivery, which includes the direct and indirect services provided to students: delivering the school counseling core curriculum, individual student planning, and responsive services. The accountability component involves the means and methods for evaluating the program's effectiveness in order to make appropriate changes and to provide students with the highest level of care. The new developments based on the 2005 version of the ASCA National Model include an increased emphasis on data-informed decision making, new tools for assessment, and more specific distinctions between direct and indirect student services, among others (ASCA, 2012).

Most states require practicing school counselors to hold a state-issued certificate, which often requires graduate coursework and continuing education credits. Some states require school counselors to hold teaching certificates or have teaching experience, whereas other states require school counselors to pass standardized tests (e.g., Praxis) before practicing in the field (Perera-Diltz & Mason, 2008).

Positions within the field of school counseling are expected to increase by 14% between 2008 and 2018 (Bureau of Labor Statistics, 2012). School counseling is an exciting and rewarding field with an increasing number of employment opportunities. Individuals considering counseling work in a school setting should also consider related vocations, such as school social work and clinical mental health counseling in schools. These professionals assist the school counselors with particularly complicated or severe cases by providing counseling to students and relevant referral information to their families.

Clinical Rehabilitation Counseling

The field of rehabilitation counseling began in the early 20th century with legislation designed to provide rehabilitation services to veterans with disabilities and to assist them in achieving their independent living and vocational goals (Sporner, 2012). In addition, the systematic practice of rehabilitation counseling (also known as vocational rehabilitation) abets individuals with cognitive, mental, developmental, physical, and emotional disabilities to attain their individual, occupational, and self-determined living goals in the most holistic settings possible through counseling (Leahy & Szymanski, 1995).

The American Rehabilitation Counselors Association (ARCA) is the main professional association for rehabilitation counselors. The Commission on Rehabilitation Counselor Certification (CRCC) focuses on quality rehabilitation counseling services to individuals with disabilities through the certification of rehabilitation counselors and the promotion of leadership in advocating for the rehabilitation counseling profession (CRCC, 2013). Rehabilitation counselors provide comprehensive counseling services in a range of counseling sites (Berens, 2009), such as private rehabilitation companies, community and private mental health counseling practices, substance abuse programs, and educational settings (high school and college/university).

Remember that within each of these specialty areas, there will be a wide variety of positions and roles you can choose from. Now that you've been introduced to the general characteristics of these seven major specialty areas, you likely have a stronger understanding of which areas seem to *fit* more for you personally at this point in your career. At the least, you might be more confident of those specialty areas that *do not fit* your desires or objectives at this time; this is good information too! You might want to go back to Reflection Exercise 4.2 to see if your answers have changed or shifted now that you have more information. In order to further this process of discovery, next we want to further explore ourselves (motivations, interests, values, etc.) and gain increased access to information about the world of work.

CAREER EXPLORATION FOR PROFESSIONAL COUNSELORS

As a counselor in training, you must begin to explore the multiple counseling settings and areas of practice available, and think about planning your career choices. You must keep in mind the fact that this developmental process involves both intrapsychic investigations (e.g., reflections on aspects of your personality that may need adjustment within a counseling role) and outward practical applications (e.g., role-play, class demonstration, and practicum/internship experiences) (Howard et al., 2006). The more experiences and interactions counselors in training have, the more opportunities they have to reflect. Hence, the best way to initially explore your career path in this field is to take advantage of the opportunities supplied to you within your graduate studies as well as to maximize personal and professional interactions (Kottler & Shepard, 2011). Generally, counseling students share that the critical incidents contributing to their professional development revolve around their engagement in experiential learning: introductory skills courses, self-development activities, incidents occurring outside of academic life affecting personal growth, field experiences and supervision, and personal counseling (Furr & Carroll, 2003). In deciding which experiential learning opportunity will benefit your discernment most, it is important to know yourself.

Getting to Know Yourself

Understanding your developing self personally and professionally begins to solidify with your investigation into and eventual choice of a field placement. These experiences are reported as the most influential on counselor development (Folkes-Skinner et al., 2010). It is critical that you, as a future professional counselor, engage in self-reflection and contemplation about your career choices. This reflection not only assists you in navigating your career path, but it also provides you an opportunity for personal and professional growth. During your program of study, you are forced to begin integrating the textbook knowledge you have gained (professional) into real-life situations and then make further sense of your individual investments and personal interests as a counselor in training. This process can be stressful, as all unknown variables are further clarified; however, supportive supervision, mentoring, and peer encouragement are key components of managing this transition (De Stefano et al., 2007; Schmidt & Adkins, 2011). For example, listening to your peers discuss their experiences working with different populations, taking the initiative to visit a variety of counseling settings, and interviewing veteran counselors can increase your understanding of your interests (Hazler & Kottler, 2005).

The concept and process of *self-understanding* can seem quite broad at times. Therefore, for the purposes of this section, we'll focus on three important aspects. First, a critical component to self-understanding is accurate emotional insight (e.g., emotional awareness). This involves one's ability to recognize how his or her values, preferences, biases, and general viewpoint in certain situations impact the emotional self intuitively. Second, an individual can utilize this awareness to regulate and monitor the emotion being felt prior to an immediate response. Involving our rational capabilities enables us to engage a third aspect of self-understanding, which is our evaluation of whether or not this intuitive emotional response is aligned with our developing value system. This process of self-understanding will begin to shift us toward an increasing amount of internal locus of control, which gives us the ability to rely on inner resources and wisdom to overcome life challenges. Ultimately, engaging in an ongoing personal reflective process and asking ourselves probing questions is critical for continued counselor development (Schmidt & Adkins, 2011). Reflection Exercise 4.3 can help you begin to clarify some of your personal characteristics and how they impact your development as a counselor.

The development of the personal and the professional aspects of the counselor cannot be successfully accomplished without a commitment to the reflective process; this process allows you to make sense of the behavioral, cognitive, and affective elements of this journey. And yes, there is a lot to reflect on. Five factors to keep in mind when considering your career trajectory include motivations, values, interests, abilities, and self-concept (Corey & Corey, 2007). While these may be equal in importance, identifying one's motivations and values does appear to require some added internal energy. Not only is it developmentally appropriate to examine your motivations for entering the field of counseling, it is also ethical. You must ask yourself which personal needs you are trying to meet through this work (Hazler & Kottler, 2005). Do you seek to be admired? Do you seek prestige? You have selfish motivations; they only become problematic when you choose not to recognize them, and then you inadvertently seek to meet them through your clients.

Reflection Exercise 4.3

INTROSPECTION

This expression has been attributed to Socrates: "An unexamined life is not worth living." As a budding counseling professional, what does this mean to you personally and professionally as you develop your counseling identity? How would attempting to embody this life philosophy influence your work with clients and your attempts at being congruent in your personal life? Do you have fears or anxieties about your own development and what that means for you as a counseling professional? Knowing how important it is for counselors to know themselves and their own blind spots, how will you commit yourself to self-knowledge and growth? What supports and resources might you seek out throughout this lifelong process?

Second, values play an important role in helping us define and clarify our personal and professional identity (Auxier et al., 2003). Beginning counselors can examine the level of congruence between their personal values and the values of the counseling profession (e.g., developmental orientation, wellness orientation). Value exploration also allows beginning counselors to further refine their underlying personal philosophy toward the work; defining and owning what exactly drives you to engage in this field can act as a cornerstone during times of frustration and challenge (Busacca, Beebe, & Toman, 2010). Utilize Reflection Exercise 4.4 to clarify some of your personal and professional interests, motivations, abilities, and values.

Reflection Exercise 4.4

IDENTITY FACTORS

As stated, the five factors to keep in mind when considering your career trajectory include motivations, values, interests, abilities, and self-concept (Corey & Corey, 2007). Take a moment now to begin, or continue, to reflect on what these five things look like for you in your life, and how these five inextricable aspects of your personal identity will color your life as a professional.

- What truly motivates you? Are these motivations authentic to your future role as a counselor and congruent with the persona you will present within a counseling setting?
- Make a list of your values in order of priority. The first on the list should be that which you value most, above all other things, and then list the rest in descending order toward other things you value but that do not reign supreme. Does one specialization within counseling align more with your top values than another area?
- Think back on the things in your life that have truly enveloped you, sparked a passion within you, and engaged you fully—mind, body, and heart. What interests you to the point of consumption, where you lose track of time and forget about compensation of any sort?
- If you had to ask a friend or a colleague to tell us about you, what would that person say are your most prominent skills, abilities, and personality characteristics? Do you see these aligning well with a particular counseling setting?
- On a scale of 1 to 10, where do you rank your overall concept of yourself? When you reflect on yourself and your capabilities both personally and professionally, what comes to mind?

Now reflect on the place where these converge: your motivation, values, interests, abilities, and self-concept. Where do you see those five things fitting within the world of work and the counseling field in particular?

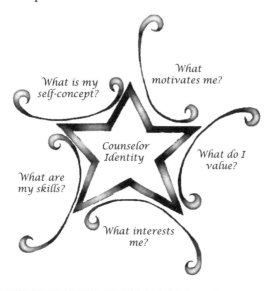

The process of understanding your identity as a counselor is something that you want to continue to review; this is what it means to be a *reflective practitioner.* Additionally, alongside this process, it is important that you inquire into and expand your knowledge about the counseling profession. Engaging in these activities concurrently gives you more information to reflect on and potentially integrate into your counselor identity. The following section reviews some suggested activities in order to help you get to know the counseling world of work.

Getting to Know the Counseling World of Work

As you have likely determined through your reading of this chapter, the counseling profession offers an enormous amount of opportunities that can sometimes be overwhelming. However, along with increasing self-knowledge, gathering additional information about the counseling world of work will be both an informative and exciting process. Here, we will focus on a few areas to consider as you seek out and begin integrating the world of professional counseling practice.

First, can you clearly delineate the differences between the different helping professions? How does a counselor's philosophy of change and clinical practice differ from that of a social worker? I find that most of my beginning counseling students aren't precisely clear on the differences and similarities between these related professions: social work, psychiatry, clinical psychology, counseling psychology, human services, and counseling. It is helpful to understand the historical background and philosophical underpinnings of these fields in order to determine whether the professional counseling orientation fits you well. Additionally, you will likely be collaborating with these other professionals in the future and it is helpful to have an understanding of their training and perspective on client issues.

Second, as you progress in your program, and if you see yourself in private practice one day, you might also begin to consider whether you envision yourself having a specialized or general practice. For instance, while some counselors could sharpen the scope of their practice to work specifically with families in which a child has been diagnosed with autism, others might have a practice focused on geriatric depression and primarily see older adult clients. A counselor in a more general practice would see a wider range of populations and work with a number of issues. There are risks and benefits to each. For example, specialized practitioners can become quite knowledgeable and adept in working within a focused practice; however, they could also begin to feel signs of burnout more quickly without exposure to various client bases. Generalizing practitioners might feel energized and excited by the unique issues brought by their clients but feel somewhat underprepared at times due to the plethora of information and methods of treatment for the varied issues they work with (Shallcross, 2012).

Third, I believe it is important for beginning counselors to make an early and honest appraisal of what range of income they expect and desire to receive upon completion of graduate school as well as years afterwards. Unfortunately, in my experience, a few students in their final semester just start to realize the actual range of salaries for entry-level counselor positions in a job market. For instance, here are the 2010 *median* annual incomes for different specialties: clinical mental health counselors ($38,150), marriage and family therapists ($45,720), school and career counselors ($53,380), substance abuse counselors ($38,120) (Bureau of Labor Statistics, 2012). Therefore, it is important for you to get salary information about counselors in different specialties early on in your graduate program in order to plan your career path.

The fourth and likely most important area to consider is professional involvement. Becoming involved with professional organizations and broader counseling initiatives is an excellent way to begin the reflective process on how you see yourself fitting in to the field as a whole and gain energy from likeminded individuals. Within the American Counseling Association (ACA), you can join one of 53 state and international branches and/or one of 19 divisions with specific foci. This type of engagement in ACA and affiliated branches and divisions, along with attending conferences and reading *Counseling Today* and peer-reviewed counseling journals (e.g., *Journal of Counseling and Development*), allows you to follow and comment on the news and legislation that influences the counseling field and participate in various other activities. These activities will enhance your knowledge of the counseling professional's world of work immensely.

Last, asking questions of or inquiring for information from practicing professional counselors is important. You should locate counselors in your areas of both interest and intrigue, and take the time to interview them about their developmental process, their personal reflections over time, their decisions at professional crossroads, and their interests in and passion for their work. Practice your counseling and interview skills while doing so! Each of these areas will help further your understanding of the field and, as you integrate these understandings with your increased self-awareness, allow you to make informed decisions about the next steps in your professional future.

Remember, finding your professional areas of interest and planning your career path do not all happen at once, and when they do happen, they are not once and for all. As you may recall, Ronnestad and Skovholt's (2003) six phases of development help you recognize that this is a process of *becoming*. Instead of focusing on the goal of having their professional future organized and finalized, graduate students have found it helpful to focus on the *next step* in their personal and professional development. For certain, you can expect struggles and challenges (Skovholt & Ronnestad, 2003), such as theoretical integration with a particular population (Lowndes & Hanley, 2010) and working within sometimes complicated administrative systems.

The benefits of joining the counseling profession are innumerable. You have the opportunity to focus on unique areas of interest and design your own career trajectory. All of this can occur while you are truly helping other people and therefore having a rewarding and meaningful occupational existence, no matter what setting you choose. As you understand at this point, these decisions come with challenges. However, each challenge presents with it another opportunity for reflection and therefore additional professional identity development—embrace them.

KEYSTONES

This chapter introduced you to the main specialty areas within the counseling profession and offered a preview into the important internal processes that take place during professional decision making. The internal processes discussed all play a role in identity formation, self-efficacy development, and cognitive complexity enhancement. The overview of each specialty area included work settings, general duties, interventions employed, potential collaborative partners, certification and licensure, and projections for future employment for professionals working in each specialty.

The specialty areas covered included the following:

- Addictions Counseling—working with individuals with compulsive behaviors and substance addiction in particular.
- Career Counseling—assisting individuals with career related developmental decisions, including but not limited to choosing a career path, deciding on future steps within a current career, and/or creating a more satisfying work experience.
- Clinical Mental Health Counseling—a broad category focusing on many aspects of mental health services, from wellness promotion to treatment for severe diagnoses.
- College and Student Affairs Counseling—working through or managing the emotional and psychological concerns that impact the academic and personal success of students in higher education.
- Marriage and Family Counseling—applying a systems perspective to helping couples and families develop means for working through conflicts in order to improve or create relationships and prevent future problems.
- School Counseling—taking a leadership position with regard to providing preventative strategies and developmental services to assist students in school settings.
- Clinical Rehabilitation Counseling—helping individuals with cognitive, mental, developmental, physical, and emotional disabilities to achieve their individual and occupational goals.

Finding a professional setting that fits is a challenging and exciting process, and the first step is enhancing self-understanding. This includes developing your emotional insight, strengthening your regulation and monitoring of your emotional responses, and engaging your rational capacities. Alongside self-understanding, other important areas of engagement were reviewed: utilizing your practical experiences, interacting with professionals, taking advantage of supervision, and getting involved with professional organizations; all of these assist the process of professional identity development and will help you clarify your future choices.

ADDITIONAL RESOURCES

Becoming Professional Counselors

American Counseling Association: www.counseling.org

King, G. (2007). Career development of counselors. *British Journal of Guidance & Counselling*, *35*(4), 391–407.

National Board for Certified Counselors: www.nbcc.org

Orlinsky, D. E., & Ronnestad, M. H. (2005). *How psychotherapists develop.* Washington, DC: American Psychological Association.

Addictions Counseling

Brooks, F., & McHenry, B. (2009). *A contemporary approach to substance abuse and addiction counseling: A counselor's guide to application and understanding.* Alexandria, VA: American Counseling Association.

International Association of Addictions & Offender Counselors: www.iaaoc.org

Master Addictions Counselor: www.nbcc.org/specialties/mac

Morgen, K., Miller, G., & Stretch, L. S. (2012). Addiction counseling licensure issues for licensed professional counselors. *The Professional Counselor: Research and Practice, 2*(1), 58–65.

Whitter, M., Bell, E. L., Gammond, P., Gwaltney, M., Magana, C. A., & Moreaux, M. (2006). *Strengthening professional identity: Challenges of the addictions treatment workforce.* Cambridge, MA: Abt Associates.

Career Counseling

Hartung, P. J. (2010). Practice and research in career counseling and development. *The Career Development Quarterly, 59,* 98–142.

National Career Development Association: http://associationdatabase.com/aws/NCDA/pt/sp/home_page

Savickas, M. L. (2011). The centennial of counselor education: Origin and early development of a discipline. *Journal of Counseling and Development, 89*(4), 500–503.

Clinical Mental Health Counseling

American Counseling Association (ACA). (2010). *Licensure requirements for Professional Counselors: A state-by-state report.* Alexandria, VA: Office of Professional Affairs.

American Mental Health Counselors Association: www.amhca.org

Colangelo, J. J. (2009). The American Mental Health Counselors Association: Reflection on 30 historic years. *Journal of Counseling and Development, 87*(2), 234–240.

Lum, C. (2010). *Licensure requirements for professional counselors.* Retrieved from http://www.counseling.org/docs/licensure/72903_excerpt_for_web.pdf?sfvrsn=2

College & Student Affairs Counseling

American College Counseling Association: www.collegecounseling.org

Gallagher, R. P. (2010). *National Survey of Counseling Center Directors.* Alexandria, VA: International Association of Counseling Services.

Hunt, J. & Eisenberg, D. (2010). Mental health problems and help-seeking behavior among college students. *Journal of Adolescent Health, 46,* 3–10.

Smith, T. B., Dean, B., Floyd, S., Silva, C., Yamashita, M., Durtschi, J., & Heaps, R. A. (2007). Pressing issues in college counseling: A survey of American College Counseling Association members. *Journal of College Counseling, 10,* 64–78.

Marriage, Couple, & Family Counseling

American Association for Marriage and Family Therapy: www.aamft.org

Goldenberg, H., & Goldenberg, I. (2012). *Family therapy: An overview* (8th ed.). Belmont, CA: Brooks/Cole.

Patterson, J., Williams, L, Edwards, T. M., Chamow, L., & Grauf-Grounds, C. (2009). *Essential skills in family therapy: From the first interview to termination* (2nd ed.). New York, NY: Guilford Press.

School Counseling

American School Counselor Association (ASCA). (2012). *The ASCA national model: A framework for school counseling programs.* Alexandria, VA: Author.
American School Counselor Association: www.schoolcounselor.org
Perera-Diltz, D. M., & Mason, K. L. (2008). Ideal to real: Duties performed by school counselors. *Journal of School Counseling, 6*(26), 1–36.

Clinical Rehabilitation Counseling

American Rehabilitation Counseling Association. (ARCA). (2013, Spring). *ARCA E-newsletter.* Retrieved from http://www.arcaweb.org/wp-content/uploads/ARCANewsletter-Spring2013 .pdf
Commission on Rehabilitation Counselor Certification (CRCC). (2013). *Welcome.* Retrieved from www.crccertification.com/
Council on Rehabilitation Education (CORE). (2013). *CACREP/CORE correspondence: CACREP Letter to Frank Lane 12-3-12.* Retrieved from http://www.core-rehab.org/Files/Doc/PDF/ WhatsNewPDFs/CACREP%20Ltr%20to%20Frank%20Lane%2012-2012.pdf

Career Exploration for Counselors

Busacca, L. A., Beebe, R. S., & Toman, S. M. (2010). Life and work values of counselor trainees: A national survey. *The Career Development Quarterly, 59*(1), 2–18.
Corey, G., & Corey M. S. (2007). *Becoming a helper* (5th ed.). Belmont, CA: Thomson.
Folkes-Skinner, J., Elliott, R., & Wheeler, S. (2010). 'A baptism of fire': A qualitative investigation of a trainee counsellors' experience at the start of training. *Counselling and Psychotherapy Research, 10*(2), 83–92.

REFERENCES

American Counseling Association (ACA). (2010a). 20/20: *A vision for the future of counseling. Consensus definition of counseling.* Retrieved from http://www.counseling.org/knowledge-center/20-20-a-vision-for-the-future-of-counseling/consensus-definition-of-counseling
American Counseling Association (ACA). (2010b). *Licensure requirements for professional counselors: A state-by-state report.* Alexandria, VA: Office of Professional Affairs.
American Psychiatric Association (APA). (2013). *Diagnostic and statistical manual of mental disorders: DSM-V* (5th ed.). Washington, DC: Author.
American School Counselor Association (ASCA). (2007). *Position statement: Crisis/critical incident response in the schools.* Alexandria, VA: Author.
American School Counselor Association (ASCA). (2012). *The ASCA national model: A framework for school counseling programs.* Alexandria, VA: Author.
Archer, J., Jr., & Cooper, S. (1998). *Counseling and mental health services on campus: A handbook of contemporary practices and challenges.* San Francisco, CA: Jossey-Bass.

Auxier, C., Hughes, F., & Kline W. (2003). Identity development in counselors-in-training. *Counselor Education & Supervision, 43,* 25–38.

Berens, D. E. (2009). Rehabilitation counseling. In Bradley T. Erford (Ed.), *The ACA encyclopedia of counseling* (pp. 446–448). Alexandria, VA: American Counseling Association.

Beutler, L. E., Malik, M., Alimohamed, S., Harwood, T. M., Talebi, H., Noble, S., & Wong, E. (2004). Therapist variables. In M. J. Lambert (Ed.), *Bergin and Garfield's handbook of psychotherapy and behavior change* (5th ed., pp. 227–306). New York, NY: Wiley.

Borders, L. D. (1989). Developmental cognitions of first practicum supervisees. *Journal of Counseling and Development, 36*(2), 163–169. doi: 10.1037/0022–0167.36.2.163

Borders, L. D. (2002). School counseling in the 21st century: Personal and professional reflections on the four focus articles. *Professional School Counseling, 5,* 180–185.

Brooks, F., & McHenry, B. (2009). *A contemporary approach to substance abuse and addiction counseling: A counselor's guide to application and understanding.* Alexandria, VA: American Counseling Association.

Brott, P. E., & Myers, J. E. (1999). Development of professional school counselor identity: A grounded theory. *Professional School Counseling, 2,* 339–348.

Bureau of Labor Statistics. (2012). *Occupational outlook handbook.* Retrieved from http://www.bls.gov/ooh/

Busacca, L. A., Beebe, R. S., & Toman, S. M. (2010). Life and work values of counselor trainees: A national survey. *The Career Development Quarterly, 59*(1), 2–18). doi: 10.1002/j.2161–0045.2010.tb00126.x

Cannon, E., & Cooper, J. (2009). Clinical mental health counseling: A national survey of counselor educators. *Journal of Mental Health Counseling, 32*(3), 236–246.

Chandler, N., Balkin, R. S., & Perepiczka, M. (2011). Perceived self-efficacy of licensed counselors to provide substance abuse counseling. *Journal of Addictions & Offender Counseling, 32*(1), 29–42. doi: 10.1002/j.2161–1874.2011.tb00205.x

Colangelo, J. J. (2009). The American mental health counselors association: Reflection on 30 historic years. *Journal of Counseling and Development, 87*(2), 234–240. doi: 10.1002/j.1556–6678.2009.tb00572.x

Commission on Rehabilitation Counselor Certification (CRCC). (2013). *Welcome.* Retrieved from http://www.crccertification.com/

Corey, G., & Corey M. S. (2007). *Becoming a helper* (5th ed.). Belmont, CA: Thomson.

Council for Accreditation of Counseling & Related Educational Programs (CACREP). (2012). *Choosing a graduate program.* Retrieved from http://67.199.126.156/template/page.cfm?id=5

Cunningham, L. (2010). *Job satisfaction and values of counselors in private practice and agency settings.* (Unpublished doctoral dissertation). University of Central Florida, Orlando.

De Stefano, J., D'iuso, N., Blake, E., Fitzpatrick, M., Drapeau, M., & Chamodraka, M. (2007). Trainees' experiences of impasses in counseling and the impact of group supervision on their resolution: A pilot study. *Counselling & Psychotherapy Research, 7*(1), 42–47. doi: 10.1080/14733140601140378

Dungy, G. J. (2003). Organization and functions of student affairs. In S. R. Komives, D. B. Woodard, Jr., & Associates (Eds.), *Student services: A handbook for the profession* (4th ed., pp. 339–357). San Francisco, CA: Jossey-Bass.

Eby, L. T., Burk, H., & Maher, C. P. (2010). How serious of a problem is staff turnover in substance abuse treatment? A longitudinal study of actual turnover. *Journal of Substance Abuse Treatment, 39,* 264–271. doi: 10.1016/j.jsat.2010.06.009

Elijah, K. (2011). Meeting the guidance and counseling needs of gifted students in school settings. *Journal of School Counseling, 9,* 3–19.

Evans, J. R., Van Velsor, P., & Schumacher, J. E. (2002). Addressing adolescent depression: A role for school counselors. *Professional School Counseling, 5,* 1096–2409.

Festinger, D. S., Rubenstein, D. F., Marlowe, D. B., & Platt, J. J. (2001). *Relapse: Contributing factors, causative models, and empirical considerations.* New Haven, CT: Yale University Press.

Folkes-Skinner, J., Elliott, R., & Wheeler S. (2010). 'A baptism of fire': A qualitative investigation of a trainee counsellor's experience at the start of training. *Counselling and Psychotherapy Research, 10*(2), 83–92.

Fong, M. L., Borders, L. D., Ethington, C. A., & Pitts, J. H. (1997). Becoming a counselor: A longitudinal study of student cognitive development. *Counselor Education and Supervision, 37,* 100–115.

Furr, S. R., & Carroll, J. J. (2003). Critical incidents in student counselor development. *Journal of Counseling & Development, 81*(4), 483–489.

Gallagher, R. P. (2010). *National survey of counseling center directors.* Alexandria, VA: International Association of Counseling Services.

Gibbons, M. M., Diambra, J. F., & Buchanan, D. K. (2010). School counselor perceptions and attitudes about collaboration. *Journal of School Counseling, 8*(34), 3–27.

Gladding, S. T., & Newsome, D. W. (2010). *Clinical mental health counseling in community and agency settings* (3rd ed.). Columbus, OH: Merrill.

Goldenberg, H., & Goldenberg, I. (2012). *Family therapy: An overview* (8th ed.). Belmont, CA: Brooks/Cole.

Hartung, P. J. (2010). Practice and research in career counseling and development. *The Career Development Quarterly, 59,* 98–142.

Hazler, R. J., & Kottler, J. A. (2005). *The emerging professional counselor.* Alexandria, VA: American Counseling Association.

Holloway, E. L., & Wolleat, P. L. (1980). Relationship of counselor conceptual level to clinical hypothesis formation. *Journal of Counseling Psychology, 27,* 539–545. doi: 10.1037/0022–0167.27.6.539

Howard, E. E., Inman, A. G., & Altman, A. N. (2006). Critical incidents among novice counselor trainees. *Counselor Education and Supervision, 46*(32), 88–102.

Hubbard, R. I., Flynn, P. M., Craddock, S. G., & Fletcher, B. W. (2001). *Relapse after drug abuse treatment.* New Haven, CT: Yale University Press.

Hunt, J., & Eisenberg, D. (2010). Mental health problems and help-seeking behavior among college students. *Journal of Adolescent Health, 46,* 3–10.

James, R., & Simons, L. (2011). Addiction studies: Exploring students' attitudes toward research in a graduate program. *Journal of Alcohol and Drug Education, 55*(2), 74–90.

Johnson, L. S. (2000). Promoting professional identity in an era of educational reform. *Professional School Counseling, 4,* 31–40.

Kaplan, D. M., & Gladding, S. T. (2011). A vision for the future of counseling: The 20/20 principles for unifying and strengthening the profession. *Journal of Counseling and Development, 89,* 367–372.

King, G. (2007). Career development of counselors. *British Journal of Guidance & Counselling, 35*(4), 391–407.

Kottler, J. A., & Shepard, D. S. (2011). *Introduction to counseling: Voices from the field* (7th ed.). Belmont CA: Brooks/Cole.

Kozina, K., Grabovari, N., De Stefano, J., & Drapeau, M. (2010). Measuring changes in counselor self-efficacy: Further validation and implications for training and supervision. *The Clinical Supervisor, 29,* 117–127.

Lambert, M. J., & Ogles, B. M. (2004). The efficacy and effectiveness of psychotherapy. In M. J. Lambert (Ed.), *Bergin and Garfield's handbook of psychotherapy and behavior change* (5th ed., pp. 139–193). New York, NY: Wiley.

Leahy, M. J., & Szymanski, E. (1995). Rehabilitation counseling: Evolution and current status. *Journal of Counseling & Development, 74*(2), 163–166. doi: 10.1002/j.1556-6676.1995.tb01843.x

Lewis, J. A., Lewis, M. D., Daniels, J. A., & D'Andrea, M. J. (2003). *Community counseling: Empowerment strategies for a diverse society* (3rd ed.). Pacific Grove, CA: Brooks/Cole.

Lowndes, L., & Hanley, T. (2010). The challenge of becoming an integrative counselor: The trainee's perspective. *Counselling and Psychotherapy Research, 10*(3), 163–172.

Martin, P. J. (2002). Transforming school counseling: A national perspective. *Theory Into Practice, 41*(3), 148–153. doi: 10.1207/s15430421tip4103_2

McGovern, M. P., Xie, H. Y., Segal, S. R., Siembab, L., & Drake, R. E. (2006). Addiction treatment services and co-occurring disorders: Prevalence estimates, treatment practices, and barriers. *Journal of Substance Abuse Treatment, 31,* 267–275.

McLellan, A. T., Hagan, T. A., Levine, M., Gould, F., Meyers, K., Bencivengo, M., & Durell, J. (1998). Supplemental social services improve outcomes in public addiction treatment. *Addiction, 93,* 1489–1499.

Miller, J. K., Todahl, J. L., & Platt, J. J. (2010). The core competency movement in marriage and family therapy: Key considerations from other disciplines. *Journal of Marital and Family Therapy, 36*(1), 59–70. doi: 10.1111/j.1752–0606.2009.00183.x

Morgen, K., Miller, G., Stretch, L. S. (2012). Addiction counseling licensure issues for licensed professional counselors. *The Professional Counselor: Research and Practice, 2*(1), 58–65.

Neimeyer, G. J., Taylor, J. M., Wear, D. M., & Buyukgoze-Kavas, A. (2011). How special are the specialties? Workplace settings in counseling and clinical psychology in the United States. *Counseling Psychology Quarterly, 24,* 43–53.

Nichols, M. P., & Schwartz, R. C. (2009). *Family therapy: Concepts and methods* (9th ed.). Needham Heights, MA: Allyn & Bacon.

Orlinsky, D. E., & Ronnestad, M. H. (2005). *How psychotherapists develop.* Washington, DC: American Psychological Association.

Paisley, P. O., & McMahon, H. G. (2001). School counseling in the 21st century: Challenges and opportunities. *Professional School Counseling, 5,* 106–115.

Parsons, F. (1909). *Choosing a vocation.* Boston, MA: Houghton Mifflin.

Patterson, J., Williams, L, Edwards, T. M., Chamow, L., & Grauf-Grounds, C. (2009). *Essential skills in family therapy: From the first interview to termination* (2nd ed.). New York, NY: Guilford Press.

Perera-Diltz, D. M., & Mason, K. L. (2008). Ideal to real: Duties performed by school counselors. *Journal of School Counseling, 6*(26), 1–36.

Pistole, M. C. (2001). *Mental health counseling: Identity and distinctiveness.* ERIC Clearinghouse on Counseling and Student Service, University of North Carolina at Greensboro.

Prochaska, J. O., & Norcross, J. C. (2003). *Systems of psychotherapy: A transtheoretical analysis* (5th ed.). Pacific Grove, CA: Brooks/Cole.

Rawson, R. A., Marinelli-Casey, P., & Ling, W. (2002). Dancing with strangers: Will U.S. substance abuse practice and research organizations build mutually productive relationships? *Addictive Behaviors, 27,* 941–949.

Ronnestad, M. H., & Ladany, N. (2006). The impact of psychotherapy training: Introduction to the special section. *Psychotherapy Research, 16*(1), 261–267.

Ronnestad, M. H., & Skovholt, T. M. (2003). The journey of the counselor and therapist: Research findings and perspectives on professional development. *Journal of Career Development, 30*(1), 5–44.

Rudd, M. D. (2004). University counseling centers: Looking more and more like community clinics. *Professional Psychology: Research and Practice, 35,* 316–317.

Savickas, M. L. (2011). The centennial of counselor education: Origin and early development of a discipline. *Journal of Counseling and Development, 89,* 500–504. doi: 10.1002/j.1556–6676.2011.tb02848.x

Schmidt, C. D., & Adkins, C. (2011). Understanding, valuing, and teaching reflection in counselor education: A phenomenological inquiry. *Reflective Practice, 13*(1), 77–96.

Scileppi, J. A., Teed, E. L., & Torres, R. D. (2000). *Community psychology: A common sense approach to mental health.* Englewood Cliffs, NJ: Prentice-Hall.

Seiler, G., & Messina, J. J. (1979). Toward professional identity: The dimension of mental health counseling in perspective. *American Mental Health Counselors Journal, 1,* 3–8.

Shallcross, L. (2012, July). Specialist, generalist, or niche provider? *Counseling Today.* Retrieved from http://ct.counseling.org/2012/05/specialist-generalist-or-niche-provider/

Sink, C. A., & Stroh, H. R. (2003). Raising achievement test scores of early elementary school students through comprehensive school counseling programs. *Professional School Counseling, 6,* 350–364.

Skovholt, T. M., & Ronnestad, M. H. (1992). Themes in therapist and counselor development. *Journal of Counseling & Development, 70*(4), 505–515.

Skovholt, T. M. & Ronnestad, M. H. (2003). Struggles of the novice counselor and therapist. *Journal of Career Development, 30*(1), 45–58.

Smith, T. B., Dean, B., Floyd, S., Silva, C., Yamashita, M., Durtschi, J., & Heaps, R. A. (2007). Pressing issues in college counseling: A survey of American College Counseling Association members. *Journal of College Counseling, 10,* 64–78.

Spengler, P. M., & Strohmer, D. C. (1994). Clinical judgmental biases: The moderating roles of counselor cognitive complexity and counselor client preferences. *Journal of Counseling Psychology, 41,* 8–17. doi: 10.1037/0022–0167.41.1.8

Sporner, M. L. (2012). Service members and veterans with disabilities: Addressing unique needs through professional rehabilitation counseling. *Journal of Rehabilitation Research & Development, 49*(8), xiii-xvii. doi: 10.1682/JRRD.2012.07.0131

Stevens, P., & Smith, R. L. (2001). *Substance abuse counseling: Theory and practice* (2nd ed.). Upper Saddle River, NJ: Prentice-Hall.

Thomas, C. P., Wallack, S. S., Lee, S., McCarty, D., & Swift, R. (2003). Research to practice: Adoptions of naltrexone in alcoholism treatment. *Journal of Substance Abuse Treatment, 24,* 1–11.

Watson, J. C., & Schwitzer, A. M. (2011). A new bridge between research and practice in college counseling and mental health. *Journal of College Counseling, 14,* 99–100.

Welfare, L. E., & Borders, D. L. (2010). Counselor cognitions: General and domain specific complexity. *Counselor Education and Supervision, 49,* 162–178.

Whitter, M., Bell, E. L., Gammond, P., Gwaltney, M., Magana, C. A., & Moreaux, M. (2006). *Strengthening professional identity: Challenges of the addictions treatment workforce.* Cambridge, MA: Abt Associates.

Winters, K., Stinchfield, R. D., Opland, E., Weller, C., & Latimer, W. W. (2000). The effectiveness of the Minnesota model approach in the treatment of adolescent drug abusers. *Addiction, 95*(4), 601–612. doi: 10.1046/j.1360–0443.2000.95460111.x

Chapter 5

Crisis Counseling and Emergency Response

ELYSIA CLEMENS

TARA HILL

ADRIA SHIPP

Events that necessitate emergency and crisis response are often unforeseen. Most of the time, an event resulting in a crisis occurs when people are not expecting it. Reflect on the events of 9/11. Had people known that a terrorist attack was about to occur, they would have rearranged their Tuesday schedule to accommodate for a terrorist attack by not going to work, taking time with their loved ones, intentionally spending their last moments doing something they loved. Instead, as the unpredictable and unforeseen events of the day unfurled, crisis spread across the globe, and emergency response was critical.

Counselors and other mental health professionals are critical in times of crisis, whether the crises occur on a national level or in a local community. In events such as 9/11 in New York City, Hurricane Katrina in New Orleans, the tornado in Moore, Oklahoma, the Columbine shootings, the Boston bombing, the Aurora movie theater shootings, and the Sandy Hook Elementary School shootings, crisis is widespread and requires widespread emergency response. During these times, a community-level crisis plan is usually put into effect. Professional counselors from community or professional organizations are called upon when a disaster occurs. These counselors are prepared to respond when a large-scale crisis happens by participating in emergency response trainings such as Disaster Mental Health Training, which is offered through the American Red Cross. In terms of a small-scale crisis, like a building fire, a suspicious person on school grounds, or violence at the workplace, emergency response organizations also have similar types of emergency response plans. Local community crisis response teams often include counselors who will provide support and assistance at the location of the crisis. House or apartment fires, car accidents, unexpected deaths, and community violence, among other events, might prompt an emergency response team to be deployed at the local level.

Whether a crisis is large or small in scale, it is important for professional counselors to understand that people are deeply impacted by the event. The Council for Accreditation of Counseling and Related Educational Programs (CACREP, 2009) proposed that counselor education programs prepare future counselors to understand "roles and responsibilities as members of an inter-disciplinary emergency management response team during a local, regional, or national crisis, disaster or other trauma-causing event" (CACREP, Standard II. G.1.c., 2009, p. 11). CACREP requires education programs to infuse content focusing on the impact that crisis can have on human growth and development (CACREP, Standard II. G.3.c.) and that students understand the principles of and be trained in proving specialized interventions to individuals in times of crisis (e.g., shootings, bombing events), disasters (e.g., tornado, earthquake) and other trauma-causing events. They are required to understand the effect of these events on individuals in the community and within school systems, including teachers, administrators, and students. Their training must include but not be limited to suicide prevention models and psychological first aid strategies (CACREP, Standard II. G.5.g., CMH.C.6, SC.C.6). In addition, CACREP requires that among their knowledge, skills, and practice, graduates from counseling education programs should demonstrate understanding of "the appropriate use of diagnosis during a crisis, disaster, or other trauma causing event" (CACREP, Standard II, CMH. K.5, 2009, p. 27).

In this chapter, you will be oriented to basic information associated with emergency response and crisis management, including the principles of, characteristics of, and interventions used in various counseling settings. You will also learn the roles and responsibilities of professional counselors in working with individuals who are impacted by crisis, disaster, and traumatic events, and in collaborating with other professionals and first responders (e.g., teachers, police officers, physicians) to assist these individuals. In addition, opportunities to acquire further training are included in this chapter (e.g., training opportunities for those interested in volunteering for the American Red Cross). Please keep in mind this chapter is just the beginning, introducing counselors in training to the literature and skills associated with emergency response and crisis management in counseling.

LEARNING OBJECTIVES

After reading the information and engaging in the reflection exercises provided in this chapter, you will be able to

1. Identify the terms commonly used in regard to crisis, including *crisis management* and *emergency response,* and the distinction between *crisis* and *disaster;*

2. Describe the emotional and psychological needs of involved individuals and responders to crisis events;

3. Differentiate between acute stress disorder and post-traumatic stress disorder, and identify when to use diagnosis appropriately during disasters and crises;

4. Discuss the roles and responsibilities of professional counselors in crisis preparedness, response, and recovery; and

5. Describe approaches and methods for working with people during emergency situations.

DEFINITIONS

As you read this chapter, it is important to have a clear definition of several terms that will be used to discuss crisis events and the impact of those events on people who experience them. We have provided definitions that may help you better understand crisis and emergency management.

Trauma

Trauma is often used to refer to "negative events that produce distress and to the distress itself" (Briere & Scott, 2006, p. 3) in psychological and physical contexts. The American Psychiatric Association (APA, 2013) defines a trauma as "exposure to actual or threatened death, serious injury, or sexual violence" (p. 271), including direct (e.g., victim of trauma) and indirect (e.g., witnessing, learning about other's trauma) experience of the traumatic event as well as repeated experience or extreme exposure to the traumatic event(s) (e.g., firefighter rescuing burn victims). From this definition, you can see how trauma impacts one's psychological, biological, and sociological functioning and well-being. It is important for persons experiencing trauma to receive proper treatment in order to mitigate associated symptoms and to resume their daily functioning.

Crisis

The definition of a crisis is tied to context. When the term *crisis* is used in the context of a system (e.g., a community, neighborhood, or school), Webster's dictionary ("Crisis," n.d.) defines it as "an unstable or crucial time or state of affairs in which a decisive change is impending; *especially:* one with the distinct possibility of a highly undesirable outcome a financial *crisis*." When the term *crisis* is used in the context of individuals, it involves their response to an event/situation or combination of events. Caplan (1964) defined crisis as "a temporary state of upset and disorganization, characterized chiefly by an individual's inability to cope with a particular situation using customary methods of problem solving, and by the potential for radically positive or negative outcome" (p. 45). Both definitions and contexts highlight that a crisis is not an event; instead, events cause crises, the result of such events is instability, and the implications or outcomes of a crisis can be significant.

Disaster

Although *crisis* and *disaster* are used interchangeably, a disaster differs from a crisis in the sense that a disaster is considered an event. The American Red Cross defines a disaster as

> an impending or occurring event that is destructive enough to dislocate people, separate family members, damage or destroy homes, and injure or kill people. A disaster produces a range and level of immediate suffering and basic human needs that cannot be promptly or adequately addressed by the affected people and prevents them from initiating and proceeding with recovery efforts. (American Red Cross, n.d.)

Disasters can be natural or human-made. Nature disasters include weather related events such as tornados, floods, or blizzards, or land events such as earthquakes. Human-made disasters include oil spills such as that of the BP Deepwater Horizon explosion in the Gulf of Mexico, 9/11, or the shooting in Arizona involving US Senator Gabrielle Giffords in 2011. Regardless of the nature of the disasters, it is important to note that disasters can lead to crises in communities and individuals.

A flood, considered a natural disaster, in a community leads to a crisis. For the communities affected by massive flooding in the Midwest in 2007 and 2011, many people were left stranded, without access to their homes, and without ways to meet basic needs. Many people lost their livelihoods, which were dependent on the natural resources in the area, such as valuable agricultural land, livestock, and fishing industries. Roads were washed out and public utilities were disrupted, leaving

---

Reflective Exercise 5.1

Please take a few moments to reflect and identify at least one situation when you considered yourself in crisis and/or experienced disaster in your life. Then, reflect on feelings associated with those situations. What are some of the needs that you had during that time? What would you have wanted or asked for to help meet some of those needs?

---

many people immediately isolated. With no electricity, no ability to travel except by canoe or kayak, and the public water system contaminated by floodwater, residents in the area lost the ability to fulfill basic needs and were unable to access community services, like emergency medical transportation. In addition to isolation and economic losses, many people affected by these floods experienced emotional and psychological tolls such as anxiety, stress, and depression (Tobin, 2005).

Disasters, both human-made and natural, result in communities and individuals experiencing crises. People in crisis are assisted by first responders and emergency officials. Often, professional counselors play a role in crisis management and relief by aiding in the recovery efforts. In the following section, you will learn about crisis management and emergency response and the roles that professional counselors can take in those efforts.

MANAGEMENT OF CRISIS, RISK, AND EMERGENCY

When a crisis arises, professional counselors are often on the front lines as first responders. You and other professional counselors are trained professionals with helping skills that allow you to assess a crisis situation and identify ways to help the individuals affected. Although there are a wide variety of situations that might result in a crisis, a crisis typically results from a situation in which individuals experience an inability to use the coping skills that have worked for them in the past. While it is common that a person in crisis may experience hopelessness, anger, grief, denial, shock, helplessness, or fear (Dass-Brailsford, 2010), others experiencing the very same crisis situation may have a very different description of their perception of the world and their feelings toward the events. While some people may struggle to find a new normal, others may display resilience (Kessler, Galea, Jones, & Parker, 2006). After a disaster or crisis event, an individual typically demonstrates resilience by assigning personal insight, purpose, and inner strength to the event (Kessler et al., 2006).

However, emergency response is not just about effective coping for individuals. It is often about assisting a community in recovery efforts. This means reconnecting people to family, friends, and other external supports such as religious and/or spiritual fellowships and other groups. Community resilience can be supported and encouraged with cultural sensitivity through the relief efforts of responders.

Crisis and Risk Management

Similar to other situations (e.g., divorces, job loss), crises can be managed. It is important that you and other professional counselors who engage in crisis and risk management have the knowledge and skills necessary to assist individuals experiencing abruptions and instabilities. Crisis and risk management include learning about prevention and preparedness in order to respond, not react, to such situations. In managing crisis and risk, specially trained professional counselors are often part of an interdisciplinary crisis team in various settings such as schools, hospitals, or community mental health agencies. Regardless of the setting, practicing prevention and preparedness is a crucial role of counselors in crisis and risk management. Prevention and preparedness requires involvement not only at an individual level but also at the family and community levels.

Prevention

Although crisis situations cannot all be prevented, prevention is an essential element of crisis response planning. Prevention includes clearly defined plans and policies to be followed prior to crisis events, which can help to increase safety and security as well as reduce risk. Professional counselors are involved in various prevention efforts depending on the settings in which they work. For example, school counselors may be asked by principals to design or participate in programs aimed to reduce bullying in schools. Clinical mental health counselors may assist in developing training programs to facilitate staff's understanding of potential barriers to compliance with a treatment protocol and how to be proactive in reducing those barriers. In especially high-risk counseling environments, the use of metal detectors may be an appropriate preventive measure to ensure the safety. Most mental health agencies have protocols in place to address clients who have demonstrated a propensity toward violent behaviors that may need immediate security attention. These plans may include a list of emergency contacts, including law enforcement authorities (e.g., sheriff and police department) in the area, or scheduling a plainclothes police officer to be in the clinic waiting room prepared to respond should an issue arise. Some schools have systems in place in which visitors' driver's licenses or government-issued identification cards are scanned before visitors are allowed to enter the building. These are all examples of crisis prevention efforts that may be in place in places where counselors work.

In addition to the prevention programs and security policies previously mentioned, mitigation that lessens the effects of a crisis is also part of prevention efforts. "Mitigation is any sustained action taken to reduce or eliminate long-term risk to life and property from a hazard event" (FEMA, 2003, p. vi). Mitigation tends to be connected to disasters and is more structural in nature than prevention. For example, areas of refuge might be identified as relatively safe rooms (e.g., rooms with two or more exit points in the basement of a building) where people may congregate if they are unable to exit a building when elevators are not an option due to an emergency situation (e.g., fire, tornado, shooting). Although hiding in a safe place does not prevent individuals from potentially being trapped in a dangerous location, it does mitigate the risk by directing all individuals to a centralized location, where rescue workers will first conduct a headcount of a group and assist individuals who are in need of help. Another example is panic buttons that may be installed to lock down a university classroom when a shooting happens. Once the alert is sounded, all classrooms will be locked, and people will be unable to enter or exit the classrooms. While the presence and correct use of a panic button does not prevent shootings, it does reduce the risk of a shooter entering other classrooms around the campus.

Prevention strategies are essential to organizations and communities, because they can potentially increase the safety of the organizations and communities as well as the individuals within those settings. Professional counselors often participate in developing or implementing the strategies (e.g., community safety prevention). While prevention is essential for reducing the risk of crises, preparedness is also needed in order to effectively manage crises and/or risky situations.

Preparedness

Preparedness involves developing a crisis plan or the protocols that should be followed if a crisis event occurs. The purpose of a crisis plan is to assist individuals, organizations, or communities when encountering a situation that requires quick decision making in order to facilitate the safety of people and property. Developing a crisis plan is a time- and labor-intensive process that includes collaboration among resource organizations in the community and takes into account specific risks and resources. A crisis plan is developed and based on the particular factors associated with locations, populations, and specific characteristics of the event.

Locations influence how individuals, organizations, and communities develop plans for crisis situations. For example, a crisis plan developed in an urban community is based on very different anticipated response times for emergency services than a plan developed in a rural community. More specific planning for an earthquake is required for a community located on a fault than for a community located in an area with no history of significant seismic activity. Target populations or key service recipients may also bring inherent risks that influence a crisis plan. For example, an outpatient alcohol or drug treatment community center has crisis plans (e.g., clinical decision trees, treatment protocols, or safety measures) for the possibility of intoxicated clients on site even if the policy is that clients will attend sessions sober.

It is important to note that being aware of the established protocols before an event occurs is essential for you as a professional counselor to effectively respond to crises and risky situations. Crisis plans often provide detailed information that is critical to the safety of all individuals involved, including staff, consumers, and first responders. For instance, in an inpatient psychiatric unit or a residential treatment facility, all personnel, including administrative, clinical, and supportive staff, are required to be familiar with an emergency or crisis response protocol that outlines a person in charge, should a crisis occur, a spokesperson to answer questions posed by the public or media, places to which the clients can be relocated, and resources that can be implemented to address safety concerns. Such protocols are important at all sites, even though the site may appear to present a low risk (e.g., a career counseling center).

In addition to crisis plans for all individuals involved or for the organization as a whole, specific crisis plans tailored to an individual's need in particular situations (e.g., suicide ideation) are also essential. For example, schools may have policies in place for assessing student suicide risk (e.g., conducted by professional school counselors or referred to a local mental health agency). Regardless of who conducts an assessment, it is important to document the process and the results in an incident report in order to provide a full description of how the crisis was managed. This documentation is used to evaluate the effectiveness of the crisis plan and to assess whether changes in the policies and/or training are necessary.

On a community level, natural disasters, such as tsunamis, tornado outbreaks, and regional flooding pose unique challenges, as the direct impacts of the disasters can also disable the resources that are central to a community's crisis plan. When local resources are disrupted, communities often rely on state and national organizations' first responders to work in conjunction mitigating the impacts of the disaster. In locations where resources may be scarce, professionals from nearby locales may be called upon to provide assessment and initial assistance to survivors immediately impacted by the event. In response to the 2007 Virginia Tech massacre, more than 200 mental health professionals from around the United States responded to a call from university officials to provide grief support and psychological first aid to students, faculty, and other university professionals in the days after the shooting (Kennedy, 2007).

A crisis plan is a critical component of effective emergency preparedness for organizations, and professional counselors play a crucial role in the development and implementation of these plans as well as in training staff about them. Whether the plan is for an organization or for a crisis on an individual level, effective response is a necessary part of the crisis and risk management process.

Emergency Response

While crisis management involves developing plans for prevention and preparedness, emergency response focuses on implementing crisis plans and providing interventions for individuals who experience crisis situations. An *emergency* is defined as "an unforeseen combination of circumstances or the resulting state that calls for immediate action ("Emergency," n.d.). Emergency response refers to interdisciplinary efforts to meet immediate and long-term needs of those impacted by a crisis situation. These interventions can be based on the following principles: (1) promoting a sense of safety, (2) promoting a sense of calm, (3) promoting a sense of self-efficacy and community efficacy, (4) promoting connectedness, and (5) instilling hope, all of which have been used in interventions for assisting people impacted by disasters and mass violence (see Hobfoll et al., 2007). Professionals can develop interventions with the five principles as a foundation that can be utilized during the disaster or crisis, immediately after it, and during recovery, with individuals or as a part of community plans.

Responses to an event that precipitates a crisis should be guided by the facility's crisis plan and policy. Even when the crisis plan is exceptionally well written, and all individuals are prepared to respond, there are opportunities for surprises, because each crisis has unique elements. For example, the crisis plan may not account for dangerous weather conditions present at the time of a crisis (e.g., bomb threat), or there may be a special event with a large number of outsiders in the building when a disaster occurs. This is a reason that organizations develop a chain of command outlined in the crisis plan. FEMA recommends that all organizations use the same terms for common roles to reduce confusion. This means that regardless of whether your organization has a president, director, or CEO at the time of a disaster the person in charge is the incident commander. And, regardless of whether your agency has a public relations professional, advertising manager, or media specialist, the title person who is in charge of all interaction with reporters and media during the time of a disaster is the public information officer. All first responders are knowledgeable of this incident command structure and prepared to function within a framework that includes these roles. This chain of command is organized to assist individuals experiencing crisis in making quick and effective decisions to respond to the situations. Regardless of an individual's beliefs about what is best, during a crisis, individuals should focus on the situation at hand and follow the crisis plan and the persons who are in charge. It is acceptable, however, to ask for clarification or point out a specific safety concern that may need attention (e.g., how should we care for the clients that are not physically capable of using the stairwell?). Similarly, remaining outwardly calm is helpful to clients and staff members. Processing, sometimes called debriefing, the crisis event afterward can be helpful.

If you have experienced some form of emergency situation (e.g., high-impact accident), you may understand that there are many thoughts and emotions going through your mind at the moment of that unexpected situation. It is important that professional counselors examine the perceptions and experiences of individuals (e.g., what went well and what can be learned is best saved for after the situation) immediately after the situation is stabilized and pressing needs have been met. Response also includes developing and implementing a plan for continued services once the immediate situation has been stabilized. Services to meet basic needs (e.g., physical or mental health needs) are likely to be part of emergency response. Coordination of the services and screening of the service providers are an important part of the response process. When an event occurs that results in a crisis, there is often an outpouring of offers to help—especially when there is significant media coverage of the event (e.g., school shooting, child abduction). Although these offers are well intended, it is important to ensure that the offers are coming from qualified providers, such as police or sheriff departments or qualified individuals trained as emergency responders. Taking the time to screen service providers is an essential task of professional counselors helping individuals in crisis, because by definition, the persons experiencing a crisis are vulnerable and may be incapable of making intentional informed choices among available services. Thus, it is the counselor's responsibility to assist with that process by screening and coordinating outside service providers.

In addition to the need to screen and coordinate service providers, there are needs for accurate communication about the crisis event. When an event (e.g., a shooting, a death, school bus accident, adverse drug reaction in a treatment facility) has a wider audience than those directly connected to the victims or those who may have been physically harmed, the counselor needs to include those who are vicariously traumatized. Part of that response typically includes communication of accurate information beyond the media coverage to dispel rumors and answer questions in a way that is respectful of victims and their families and considers pertinent laws related to privacy.

Rumors about and/or misunderstandings of the crisis event can occur and may contribute to heightened anxiety of people in the surrounding community. For example, if a patient on an inpatient psychiatric unit has a seizure in a location witnessed by other patients, there could be rumors that it was an adverse reaction to medication prescribed by an onsite physician, and that could result in widespread refusal among the patients to take prescribed medication. Another example could be that if parents see law enforcement's presence at a high school while picking up their children, other parents may be misinformed about the nature of the situation, resulting in numerous phone calls to school personnel from worried and concerned parents. Planning for communication is essential, as there are Health Insurance Portability and Accountability Act /Family Educational Rights and Privacy Act (HIPAA/FERPA) guidelines around patient/student privacy, and there is a need to decrease anxiety in the milieu. Thus, a coordinated and accurate message developed by an incident commander or official is essential to meet the goals of responding to the vicarious trauma that may have occurred and protecting the rights of others. Information about HIPAA and the specific regulations around management of health information and records during disaster events can be found at www.hhs.gov/ocr/privacy/. Information about FERPA can be found at www2.ed.gov/policy/gen/guid/fpco/ferpa/index.html.

To combat the possibilities of rumors and disinformation, the Centers for Disease Control and Prevention (n.d.) developed training regarding their crisis and emergency risk communication (CERC) principles and guidelines, which they developed to assist officials in planning for providing effective communication during disasters and emergencies. A CERC plan is based on the philosophy "Be first. Be right. Be credible" (as cited in American College Health Association, 2011, p. 439). Because of the sensitive nature of information that often is shared, professional counselors may play several key roles, from assisting in drafting a statement to delivering the statement, meeting with primary survivors and their friends and families, providing psychological first aid to those in need, and acting as the incident commander.

Recovery

After experiencing a crisis or disaster, individuals enter a period called recovery. If you or your love ones have tried to recover from a crisis or disaster, you may know that the recovery process is not easy. Recovery from a crisis situation takes on many forms and begins with a caring, supportive, and reflective environment. Just as each individual responds differently to precipitating events, recovering from a crisis is personalized and varies from one person to another. While some persons may have a very visible and immediate emotional response, others may have a delayed or masked reaction. Regardless of how responders react to the crisis situation, it is critical for counselors to understand that these individuals need mental health recovery. Responding to the mental health needs of individuals is discussed in greater detail in the next section of this chapter.

When discussing recovery, it is important that you understand the concept of *psychological resilience.* Psychological resilience refers to one's ability to cope with hardship or to adjust to change and to resume one's normal functioning without showing negative impacts. The American Psychological Association defines *resilience* as "the process of adapting well in the face of adversity, trauma, tragedy, threats, or even significant sources of stress—such as family and relationship problems, serious health problems, or workplace and financial stressors. It means 'bouncing back' from difficult experiences" (n.d.). You may wonder why some people adapt well to change, while others may not be able to do so. For example, some children who witnessed the shootings at Sandy Hook Elementary School resumed their normal functioning (e.g., playing after school) without showing any emotional difficulties, while others presented symptoms of acute stress disorder (e.g., having nightmares, excessive crying and tantrums). It is essential to remember that developing resilience is an ongoing process that requires individuals to exercise their internal (e.g., emotional strengths) and external (e.g., family, friends) sources of support in order to cope with adverse situations.

Recovery is not a short-term process. Rather, recovery may include intentional efforts to remember, to reflect, and to recognize the impact and importance of the events that created a crisis for individuals and communities. Memorial and anniversary events should be planned in consultation with those individuals and/or families most directly impacted to ensure that the efforts at healing are consistent with their wishes. In particular, it is helpful for professional counselors to consider the history of such events and how the recovery might impact those who may have experienced similar events in the past. In addition, it is critical for counselors to recognize that the most important part of the recovery deals with reflecting on the events that occurred in order to strengthen the crisis prevention and preparedness. This reflection may include implementing additional prevention or mitigation efforts. For example, reviewing an incident report that explains the steps taken to ensure the safety of a suicidal student helps to assess the appropriateness of the policies, protocols, and security measures. This review process is a common and essential part of the crisis management and response plan. Adjustments to protocols and the inclusion of additional details in crisis plans are common outcomes of this reflective process.

The role of the professional counselor during a disaster is to participate in the emergency response as a first responder and provide assistance and support to the first responders. It is imperative for professional counselors to be adequately knowledgeable about how to engage those who are involved and understand the impacts of crises and disasters on individuals and communities. During recovery, professional counselors can play an important role in helping individuals recover from disasters. Typically, professional counselors volunteer working under a responding organization such as the American Red Cross to help survivors meet their basic needs. The next section will explain the emotional impacts of disasters

Reflective Exercise 5.2

In the first reflective exercise, you were asked to identify at least one situation when you considered yourself in a crisis and/or experienced a disaster in your life. Since that time, what changes have you made in preparation for the chance that you may experience a similar situation in the future? What actions have you taken to reduce your risk of being in a similar situation again?

and their effects on individuals' and communities' abilities to meet their basic needs, and it will provide important information about the counseling process in such situations, which includes informed consent and rapport building.

IMPACTS OF CRISES AND NATURAL DISASTERS

While saving lives, stabilizing injuries, and maintaining community safety are the first goals in response interventions for first responders during disaster and emergency events (US Department of Homeland Security, 2008), those goals also include meeting the basic needs of the survivors affected by the event. The impact of crises and disasters can take emotional, social, and physical tolls on individual and community levels. Rao (2006) indicates that both the specific aspects of the crisis event and the way people are affected by and perceive the event determine the human impact of the disaster. Essentially, psychological and physical vulnerabilities are exposed when basic resources are depleted by disasters and emergency events.

Considerations for Basic Needs

When individuals encounter a crisis, not only do they typically experience a wide range of emotional reactions (e.g., fear, uncertainty, sadness), but also they may experience a shift in their sense of security, especially if their ability to meet their basic needs is in jeopardy. For example, individuals who experience a tornado in their community may lose access to food, water, and shelter if their homes and communities are destroyed. Maslow (1943) discussed the importance of basic needs and designed a hierarchy of them that included, at the most basic, physiological needs (e.g., for air, food, and water). Beyond that, safety of body, family, health, and property are next, and beyond that, a sense of love or belonging that includes friendship, family, and sexual intimacy. At the top of the hierarchy of needs are esteem and self-actualization. Esteem includes an individual's sense of confidence, achievement, and self-respect, while self-actualization, which is the highest level of human need, includes a sense of morality, spontaneity, and lack of prejudice. Maslow (1943) noted that the needs at the bottom of the hierarchy had to be fulfilled before individuals could progress to meet higher-order needs. For example, individuals need to have food and shelter before they can have a sense of security or the ability to make sound moral choices. The latter may be an explanation for the looting that was prevalent following Hurricane Sandy in 2012, the tornado in Moore, Oklahoma, in 2013, and other crisis events. Looting is a common behavior during times of crisis in otherwise lawful communities. For various reasons, disaster events may be mishandled, and communities may be ill-prepared to cope and fall into chaos. People may feel desperate to meet their basic needs or concerned that their ability to meet their basic needs may be in jeopardy. Looting for food and other necessities is an illustration of the efforts of people to meet their basic needs, and it underscores the need for both effective crisis management and emergency response plans.

Community Impacts

Among the many factors that contribute to a comprehensive community response to a disaster or emergency is that everyone is equally served. When protective factors such as social supports, community bonds, financial assistance, emotional care, and emotional and spiritual connections such as family and religious organizations are available and accessible to survivors, it is likely that the emergency event will remain a manageable crisis. When these protective factors are unavailable or accessibility to them is delayed or limited, communities may erupt into chaos (Dass-Brailsford, 2010). This logic is often drawn when considering the 1992 Rodney King riots in South Central Los Angeles. In this situation, four White police officers were acquitted by a jury of police brutality against an African American, Rodney King. The only information most of America had about this incident was a nighttime home video of 25-year-old Rodney King on his knees, sometimes falling to the street, surrounded by several police officers, three of whom struck him up to 50 times (see www.youtube.com/watch?v=SW1ZDIXiuS4 for the ABC clip). The safety and security of this community was questionable prior to the incident of police brutality, and the courts validated the community's perception that they were not safe even from the police by acquitting the officers, which furthered racial tensions. Citywide riots were the result.

In 1995, an Australian farming community struggled with a disease that affected its major agricultural commodity; this led to a loss of nearly all of the economic viability in the region. An entire community's ability to meet its basic needs was

---

Reflective Exercise 5.3

What do you think were the needs of the community in South Central Los Angeles during and after the riots? What suggestions would you make to meet these needs?

---

unstable. Residents reported that because of the nature of the outbreak, this agricultural disaster "destroyed social cohesion," leading to fragmentation and provoking "disharmony to social relationships" (Hood & Seedsman, 2004, p. 58).

A community's ability to return to predisaster functioning depends on many factors, including coping skills, supports, and ability to meet basic needs, as well as the timing of rescue and recovery. One of the most prominent criticisms that emerged from Hurricane Katrina survivors was that response and rescue efforts lagged, allegedly due to the socioeconomic status of the communities hardest hit by the storm and subsequent levee failures (Dass-Brailsford, 2010). While this may be true for the immediate emergency response, the long-term perception and impact of the crisis varies from person to person and community to community (Mallick, Rahaman, & Vogt, 2011). The Lower Ninth Ward was among the areas most impacted by Hurricane Katrina in 2005, and it included a region of New Orleans most densely settled by Vietnamese immigrants. In this immigrant community, Vu and VanLandingham (2012) found remarkable rates of rapid improvement in mental and physical health after the initial stress of the crisis. The authors attributed the rapid resilience in part to strong community organizational support, extended family involvement, and previous experience. They indicated this rapid resilience resulted from a feeling of being a part of a larger community of refugees who escaped a war-torn nation, triggering several relocations (Vu & VanLandingham, 2012).

Enduring a natural disaster, a community may experience a sense of collective efficacy, and through coordinated efforts, join together to respond and recover despite depletion of local resources and absence of emergency services. In 1996, the 100 full-time residents of Buffalo Creek, Colorado, experienced a devastating forest fire, resulting in conditions prone to flash flooding. Three months later, a storm producing massive rains triggered the feared flash floods throughout the small community. Because of the loss of infrastructure and the absence of a formal governing body, residents formed a crisis response team to work with regional officials to meet basic needs, secure grant funding, and secure other necessary provisions to rebuild their community (Benight, 2004). In a study exploring the impact of the natural disaster on the community, Benight found that, after a year, members of the community of Buffalo Creek believed they could deal well with future disasters, and this belief had a buffering effect on the psychological distress experienced as a result of the crisis.

Important implications for how counselors can help come from studies about community impacts. Mallick, Rahaman, and Vogt (2011) point out that often communities already have informal inherited customs and processes for preparing for natural disasters. Often in efforts to develop disaster management plans, the impacts at the community level are an afterthought and not addressed (Mitchell, Stewart, Griffin, & Loba, 2004). Regardless of its level of elaboration, extensiveness, and detail, a plan will lack functionality if it does not take into account the cultural practices of community members. Including community leaders and residents in preparedness planning or practices can assist in developing a sense of solidarity, social cohesion and social integration (Mallick et al., 2011; Schouten, Callahan, & Bryant, 2004; Watson, Brymer, & Bonanno, 2011).

Professionals specializing in disaster management are calling for greater comparative predisaster assessment data, which would require that communities be evaluated prior to crisis events. Of course, logically, it is difficult for all of us to predict the devastating effects of storm outbreaks or terrorist attacks on communities. However, we know that some common characteristics exist among certain types of events (e.g., earthquakes on the US West Coast, political tensions in some areas of the Middle East potentially resulting in civil wars and terrorism, and West African, Asian, and Australian monsoonal rains triggering mudslides). These characteristics include time frame, location, and general demographics of the population who will be impacted. Having predisaster comparative data for culturally specific populations will aid counselors in developing evidence-based preparedness plans and interventions that are ethnoculturally focused (Watson et al., 2011).

Individual Impacts

It is essential that you as a professional counselor are aware of how crisis events impact individuals' ability to meet their basic needs (e.g., they have no other clothes to wear, shortage of food, fear, sense of safety). Although professional counselors see the need to process individuals' feelings associated with traumatic events, at times the most important task for professional counselors may be distributing clean water, food, and clothes or offering assistance to individuals who are searching for information about loved ones who have not been found.

According to Maslow's (1943) hierarchy of needs, the first level of basic needs includes physiological requirements such as food, water, and breathing. Once the basic needs and the need for safety are adequately satisfied, an assessment of mental health needs can take place. However, while this is often the time that emotional needs can begin to emerge, once long-term temporary shelter is secured, support services may be discontinued, leaving survivors feeling disconnected from further services (Thara, Rao, & John, 2008).

While all disasters result in crises, only some crises develop into trauma for individuals (Dass-Brailsford, 2010). That is, not all individuals' experiences result in negative emotional and psychological symptoms that rise to the degree of clinical diagnosis (Watson et al., 2011). Still, it is normal to have an emotional and psychological response to a crisis event. Often these emotional responses are paired with physical or somatic complaints, such as headaches, stomachaches, and other body aches and pains. Commonly reported emotional responses to crisis events include nervousness, anger, fear, helplessness, hopelessness, distress, grief, shame, desperation, anger, confusion, forgetfulness, anxiety, depression, feelings of loneliness and isolation, and feeling lost, among other negative feelings (Burnham, 2009; Daniels, 2002; Dass-Brailsford, 2010; Hood & Seedsman, 2004; Rao, 2006; Suomalainen, Haravuori, Berg, Kiviruusu, & Marttunen, 2010). Similar to students, teachers, principals, and other school professionals are emotionally impacted and affected by school violence, such as shootings and bomb threats. Several studies found that students and school employees alike have experienced emotional and psychological symptoms such as fear, avoidance, and hypervigilance after school related emergencies (Daniels, 2002; Suomalainen et al., 2010).

In 1995, in an Australian farming community where raising sheep was a mainstay of the economy, a disease devastated the sheep herds. As a result of this agricultural disaster, mental health workers reported that members of the community experienced signs and symptoms of grief, loss, depression including thoughts of suicide, and post-traumatic stress disorder (Hood & Seedsman, 2004).

The 1998 Swissair Flight 111 tragedy off the coast of the Canadian province of Nova Scotia reveals another dimension of the disaster and emergency concept. In this event, tragically, 229 people were killed after taking off from New York heading to Switzerland. This event was not a natural disaster that impacted the people of the Nova Scotian communities, nor was it a terrorist attack that affected the livelihoods of the residents. This event did not directly injure or kill or cause property loss or damage to any member of the small coastal towns tasked with the massive rescue and recovery efforts. However, this disaster depleted community resources, diverted relief and public service workers from their work in the community, and overloaded the towns with rescue personnel, media people, military reservists, construction workers, and grieving family members (Mitchell et al., 2004). Community rescue and recovery volunteers were interviewed about their experiences and shared that their communities and lives were overtaken by the search efforts (Mitchell et al., 2004). Mitchell et al. found that after spending hours, days, and weeks assisting in recovering severed body parts off of the shore and consoling bereaved family members, the resident volunteers avoided seeking help despite its availability and their needs, instead opting for a code of silence. Some volunteers reported an emotional and intellectual split when dealing with the disaster (Mitchell et al., 2004; Taylor & Frazer, 1982). The researchers frequently referred to the cultural value of inner strength and stoicism but cautioned readers to question the silence as also a sign of trauma (Mitchell et al., 2004). This study brings to light the effects of disaster on first responders.

Cultural links seem to have an impact on level of distress after disasters. After the magnitude 7.0 earthquake in Haiti in 2010, Haitian Americans with strong connections to family and friends who were direct victims of the disaster were more likely than other Americans to experience distress (Allen, Marcelin, Schmitz, Hausmann, & Schultz, 2012). Similarly, another study found that in a group of immigrant survivors of a disaster, those with the least acculturation (strong orientation to country of origin) were more likely to experience distress (Vu & Van Landingham, 2012).

Mental Health Needs During Crises and Disasters

The definition of *crisis* applied to an individual is "a temporary state of upset and disorganization, characterized chiefly by an individual's inability to cope with a particular situation using customary methods of problem solving, and by the potential for radically positive or negative outcome" (Caplan, 1964, p. 45). Embedded in this definition is a great deal of key information that can help counselors respond to clients experiencing a crisis and conceptualize their needs. A crisis is, by definition, temporary, and is not a persistent mental illness. Instead, crisis is a point in time when clients are experiencing a change from their typical level of functioning as a result of a precipitating event or combination of events.

Generally, the client's typical way of coping with challenges or problem solving does not work in the crisis situation because of the overwhelming circumstances, lack of individual preparedness, and a sense of helplessness. Although there are differences in coping styles, individuals facing crises are likely to be shocked and incapacitated, and they recognize that they are unable to solve their own problems. Therefore, it is likely that the client will need to learn new ways of coping in order to get past the crisis situation. In this case, professional counselors are trained to implement a risk assessment and to take a more directive approach to counseling when working with clients who are experiencing crises. In this section, you will learn about the mental health needs of people who are traumatized by disasters. Two diagnoses that are common for this group are posttraumatic stress disorder and acute stress disorder, In addition, you will learn about common crisis management strategies for assisting people with coping after disasters.

Mental Health Assessment

Disasters can have profound effects on people. However, most people have emotional responses that are normal reactions to disaster experiences, and they do not require the assistance of mental health professionals to manage. These normal reactions are typically temporary, and survivors are able to utilize their usual coping skills to deal with the stresses brought on by the crisis. However, at times the emotional responses may be significantly distressing and require professional counselors to assist with processing the associated feelings (e.g., fear, terror) and/or physicians to prescribe medication to reduce symptoms (e.g., insomnia). It is essential that counselors consider assigning a diagnosis only when there is evidence of reactions or symptoms that "cause clinically significant distress or impairment in social, occupational, or other areas of functioning" (APA, 2013, p. 8). This statement highlights the importance of the term *clinical significance* as defined in the DSM IV-TR; this is an essential criterion for all diagnoses.

Post-traumatic stress disorder (PTSD) and acute stress disorder (ASD) are the most common diagnoses associated with disasters (e.g., volcano eruption, earthquakes) and other trauma-causing events (e.g., car crash, fire). These two diagnoses are closely related in criteria with the main distinction being the time lapse between the event and the clinically significant stress response. According to the DSM IV-TR (APA, 2013), ASD occurs within four weeks of the event, meaning that the symptoms occur immediately after the event and last for a maximum of four weeks. ASD criteria reflect the immediate effects of the event (Daniels, Bradley, & Hays, 2007). In contrast, the criteria for PTSD tend to be reflective of longer term emotional effects of the event, and symptoms last for more than four weeks (APA, 2013). Both ASD and PTSD are diagnoses that can be appropriate when an individual is exposed to a significant traumatic stressor and the reaction is an intense emotional response to this trauma. Common to both diagnoses are (1) exposure to a perceived life-threatening event provoking an intense emotional response, (2) a recurrence of the event through images, flashbacks, dreams, thoughts, or distress upon unexpected reminders of the event, (3) attempts to avoid any place, situation, or experience that may remind the individual of the event, (4) numbing of emotions and reactions, and (5) an increased sense of arousal, including anxiety, poor concentration, insomnia, and exaggerated startle response, among other symptoms (APA, 2013). ASD has an additional criterion that is not found in PTSD; this is dissociative symptoms, such as derealization or reduced awareness of surroundings. In addition to the differences in onset and duration and this one extra criterion for ASD, a final distinction between ASD and PTSD includes the number of criteria necessary for diagnosis.

CASE ILLUSTRATION 5.1

A second-semester freshman is referred to the college counseling center by her advisor due to a sudden and marked decline in performance in most of her classes and attendance issues over the last six weeks. First semester she performed well and appeared to be adjusting well to college. Early in second semester she was at a party, and the house caught on fire. Although everyone survived, she was trapped in the crowd and unsure if she would be able to exit the building. She reports symptoms of frequently reliving the fire experience and feeling the sense of panic and fear associated with thinking she might die. She indicates that this is a problem especially when she is in a confined space with multiple people, which keeps her from attending classes—especially those held in large lecture halls—unless she can get the seat by the door. She reports going to class each day but not being able to go in and sit down if there are too many people already in the room or the two seats by the door are already taken. Even if she does get a seat by the door, she reports feeling on edge the whole time and sometimes thinking she smells smoke. She says that although she no longer attends house parties, her close friends also do not attend, so her social life has not been affected to the same degree as her academic performance.

This case example is illustrative of a presentation of criteria for PTSD. The full criteria for these diagnoses are available in the DSM-IV-TR and also on the National Center for PTSD website (www.ptsd.va.gov/professional/index.asp). Both resources provide a great deal of information for professionals on the assessment and treatment of PTSD.

Individuals with ASD present similar diagnostic criteria. A key difference between the two diagnoses is the duration of symptoms. As noted previously, PTSD criteria include the presence of symptoms for four weeks or longer. ASD differs in that the criteria state that the pattern of symptoms "must occur within 4 weeks of the traumatic event and resolve within that 4-week period" (American Psychiatric Association, 2013, p. 467).

Please note the tentative language that is used in the case example "may consider an ASD diagnosis." Revisiting the definition of a crisis, Caplan (1964) stated that crisis is a temporary state. Although diagnoses such as ASD parallel this temporary aspect, it is critical to consider the American Counseling Association's Ethical Code (2005) and all aspects of diagnostic criteria before making a diagnosis. Key questions in times of crisis might include the following:

> ## CASE ILLUSTRATION 5.1-CON,
>
> Since the freshman was first seen a week after the fire and reported these symptoms, a counselor might consider an ASD diagnosis to conceptualize the symptoms. Through treatment, the student might be able to develop coping skills to alleviate the symptoms, and if they resolve to the point of being no longer clinically significant within four weeks of the fire (traumatic event), the diagnosis of ASD may be appropriate. If symptoms persist beyond four weeks, the counselor is likely to consider a diagnosis of PTSD.

1. Will making or reporting a diagnosis cause harm to the client? (ACA, 2005, E.5.d.)

2. Are these symptoms truly clinically significant as defined by the DSM IV-TR? If the answer is "no," then the client has not met criteria for a diagnosis.

3. Are you using appropriate techniques to assess this information?

It is recognized in the DSM IV-TR that assessing whether the clinical significance criterion is met "is an inherently difficult clinical judgment" (APA, 2013, p. 8). Client self-report may not be sufficient to fully determine if clinical significance is met. It is important to keep in mind that some clients, with support, can recover from crises without ever fully meeting criteria for a diagnosis, and other clients do not meet full criteria and yet benefit from a diagnosis (e.g., increased access to mental health care). It is essential to consider the individual and her strengths, coping resources, social support, and interpretation of the event. Each person will respond to the aftermath of a disaster or crisis-causing event differently, and each person's needs for treatment will be unique to her response and recovery-related strengths and resources.

SERVING OTHERS AT TIMES OF CRISIS

Most counselors are used to following certain procedures when beginning their work with a new client. It is typical to obtain informed consent with clients, conduct an extensive initial assessment, and establish rapport during the first few sessions. However, during a crisis or disaster situation, these aspects of counseling may look very different.

Informed Consent

Informed consent for treatment, which concerns clients' rights, is considered a part of the crisis counseling process. In the case of disaster and emergency response, the American Red Cross acknowledges that using typical procedures for obtaining informed consent is often not possible, as individuals may not be able to make informed decisions at the time of crisis. This, however, does not mean that counselors should minimize the importance of professional practice and manners, such as introducing oneself, telling the client about one's credentials and training, and stating one's role in the crisis response. For example, a counselor should introduce herself: "My name is Jane. I am a licensed professional counselor in the State of Colorado, and I am volunteering with the American Red Cross." It is also critical that counselors provide clients with choices and freedom to choose whether they would like to engage in the therapeutic exchange, because this is consistent with the ethical principle of autonomy. Counselors can introduce the client's freedom to choose by saying, "I noticed that you have been crying and upset, and if it is ok with you, I would like to ask you a few questions to see if I can help you cope. Is it okay if we talk about what you are you are going through?" This process is essential in building a working relationship, rapport, with the client.

Rapport

Relationship is the most critical factor in counseling. Although the client is facing a crisis situation, building rapport is essential. In a situation that feels chaotic, building rapport may begin with simple gestures, such as moving to a more private space so that the individual feels less exposed. In an ideal setting, that would be a comfortable office space; however, that is not always readily available. A simple solution may be that counselors adjust how they and their clients are positioned. For example, if the client is with a group of people when the conversation is initiated, the counselor may stand to the outside of the group so that the client's back is to the group, thereby blocking most of the client's voice from being overheard. Another option may be to step slightly away from the group into a corner of the room, thus allowing for slightly more privacy. It is important that the counselor allow the traumatized person to be in a less visible or chaotic area (e.g., in a tent, under a tree, or behind a visual barrier) and avoid facing the majority of the people, the accident scene, or emergency responders. These strategies may help individuals experiencing crisis to feel less exposed and can be helpful in rapport building.

Risk Assessment

Conducting risk assessment is essential in crisis counseling. Although it is difficult to assess who is most at risk when a crisis arises, you must consider the individual's

---

Reflective Exercise 5.4

The link below is to a BBC audio broadcast of the stories and reflections of staff assigned to the Superdome during Hurricane Katrina. These reflections were shared at the five-year anniversary of Katrina, and they provide insight into the lived experience of those who experienced a disaster firsthand as simultaneous responders to and victims of a natural disaster. Please take some time and journal your thoughts and feelings about and responses to these stories.

www.bbc.co.uk/worldservice/programmes/2010/07/100708_outlook_superdome .shtml

---

context as well as evaluate her response (both immediate and long-term) to the crisis situation in order to determine the level of risk the person is experiencing. At the most basic level, changes in a person's behavior or affect can be indicators that she is interpreting an event as a crisis, particularly if those changes are in concert with known warning signs of a crisis.

Warning signs

Any significant departure from a person's normal way of behaving and feeling may be an indicator that she is experiencing an event crisis. Examples of changes in behavior include (a) engaging in more risk-taking behaviors than is typical (e.g., risky stock market investments, drinking and driving, high-risk sexual behaviors), (b) a marked decline in performance (e.g., poor attendance at school or work, grades dropping), and (c) atypical behaviors (e.g., starting to use drugs, giving away prized possessions, purchasing a gun, or collecting medications). Because crisis is a temporary state, recognizing a crisis includes looking for changes that are temporary departures from what is normal for a given person. Other behavioral changes may include a shift in how a person engages with others. Distancing from close friends and spending lots of time with new friends whose behavior does not reflect the person's values (e.g., new friends that drink a lot more, dress differently) may be a warning sign of a crisis. Similarly, behaving more irritably or no longer participating in activities with friends and family could be another warning sign that a person is experiencing crisis.

Emotional responses

Individuals experiencing crisis may report feeling hopeless, overwhelmed, trapped, guilty, and/or indifferent. These feelings may be affected by the way they interpret the crisis, their culture, and their coping skills. Individuals may find they lose interest in activities that were previously enjoyable and/or exhibit dramatic changes in their mood or affect. For example, someone who previously met friends for dinner once a week and was generally described as outgoing and friendly may cancel plans and withdraw.

It is important that you as a professional counselor understand the distinctions between individuals' emotional response during crisis and symptoms of mental disorders (e.g., mood disorders). For instance, if a person with dysthymic disorder (a mood disorder characterized by more than two years of depressed mood) continues to report a level of hopelessness similar to what she has experienced for a long time, this would be less likely to be conceptualized as exhibiting warning signs of a crisis based on feelings of hopelessness alone. However, if there are additional signs or a marked change in those feelings of hopelessness, it is essential that the professional counselor further assess the feelings of hopelessness that the client presents.

As mentioned in this section, changes in how people behave, feel, and act toward others are warning signs that they may be at risk as a result of experiencing a crisis situation. These warning signs could be evidence that a person is experiencing stress and that typical ways of coping are not working in this situation. Although these changes may be symptoms of experiencing a crisis, they need to be interpreted with caution, just as the warning signs of a tornado (e.g., dark, greenish sky, or hail without rain) do not necessarily mean that a tornado will absolutely develop nearby. Warning signs are simply the indicators that it is important for professional counselors to attend to; they must then inquire for further necessary information, assess for safety, and only then provide support to individuals whom they determine are in need of help.

Risk factors

Risk factors are different from warning signs. While warning signs are the indicators that a person may experience stress during and/or after a crisis situation, risk factors are the characteristics of a person or situation combined with the statistical likelihood that people with similar profiles in similar situations will experience a crisis. For the purposes of this chapter, we describe risk factors specifically to suicidality, as this is one crisis that beginning counselors often encounter in their practica and internship experiences. Further, suicidality is important to assess when there are disasters or other crisis events in the community. A well-known mnemonic device for assessing risk factors of suicide is SAD PERSONS (Patterson, Dohn, Bird, & Patterson, 1983). SAD PERSONS include the following:

S = Sex. Females who attempt suicide (34%) are more likely to have a history of previous attempts than males (16%) (Centers for Disease Control and Prevention, n.d.).

A = Age. Suicide was the third-leading cause of death for people ages 15 to 24 in 2009 (National Center for Health Statistics, 2011).

D = Depression. People experiencing depression, particularly in combination with substance abuse (see *E* in sad persons), are at greater risk for suicide. The lifetime risk for people with clinically significant depression ranges from 6% to 25%, but if depressed individuals received treatment, they are likely to have a lower risk for suicide (American Association of Suicidology, 2012).

P = Previous Attempt. Those who have previously attempted suicide are more likely to try it than those who have never attempted it (Centers for Disease Control and Prevention, n.d.).

E = Ethanol Use. As reported in 2007, the three leading methods of suicide were firearms, strangulation/hanging, and poisoning (Centers for Disease Control and Prevention, National Violent Death Reporting System, n.d.). Individuals with a known history of substance abuse or dependency accounted for less than half of the poisoning suicides by alcohol and/or drug overdose (Centers for Disease Control and Prevention, National Violent Death Reporting System, n.d.).

R = Rational Thought Loss. Experiencing psychosis is considered one of the symptoms of individuals experiencing a crisis event and is a risk factor for suicide. Psychosis may present in the form of hallucinations (e.g., hearing or seeing things others do not) or delusions, where the client misinterprets reality (e.g., the song being played on the radio when she gets into the car is a message meant just for her).

S = Social Support Lacking. Another risk factor is lack of support systems, for example, a person who does not have close friends or strong affiliation with an aspect of the community is at higher risk.

O = Organized Plan. The more organized and thought out the plan for committing suicide (e.g., place, means, time, what needs to happen beforehand), the greater the risk of suicide. In a study of 151 depressed adult patients with a history of suicide attempts, Nakagawa et al. (2009) found that there was a significant relationship between the degree of lethality and how much prior planning was involved in the suicide attempt.

N = No Spouse. Individuals who have lost significant others (e.g., spouses, partners, parents) are likely to be more vulnerable than individuals who have strong and supportive relationships.

S = Sickness. Severe and chronic illnesses (e.g., cancer) constitute one of the risk factors, as clients may be at the mercy of the medical establishment, buried in insurance paperwork and hospital bills, and at times even confused about disability benefits. Any and all of these situations can create a sense of hopelessness and helplessness. Many studies (Conwell et al., 2010; Juurlink, Herrmann, Szalai, Kopp, & Redelmeier, 2004; Voaklander et al., 2008) have shown that suicides within the elderly population have been particularly associated with medical illnesses. Similarly, nonelderly adults with medical illnesses and physical disabilities (e.g., HIV/AIDS, chronic pain) are also at risk of suicidal behavior (Bullman & Kang, 1996; Cheatle, 2011; Cooperman & Simoni, 2005; Davis, Koch, Mbugua, & Johnson, 2011).

The SAD PERSONS mnemonic has been adapted to apply to children and adolescents by adjusting the last two letters, *N* and *S* (Juhnke, 1996): N = negligent (or abusive) parents, and S = school problems as well as sickness. Counselors can utilize SAD PERSONS as an initial assessment with children and adolescents who are affected by disasters as a method not only to assess risk for suicide and possible interventions but also to express authentic care and concern, which can build rapport, an essential component of psychological first aid.

It is important that you are aware that although warning signs can help counselors recognize when a client is in crisis, and risk factors can help gauge the propensity of a person to engage in a behavior associated with crisis such as suicidality, these are not comprehensive screening tools. Further, a person who does not outwardly display warning signs and does not have any known risk factors may still have suicidal thoughts and/or commit suicide. Professional counselors must rely on their clinical skills, consultation, supervision, and professional judgment when encountering individuals who have experienced a crisis and assess for suicidality when appropriate.

Disasters and crisis events can have emotional and psychological impacts on people that can vary from the minimally troublesome, in which the individual expresses resilience and copes adequately with the unexpected stressors, to the significantly disruptive, causing impairment in one or more domains of the individual's life and possibly triggering symptoms worthy of a suicidal ideation or a diagnosis of mental illness. Regardless of the severity of the emotional response, professional counselors should be knowledgeable of the risks and warning signs for suicide and the symptoms and criteria for mental illness diagnosis and possess the skills necessary to apply that information to the individuals being serviced.

It is important to consider how each individual's perception of the event impacts her emotional response. This will be explored in the next section.

CRISIS MANAGEMENT AND EMERGENCY RESPONSE WITH DIVERSE POPULATIONS

A crisis is not an event but instead the interpretation of an event or situation. What constitutes a crisis can be markedly different from one person to another, depending on the factors that might be influencing the situation. Age, gender, culture, past experiences, economic resources, proximity to a support system, geographic location, and many other variables can influence how people react to a crisis, as can their perception of the magnitude of the event they are experiencing (Allen et al., 2012; Dass-Brailsford, 2010; Mallick et al., 2011; Thara et al., 2008; Vu & VanLandingham, 2012).

In some crisis situations, few people are directly impacted (e.g., intimate partner violence, an unexpected death, a fatal diagnosis), while other crises impact entire communities (e.g., natural disasters, acts of terrorism, stock market crashes). Regardless of how many are initially affected, there is often a ripple effect that spreads from those who are directly affected to those who are less directly affected. For example, those who respond to a disaster may have emotional reactions to the aftermath of the event once they leave the disaster scene. Community members who have experienced a recent loss or have ties to those directly impacted may also be surprised by the intense emotional reaction they may experience. It is important that professional counselors are aware that both direct and indirect impacts can create situations in which an individual experiences a crisis.

Furthermore, individuals experiencing the same crisis-precipitating situation may have very different reactions to and perceptions of the event. For example, two students who witness a school shooting may have very different experiences during and after the event. Two families who have unexpectedly lost a loved one at the hands of another person may respond in dramatically different ways. Two people involved in the same terrifying natural disaster may disclose similar experiences during the crisis situation; however, the feelings each person describes after the crisis can be extremely different. These are important clarifications for professional counselors, because there is not one *right* way to approach treatment for those involved in a crisis situation. It is most important that professional counselors establish rapport with and instill hope in their clients, as well as create a treatment plan that fits with each individual's unique needs.

Specifically, for children in a disaster, Baggerly and Exum suggest a three-phase approach:

a. Identifying children's typical and clinical symptoms after a natural disaster

b. Training parents and teachers in basic interventions

c. Implementing developmentally appropriate clinical interventions that integrate play (2008, p. 80).

Reflective Exercise 5.5

You are the chair of your school's crisis response team, which includes eight members: the principal (vice chair), three faculty members (with at least one teacher representing students from each level), the manager of the facilities department, the school nurse, one member representing the professionals assisting in the daily functioning of the school (e.g., the librarian, administrative assistants, cafeteria workers, classroom paraprofessionals), and one parent. As the chair, you have several responsibilities. In times of crisis and emergencies, you are the appointed incident commander. Yearly, you lead your team in a careful and thorough review of your school's policy and procedure manual for emergency management, and subsequently you propose updates to the principal and administration for their approval. At monthly meetings with your team, you review recent incident reports to evaluate and improve your planning and preparedness efforts. The review involves assessing personnel policy adherence, incident outcomes, and training needs as well as follow-up with all involved school personnel regarding the circumstances of the incident, if necessary.

It is an ordinary Tuesday morning when you are faced with the following dilemma:

8:00 a.m.—The starting bell rings.

8:02 a.m.—You receive a call on your office phone. The principal informs you that at 7:51 a.m., a student walking to school was struck and killed by a car driven by a drunk driver. The student's parents have been notified. Several other students saw the incident but returned home to be with their families. A police car is in front of the school, and students are becoming restless and excited about what is happening. Rumors are beginning to circulate. The principal asks you if he should be drafting a statement to broadcast to the school with the morning announcements and Pledge of Allegiance.

As the incident commander and processional counselor, there are many things for you to consider.

First, please take a moment to reflect on communicating to those concerned about the incident.

What is your plan for communicating with the students and other school professionals about this event? How do you, as the incident commander or the authoritative body in any emergency, communicate to the people involved about emergencies? What is the best way to deal with sharing emergency information in a school setting? Take a few minutes to compose a statement about the incident. Some aspects to consider may include the age and developmental level of the students, the relationship of the students and school professionals to the deceased, the academic daily schedule, your established emergency management plan, and available resources. Who will communicate this information? Who is best to be included as the information is shared?

Second, as you think about a plan for this type of incident, please consider the following:

Who will be impacted by this event? What are their needs? Assuming that you have available resources, what will you do to fulfill their needs? Employing an all-hazards approach within a school setting involves each department having a plan to address the needs of the students during a disaster or emergency event (American College Health Association, 2011). What might be some ways that different departments (e.g., facilities, library, cafeteria, specialties, and admin-istrative assistants) could assist students and school professionals during this emergency situation?

CRISIS TRAINING OPPORTUNITIES FOR COUNSELORS

When a crisis situation is created or a disaster presents itself, professional counselors can offer help to the victims of the unfortunate event. You as a professional counselor can effectively respond to these demands by being trained in crisis counseling. There are a variety of trainings offered to professional counselors to enhance their knowledge and skills in working with individuals experiencing crises.

Trainings and Workshops Offered Through Professional Organizations

Because of the unique psychological needs of people who are experiencing a crisis in the aftermath of a disaster—whether it be natural, human-made, or due to mass violence, any one providing mental health support to survivors should receive specialized training (Dass-Brailsford, 2010). American Red Cross partners with the American Counseling Association (ACA) to provide Red Cross disaster mental health volunteer training (ACA, n.d.). Members of the ACA can receive free training at the ACA annual conference and can then be deployed by the Red Cross locally and nationally. (For additional information, go to www.counseling .org/knowledge-center/trauma-disaster).

At www.jhsph.edu/research/centers-and-institutes/johns-hopkins-center-for-public-health-preparedness/training/NIMS.html, the National Incident Management System (NIMS) offers online training for dealing with mental health issues associated with disasters. The online training covers reasons for disaster mental health intervention, disaster mental health planning, an introduction to mental health and disaster preparedness, mental health consequences of disaster, psychological first aid competencies for public health workers, psychology and crisis response, psychology of terrorism, roots of terrorism, and self-care (Johns Hopkins Bloomberg School of Public Health, n.d.).

The Federal Emergency Management Agency (FEMA) provides a series of modules for online training for Community Emergency Response Teams (CERT), including Module 4: Disaster Medical Operations, which includes lessons on "Principles and Guidelines for Victim Care" and "Disaster Psychology." FEMA's course menu is available at www.citizencorps.gov/cert/IS317/; go to www.fema.gov/pdf/emergency/nrf/nrf-esf-08.pdf for additional information on FEMA's CERT programs.

The Centers for Disease Control and Prevention dedicates a page to mental health at www.cdc.gov/mentalhealth/, where mental health basics and resources are given. At http://emergency.cdc.gov/CERC/cerc.asp, CDC highlights in-person training with a module on "Psychology and Use of Risk Communication Principles in a Crisis." On-demand trainings are also offered at http://emergency.cdc.gov/CERC/ondemandtraining.asp, with a particular webinar titled "Crisis & Emergency Risk Communication Course (CERC)" that focuses on communication principles for use in emergency situations.

The National Association of School Psychologists sponsors a program called PREPaRE that is focused on training for emergencies in school environments (www.nasponline.org/prepare/faqs.aspx). Additional resources are provided at www.nasponline.org/resources/crisis_safety/index.aspx; this site includes, but is not limited to, resources on crisis response, trauma, and natural disasters.

Crisis response training (CRT) is provided by the National Organization for Victim Assistance (NOVA) at www.trynova.org/help-crisis-victim/crisis-training. This site includes basic CRT training, advanced CRT, and a trainer of trainers program. Training manuals are also available on this site.

The Substance Abuse and Mental Health Services Administration (SAMHSA) has an education and training page (www.samhsa.gov/dtac/education.asp) offering webcasts, online training sites, and field events. The webcast list includes "Deployment Supports for Disaster Behavioral Health Responders Podcast," a 30-minute podcast to prepare behavioral health responders to confront unique situations. Other podcasts include subjects on self-care for disaster behavioral health responders, best practices for disaster behavioral health responders, and building awareness of disaster behavioral health. Podcasts last anywhere from 30 to 60 minutes, and webinar series are also offered.

The American Red Cross is a reputable national organization with years of experience in crisis and disaster preparedness. It offers disaster mental health training around the United States. Generally, this training is offered through state counseling associations as a preworkshop session during each state association's annual conference. In addition to the training, the American Red Cross has local chapters throughout the United States. These chapters provide an opportunity for professional counselors to become involved in their communities working with crisis or emergency response teams composed of professionals from various disciplines. The ACA also offers a wide variety of resources for professional counselors looking for additional reading materials to learn about crisis response.

Conference sessions on the topic of crisis management and crisis counseling are often offered at the state and national levels. It can be extremely helpful for fellow professional counselors to learn from the experiences of professional counselors who have been through a crisis situation, because these counselors are able to share their experiences in working with clients during a crisis. This information can be invaluable to other professional counselors in terms of future preparedness.

In terms of suicide management, the QPR Institute offers suicide trainings designed for all levels of mental health professionals. These trainings include suicide prevention trainings for a variety of professionals, including EMS/firefighters, nurses, school counselors, mental health and substance abuse professionals, and specialists in counseling suicidal people. The website provides a wealth of information on each course, including specifying what each training's focus is. Further information can be found at www.qprinstitute.com/. In addition, the American Association of Suicidology provides webinars and trainings on crisis worker skills. This includes a webinar entitled "Recognizing and Responding to Suicide Risk" and individual certification in crisis working. You can find more information about these trainings by going to www.suicidology.org/home.

KEYSTONES

Not everyone responds to a disaster or crisis-causing event in the same way; therefore, it is important to tailor crisis response to meet individual clients' needs. It is crucial for professional counselors to be aware that

- A crisis comes in many forms and can impact only a few individuals or have a wide reaching impact. Regardless, the crisis is significant for those involved, whether directly or indirectly.
- Counselors sometimes respond to crises individually and are sometimes part of a larger team of professionals working together.

- Counselors are impacted by crises as well, and will need to have a plan for debriefing, processing, and self-care after helping others who have been involved in a crisis situation.
- A crisis event is not one that individuals typically recover from within days or weeks.
- Counselors can offer hope during a crisis by establishing rapport, building trust, assessing needs, and creating a plan for moving forward.

ADDITIONAL RESOURCES

Suicide and Emergency Response Hotlines

American Red Cross 1–800-RED CROSS (733–2767)
Boystown 1–800–448–3000
Trevor Project (For LGBTQ Youth) 1–866–488–7386
Vet2Vet (Veteran's Crisis Hotline) 1–877-Vet2Vet (838–2838)

Websites

American Association of Suicidology www.suicidology.org/home
American Citizen Corps www.citzencorps.gov/citizencorps/partners/paindex.shtm
Federal Emergency Management Agency www.fema.gov/
Foundation for Suicide Prevention www.afsp.org/
National Center for Post-Traumatic Stress Disorder www.ptsd.va.gov/professional/index.asp
Substance Abuse and Mental Health Services Administration www.samhsa.gov

REFERENCES

Allen, A., Marcelin, L. H., Schmitz, S., Hausmann, V., & Schultz, J. M. (2012). Earthquake impact on Miami Haitian Americans: The role of family/social connectedness. *Journal of Loss and Trauma, 17*(4), 337–349, DOI: 10.1080/15325024.2011.635577

American Association of Suicidology (2012). *Facts about Suicide and depression.* Retrieved from http://www.suicidology.org/c/document_library/get_file?folderId=262&name=DLFE-529.pdf

American College Health Association, Emergency Public Health Threats and Emergency Response Coalition and Campus Safety and Violence Coalition. (2011). Emergency planning guidelines for campus health services: An all-hazards approach. *Journal of American College Health, 59*(5), 438–449.

American Counseling Association (ACA). (n.d.) *ACA and the American Red Cross.* Retrieved from http://www.counseling.org/sub/dmh/redcross.aspx

American Counseling Association (ACA). (2005). *ACA code of ethics.* Washington, DC: Author.

American Psychiatric Association (APA) (2000). *Diagnostic and statistical manual of mental disorders,* (4th ed., text revision). Washington, DC: Author.

American Psychiatric Association (APA). (2013). *Diagnostic and statistical manual of mental disorders: DSM-V* (5th ed.). Washington, DC: Author.

American Psychological Association. (n.d.). *The road to resilience.* Retrieved from http://www.apa.org/helpcenter/road-resilience.aspx#

American Red Cross. (n.d.). Disaster Services. Retrieved from http://www.ehdoleredcross.org/index.php/site/info/822/

Baggerly, J., & Exum, H. A. (2008). Counseling children after natural disasters: Guidance for family therapists. *The American Journal of Family Therapy, 36,* 79–93. DOI: 10.1080/01926180601057598

Benight, C. C. (2004). Collective efficacy following a series of natural disasters. *Anxiety, Stress and Coping, 17*(4), 401–420. DOI: 10.1080/1061580051233128768

Briere, J., & Scott, C. (2006). *Principles of trauma therapy: A guide to symptoms, evaluation, and treatment.* Thousand Oaks, CA: Sage.

Bullman, T. A. & Kang, H. K. (1996). The risk of suicide among wounded Vietnam veterans. *American Journal of Public Health, 86,* 662–668.

Burnham, J. J. (2009). Contemporary fears of children and adolescents: Coping and resiliency in the 21st century. *Journal of Counseling & Development, 87,* 28–35.

Caplan, G. (1964). *Principles of preventative psychiatry.* New York, NY: Basic Books.

Centers for Disease Control and Prevention. (n.d.). *Crisis and Emergency Risk Communication (CERC).* Retrieved from http://emergency.cdc.gov/cerc/

Centers for Disease Control and Prevention, National Center for Injury Prevention and Control. (n.d.). *Web-based injury statistics query and reporting system* (WISQARS). Retrieved January, 2012, from http://www.cdc.gov/ncipc/wisqars

Centers for Disease Control and Prevention. National Violent Death Reporting System. (n.d.). *National suicide statistics at a glance: Number and percentage of suicides for persons ages 10 years and older, by sex and associated circumstances—National Violent Death Reporting System, 16 states, 2009.* Retrieved from http://www.cdc.gov/ViolencePrevention/suicide/statistics/reporting_system.html

Cheatle, M. D. (2011). Depression, chronic pain, and suicide by overdose: On the edge. *Pain Medicine, 12 Supplement,* S43–S48.

Conwell, Y., Duberstein, P. R., Hirsch, J. K., Conner, K. R., Eberly, S., & Caine, E. D. (2010). Health status and suicide in the second half of life. *International Journal of Geriatric Psychiatry, 25,* 371–379.

Cooperman, N., & Simoni, J. (2005). Suicidal ideation and attempted suicide among women living with HIV/AIDS. *Journal of Behavioral Medicine, 28,* 149–156.

Council for Accreditation of Counseling and Related Educational Programs (CACREP). (2009). *2009 Standards.* Retrieved on September 3, 2012 fromhttp://cacrep.org/doc/2009%20Standards%20with%20cover.pdf.

Crisis. (2011). In *Merriam-Webster.com.* Retrieved October 12, 2012, from http://www.merriam-webster.com/dictionary/crisis

Daniels, J. A. (2002). Assessing threats of school violence: Implications for counselors. *Journal of Counseling & Development, 80,* 215–218.

Daniels, J. A., Bradley, M. C., & Hays, M. (2007). The impact of school violence on school personnel: Implications for psychologists. *Professional Psychology: Research and Practice, 38,* 652–659. DOI: 10.1037/0735–7028.38.6.652

Dass-Brailsford, P. (Ed.). (2010). *Crisis and disaster counseling: Lessons learned from Hurricane Katrina and other disasters.* Thousand Oaks, CA: Sage.

Davis, D. J., Koch, D. S., Mbugua, A., & Johnson, A. (2011). Recognizing suicide risk in consumers with HIV/AIDS. *Journal of Rehabilitation, 77,* 14–19.

Emergency. (n.d.). In *Merriam-Webster.com.* Retrieved October 12, 2012, from http://www.merriam-webster.com/dictionary/emergency

Federal Emergency Management Agency (2003). Integrating manmade hazards into mitigation planning. Washington, DC: Author. Retrieved from http://hazardmitigation.calema.ca.gov/docs/howto7 Integrating Manmade_Hazards.pdf

Hobfoll, S.E., Watson, P. J., Bell, C. C., Bryant, M. J., Brymer, M. J., Friedman, M., . . . & Ursano, R.J. (2007). Five essential elements of immediate and midterm mass trauma interventions: Empirical evidence. *Psychiatry, 70*(4), 283–315.

Hood, B., & Seedsman, T. (2004). Psychosocial investigation of individual and community responses to the experience of Ovine Johne's disease in rural Victoria. *Australian Journal of Rural Health, 12,* 54–60.

Johns Hopkins Bloomberg School of Public Health. (n.d.). National incident management system (NIMS) training for public health departments. Retrieved from http://www.jhsph.edu/research/centers-and-institutes/johns-hopkins-center-for-public-health-preparedness/training/online/nims.html

Juhnke, G. A. (1996). The adapted–SAD PERSONS: A suicide assessment scale designed for use with children. *Elementary School Guidance & Counseling, 30*, 252–259.

Juurlink, D. N., Herrmann, N., Szalai, J. P., Kopp, A., & Redelmeier, D.A. (2004). Medical illness and the risk of suicide in the elderly. *Archives of Internal Medicine, 164*, 1179–1184.

Kennedy, A. (2007). We are Virginia Tech. *Counseling Today.* Retrieved from http://ct.counseling.org/2007/04/we-are-virginia-tech/

Kessler, R. C., Galea, S., Jones, R. T., & Parker, H. A. (2006). Mental illness and suicidality after Hurricane Katrina. *Bulletin of the World Health Organization, 84*, 930–939.

Mallick, B., Rahaman, K. R., & Vogt, J. (2011). Social vulnerability analysis for sustainable disaster mitigation planning in coastal Bangladesh. *Disaster Prevention and Management, 20*(3), 220–237. DOI: 10.1108/09653561111141682

Maslow, A. H. (1943). A theory of human motivation. *Psychological Review, 50*, 370–396.

Mitchell, T., Stewart, S. H., Griffin, K., & Loba, P. (2004). "We will never ever forget": The Swissair Flight 111 disaster and its impact on volunteers and communities. *Journal of Health Psychology, 9*, 245–262. DOI: 10.1177/1359105304040890

Nakagawa, A., Grunebaum, M. F., Oquendo, M. A., Burke, A. K., Kashima, H., & Mann, J. J. (2009). Clinical correlates of planned, more lethal suicide attempts in major depressive disorder. *Journal of Affective Disorders, 112*, 237–242.

National Center for Health Statistics. (2011). *Table 39: Death rates for suicide, by sex, race, Hispanic origin, and age: United States, selected years 1950–2009.* Retrieved from http://www.cdc.gov/nchs/data/hus/2011/039.pdf

Patterson, W. M., Dohn, H. H., Bird, J., & Patterson, G. A. (1983). Evaluation of suicidal patients: The SAD PERSONS scale. *Psychosomatics: Journal of Consultation Liaison Psychiatry, 24*, 343–349. DOI: 10.1016/s0033–3182(83)73213–5

Rao, K. (2006). Psychosocial support in disaster-affected communities. *International Review of Psychiatry. 18*, 501–505. DOI: 10.1080/09540260601038472

Schouten, R., Callahan, M. V., & Bryant, S., (2004). Community response to disaster: The role of the workplace. *Harvard Review of Psychiatry, 12*(4), 229–237. DOI: 10.1080/10673220490509624

Suomalainen, L., Haravuori, H., Berg, N., Kiviruusu, O., & Marttunen, M. (2010). A controlled follow-up study of adolescents exposed to a school shooting: Psychological consequences after four months. *European Psychiatry, 26*, 490–497. DOI: 10/.1016/j.eurpsy.2010.07.007

Taylor, A., & Frazer, A. (1982). The stress of post-disaster body handling and victim identification work. *Journal of Human Stress, 8*, 4–12.

Thara, R., Rao, K., & John, S. (2008). Assessment of post-tsunami psychosocial training programmes in Tamilnadu, India. *International Journal of Social Psychiatry, 54*, 197–205. DOI: 10.1177/0020764008090421

Tobin, G. (2005). Distress and disasters: Positive outcomes of the great Midwestern floods of 1993. *Journal of Contemporary Water Research & Education,. 130*, 49–60.

US Department of Homeland Security. (2008). National Response Framework. Retrieved from http://www.fema.gov/pdf/emergency/nrf/nrf-core.pdf

Voaklander, D. C., Rowe, B. H., Dryden, D. M., Pahal, J., Saar, P. & Kelly, K. D. (2008). Medical illness, medication use and suicide in seniors: A population-based case-control study. *Journal of Epidemiology & Community Health, 62*, 138–146.

Vu, L. & VanLandingham, M. J. (2012). Physical and mental health consequences of Katrina on Vietnamese immigrants in New Orleans: A pre- and post-disaster assessment. *Journal of Immigrant Minority Health, 14*, 386–394. doi: 10.1007/s10903–011–9503–011–9504–3

Watson, P. J., Brymer, M. J., & Bonanno, G. A. (2011). Postdisaster psychological intervention since 9/11. *American Psychologist, 66*(6), 482–492. DOI: 10.1037/a0024806

Chapter 6

Multiculturalism and Social Justice in Professional Counseling

MANIVONG J. RATTS

ALEXA WAYMAN

Counseling is a field that is continuously evolving with the zeitgeist of the times. The changes that occur in the profession are a microcosm of the changes in society. As society becomes more diverse, professional counselors are required to practice multicultural and social justice counseling in order to serve clients with unique backgrounds. Multicultural and social justice counseling, often referred to as the fourth and fifth forces in counseling, follow the psychoanalytic, cognitive-behavioral, and existential-humanistic forces in the field. Both multicultural and social justice counseling grew out of discontent with predominant counseling theories that are not adequately serving the needs of historically oppressed and diverse client populations. Predominant counseling theories place less emphasis on the relevance of cultural factors and the role of social context in human development, focusing solely on intrapsychic approaches. Counselors operating from a traditional model of helping may not be adequately equipped to work with culturally diverse populations and may lack skills to attend to the social ills that hinder client development. Consequently, culturally diverse clients often leave counseling unsatisfied, believing their problems reside within them and that they needed to be fixed.

This chapter provides an overview of the multicultural and social justice counseling perspectives. You will learn the need for professional counselors to operate from a multicultural and social justice framework as well as the relevance of culturally responsible social advocacy. Both the multicultural counseling competencies (MCCs) and the advocacy competencies are highlighted, as are their relevance to the role of the professional counselor. Last, you will learn about ethical concerns and dilemmas within the context of counseling services in a pluralistic society. Reflection exercises and case studies will enhance your learning about multiculturalism and social justice in counseling.

LEARNING OBJECTIVES

After reading this chapter and completing the activities provided in it, you will be able to

1. Identify the major events that have shaped the multicultural and social justice counseling movements,

2. Describe the components of the MCCs,

3. Describe the components of the advocacy competencies,

4. Discuss the relevance of multiculturalism and social justice in counseling, and

5. Consider the importance of being a change agent in counseling.

MULTICULTURAL COUNSELING: THE DEVELOPMENT OF A FOURTH FORCE

Although multicultural counseling has been presented in counseling discourse as the fourth force within the last two decades, you can find evidence of cross-cultural interactions, and the necessity of exploring different methods of relating, dating throughout the history of civilization. For example, Herodotus recognized the vigor in diversity and "set forth the famous dictum 'custom is stronger than law' in order to explain why conquerors have so much trouble getting conquered peoples to adopt to the conqueror's law" (Jackson, 1995, p. 4).

The literature on multicultural counseling did not proliferate until the 1960s for several reasons. Segregation, racism, and discrimination in greater society, and thus manifesting within the American Personnel and Guidance Association

(APGA, former title of the American Counseling Association), limited the drive to focus on best practices for counseling culturally diverse populations. The "melting pot" metaphor was also the dominant ideology of the time within the United States (Sue & Sue, 2013). This metaphor was rooted in the belief that people from different cultural groups could coexist and form into a common culture by identifying similarities across groups and ignoring differences among groups and between individuals. This philosophy manifested in the erroneous and predominant belief that counseling theories, research, and practices need not be adapted for culturally diverse populations, the belief being that counseling that is thoughtfully grounded in one or more theoretical orientations is effective counseling, regardless of a client's sociocultural background. Patterson (1996) criticized counselors who modified the counseling process to fit different cultures and instead argued that there were universal aspects of counseling that are applicable to all cultures. Though Patterson's line of thought persists among some counselors today, prior to 1970, there simply was not consideration given to the ways in which basic counseling theories simply do not apply to large numbers of people.

Although the melting pot metaphor was central to the development of counseling services, it has never been a reality in the United States. Even in the face of oppression and pressures to assimilate into the dominant culture, immigrant and underrepresented racial and ethnic groups have retained their cultural distinctions and practices and created subcultures fostered in schools, churches, and community centers in neighborhoods where minorities reflect the majority. Assimilation counseling was prevalent before the 1960s, reflective of the greater societal norms and standards, but just like the melting pot was made impossible by the inherent strength of engrained culture, assimilation counseling proved ineffective for, and at odds with, individuals of diverse heritages (Jackson, 1995).

The civil rights movement forced the counseling profession to see its imperfections. Specifically, it illustrated the flaws inherent in traditional counseling theories when applied to clients of color, as questions about the relevance of predominant helping paradigms began to appear in the literature. The multicultural movement led to legislation within the APGA that called for standards of guidance and counseling of persons who were "culturally disadvantaged" (Hoyt, 1967, p. 625). The use of the term "culturally disadvantaged" is a reflection of the times when people of color were still considered deviant and abnormal rather than a variation of society.

The 1970s marked the formation of the Association of Non-White Concerns (ANWC), which consisted mainly of African American members of the APGA. However, it was not until 1972 that ANWC became an official division of the American Counseling Association (ACA) (McFadden & Lipscomb, 1985). Formation of the ANWC led to the development of the *Journal of Non-White Concerns* (*JNWC*). The *JNWC* changed the focus of counseling scholarship and ultimately counseling practices. Articles published in the *JNWC* gave credence to a culture-centered approach. At the time, counseling literature called for approaches that required clients of color to align with counselors' theoretical orientations. This practice often led counselors to ignore the relevance of cultural factors and misdiagnose the experience and repercussions of racism as mental illness (Albee & Joffe, 2004). The multicultural perspective shifted this responsibility to counselors. Theories and approaches needed to accommodate clients' culturally diverse backgrounds. With this, the idea that counselors are called to question their own perspectives and examine how their perceptions and biases influence the counseling relationship began to take shape.

As you can imagine, during early 1980s, US society became more diverse. This situation presented an urgent need for professional counselors to develop cultural competencies for use when working with diverse clients. For this reason, in the 1980s and 1990s, multicultural counseling continued to flourish. In 1985, the ANWC changed its name to the Association for Multicultural Counseling and Development (AMCD) to better reflect the movement's broader focus on oppressed racial groups in addition to nonwhites and on the dual experience of sexism and racism. These decades also marked a period in which the multicultural perspective began to be seen as mainstream in the counseling profession. Rather than viewing this perspective as an add on, Pedersen (1991) presented the idea that "multiculturalism is relevant throughout the field of counseling as a generic rather than an exotic perspective" (p. 6) and, thus, should be considered as a fourth force of the counseling profession. Additionally, in 1996, the AMCD adopted the MCCs (Arredondo et al., 1996). The MCCs provide standards for counselor training and practice.

Exercise 6.1

THE COMPLEXITIES OF DIVERSITY

The melting pot paradigm led culturally encapsulated counselors to be ethnocentric in practice, utilizing one-size-fits-all approaches. The multicultural movement challenged this belief by adopting a cultural mosaic perspective, in which differences were acknowledged as much as similarities.

1. Take a few minutes to write on paper the multiple facets that form your own identity (e.g., race, ethnicity, gender, sexual orientation, gender identity, gender expression, disability status, religious/spiritual orientation, socioeconomic status, parental status).

2. To the extent that you are comfortable, share the various aspects of your identity with a classmate, peer, or colleague. In what ways are you the same? In what ways are you different?

3. What aspects of your identity are you most conscious of on a daily basis? What aspects of your identity are you least conscious of on a daily basis? Why?

4. How have the various aspects of your identity shaped your lived experiences and worldview?

The 21st century brings a broader and more complex perspective to the multicultural counseling movement. For example, there is increased attention on global and international affairs, which has led the US society to put more explicit efforts toward understanding different cultural backgrounds. As a result, both the ACA and the AMCD have developed international outreach efforts that extend to Africa, Asia, and the Middle East, among other regions. The globalization of the counseling profession coincides with technological advance in the United States. The progress and prevalence of economic globalization has led to the realization that counseling methods can and should diversify in order to be applied to other nations.

At the beginning of the 21st century, scholars in the United States also found a greater commitment to understanding the complexities of human diversity and the intersection of race, ethnicity, gender, sexual orientation, economic status, age, and religious identity. McNeill and Gallardo (2009) argued that it is important to conceptualize and recognize clients according to the multiple ways in which they conceptualize themselves, because this allows counselors to gain a deeper understanding of client experiences. A study conducted by Jones and McEwen (2000) explored how aspects of human diversity (e.g., race, ethnicity, gender, sexual orientation) interact and the salience of people's identities at a given period of time (and the ways in which individuals interact with the stigmas that prevail in society at that time). The results of their study indicated that social context influences whether people are aware of certain aspects of their identity. In addition, participants in this study indicated being conscious of aspects of their identity when they were made to feel different or marginalized.

MULTICULTURAL COUNSELING COMPETENCIES

As mentioned, during early 1980s, the US society became more diverse, which inadvertently forced professional counselors to develop cultural competencies for working with diverse clients. Sue et al. (1982) issued a historic call to the profession asserting the need for competence in multiculturalism across all counseling practice and education. This ethical mandate formed the foundation for later literature and standards for multicultural competence. In 1991, the AMCD commissioned Sue, Arredondo, and McDavis to develop multicultural competencies for the profession. The belief was that counselors need a minimal level of competency to effectively work with culturally diverse clients. The work of Sue et al. led to the development of the MCCs. The MCCs are arguably one of the most substantial developments in counseling and psychology. The creation of the MCCs was considered so significant that it was published in both the *Journal of Counseling and Development* and the *Journal of Multicultural Counseling and Development* in 1992.

Exercise 6.2

OPERATIONALIZING THE MULTICULTURAL COUNSELING COMPETENCIES

There are three domains to the MCCs: The *attitudes* domain calls counselors to reflect on their own experience in the world; the *knowledge* domain calls counselors to critically analyze how others experience the world; and the *skills* domain requires counselors to practice in ways that ethically demonstrate multicultural competence.
   In a small group, reflect on and discuss the following questions.

1. Given your understanding of these three domains, discuss (without using academic jargon) the MCCs and their relevance in counseling.

2. Think about the population or community that you want to work with in the future. What aspects of the MCCs will you find easy to maintain in your practice with this population? What particular competencies will be more challenging to implement?

3. What are some limitations of the MCCs? How will you address these limitations in your own practice?

4. How do you integrate the multicultural perspective into your theoretical orientation?

5. What are ways in which you can enhance your awareness in each of the three areas of competence in the MCCs?

   a. Attitudes and Beliefs

   b. Knowledge

   c. Skills

Looking at the evolution of society and its changing demographics, you can see how multicultural competence has become essential in all work that involves interacting with others, and especially in counseling. At all times, when you provide counseling for individuals as a professional counselor, you are called to cultivate your understanding of the client's perspective, and recognize the ways in which the client is impacted by her environment. Taking a client's perspective is a theme throughout humanistic theories of counseling, especially in existential counseling, where we are involved in a genuine encounter with an individual. This is an experience Van Kaam (1966) describes as sharing "the life of the other, the existence of the other, his[/her] way of being in the world" (p. 16). If you truly seek to achieve a therapeutic relationship where you can deeply understand your client's point of view, you must strive to achieve multicultural competence.

Cornish, Schreier, Nadkami, Metzger, and Rodolfa (2010) defined multicultural competence as "the extent to which a psychotherapist is actively engaged in the process of self-awareness, obtaining knowledge, and implementing skills in working with diverse individuals" (p. 7). Rubin et al. (2007) described competencies as "complex and dynamically interactive clusters of integrated knowledge of concepts and procedures; skills and abilities; behaviors and strategies; attitudes, beliefs, and values; dispositions and personal characteristics; self-perceptions; and motivations that enable a person to execute a professional activity with myriad potential outcomes" (p. 453). Ratts and Ford (2010) added, "Competencies are critical to a profession because they help to determine best practice, standards of service, and professional qualifications" (p. 22). Ratts (2011) noted that "the MCCs were created in an effort to reduce bias in counseling and to help professional counselors develop the requisite awareness, knowledge, and skills needed to provide culturally sensitive and appropriate counseling for their diverse clientele" (p. 28).

The MCCs are categorized into three areas: (1) counselors' awareness of their own assumptions, values, and biases; (2) an understanding of the worldviews of culturally diverse clients; and (3) a commitment to using culturally appropriate intervention strategies and techniques (Sue, Arredondo, & McDavis, 1992). Counselor awareness, knowledge, and skills form the three elements that make up the foundation of the MCCs.

Since their inception, the MCCs have revolutionized counselor training and standards of practice. It is now mainstream to consider the relevance of cultural issues in the therapeutic relationship. You also see elements of the MCCs throughout the 2005 ACA code of ethics. For instance, section B.1.a. states counselors must "maintain awareness and sensitivity regarding cultural meanings of confidentiality and privacy. Counselors respect differing views toward disclosure of information. Counselors hold ongoing discussions with clients as to how, when, and with whom information is to be shared" (American Counseling Association, 2005, p. 7). This call to multicultural competence is not only ethical but also a means of allowing all individuals to feel comfortable in a counseling environment and, thus, preserving the necessity of our profession in a country that is increasingly diverse. Arredondo et al. (1996) contend that retention rates in counseling culturally diverse clients are extremely low due to the inability of counselors to offer culturally relevant services.

The demographics in the United States are shifting, and as collective underrepresented groups grow into the majority, professional counselors are called to adopt multicultural practices in order to maintain the progress and relevance of the counseling field. The essential nature of how counselors interact with clients—from a place of understanding and respect—was not developed by the MCCs, but the MCCs do specify the nature of this relationship. Case Illustration 6.1 will help you better understand how the MCCs can assist professional counselors to effectively address the needs of diverse client populations.

CASE ILLUSTRATION 6.1

MULTICULTURAL CONSIDERATIONS

In the movie *Real Women Have Curves* (Cardoso, 2002) Anna, a Latina female high school senior, struggles with whether to attend college or work in the family tailoring business upon graduation. Anna lives in a working-class southside neighborhood in Los Angeles. She rides a bus an hour each way from her poverty-stricken neighborhood to attend an elite predominately White private school in Beverly Hills, California. Anna is one of the few students of color at the school, and she has an academic scholarship. Her grades would allow her to attend the top universities in the country. However, Anna's working class family wants her to help sew dresses in the family's tailoring business after graduation. Anna is experiencing conflict between wanting to please her family and wanting to attend college. She sees college as a means out of poverty and of eventually helping her family. College is a foreign and abstract concept for Anna's family. Consistent with Latino cultural values and beliefs of collectivism, Anna's family's needs take precedence over her individual needs.

The above case study illustrates the struggles many first generation Latino families experience when immigrating to the United States. Latino families often come to the United States in search of better economic opportunities. Upon arrival, children experience a different America than their parents do. Latino youth develop a bicultural worldview as they become acculturated into US culture. This experience can create tension between parents and their children because of the cultural divide in the home. Counselors who understand and integrate cultural factors into their work with such clients will likely be more effective than those who ignore the relevance of culture.

Now it is time for you to answer the following questions:

1. What cultural factors make Anna's situation different from that of her White peers?

2. What are the consequences of working from an ethnocentric perspective with Anna and her family?

3. What challenges might you experience if you were Anna's and her family's counselor?

4. How might your own values, beliefs, and biases influence your counseling with Anna and her family?

As the case study illustrates, cultural factors play a significant role in people's lives. Children who grow up in collectivistic families, but attend schools that promote individualism, are likely to experience some form of conflict. It is thus important that counselors acknowledge this struggle with such clients. When culture is ignored, counselors run the risk of doing more harm than good. For instance, it can be easy to devalue Anna's parents' belief system and encourage her to attend college. This approach is likely to occur when counselors are not privy to the complex ways in which culture impacts client's lives. It is this belief that led to the evolution of the multicultural movement in counseling.

The monumental evolution in counseling beginning in the late 20th century marks the beginning of a shift that will continue to call counselors to enhance their own understanding of multicultural and intersecting identities in order to engage in healthy therapeutic relationships (Sue & Sue, 2013). This shift is essential for counselors to maintain provision of relevant services as society continues to diversify. Multicultural counseling competence is an ethical mandate for counselors, because when counselors are not aware of cultural differences, there is an inevitable deficit in the counseling relationship. Counselors are called to ascertain a client's presenting issues given an understanding of their worldview and their experience in the world. As counselors become aware of the multiple vehicles of oppression that are at play in society, and the effects they have on a client's life, acting in the best interest of the client becomes a multifaceted task. Not only are counselors called to work to promote growth within the counseling relationship, but they are also called to act in society at large to promote equity. This idea is leading the counseling field to explore the fifth force in counseling: social justice.

SOCIAL JUSTICE COUNSELING: DEVELOPMENT OF THE FIFTH FORCE IN COUNSELING

As previously presented in the last section, an increase of diversity in the US society during the latter half of the 20th century influenced the counseling profession. Consequently, such scholars such as Pedersen (1991) identified multiculturalism as the fourth force in counseling. Ratts, D'Andrea, and Arredondo (2004) proposed the concept of social justice as the next, fifth, force of the counseling profession, because it changed how counseling had traditionally been practiced. Professional counselors were now called to provide both individual counseling and advocacy counseling outside the office setting. Kiselica and Robinson (2001) noted that social justice has a long history in the counseling profession. The social justice perspective is best reflected in the 1971 special issue of the *Personnel and Guidance Journal* (the predecessor to the *Journal of Counseling and Development*), titled *Counseling and the Social Revolution* (Lewis, Lewis, & Dworkin, 1971). This special issue highlighted the need for counselors to use advocacy to address oppressive systemic barriers and to consider the relevance of being a change agent, calling for counselor preparation programs to equip counselors with the skills to address social injustices experienced by clients. Other publications ensued during this era speaking to the need for counselors to be advocates for social and political change (Baker & Cramer, 1972; Dustin, 1974; Hutchinson & Stadler, 1975; Ponzo, 1974). These publications mark a significant shift in the counselor role. Rather than provide traditional therapy, which focuses on the internal world of the client, counselors were called to attend to the external world of the client.

The 1980s presented a shift away from advocacy for clients to advocacy for the profession (Fouad, Gerstein, & Toporek, 2006). You will find more information about advocacy for the profession of counseling in Chapter 12 of this textbook. The need to advocate for the profession was due in part to the increasing influence of managed care industries, the psychiatry profession, and education administrators on the role of professional counselors. For instance, managed care industries began to dictate the number of sessions available to clients each year. The field of psychiatry dictated what was considered a mental health issue with the publication of the *Diagnostic and Statistical Manual* of mental disorders. Principals in K–12 schools largely determined the role of professional school counselors.

Lee and Walz (1998) published the book *Social Action: A Mandate for Counselors,* in 1998. This book made a case for the need for counselors to be social change agents and the significance of advocacy counseling. In this book, Lewis and Arnold (1998) wrote a chapter detailing the distinction and connection between multiculturalism and social justice advocacy. They indicated that multicultural competence was limiting if it did not also include a focus on social justice advocacy, because many of the issues that oppressed clients bring to therapy are systemically based. In 1997, the Association for Gay, Lesbian, and Bisexual Issues in Counseling (the predecessor to the Association for Gay, Lesbian, Bisexual, and Transgender Issues in Counseling) became a division of the ACA. This marked the profession's commitment to human rights of LGBTQ individuals and communities.

In the early 2000s, professional counselors began to see the social justice perspective become more legitimized and integrated in counseling, beginning with a book edited by Lewis and Bradley (2000), *Advocacy in Counseling: Counselors, Clients, and Community.* That same year, Jane Goodman, then president of the ACA, commissioned a taskforce to focus on developing advocacy competencies for the field (Ratts, 2006). The work of the taskforce led to a document called *The Advocacy Competencies,* which the ACA governing council adopted (ACA Governing Council, 2003). A special section on the advocacy competencies was developed and published in the summer of 2009 in the *Journal of Counseling and Development,* the flagship journal of the ACA. Counselors for Social Justice (CSJ) also became a division of the ACA in 2002. The mission of CSJ is to promote issues of justice and equity within society. Social justice counseling was a paradigm unto itself, distinct from the psychoanalytic, cognitive-behavioral, existential-humanistic, and multicultural paradigms, because of its emphasis on balancing individual counseling with social justice advocacy. In 2010, a special issue on social justice titled *Social Justice: A National Imperative for Counselor Education and Supervision* was published in *Counselor Education and Supervision*, the leading journal on counselor preparation and training. This special issue called on counselor educators and supervisors to consider ways to integrate social justice into their training programs.

Exercise 6.3

SOCIAL JUSTICE COUNSELING—AN OVERVIEW

The movement toward a social justice perspective in counseling evolved in response to the impact of oppression on clients. As counselors started to work with culturally diverse clients, they began to realize that the mental health problems clients presented were often a result of factors outside the client, such as racism, sexism, heterosexism, classism, ageism, and religious oppression. This realization led to calls to address systemic barriers that impede clients' academic, career, and personal/social development. This shift in how client problems are understood has revolutionized how counseling is practiced.

(Continued)

(Continued)

1. Do you agree that social justice counseling should be considered a fifth force in counseling?

2. Describe two events that have shaped the social justice perspective in counseling.

3. Privilege and oppression permeate all aspects of society, including the counseling relationship. Given this perspective, how has your lived experience been shaped by privilege and oppression?

4. Terms such as *advocate, change agent,* and *community activist* are being used with increasing frequency to describe professional counselors. How might these terms align with your professional identity as a counselor?

5. Consider ways you can work to enhance your perspective on the experience of oppression from all angles. If you intend to work with a particular oppressed client population, what are some activities you could engage in to inform your understanding of this group?

ADVOCACY COMPETENCIES

Ratts, Toporek, and Lewis (2010) noted, "While the roots of the profession of counseling have acknowledged the significance of external forces in clients' lives, the extent to which counselors have focused attention on these external barriers has fluctuated and been influenced by the zeitgeist of the time" (p. 11). The lack of a well-thought-out advocacy framework makes it difficult for helping professionals to enact advocacy strategies in meaningful ways. A conceptual framework for implementing advocacy strategies can go a long way in helping counselors attend to both individual and contextual factors. This belief led to the development of the advocacy competencies in counseling.

The advocacy competencies provide helping professionals with a framework to advocate with and on behalf of clients. Within the advocacy competencies, advocacy occurs at the micro, meso, and macro levels (Ratts, Toporek, & Lewis, 2010). Micro-level advocacy strategies focus on empowering clients at the individual level. These may include working with clients by helping them understand their situation in context and developing self-advocacy skills. Meso-level advocacy interventions entail working at the school and community levels outside the traditional office setting. Such interventions may include collaborating with community and religious leaders to address issues that may impede client development. Macro-level advocacy involves bringing client issues to the public eye by working at the public arena level. This means using social media to enact change and working with legislators to change or eradicate social policies that impede client development.

The advocacy competencies are instrumental in helping counselors address client issues on an individual and systemic scale. Specifically, the competencies encourage counselors to consider whether individual-level or systemwide interventions are needed. While this has made counseling more complex than it has been in the past, this multilevel approach is more likely to address the root of client problems, because it considers clients and their environment.

ETHICAL CHALLENGES TO MULTICULTURAL AND SOCIAL JUSTICE COUNSELING

Multicultural and social justice counseling are creations of the profession of counseling to respond to diverse cultural groups in the US pluralistic society. Since the mid-1990s, multiculturalism and social justice have become an integral part of professional counseling. According to the ACA code of ethics (2005), it is unethical for professional counselors to practice counseling without considering the relevance of multiculturalism and social justice. Professional counselors who fail to integrate multicultural and social justice perspectives into their clinical work run the risk of misdiagnosing cultural factors as mental illnesses and mislabeling environmental barriers as residing inside the client. For instance, in the book *The Spirit Catches You and You Fall Down,* Fadiman (1997) describes the damage to individuals and families by well-intentioned helping professionals that occurs when cultural and contextual factors are ignored. In the story told in this book, White helping professionals ignore a Hmong patient and her family's cultural practices and spiritual beliefs. Specifically, helping professionals mislabel the family's cultural beliefs and practices as irrational, and they impose Western medical practices, steeped in the scientific method, on the patient. This approach led the family to mistrust helping professionals. From this story, it is clear that good intentions of professional counselors are not sufficient. Rather, it is essential for counselors to understand and respect the client's cultural background in order to effectively work with the client.

It is important for you to understand that the mandate for a multicultural and social justice counseling perspective does not come without its challenges. Significant ethical challenges arise when one operates out of a multicultural and social justice framework. We highlight these ethical challenges in this section.

Referring Culturally Diverse Clients

The MCCs encourage counselors to be knowledgeable and sensitive to a client's cultural background. The ACA code of ethics (2005) also states the importance of cultural competence in helping professionals. Section A.11.b of the code suggests counselors should refer clients when they are practicing outside the scope of their competence. This specific aspect of the ethical code is often used as a reason to refer culturally diverse clients to other professionals. Being culturally competent with every client is so challenging as to be impossible. It is important to refer culturally diverse clients to professionals that may be more competent and effective in working with particular clients. The ethical dilemma and challenge occurs when counselors find themselves continually referring culturally diverse clients to other professionals. When this becomes a pattern with specific client populations, counselors run the risk of being unethical. Counselors have an ethical responsibility to seek professional development when they lack adequate knowledge and skills. Further training can increase counselors' sense of cultural awareness, knowledge, and skills with specific client populations. Professional development is important, because it ensures the provision of counseling services is accessible for everyone.

Oppressed Counselors Working With Privileged Clients

A majority of the multicultural counseling literature refers to how counselors can work with culturally diverse clients. However, when we read the multicultural counseling literature with a critical eye, it becomes apparent that the literature refers to counselors from privileged groups. What is lacking in the literature is a more balanced focus on the challenges counselors from oppressed groups experience when working with clients from both privileged and oppressed groups. This is an ethical issue, because counselors from oppressed groups have a fundamentally different experience than counselors from privileged groups have in the therapeutic realm. Counselors from oppressed groups must navigate issues of power and privilege within the therapeutic relationship from a place of nondominance or ambiguity. Coming from a place of being one-down can be challenging for counselors who seek to have parity with their clients.

Cultural Clash Between Counselor and Client

The ethical codes of the counseling profession are value laden in that counselors are required to uphold certain beliefs and standards, especially those in relation to withholding judgment and freeing oneself from stereotypes and assumptions. For example, section C.5 of the ACA code of ethics (2005) states that counselors do not condone discrimination "based on age, culture, disability, ethnicity, race, religion/spirituality, gender, gender identity, sexual orientation, marital status/partnership, language preference, socioeconomic status, or any basis proscribed by law" (p. 10).

This statement challenges counselors to align counseling services to meet the needs of all clients, especially those who are not part of the dominant culture. The challenge for counselors is when their values, beliefs, and worldviews do not match those of their clients. When this occurs, it can be easy for counselors to want clients to see the world in the same way they do. Professional counselors may even mislabel cultural differences as abnormal rather than healthy, because the differences do not align with their worldview. The ethical dilemma counselors face in such situations is how to respect clients' values, beliefs, and worldview as variations of what society offers rather than as deviations. In the face of multicultural challenges, culturally responsive supervision is advised. Culturally responsive supervision is supervision between a culturally competent supervisor and a supervisee. Culturally responsive supervision helps counselors explore their internal values and beliefs, so they may best determine how to work with culturally diverse clients.

Articulating Professional Boundaries

Multicultural and social justice oriented counselors use both individual counseling and advocacy counseling. Counseling skills are utilized in both traditional and nontraditional ways. The counseling office has expanded to include the community, and "clients" have been reconceptualized to include families, religious figures, community leaders, legislators, and school staff. The combination of individual counseling and advocacy counseling makes it critical that counselors explain professional boundaries to clients early on in the counseling process. Taking initiative on articulating professional boundaries with clients can prevent ethical dilemmas and misunderstandings about the counselor role.

Balancing Individual Counseling and Advocacy Counseling

Finding the right balance between individual counseling and advocacy counseling can be a challenge. What is the percentage of time that should be devoted to individual work and advocacy work over the course of a day? What is realistic, attainable, and in the best interest of clients? Determining how to make that seamless connection between individual and advocacy work is critical. Some counselors may find themselves doing more advocacy work than others, and vice versa. The percentage of time devoted to individual counseling and advocacy counseling should be based on the needs of the client, the setting in which a counselor works, the counselor's level of professional competence, and what is realistic for the counselor. In situations where counselors are not able to provide advocacy work, they may want to consider collaborating with other organizations that can offer this service.

Maintaining Professional Identity

Critics of the social justice movement argue that advocacy counseling is really social work (Hunsaker, 2011). What is interesting is that social workers also provide individual counseling. Yet, we do not hear proponents of our profession saying that individual counseling and therapy should be relegated to the counseling profession. We agree that social workers have a history and tradition of doing community-based work. As the social work profession evolved, it became increasingly clear in the field that clients could also benefit from individual counseling. The opposite is occurring within the counseling profession, where counselors realize the benefits of advocacy work. The distinction lies in how each guild determines whether individual counseling and/or advocacy counseling is needed. Social workers may start with advocacy work and then determine that clients would benefit from individual counseling, whereas counselors may begin with individual counseling and then determine that advocacy counseling is warranted. There are strengths to both professions. Drawing the best from each profession while maintaining one's professional identity better equips helping professionals for the realities of today's world.

Lack of Advocacy Training

You are living in an era where calls for counselors to provide advocacy counseling outweigh the number of advocacy competent counselors. This gap is due in large part to the lack of systematic advocacy training efforts in counselor education programs (Chang, Crethar, & Ratts, 2010). The current call for advocacy counseling creates a situation akin to the early days of the multicultural counseling movement, when professional counselors were expected to provide culturally competent services without adequate training. Professional counselors who are not adequately equipped to provide advocacy counseling risk running into ethical challenges, because they lack theoretical knowledge and practical skills. For this reason, we encourage you to seek professional development opportunities outside what the counseling profession can offer.

There are many challenges when counselors integrate multiculturalism and social justice into their practice. Determining when to refer culturally diverse clients to other professionals, working through cultural clashes between clients and counselors, clarifying the counselor's professional identity, maintaining professional boundaries, identifying ways to balance individual counseling with advocacy work, and gaining further training in advocacy compound the issues that counselors must address. How these challenges are addressed will impact the future direction of the multicultural and social justice perspectives in counseling.

CRITIQUE OF THE MULTICULTURAL AND SOCIAL JUSTICE COUNSELING MOVEMENTS

Patterson (1996, 2004) speaks out against the MCCs, arguing that multicultural counseling competence is not black and white and cannot be enumerated in a set of standards. Rather, competence is achieved through a genuine understanding of a client and her perspective on an individual level. This, Patterson argues, is not about studying a given culture in an anthropology or sociology class, but rather, experiencing directly and for a long period of time the way your client lives and develops perspective on the world. Professional counselors cannot assume competence in working with specific populations simply because they have taken one school course on the minority population with whom they plan to work. Professional counselors have to strive to immerse themselves in the cultures of their clients, and also take a close look at the systems at play in greater society that function to oppress their potential clients.

Patterson's (1996, 2004) argument is certainly not without reason, and as professional counselors endeavor to adhere to the MCCs, you must keep in mind basic counseling ethical standards. If you are not fit to work with a client who is of a different culture, you should refer that client to someone who may be better suited. If you are not able to genuinely empathize with your client's experience, you are not providing adequate counseling services. The educational experiences that you seek in order to prepare yourself to work with a given population should be carefully assessed in relation to the extent to which you are able to cultivate your understanding. You have to find ways to immerse in the culture for sustained periods of time, forming relationships with a number of individuals who identify with the diverse group with whom you plan to work.

Patterson (2004) asserted that the experience in therapy is not determined by a technique, but rather, by a relationship that is grounded in empathy and warmth. Unfortunately, Patterson failed to recognize that all professional counselors have their own inherent biases that can hinder them in fully being able to develop genuine and empathetic relationships with clients. A very important element of the MCCs is that counselors are called to look at their own inherent biases and at the ways that they have experienced the world, and to cultivate an understanding of the ways in which these perceptions and experiences influence relationships and judgments. Without the competencies to remind us to be introspective on this level, we risk not providing effective counseling, and even harming our clients.

As for the social justice and advocacy aspect of professional counseling, in order to deeply address the social injustices that any of your clients may face and be affected by, you cannot disengage from the societal structures that exist. As a professional counselor, working in the best interest of the client can manifest in the form of advocacy at the micro, meso, and macro levels. Many in the field do not currently recognize the practice of advocacy work as part of the conventional counselor role. But, if we want to get at the roots of client issues, we have to accept that. Especially given the current state of our nation, often we will be called to look beyond the internal problems of our clients.

As you start to see the multicultural and social justice counseling models as paradigms that permeate your professional counseling practice, you will be called to seek out greater understanding through your practicum and internship, developing connections with diverse communities, and expanding your perspective through self-analysis and genuine relationships. Such experiences will further facilitate your understanding of the applications of the multicultural and social justice counseling, and ultimately, they will help foster your advocacy efforts for the clients you serve.

ADVOCATING FOR CLIENTS

At its core, social justice counseling is about advocacy with, and on behalf of, clients. Counselors can use their positions in society to create a better world for clients and communities through advocacy. The problems clients present can no longer be viewed through the narrow lens that counseling has used in the past. When counselors view client problems in a larger context, they begin to comprehend the need for advocacy.

As previously mentioned, advocacy is important and should be integrated into every aspect of a counselor's professional practice at the micro, meso, and macro levels. Micro-level interventions focus on empowering clients within the traditional office setting. Meso-level interventions address clients and their surrounding social systems. Macro-level interventions address social and political policies affecting clients. Advocacy can address client problems as well as the state of the social systems that impact clients. Below are various examples of how you can advocate for clients at the individual and institutional levels:

Meso Level (Client-Level Interventions)

- Display a "Safe Space" or "Hate-Free Zone" emblem in your office.
- Use culturally sensitive, respectful, and inclusive language.
- Be genuine and authentic in acknowledging the daily struggles that culturally diverse client populations experience.
- Use a biopsychosocial approach to understanding client problems.
- Help clients to see their situation within a larger context by examining how oppression is connected to their presenting problems.
- Allow clients to educate you on their worldview and cultural way of being.
- Educate clients on such concepts as internalized oppression and systemic oppression.
- Distinguish between internalized oppression and mental health problems.
- Use culturally sensitive helping theories.

- Integrate clients' worldview into the helping process.
- Equip clients with the awareness, knowledge, and skills to navigate their world.
- Share with clients your knowledge of community resources, services, and costs.
- Involve clients at all levels of the counseling process.

Meso Level (Client-Level and Systems-Level Interventions)

- Assess the needs of clients, and arrange, coordinate, or advocate for services that address client needs.
- Assesses the strengths and weaknesses of environmental systems.
- Connect clients with community resources, services, and opportunities.
- Intervene at the systems level to support existing clients in addressing issues of concern.
- Serve as a liaison between clients and client systems.
- Use professional counseling skills to expand client access to resources.
- Use professional counseling skills to enhance community resources and environmental systems.
- Collaborate with community and religious leaders on client issues.
- Use technology to bring client issues to public awareness.

Macro Level (Systems-Level Interventions)

- Collaborate with legislators to address social policies affecting clients.
- Contribute to the creation of social policy.
- Address and change systemic barriers affecting clients.
- Organize others, create events, and collaborate with others to lead rallies and movements to address client issues.

Exercise 6.4

BALANCING INDIVIDUAL COUNSELING WITH ADVOCACY COUNSELING

The role of the counselor in everyday society is shifting. Our perceptions of what a counselor does on a daily basis change as we look at the systems that are controlling our clients' outlooks and experiences of life. Where counselors used to spend most of their time in the office, they are now being called to step out into the community to confront systems of oppression through social action and advocacy.

1. What are the benefits to clients when counselors work at large in the greater society to advocate for equity for their clients?

(Continued)

(Continued)

2. Provide an example of when you might be called to advocate for your client outside of the traditional counseling relationship.

3. What strengths do you bring to being an advocate and change agent?

4. What are challenges to balancing individual counseling with social justice advocacy?

KEYSTONES

One cannot fully grasp the idea of diversity in the world without noting the intensity of oppression that individuals experience for being different from others, or without sensing the inherent call to action to work to remedy it. In your practice as a professional counselor, if you are practicing true empathy, a requisite in the counseling field, it is wrong to not actively seek ways in which you can empower individuals beyond the empowerment they receive from fundamental counseling responses and dialogue. As soon as you, as a professional counselor, recognize the ethical mandate in the profession to serve as an advocate as well as an individual counselor, you can work to achieve a balance between the two areas of focus in your work.

The future of the counseling profession is bright when you consider the impact multicultural and social justice lenses have had, and continue to have, on the field. Both perspectives have transformed how clients' presenting concerns are conceptualized, the types of strategies used, and the role of the professional counselor. Multicultural and social justice counseling perspectives offer counselors practical tools to work with culturally diverse clients in both traditional and nontraditional settings. Without knowledge of the concepts and skills associated with multiculturalism and social justice, counselors will be ill equipped to work with clients whose presenting issues are culturally and externally driven. As long as oppression exists, to whatever degree, you as a professional counselor are required to continually cultivate your understanding of multicultural and social justice counseling perspectives, which have been developed to ensure that you are providing the highest possible quality of counseling for all individuals. The following are keystones gleaned from this chapter:

- All interactions are multicultural processes.
- Counseling is a sociopolitical process.
- A biopsychosocial approach is comprehensive, because it considers a multitude of issues that impact clients.
- Multiculturalism and social justice are two sides of the same coin; they are complementary forces that are needed for ethical clinical practice.

- The multicultural counseling competencies form the foundation of multicultural counseling.
- The advocacy competencies form the foundation of social justice counseling.
- Counseling is not, and cannot be, a value-neutral process.
- Counseling can either support a dominant status quo or it can dismantle oppressive systems that impact clients.
- Multiculturalism and social justice are new paradigms that need to be considered in all aspects of the counseling profession.

REFERENCES

ACA Governing Council. (March 20–22, 2003). *ACA governing council minutes.* Anaheim, CA. Retrieved from http://www.counseling.org/Sub/Minutes/Governing_Council/2003_0320.pdf

Albee, G. W., & Joffe, J. M. (2004). Mental illness is NOT "an illness like any other." *The Journal of Primary Prevention, 24*(4), 419–436.

American Counseling Association (ACA). (2005). *ACA code of ethics.* Alexandria, VA: Author.

Arredondo, P., Toporek, R., Brown, S. P., Sanchez, J., Locke, D. C., Sanchez, J., & Stadler, H. (1996). Operationalization of the multicultural counseling competencies. *Journal of Multicultural Counseling and Development, 24*(1), 42–78.

Baker, S. B., & Cramer, S. H. (1972). Counselor or change agent: Support from the profession. *Personnel and Guidance Journal, 50*(8), 661–665.

Cardoso, P. (Director). (2002). Real women have curves [Motion picture]. United States: HBO.

Chang, C. Y., Crethar, H. C., & Ratts, M. J. (2010). Social justice: A national imperative for counselor education and supervision. *Counselor Education and Supervision, 50*(2), 82–87.

Cornish, J., Schreier, B., Nadkami, L., Metzger, L., & Rodolfa, E. (2010). *Handbook of multicultural counseilng competencies.* Hoboken, NJ: John Wiley & Sons.

Dustin, R. (1974). Training for institutional change. *Personnel and Guidance Journal, 52*(6), 422–427.

Fadiman, A. (1997). *The spirit catches you and you fall down: A Hmong child, her American doctors, and the collision of two cultures.* New York, NY: Farrar, Straus, and Giroux.

Fouad, N. A., Gerstein, L. H., & Toporek, R. L. (2006). Social justice and counseling psychology in context. In R. L. Toporek, L. H. Gerstein, N. A. Fouad, G. Roysircar, & T. Israel (Eds.), *Handbook for social justice in counseling psychology: Leadership, vision, and action* (pp. 1–16). Thousand Oaks, CA: Sage.

Hoyt, K. B. (1967). Attaining the promise of guidance for all. *Personnel and Guidance Journal, 45*(1), 624–630.

Hunsaker, R. C. (2011). Counseling and social justice. *Academic Questions, 24*(3), 319–340. Retrieved from http://www.springer.com/education+%26+language/higher+education/journal/12129

Hutchinson, M. A., & Stadler, H. A. (1975). *Social change counseling: A radical approach.* Boston, MA: Houghton Mifflin.

Jackson, M. L. (1995). Multicultural counseling: Historical perspectives. In J. G. Ponterotto, J. M. Casas, L. Suzuki, & C. M. Alexander (Eds.), *Handbook of multicultural counseling* (pp. 3–16). Thousand Oaks, CA: Sage.

Jones, S. R., & McEwen, M. K. (2000). A conceptual model of multiple dimensions of identity. *Journal of College Student Development, 41*(4), 405–414.

Kiselica, M. S., & Robinson, M. (2001). Bringing advocacy counseling to life: The history, issues, and human dramas of social justice work in counseling. *Journal of Counseling and Development, 79*(4), 387–398.

Lee, C. C., & Walz, G. R. (Eds.). (1998). *Social action: A mandate for counselors.* Alexandria, VA: American Counseling Association.

Lewis, J., & Arnold, M. S. (1998). From multiculturalism to social action. In C. C. Lee & G. R. Walz (Eds.), *Social action: A mandate for counselors* (pp. 51–65). Alexandria, VA: American Counseling Association.

Lewis, J., & Bradley, L. (Eds.). (2000). *Advocacy in counseling: Counselors, clients, and community.* Greensboro, NC: ERIC Clearinghouse on Counseling and Student Services.

Lewis, M. D., Lewis, J. A., & Dworkin, E. P. (1971). Counseling and the social revolution [Special issue]. *Personnel and Guidance Journal, 49*(9).

McFadden, J., & Lipscomb, W. D. (1985). History of the Association for Non-White Concerns in personnel and guidance. *Journal of Counseling and Development, 63,* 444–447.

McNeill, B. W., & Gallardo, M. E. (Eds.). (2009). *Intersection of multiple identities: A casebook of evidence-based practices with diverse populations.* New York, NY: Routledge.

Patterson, C. H. (1996). Multicultural counseling: From diversity to universality. *Journal of Counseling and Development, 74,* 227–231.

Patterson, C. H. (2004). Do we need multicultural counseling competencies? *Journal of Mental Health Counseling, 26*(1), 67–73.

Pedersen, P. B. (1991). Multiculturalism as a generic approach to counseling. *Journal of Counseling and Development, 70*(1), 6–12.

Ponzo, Z. (1974). A counselor and change: Reminiscences and resolutions. *Personnel and Guidance Journal, 53*(1), 27–32.

Ratts, M. J. (2006). *Social justice counseling: A study of social justice counselor training in CACREP-accredited counselor preparation programs.* Doctoral dissertation, Oregon State University. Dissertation Abstracts International, 67, 1234. Corvallis.

Ratts, M. J. (2011). Multiculturalism and social justice: Two sides of the same coin. *Journal of Multicultural Counseling and Development, 39*(1), 24–37.

Ratts, M., D'Andrea, M., & Arredondo, P. (2004). Social justice counseling: Fifth "force" in field. *Counseling Today, 47*(1), 28–30.

Ratts, M. J., & Ford, A. E. (2010). Advocacy competencies self-assessment survey. In M. J. Ratts, R. L. Toporek, & J. A. Lewis (Eds.), *ACA advocacy competencies: A social justice framework for counselors* (pp. 21–28). Alexandria, VA: American Counseling Association.

Ratts, M. J., Toporek, R. L., & Lewis, J. A. (Eds.). (2010). *ACA advocacy competencies: A social justice framework for counselors.* Alexandria, VA: American Counseling Association.

Rubin, N. J., Leigh, I. W., Nelson, P. D., Smith, I. L., Bebeau, M., Lichtenberg, J. W., . . . Kaslow, N. J. (2007). The competency movement within psychology: An historical perspective. *Professional Psychology: Research and Practice, 38*(5), 452–462.

Sue, D. W., Arredondo, P., & McDavis, R. J. (1992). Multicultural counseling competencies and standards: A call to the profession. *Journal of Multicultural Counseling and Development, 20*(2), 64–89.

Sue, D. W., Bernier, Y., Durran, A., Feinberg, L., Pedersen, P. B., Smith, E. J., & Vasquez-Nuttal, E. (1982). Position paper: Cross-cultural counseling competencies. *The Counseling Psychologist, 10,* 45–52.

Sue, D. W., & Sue, D. (2013). *Counseling the culturally diverse: Theory and practice* (6th ed). Hoboken, NJ: John Wiley & Sons.

Van Kaam, A. (1966). *The art of existential counseling: A new perspective in psychotherapy.* Wilkes-Barre, PA: Dimension Books.

Vera, E. M., & Speight, S. L. (2003). Multicultural competence, social justice, and counseling psychology: Expanding our roles. *The Counseling Psychologist, 31*(3), 253–272. doi: 10.1177/0011000003031003001

Chapter 7

Counselor Supervision

Melissa Odegard-Koester

Varunee Faii Sangganjanavanich

Verl T. Pope

When one typically thinks of supervision or a supervisor, one usually thinks of an employer or a manager who holds a higher status and perhaps has more authority than a supervisee within the professional relationship. However, in the field of counseling, the status difference accounts for only a small part of the relationship. The nature of the relationship in counselor supervision is different and complex, because it involves multiple parties, including the client, supervisee, and supervisor. This professional relationship is developed to ensure that counselors ethically and effectively implement the knowledge and skills pertinent in their service to clients. It also exists to help counselors develop their critical reflection and professional development. This professional relationship is referred to as *supervision, counselor supervision,* and/or *clinical supervision.* Therefore, in this chapter, you will see these terms being used interchangeably.

While counselor education programs provide counseling students with the didactic instructions and training necessary to become effective counselors, counselor supervision is the primary means through which counselors-in-training (CITs) are provided an opportunity to develop counseling skills and clinical competencies. After receiving their counseling degrees, counselors continue to pursue licensures and certifications, which require them to engage in supervision to enhance their clinical competencies and professional development.

Counselor supervisors are required to possess not only an effective set of counseling skills but also additional supervision skills to facilitate the development of CITs. The Council for the Accreditation of Counseling and Related Educational Programs (CACREP, 2009) suggested that counselors should have an understanding of counseling supervision models, practices, and processes. Therefore, the purpose of this chapter is to provide you the foundational knowledge of counselor supervision. You will obtain information regarding the definitions, purpose, methods, and theoretical models of supervision. You will also learn about current trends in and studies of supervision in the field of counseling as well as the professional issues that relate to counselor supervision. In addition to the foundation knowledge, you will have an opportunity to engage in multiple exercises and reflections to enhance your understanding of counselor supervision in various contexts. Practical resources will be introduced to you at the end of this chapter.

LEARNING OBJECTIVES

After reading and engaging in reflection exercises provided in this chapter, you will be able to:

1. Describe the definitions, purpose, and characteristics of supervision,

2. Identify major theoretical models of supervision; and

3. Discuss effective roles and functions of clinical supervisors.

DEFINITION AND PURPOSE OF SUPERVISION

What creates an effective counselor? To answer this question, Brendel, Kolbert, and Foster (2002) suggested that an effective counselor uses a process incorporating the evaluation of complicated interpersonal/multicultural interactions, an appreciation for (and ability to select) appropriate responses, and principled decision making. Rogers (1975) stated that an effective counselor is defined as one who possesses "the qualities of positive regard and therapeutic congruence which together with empathy . . . promotes the therapeutic process" (p. 2). In other words, for you as a counselor to be effective, you must first be able to develop a therapeutic relationship with clients and understand their worldview. Upon establishment of a trusting relationship, you can accurately assess the readiness of the client, develop a plan to address the client's presenting issue, and facilitate the counseling process that promotes change in the client.

What creates an effective counseling supervisor? Lambert and Ogles (1997) suggested that those supervisors who exhibited qualities such as expertise, trustworthiness, and the ability to create facilitative conditions like empathy, genuineness, and positive regard were more effective as supervisors. That is, supervisors are required to understand the characteristics, the knowledge, the experiences, the skills, and the values that make up effective counselors. Supervisors then use effective teaching, which facilitates counselor knowledge and enhances counselor skills. The supervisor mentors the CITs to promote professional identity and integrate other supervisory roles to help beginning counselors become as effective as they can be.

Definition

In most professions, *supervision* refers to a hierarchical and evaluative relationship between two individuals or parties, with one being an individual with more experience and holding higher status and the other being an individual with less experience and holding lower status in a given professional relationship. In counseling, the supervisory relationship involves the aforementioned aspect; however, the relationship is more complex and delicate in nature. Although supervision requires an element of evaluation and overseeing from a supervisor, it also encompasses facilitating the professional and personal development of a supervisee. Bernard and Goodyear (2009) stated,

> Supervision is an intervention provided by a more senior member of a profession to a more junior member or members of that profession. This relationship is evaluative and hierarchical, extends over time, and has the simultaneous purposes of enhancing the professional functioning of the more junior person(s); monitoring the quality of professional services offered to the clients that she, he, or they see; and serving as a gatekeeper for those who enter a particular profession (p. 7).

A similar concept proposed by Maki and Delworth (1995) defined supervision in rehabilitation counseling as "a distinct intervention, the use of which requires the trained supervisor to have specific knowledge and skills in multiple domains, including, but not limited to, education, consultation, and counseling" (p. 293). The above definitions incorporate the competency of the supervisor as well as the importance of facilitating the professional development of the counselor through the evaluative role of the supervisor. Specific to counselor education programs, CACREP (2009) defined supervision as

> a tutorial and mentoring form of instruction in which a supervisor monitors the student's activities in practicum and internship, and facilitates the associated learning and skill development experiences. The supervisor monitors and evaluates the clinical work of the student while monitoring the quality of services offered to clients (p. 63).

This definition focuses on supervision in counselor preparation programs in which a supervisor or an instructor oversees CITs during their clinical experiences, including practicum and internship. The nature of this type of supervision is instructional and skill focused (Ronnestad & Skovholt, 1993). During the CITs practicum training, the supervisor's primary role is teacher. The supervisor monitors the clinical work of the student through viewing live recordings of the services the student provides to a client. Early on in a student's development, there is a tendency for the student to desire structure and specific feedback on the skills performed (Ronnestad & Skovholt, 1993). While feedback is essential in order for supervision to be effective, it is important that the supervisor consider student development while integrating specific feedback. For example, as you continue to expand your clinical skills and experiences, the role of your supervisor may shift from teaching to being more consultative in nature.

Based on these definitions, supervisors are required to be experienced counselors who possess counseling competencies outlined by the profession and who demonstrate evaluative skills to assess and enhance the competencies of supervisees. As gatekeepers to the profession, supervisors have the responsibility of ensuring that clients are receiving quality service and care. Due to the significant responsibility supervisors have in ensuring quality service and care is provided to clients, you may wonder how supervisors go about implementing their supervisory roles. In this section, we further discuss the purpose of supervision in order to gain a broader understanding of how supervisors implement their roles in the supervisory process.

Purpose of Supervision

Because of the multiple roles a supervisor plays in the supervisory relationship, it is important to consider the literature in order to glean more information about the purpose of supervision. According to Borders (1991), a primary purpose of supervision is to enhance counselor development. It is through teaching, counseling, and the integration of consulting skills that the supervisor can work with counselors toward mutually agreed-upon goals. Borders (1991) further contends that although skill enhancement is often a specified goal, the supervision process also encourages greater self-awareness and an integrated professional and personal identity as a counselor.

Ultimately, if the supervisor focuses on skill enhancement and facilitating a greater self-awareness, it is likely that the counselor's competence will be increased. Another purpose of supervision is then to facilitate the development of counselors' competence as they work with clients. Essentially, the supervisor works to challenge, stimulate, and encourage counselors to become more competent in their work with clients (Bradley & Ladany, 2001). Like many counselors, supervisors integrate their personal styles into their work with supervisees. Ladany, Walker, and Melincoff (2001) assert that supervisory styles influence the supervision process. To illustrate, in a study that Ladany et al. conducted of supervisors (2001), they discovered that supervisors who believed they were warm and supportive were also likely to view the supervisory relationship as mutually trusting. The results of the study suggested that it is important for supervisors to be flexible in their approach to supervision due to various styles contributing in unique ways to the supervisory relationship.

In addition to supervisors being flexible in their approach as they consider the purpose of supervision, it is important that they consider *how* they might foster supervisee professional development. The counselor supervisor enhances supervisee professional development through a variety of means. Some of these include teaching therapeutic skills; encouraging compliance with legal, ethical, and professional standards; providing ongoing feedback and evaluation; and providing professional experiences appropriate to the supervisee (Loganbill, Hardy, & Delworth, 1982). The counselor supervisor ensures client welfare through consistent monitoring. Monitoring of client welfare can be assessed through observing live counseling sessions, watching videotaped sessions, and the self-report of the supervisee.

UNIQUE CHARACTERISTICS OF SUPERVISION

Supervision has unique characteristics that are different from counseling. Although counseling and supervision both require a practitioner to master counseling skills and possess clinical competencies in order to develop interpersonal relationships with clients, there are some aspects of supervision that are different from counseling. Therefore, you as a future counseling supervisor will need to learn four aspects of supervision that require the supervisors to assume different roles.

Four Aspects of Supervision

Counseling

In supervision, the therapeutic work (i.e., counselor role that the supervisor embraces) should serve only to increase the supervisee's effectiveness with the client (Neufeldt & Nelson, 1999). For example, the supervisee may have unresolved childhood issues (e.g., abandonment, parental divorce) that may impact her ability to treat young children. If the supervisor believes the supervisee is in need of sorting through a personal issue through counseling, it is the ethical responsibility of the supervisor to refer the supervisee to a professional counselor (ACA, 2005).

Consulting

Supervision is complex in nature and involves multiple parties and systems, including the supervisor, supervisee, and client (Bernard & Goodyear, 2009). Assuming that the supervisor has more clinical experience and a higher level of clinical skill than the supervisee, the supervisee relies on the supervisor's experience and skills to benefit her work with clients. When needed, the supervisor functions as a consultant to the supervisee. That is, the supervisee consults with the supervisor to gain a deeper knowledge or better understanding of a particular issue related to the client. For example, the supervisee may need to consult with the supervisor about working with drug and alcohol abuse in teenagers in order to gain specific knowledge for use with a teenage client who is experimenting with drugs and alcohol. It is important for the supervisee to receive direct consultation from a more senior clinician in order to monitor the quality of service delivery.

Instructing

Direct instruction is also a part of supervision. The supervisee sometimes needs structured guidance from the supervisor in order to learn particular material (e.g., research related to the client's presenting issue) and to develop specific skills (e.g., reflection of feelings). The supervisor utilizes didactic (e.g., lecture) and experiential (e.g., activities) instruction to facilitate the supervisee's understanding of many aspects of clinical work, including case conceptualization, skills development, and treatment planning. For example, the supervisor may decide to give a lecture about cognitive behavioral therapy (didactic instruction) in order to promote the supervisee's case conceptualization skill. The supervisor may also role-play (experiential instruction) with the supervisee to show how to implement relaxation techniques with the client.

Evaluating

It is important for you to remember that although the supervisor works indirectly with the client, the supervisor is directly responsible to the client and for the client's welfare (ACA, 2005). The supervisor holds both authoritative and evaluative roles when working with the supervisee to ensure the quality of service provided to the client. As mentioned earlier, this evaluative role allows the supervisor to become a gatekeeper for the profession. Specifically, supervisors as gatekeepers have a responsibility to protect the welfare of families and individuals seen by students and supervisees (Baltimore, 1998). In order for supervisors to serve in the role of gatekeeper, it is imperative that they evaluate the services their supervisees are providing to their clients. Evaluation is one function of supervisors, and thus supervisors have an ethical responsibility to provide both honest and critical feedback to their supervisees (Bernard, 1987). Supervisors consider the ACA code of ethics (2005) in addition to professional standards of practice (CACREP, 2009) when giving feedback to their supervisees.

While evaluation is an important role in the gatekeeper function of the supervisor, the supervisor also considers the ongoing, working relationship with the supervisee. Supervision encompasses various aspects of counseling and consultation, including nurturing, instructing, and role-modeling. The supervisor works to facilitate awareness, help CITs focus on specific learning goals, and help CITs use their strengths to develop their abilities in areas where they are less competent (Borders, 1991). The ongoing supervisory relationship with the supervisee focused on the aforementioned aspects does not occur in a vacuum; rather it is a process that evolves between the supervisor and supervisee.

Process of Supervision

Supervision is a process-oriented task (Borders, 1991). Supervisors are responsible to facilitate the supervision process to promote supervisees' professional and personal growth. The supervisor first teaches therapeutic skills; this can be done through didactic instruction and individual supervision. Through homework assignments the supervisee enhances didactic knowledge and learns how to apply that knowledge in a therapeutic way. Second, the supervisor provides ongoing feedback to the supervisee. The supervisor monitors the work that the supervisee is doing by watching live or in recording the counseling sessions that the supervisee is conducting with clients. The supervisor then provides the supervisee feedback on how to be more effective in the therapeutic process. Third, the supervisor monitors the

---

Exercise 7.1

EVALUATION OF SUPERVISEES

Directions: As mentioned earlier in this chapter, supervisors have an evaluative function when working with supervisees. In which domains do you think supervisors evaluate supervisees? Once you list all of those domains, please discuss why those domains are important to evaluate. You may compare your answers with your classmates and/or study partners and may begin an interesting conversation concerning supervisors' evaluation of supervisees.

Exercise 7.2

SUPERVISION GOALS

Directions: Consider the twofold purpose of supervision: facilitating professional development and ensuring client welfare. Imagine for a moment that you were going to select the perfect counselor supervisor; what are your primary concerns as you embark on this supervision journey? Write down three goals that you think are imperative to your professional development as a counselor. In addition, write down three goals that will help you ensure client welfare. After you review your six goals, rank order your goals, and practice communicating with your supervisor your goals for and expectations of the supervisory relationship.

---

supervisee's work as it relates to client welfare and verifies that the client is receiving increasingly effective services. Fourth, the supervisor provides other professional experiences appropriate for the profession that include professional development, memberships in professional organizations and the experiences and endorsements needed to obtain professional certification and licensure. Last, the supervisor monitors the supervisee for compliance with legal, ethical, and professional standards (Bernard & Goodyear, 2009).

THE NATURE OF THE SUPERVISORY RELATIONSHIP

If you can recall your personal experience in working with an employer, manager, or teacher, you may be able to think of at least one interesting story regarding your working relationship. You may find that a good working relationship helps you enjoy your work and vice versa. As mentioned in Chapter 1, as it is in counseling and working with clients, relationship is the most critical component in supervision and when working with supervisees (Carifio & Hess, 1987; Ladany et al., 2001; Ronnestad & Skovholt, 1993). Various scholars have noted the importance of the supervisory relationship. Carifio and Hess (1987) suggested that an ideal supervisor is one who shows respect, genuineness, and self-disclosure when working with supervisees. Along the same line, Campbell (2000) stated that in order to build a successful working alliance with supervisees, relationship skills are essential in facilitating effective supervision.

Once a supervisor builds trust and rapport with a supervisee, the supervisory relationship becomes a positive exchange for an experiential learning process between the supervisor and supervisee. The supervisor assists the supervisee in developing therapeutic and professional competence through intentionally using skills that promote the process of professional development of the supervisee (Campbell, 2000). In counseling, the client works through a variety of issues with counselors. Analogously, in supervision, the supervisor helps the supervisee improve skills and develop new areas of competence in order to work with clients effectively (Borders, 1991).

Parallel Process in Supervision

Because the supervision relationship involves the supervisor, supervisee, and client, it is not surprising that the potential of the parallel process exists within the exchanges among them (Morrissey & Tribe, 2001). Parallel process is an intrapsychic phenomenon that unconsciously occurs on the part of the supervisee. This originates in a relationship in one setting with the client and is reflected in a relationship in a different setting with the supervisor (Jacobsen, 2007). The process reflects the interpersonal relationships of both the supervisee and the client (Bernard & Goodyear, 2009). There are three elements that help define parallel process: It is triggered by the client or some facet of the client's relationship with the supervisee, it is not within the supervisee's awareness, and the supervisee is the means of expression regarding the process from the counseling relationship to the supervisory relationship (Bernard & Goodyear). For the supervisee, parallel process often manifests as a characteristic of the client portrayed by the supervisee in the context of supervision (Jacobsen, 2007; Schneider, 1992).

Consider, for example, that the supervisee is struggling with the client on an issue that the supervisee may herself be struggling with. This may result in some level of transference between the client and the supervisee. More than likely, the counselor is not aware that she is essentially presenting the same characteristic in supervision that the client brings to counseling. This is an example of parallel process occurring in the context of the supervisory relationship. In a study conducted by Jacobsen (2007), the results indicated that when supervisors recognized parallel process, they first quietly observed and then pointed out the parallel process directly, while trying to maintain the supervisory alliance. As mentioned earlier, a supervisee may be struggling with how to proceed with a client on an issue that the supervisee may also be struggling with. One of the roles of the supervisor, in this instance, would be to address the conflict the supervisee has with the client and consider ways the supervisee may move forward. Through addressing the conflict, the hope is that the therapeutic alliance will be enhanced, so the supervisee can facilitate positive change with their client.

You may wonder how a supervisor would expect to address this concern. Ideally, the supervisor would recognize this issue with the supervisee and help the supervisee deal with this dissonant experience. For example, the supervisor could facilitate an awareness of the anger presented in both the supervision context and the counseling session. Following this identification of anger, the supervisor could help the supervisee consider how the anger could prevent the counseling relationship from being effective. Effective supervisors are aware of the challenging contexts that present themselves in the supervisory relationship and know how to provide feedback that facilitates the development of the supervisee. Thus, the working alliance between the supervisee and supervisor is essential when considering the development of the supervisee (Ladany et al., 2001).

Supervisory Working Alliance

While building rapport is important to the supervisory relationship, the nature of the relationship between supervisor and supervisee is different from the relationship fostered between counselor and client. Because the relationship between the supervisor and supervisee is evaluative in nature, the relationship is a working alliance rather than a therapeutic enterprise. Many authors (Carifio & Hess, 1987; Ladany et al., 2001; Ronnestad & Skovholt, 1993) have claimed that when the supervisory working alliance is well established, a strong emotional bond between the supervisor and supervisee is likely to be present (Ladany, Ellis, & Friedlander, 1999). Bordin (1983) described the supervisory working alliance as a collaboration for change that includes the agreed-upon goals, tasks, and bonds that are developed in supervision.

Numbers of factors are suggested to have an influence on a supervisory working alliance. Ladany et al. (2001) found that there was a relationship between supervisory styles and the supervisory working alliance. For example, the results of their study suggested that supervisors who adopted an attractive style (warm, supportive, and open) were likely to view themselves as having a stronger emotional bond with their supervisee (Ladany et al., 2001). Other factors, such as supervisor characteristics, can also play a role in developing the supervisory working alliance. Supervisor characteristics that are considered positive when developing the working alliance include being nonjudgmental, providing validation, supporting exploration, imparting an empathic attitude, and normalizing anxiety and tension (Worthen & McNeill, 1996).

Furthermore, Magnuson, Wilcoxon, and Norem (2000) found in their interviews with experienced counselors several overarching principles that impacted the supervisory working alliance negatively. The overarching *lousy supervisor* principles include being unbalanced in approach, providing developmentally inappropriate supervision, and an intolerance of differences. Similarly, Fong and Lease (1997) assert that there are several factors that influence the supervisory relationship negatively. Some of these include unintentional racism, miscommunication, insensitivity to supervisees' nonverbal cues, racial/ethnic issues that are not discussed, gender bias, and an overemphasis on cultural explanations for psychological difficulties (Fong & Lease, 1997; Killian, 2001; Lopez, 1997). On the other hand, when supervisors exhibit a style that communicates sincere attention to cultural and racial factors as well as vulnerability, supervisees view the supervisors as facilitators of a culturally responsive supervisory relationship (Killian, 2001). In turn, a supervisor who is multiculturally competent facilitates a positive supervisory working alliance within the supervisory relationship (Inman, 2006).

To foster a strong working alliance with the supervisee, it is important that the supervisor be aware of both the positive and negative contributing factors stated above. Supervisors can continue to improve the working alliance with their supervisees through facilitating an open discussion surrounding the supervisee's goals and expectations, the method of evaluating the relationship, and plans to address supervisory relationship problems as they arise (Campbell, 2000).

It may seem obvious, but like counseling, supervision occurs in a relational context, thus making the supervisory relationship of utmost importance. Numerous factors affect the relationship, including issues that constitute a healthy relationship, the influence of individual and developmental differences, and many others (Borders & Leddick, 1987). These elements interrelate and affect one another in the development and maintenance of the supervisory relationship.

You, by now, understand that the supervision relationship is not uniform or static; as with any system, it is always changing and developing. While there are many similarities between the counseling relationship and the supervisory relationship, there are some significant differences you may want to consider. If a counselor is successful, then she has helped the client become a more effective person who will live her life in a more effective way. If a supervisor is successful, then the supervisee becomes a peer and a colleague. It is this narrower desired outcome that creates the further need for more focused evaluation. This more focused evaluation has the effect of increasing the difference in responsibility and power in the supervisory relationship (Berger & Buchholz, 1993). Therefore, it is imperative that the supervisor be aware of the power differential existent in supervision.

Power Differential in Supervision

Recall again your current or previous relationship with your employer, supervisor, or teacher. One thing you may be able to point out is the power difference between you and this person, which underscores and influences the nature of your relationship with her. Supervisors hold multiple roles when working with supervisees. One of their most important roles is an evaluative role. Although the supervisory working alliance is central to the relationship, it is important that supervisors recognize the power differential between themselves and their supervisees based on the evaluative function of the supervisor. Such a function forces supervisors to serve as gatekeepers who determine the professional fitness of the supervisees. Supervisors are responsible for constructively providing ongoing feedback to the supervisees in order to facilitate professional competencies, including knowledge, attitudes, and skills in becoming professional counselors (ACA, 2005; CACREP, 2009).

The supervisor is responsible for monitoring the supervisee's progress with clients and at the same time encourages the progress of the supervisee's professional development. The developmental level of the supervisee impacts the way in which the supervisor proceeds in the supervisory relationship. It is critical for the supervisor to consider whether the supervisee will benefit more from intentional direction or from a consultative role with the supervisee. In addition, the supervisor should be able to identify when a particular supervisee is not able to be effective professionally. When this is identified, it is important for the supervisor to consider the appropriate actions. In the next section, you will learn more about the development of counselors and the role of supervisors in responding to such development.

STAGES OF COUNSELOR DEVELOPMENT

In order to facilitate the professional growth and development of the supervisee, it is imperative that the supervisor take the developmental level of the supervisee into consideration. The counselor's level of development is important to consider, because it impacts the way in which the supervisor approaches the supervisee (Bernard & Goodyear, 2009). Effective supervisors know the growth level of each supervisee and modify their techniques to facilitate growing autonomy in each. Consider, for a moment, counselor development on a continuum, particularly as it relates to counselors who are in counselor training programs. Imagine a continuum that starts at point A, the novice or beginning counselor development level, and ends at point B, the expert practitioner counselor development level (Bernard & Goodyear, 2009). One would suspect that a novice or beginning counselor would exhibit the following characteristics: lack of confidence in self, fear of whether the *right* counseling skills are integrated, and little tolerance of ambiguity, for example. The expert practitioner would be more likely to trust her own judgment, tolerate ambiguity, and not be set on the *right* way to integrate skills with a particular client. One would assume that beginning counselors tend to lean on the novice side of the continuum. It is important that counselor supervisors consider these characteristics when working with supervisees to promote their professional and personal development. Stages of counselor development inform supervisors regarding characteristics that may be observed during each developmental stage.

Similar to clients, supervisees have unique needs and working styles. Although several supervisees may enter supervision at the same time, each has a different starting point. Supervisors are responsible to understand the developmental processes of the supervisees in order to help them progress to be effective counselors. Therefore, it is helpful to conceptualize counselor development in three stages and to consider how the supervisor addresses working with the supervisee in a developmental context.

In the beginning stage of counselor development, the supervisee is dependent on the supervisor and is also imitative in nature (Loganbill ct al., 1982). The supervisee demonstrates a need to rely on the supervisor's guidance and directions. Through observation, the supervisee begins to adopt the supervisor's counseling style and thought pattern with the intent of achieving clinical competence. However, there is a lack of self-awareness and categorical thinking on the part of the supervisee. New supervisees can fit in several continuums, for example, high to low motivation, high to low anxiety, high to low tolerance for ambiguity, high to low self-awareness, and high to low independent thinking may be present in supervisees. To respond to the unique needs of supervisees who are in the beginning developmental stage, supervisors (a) provide concrete structure, direct guidance, and positive feedback (b) attend to presenting and underlying anxiety of the supervisees, and (c) focus on the clinic context (e.g., the client's presenting issue) rather than the supervisee self.

In the second stage of counselor development, difficulties within the supervisee and the supervisory relationship tend to occur (Loganbill et al., 1982). In this stage, the supervisee is striving for independence and developing clinical competence. In the process of gaining autonomy, the supervisee shows more assertiveness toward the supervisor, such as asking challenging questions and questioning the supervisor's professional judgment. The supervisee also demonstrates fewer imitative behaviors and starts to present her working style by trying out new therapeutic models or techniques or branching out of the supervisor's way of clinical practice. However, while moving toward becoming more independent and competent, the supervisee still has needs for the supervisor's guidance. During the classic dependency/autonomy conflict stage, it is critical that the supervisor understands such internal conflict and provides empathy to the supervisee. It is also important that the supervisor fosters a safe learning environment, in which the supervisee is encouraged to participate in trial and error, versus a punitive situation. In addition to encouragement, the supervisor shows flexibility, approaches the supervisee and supervision rationally, and promotes the supervisee's autonomy. The supervisor also focuses on application of counseling theory by offering constructive feedback to the supervisee and challenging the supervisee when needed for her personal growth and professional development.

When reaching the third, last, stage of counselor development, the supervisee experiences autonomy, stability, and growth (Loganbill et al., 1982). This stage centers on the supervisee's personal sense of professional identity and self-confidence. The supervisee's motivation is more stable, autonomy is not threatened, the relationship between self and other is more congruent, and the supervisee is able to be more objective with clients. The supervisor at this stage helps balance dependency and independence, cultivates personal and professional strengths, and promotes accountability in the supervisee. The supervisee may move beyond the formal or regular scheduled supervision session and may seek help with specific client cases. The supervisory relationship is more collegial than authoritative. The supervisor works to broaden the supervisee's repertoire, and the focus is toward an integration of all aspects of a counselor's professional development (Stoltenberg, McNeill, & Delworth, 1997). In addition to the supervisor considering the developmental level of the supervisee, there are various supervision theories or models from which supervisors choose to assist them in proceeding intentionally in the supervisory relationship.

Exercise 7.3 is designed for you to further understand counselor development.

Exercise 7.3

COUNSELOR DEVELOPMENT EXERCISE

Directions: Consider where you are currently in your counselor development. Where would you place yourself on the following continuums?

High _____ to Low Motivation
(Highly motivated supervisees might consider a client's multiple systems and complexity when addressing client issues, while a supervisee with lower levels of motivation might easily give up when presented with a client's complex concern.)

High _____ to Low Anxiety
(Highly anxious supervisees may be overly concerned with how they proceed in addressing client concerns and issues, while supervisees with low anxiety would not allow their nerves to get in the way of integrating an intervention.)

High _____ to Low Fear of Failure
(Highly fearful supervisees may be immobilized when considering how to proceed with a client concern, while supervisees who have less fear of failure trust themselves when utilizing an intervention.)

High _____ to Low Tolerance for Ambiguity

(Supervisees with a high tolerance for ambiguity may be more willing to address client concerns creatively and flexibly, while those who have a lower tolerance would have difficulty addressing client concerns unless they were able to follow a concrete and guided plan when addressing those concerns.)

High _____ to Low Independent Thinking

(Highly independent supervisees rely less on their supervisors for direct guidance in their work with clients, while those with lower independence rely heavily on their supervisors for guidance.)

High _____ to Low Abstract Thinking

(Supervisees who engage abstract thinking at higher capacities tend to address working with their clients while considering multiple domains and engaging creative interventions. Those supervisees who engage less abstract thought in their work with clients tend to stick to concrete interventions.)

High _____ to Low Self-Awareness

(Supervisees with high levels of self-awareness are able to identify their limitations when working with clients, while those with little self-awareness may not be aware of their limitations when working with clients.)

High _____ to Low Ability to Empathize

(Supervisees with a high ability to empathize are able to easily identify with client concerns, while those who have lower empathy find it difficult to identify with client concerns.)

Reflect on the following questions:

1. After reviewing where you placed yourself on each of the above continuums, what areas are you lowest in?

2. How would you go about strengthening the areas that are lower?

3. Pick one continuum that you find the most challenging in your counselor development and come up with three goals to strengthen that area.

MODELS OF CLINICAL SUPERVISION

In addition to considering stages of counselor development, it is important that counselor supervisors attend to supervision theories and models. Just as a counselor has a theory that provides a framework for her work with clients, it is also imperative for counselor supervisors to have a framework or mode of operation as they consider how they work with their supervisees. There are multiple existing theories that are available for counselor supervisors to utilize to facilitate counselor development and professional competencies. In this section, major theoretical models of clinical supervision are presented. These models include developmental models, a discrimination model, a systems model, and psychotherapy-based models of supervision.

Developmental Models of Supervision

Developmental models of supervision hold to the notion that all individuals are continually growing, yet sometimes they don't grow in a smooth manner. At times they progress faster and at times slower, and sometimes individuals get stuck. Developmental models take into account a supervisee's experiences, values, previous training, and genetic predisposition, among others factors, and they focus on the strengths and areas for growth of each individual (Bradley & Ladany, 2001). The purpose of developmental models is to maximize and identify growth needed for the future. When using these models, it is typical to be continually identifying new areas of growth in a lifelong learning process.

Historically, developmental models of supervision have been the most researched and visible in clinical supervision (Stoltenberg et al., 1997). Developmental models are typically aimed at describing the level of a student in a training program (Goodyear & Bernard, 1998); for example, a student may be at the beginning level versus at the practicum or internship level. Similar to other developmental theories (e.g., life span theories), the developmental models of supervision assume that the supervisees cycle and recycle through stages of development (Loganbill et al., 1982). These stages of development can help the supervisor understand a supervisee's characteristics and abilities in order to assist them in their work with clients.

There are multiple development models that counselor supervisors may consider in the context of working with supervisees. For the purposes of this chapter, selected developmental supervision models are described in the following sections. These developmental models are included in this chapter due to their influence in counselor supervision: the integrated developmental model (IDM); the Loganbill, Hardy, and Delworth model; and the Ronnestad and Skovholt model.

The integrated developmental model

The IDM emerged from Hogan's (1964) work as developmental constructs were more formally integrated into a supervision model (Stoltenberg et al., 1997). Initially, the IDM was identified as the counselor complexity model, and due to subsequent research and some critiques, the explicit cognitive component was excluded (Bernard & Goodyear, 2009). The IDM can currently be understood as a conceptual framework that assists supervisors in understanding the various experience levels of supervisees (Stoltenberg, 1981; Stoltenberg, McNeill, & Delworth, 1998).

Because the IDM is aimed to facilitate the supervisor's understanding of the supervisee's development, the model considers various levels for supervisor conceptualization. Stoltenberg et al. (1998) identified four levels of counselor development. In the first level, the supervisee has limited training or experience, has high anxiety, is egocentric, and is dependent on the supervisor (Stoltenberg et al., 1998). In the second level, the supervisee begins to transition from being dependent to less dependent on the supervisor. In this level, the supervisee also starts to be less imitative of the supervisor. Often, the supervisee may fluctuate from higher to lower levels of confidence. In the third level, the supervisee focuses on a more personalized approach to counseling and understanding how to integrate *self* into the counseling relationship (Stoltenberg et al.). While supervisees may question their effectiveness from time to time as counselors in the third level, they do not become immobilized in their work with clients. In the integrated level, supervisees have integrated themselves across the multiple domains of treatment, conceptualization, and assessment. In other words, they take a personalized approach as they practice with their clients. There is also a strong awareness of strengths and limitations by the supervisee (Stoltenberg et al.).

To identify the developmental level of supervisees, Stoltenberg et al. (1998) suggested a need for counselor supervisors to assess the supervisees in three areas, including self/other awareness, motivation, and autonomy. Identifying the supervisee's developmental level can assist the counselor supervisor in identifying an appropriate mode of intervention with the supervisee. According to Stoltenberg et al., in order to promote the supervisee's professional competencies, it is imperative that counselor supervisors consider the various domains of professional functioning. For example, a counselor supervisor will consider how confident a supervisee is in carrying out therapeutic interventions (intervention skills competence).

Another developmental model with influence in the field of clinical supervision is Loganbill, Hardy, and Delworth's (1982) model.

Loganbill, Hardy, and Delworth's model

Similar to Stoltenberg's IDM, this model (Loganbill et al., 1982) includes three stages of counselor development: the stagnation, confusion, and integrative stages. There are supervisory issues that can manifest during these stages, and Loganbill et al. suggested that the supervisor assess how the supervisee experiences these issues in order to facilitate movement to the next stage of development. However, unlike Stoltenberg, these authors believe that supervisees cycle and recycle through stages.

The stagnation stage is characterized by a supervisee's unawareness of difficulties or deficits. The supervisee at this stage is likely to engage in concrete thinking when working with clients and may become stuck in a particular area (Loganbill et al., 1982). The confusion stage can be defined as instability, disorganization, and conflict, for example. In this stage the supervisee recognizes that the answers may not come from the supervisor, and the supervisee can become frustrated as a result. The integration stage can be defined as the "calm after the storm" (Loganbill et al., 1982, p. 19), where the supervisee shifts to becoming flexible, realistic, and aware of her strengths and weaknesses.

Ronnestad and Skovholt's model

Ronnestad and Skovholt (1993) were the first to uncover developmental themes from a qualitative research study. Their initial conceptualization of counselor development was based on interviews with 100 counselors and therapists who ranged in their experiences from first-year graduate students to 40 years beyond graduate school (Ronnestad & Skovholt, 1993). Recently, they have offered a more refined model based on previous feedback, reinterviewing counselors, and their own reanalyses of the data (Ronnestad & Skovholt, 2003). Currently their model can be conceptualized as six phases of development and 14 themes of therapist-counselor development (Ronnestad & Skovholt, 2003).

Ronnestad and Skovholt's model corresponds to the IDM (Stoltenberg et al., 1998) described earlier in this section. For illustration purposes, the six phases will be succinctly described, and one theme will be illuminated as an example. In the lay helper phase, the novice will be ready to assist the individual with the problem and have a tendency to be sympathetic or overly involved. In the beginning student phase, the supervisee can be described as vulnerable, dependent, and needing encouragement or support from supervisors. In the advanced student phase, the supervisee is functioning at a basic professional level through integrating a more conservative or cautious style. In the novice professional phase, a new graduate supervisee will begin to integrate her personality into treatment. In the experienced professional phase, which typically includes those with several years of clinical experience, the supervisee tends to find ways to authentically integrate her values and personality into the therapeutic relationship. The final phase, senior professional, includes those individuals who have 20 or more years of experience who develop very individualized and authentic approaches (Ronnestad & Skovholt, 2003).

All developmental supervision models emphasize the importance of the supervisor's assessment and understanding of the supervisee's developmental level. Developmental supervision theorists (e.g., Loganbill et al., 1982; Ronnestad & Skovholt, 2003; Stoltenberg et al., 1998) believe that although each individual is unique, supervisees cycle through similar stages of development. Understanding the supervisee's developmental stage can assist the supervisor to develop and utilize appropriate supervision interventions that ultimately promote the supervisee's growth and development. A social role model (Bernard 1979, 1987) can also assist supervisors as they consider working with supervisees effectively.

Discrimination Model of Supervision

The discrimination model (Bernard, 1979) was introduced in the late 1970s due to the sparse literature and research surrounding the process of supervision during that time. By this time, there were models in existence that were developmental in nature (Fleming, 1953; Hogan, 1964); however, they were brief and lacking in detail. With her model, Bernard intended to train counselors in a systematic manner. Included in this model were three separate foci for supervision as well as three supervisory roles. The three separate foci for supervision included the supervisee's intervention skills (what the supervisee is doing in session), conceptualization skills (how the supervisee understands what is occurring in session), and personalization skills (how the supervisee manages personal concerns and countertransference responses in session). The supervisory roles included those of teacher, counselor, and consultant.

The teacher role may be more directive in nature, while the consultant role may be more facilitative, for example. On the other hand, if the supervisor elects to utilize the counselor role, she may assist the supervisee in discovering what prevents her from integrating certain skills in session. These concepts were introduced for use throughout the various roles that the supervisor takes on with students to gauge student growth in understanding of conceptualization, integration of process skills, and personalization of individual and client issues.

For example, if a supervisee came into supervision struggling with implementing systematic desensitization with a client because the supervisee had never learned desensitization techniques, the supervisor could teach the counselor relaxation techniques, successive approximation, hierarchy building, and the desensitization process (Bernard, 1979). This is an example of the *teacher role* that the supervisor would take on, while the counseling function represents the *intervention* a supervisee might utilize. Bernard (1979) cautions supervisors not to oversimplify specific roles with functions in the discrimination model. She further states that if a supervisee is deficient in intervention skills, the teaching role may not always be the most useful approach in supervision. That is, some counselors may be uneasy with certain intervention skills, because these skills do not fit the counselor's values or beliefs, and thus the supervisor might consider the role of *counselor* instead of *teacher*. The discrimination model is contextual in that it allows the supervisor nine options to consider framing the supervisory relationship (Bernard, 1979).

These choices allow room for supervisors to select a range of approaches that fit a variety of counselor functions (Bernard, 1979). Many supervisors have integrated Bernard's model of supervision over the years to assist in their supervision with counselor trainees (Bernard & Goodyear, 2004).

Systems Model of Supervision

Another supervision approach that can assist supervisors in understanding how to work effectively with supervisees is Holloway's (1995) systems model. The systems model of supervision was intended to provide supervisors with a common language, even among those supervisors who operate from different theoretical orientations. The systems approach to supervision or SAS model considers the relationship as the core factor throughout the process of supervision. The supervision relationship is one of seven factors (also known as dimensions); the other six factors include the institution, the supervisor, the client, the trainee, the tasks of supervision, and the functions of supervision. A primary goal of supervision in this model is to enhance the professional development and skill of the counselor trainee (Holloway). In order to accomplish this goal, it is important for the supervisor to recognize how the factors that compose this model mutually influence one another and that they are highly interrelated. The supervisor is then able to consider the tasks of supervision effectively and to help counselor trainees assess counseling skill, case conceptualization, professional role, and emotional awareness, and conduct a self-evaluation.

Psychotherapy-Based Models of Supervision

While some supervisors operate from supervision-based models, others choose to work from a basis of counseling theory. Psychotherapy approaches to supervision align very closely with the counseling theories for which they are named. Counselors that adopt a particular brand of counseling, for example Adlerian, solution-focused, or behavioral, often believe that the best supervision is an analysis of the practice for true adherence to the theory. There are some advantages and disadvantages of theory-based models. When the supervisor and the supervisee share the same orientation, modeling is maximized, and the theory is more integrated into the training. Several of the theoretical models of supervision that are utilized include the psychodynamic, person-centered, cognitive-behavioral, systemic, and constructivist approaches to supervision (Bernard & Goodyear, 2009). For illustration purposes, psychodynamic, person-centered, cognitive-behavioral, and the constructivist models of supervision will be further discussed.

Psychodynamic theories (e.g., Freud, 1895/1966; Jung, 1959) focus on the individual's internal process. Psychodynamic theorists (e.g., Jung and Freud) believe current human experiences and functioning are connected to one's past, especially one's upbringing. As a result, the treatment emphasizes the importance of examining one's past, which is deeply connected to psychological processes of individuals. Similar to psychodynamic therapy, a psychodynamic model of supervision would consider both unconscious motivations and the formative role of childhood development and experiences and their impacts on the supervisee (Bomba, 2011). One primary goal of psychodynamic theory is to facilitate a learning process that assists supervisees with addressing conflict between themselves and their supervisors in order to benefit future work with clients (Bordin, 1983). The roles of psychodynamic supervisors are then to attend to the evolving nature of the supervisory relationship while also addressing any parallel process that occurs between the supervisor–supervisee relationship and the supervisee–client relationship (Bomba, 2011).

A person-centered model of supervision is similar to person-centered counseling because of the emphasis on the facilitative conditions of genuineness, empathy, and warmth (Bernard & Goodyear, 2009). Just as Rogers (1975) believes that the relationship between the client and counselor is central to counseling, person-centered supervision highlights the importance of the supervisee–supervisor relationship. The focus of this model of supervision encourages the development of a trusting relationship that facilitates core conditions—unconditional positive regard, empathy, and congruence—to exist in supervision. The ideal supervisee in this supervision model is one who is able to differentiate self and move toward self-actualization. Differentiation of self refers to a supervisee's ability to accept self and client as the supervisee works with the client through the therapeutic process (Patterson, 1983). Essentially, supervisees are moving toward self-actualization as they integrate acceptance of self. In the context of supervision, differentiation and self-actualization are critical, because supervisors are in a position to model their own individuality while remaining in a significant and effectual relationship with their supervisees (Hill, Hasty, & Moore, 2011). Ultimately, the supervisee then has the potential to model and offer an environment in which clients can change. Therefore, the goal of supervision is to facilitate differentiation of self and self-actualization throughout the supervision process. In essence, the role of the supervisor is to model trust in self in order for the supervisees to embrace themselves in the supervision process.

In contrast to supervisors using a person-centered model of supervision, supervisors using a model based on cognitive–behavioral therapy (CBT) are more specific and systematic in terms of both their goals and processes (Bernard & Goodyear, 2009). In the beginning of each supervision session, the supervisor is likely to negotiate with the supervisee a plan of action for the supervision session. The CBT supervisor will also continuously monitor the supervisee's clinical progress. Some of the tools supervisors may employ include Socratic questioning and challenging the supervisee's cognitions and misperceptions (Rosenbaum & Ronen, 1998). Supervisors who operate from a CBT model are concerned with how supervisees demonstrate their theoretical skills and see themselves being responsible for facilitating a fruitful learning environment for supervisees.

Essentially, a goal of CBT-based supervision is to examine the thinking, feeling, and doing parts of the supervisee simultaneously (Woods & Ellis, 1997). As the supervisor does this in the context of the supervisory process, irrational thinking can be identified and addressed in supervision. The role of the supervisor, then, is to model CBT in supervision in order for the supervisee to engage clients in the same manner. It may also be helpful for the supervisor to consider identifying generalizing words such as *always, never,* or *must* to further explore, as these words are typically used by supervisees when discussing their work (Campbell, 2000).

A constructivist approach to supervision operates under the assumption that reality is based on the context, or the individual's environment and needs. In other words, truth, for an individual, is a construction that is grounded in social interactions and experiences (Bernard & Goodyear, 2009). If truth (reality) is based on constructions, then there is a potential for multiple truths to exist based on the context of the individual. With this lens in mind, it is no surprise that constructivist supervisors rely heavily on consultation with the supervisee in order to maintain relative equality and focus on the supervisee's strengths.

For illustration purposes, a solution-focused model of supervision will be illuminated as it aligns with a constructivist supervision orientation. A solution-focused form of therapy can be applied to supervision, because it helps empower the supervisee and encourages work between the supervisor and supervisee to be conducted in a collegial manner (Campbell, 2000). One major assumption of solution-focused therapy is the recognition of the resources and strengths supervisees have to solve their own problems (Juhnke, 1996). A goal of the supervisor then is to focus on how well supervisees do with their clients, identifying primarily their strengths. The supervisor moves out of the teacher role and into more of a cooperative role, showing respect for the supervisee's resources (Campbell, 2000). In addition to identifying the strengths of the supervisee, a solution-focused supervisor's role would also include facilitating small changes or having the supervisee try something new with a client (O'Hanlon & Weiner-Davis, 1989). This form of supervision can be reassuring and encouraging to supervisees, as it focuses not just on constructive feedback but also on the strengths that the supervisees possess.

Exercise 7.4

SUPERVISION MODEL EXERCISE

Imagine that you are a counseling student who is in practicum. You are working with a client who presents as suicidal on a video recording that you have taped and present in your next supervision session. You are not sure if you should conduct a suicide assessment with this particular client, and you wonder what might be the most appropriate intervention. However, you are not overly concerned with the client and don't believe that the client is truly at risk. You show your tape to your supervisor and you state that the client has a history of suicidal ideation but has no history of attempts. This indicates to you that there is not truly a reason for concern. However, your supervisor is concerned, and she suggests some procedures associated with suicide assessment that she thinks you need to complete with the client in order to protect the client, you, and your supervisor. After the supervisor checks in with you the following week in supervision, you state that you have not implemented a suicide assessment.

1. How do you think your supervisor should handle this situation?

2. What supervision model do you think would help your supervisor address the situation? List the major components of the model.

3. How do you think a supervisor would handle the situation differently with an internship student?

4. List some of the implications for the supervisor and the supervisory relationship.

SUPERVISOR TRAINING AND CREDENTIALS

Supervisors hold multiple responsibilities to clients and supervisees. Such responsibilities require supervisors to possess qualities that facilitate the counselor's professional and personal development as well as protect the client's welfare. Regardless of their supervisory theoretical models and approaches, supervisors are expected to demonstrate knowledge and understanding of supervision as well as to master supervisory skills.

As previously mentioned, although the utmost purposes of counseling and supervision align (in both cases, the utmost purpose is protecting the welfare of clients), much of the knowledge and many of the skills used in supervision are different from those used in counseling. In supervision, supervisors need to understand counselor development and to be able to identify the developmental stages of the supervisees, each of whom is unique. Supervisors are also required to be knowledgeable of supervision theoretical models and approaches in order to conceptualize supervisory goals and interventions when working with supervisees. Importantly, supervisors are expected to have additional skills beyond counseling skills to complete supervisory tasks and to assume the role of gatekeeper.

Because the supervisor has the added task of gatekeeping, it is important that supervisors have the set of skills necessary to implement this role effectively. In addition, because the clinical supervisor is first and foremost a person who helps counselors develop their professional competencies, the supervisor must also be able to demonstrate both effective clinical skills and facilitative supervisory skills to foster the development of the supervisee. Supervisors are expected to evaluate counselors and their implementation of competence in skill and professional development. For this reason, it is important for supervisors to have appropriate and sufficient training in supervision. To be an effective supervisor, most supervisors go through additional training specifically in the modalities and techniques associated with supervision that are beyond effective clinical counseling skills. In addition to requiring training and experience for supervisors to be granted supervisory credentials initially, licensing agencies also require supervisors to obtain a minimum number of continuing education units (CEUs) in each renewal period (e.g., three years) in order to maintain the integrity of current knowledge and practice in supervision.

At the national level, the Center for Credentialing and Education (CCE) offers the Approved Clinical Supervisor (ACS) credential for qualified supervisors. The ACS is a national credential that requires specific training in supervision, mastery of supervision skills, and conforming to the supervisor code of conduct. This credential is gaining increased recognition by supervisors and state licensing boards.

At a state level, there are credentials offered for supervisory status. In many states (e.g., Ohio, Texas), licensing boards require supervisors to obtain supervision training, to have experiences in supervision of supervision (e.g., supervising a clinical supervisor), and to attest to the ethical codes of supervisors before becoming licensed supervisors or approved supervisors by the board. Following the completion of an advanced degree in counseling, and many times before a candidate obtains licensure or certification, she is required to have postdegree supervision. Different jurisdictions have different requirements for the supervision. For example one state may require that a newly graduated counselor obtain 3,000 hours of post–master's degree supervised experience. State licensing boards dictate the credentials of supervisors and may require that that supervised experience be registered or approved by the board before it is implemented. While the board may have some conditions for the supervisory relationship, it is still voluntary in nature. However, if the counselor had to respond to a complaint or if there were specific ethical issues that a counselor had to respond to, state licensure boards may require the counselor to have supervision from an assigned supervisor. This situation is considered involuntary supervision and is imposed by a certifying or licensing board as a result of failure to abide by the ethics or standards of practice required of the counselor. The nature of these supervisor relationships is expected to be more difficult. In many respects, it parallels those of involuntary clients who are coming in to counseling as a result of probation or court order.

Whether working with involuntary or voluntary supervisees, effective supervisors have characteristics similar to those of effective counselors. These include empathy, tolerance for ambiguity, flexibility, genuineness, nonjudgmental respect, and emotional awareness. Supervisors have additional skills of recognizing and fostering growth not only in the client but also in the supervisee.

ETHICAL AND LEGAL ISSUES IN SUPERVISION

Similar to counselors, supervisors can expect to encounter ethical dilemmas in supervision. However, unlike counseling, supervision brings different kinds of challenges. Supervisors are involved not only in the supervisee–supervisor relationship but also in indirect service to the client, and they are responsible for the client welfare.

Although there is a similarity between ethical and legal issues in supervision, they are not necessarily the same. Ethics hold the supervisor to a predetermined high standard, whereas legal standards are sometimes minimal (Disney & Stephens, 1994). Individuals many times make discussions based upon morals and values. Morals and values are based upon the perspective of what is right and wrong in the context of the decision maker and the decision to be made. They involve an evaluation of actions based upon cultural contexts, norms, or religious standards. Ethics becomes an agreed-upon set of "morals" for the profession that establishes a way of interacting professionally: What does the profession see as being ethical? Therefore, ethics looks to best practices and a professionally agreed-upon ethical code that governs the professional actions of counselors and supervisors.

Legal issues in counseling and supervision are derived from laws passed by governments in order to regulate the profession with the sole purpose of protecting the public. Legal issues can also come from case law or a court precedent, which is a compilation of court rulings that influence the practice of the profession (Disney & Stephens, 1994). Counselors and supervisors risk legal sanctions if they violate the law or court precedent.

Vicarious liability is more likely to make its appearance in a supervisor–supervisee relationship than in other forms of counseling. In this type of liability, the supervisor is held liable for the actions of the supervisee, even when the supervisor does not suggest the actions to the supervisee or is not aware that the supervisee was performing such actions. In this case, the supervisor is liable for failing to provide supervision at a level that would prevent malpractice (Disney & Stephens, 1994). Vicarious liability is the kind of case most likely to be faced by supervisors and constitutes supervisor malpractice. From a legal perspective, the supervisor must have reasonable control and authority over the supervisee and is responsible for the actions of the supervisee.

Finally, it is the responsibility of supervisors to know and apply the appropriate laws and regulations and ethical codes that apply to them. For example, if a supervisor was practicing in a particular state, it would be her responsibility to know, understand, and apply the laws and regulations of that particular state. Many of these regulations can be found on the states' licensing boards' websites. The Association for Counselor Education and Supervision (ACES) maintained independent supervision ethics until 1993; however, these ethics were incorporated into the American Counseling Association's code of ethics (ACA, 2005, section F). Therefore, any ACA or ACES member must adhere to these ethics.

Many counselors and supervisors also seek and obtain certification as counselors or as supervisors. It is important to note that if advanced certification is obtained, then the supervisor must also be knowledgeable of and follow the ethical standards of the certifying agency. For example, if a counselor holds the national certified counselor (NCC) credential, then she must abide by NBCC Code of Ethics (NBCC, 2005). If a supervisor has obtained certification as an approved clinical supervisor (ACS), then the ACS code of ethics must be applied to her practice of supervision (CCE, 2008). As is the case with counseling, ethics provides an articulation of the generally accepted practice of clinical supervision.

Exercise 7.5

ETHICAL AND LEGAL ISSUES IN SUPERVISION

Dr. Jones is an assistant director of a community mental health agency and has practiced as a licensed professional counselor with supervisor designation (LPC-S) for almost five years. The agency provides various individual and group counseling services, including anger management counseling for court ordered clients. The agency has a strong connection to the community as well as the local judicial system.

This afternoon, one of the staff counselors in the agency, Austin, brought up a client issue that is concerning to Dr. Jones. Five weeks ago, Austin began working with a new court ordered client, Tamara, a 36-year-old African American single mother, who had been referred by the court for 10 anger management sessions. Tamara was charged with domestic violence (beating her live-in boyfriend and causing physical injuries) and went to jail for three days. Because Tamara was in jail, the state's children's services agency placed her three children in foster homes. Tamara is currently working with a social worker (case manager) to obtain full custody of her children. Tamara has signed a release of the information for the court/judge and case manager.

Austin has notice a pattern of missing and rescheduled sessions since Tamara entered the treatment. Austin has also observed that Tamara seemed disengaged and resistant during the sessions. Tamara generally talked about her everyday life; little of her anger issues was mentioned.

Tamara called Austin two days ago and told him her boyfriend, JJ, had committed suicide, and she would not be able to attend the upcoming counseling session. Tamara said her boyfriend was playing with a gun with his friends in the basement and accidentally shot himself. Austin asked Tamara whether she was okay, and Tamara insisted she was fine and did not cry. Tamara and Austin agreed that she would attend the session tomorrow in order to process the situation. After he hung up the phone, Austin felt that Tamara did not react like a person who has just experienced an unthinkable situation.

Tamara showed up yesterday as scheduled (Session 3). During the session, Tamara seemed confused and presented different versions of JJ's death. At first, Tamara said the police ruled the death homicide. Then, Tamara said the police had begun their investigation. Tamara spoke minimally about her feelings of loss, even when Austin directly asked her about them. Tamara asked Austin to release a record of attendance to her case manager and attorney, with whom she was working to obtain a full custody of her children. When Austin asked why she made this request, Tamara said, "They asked for that." Tamara is scheduled for another session next week (Session 4).

Mark is one of the staff counselors who has worked with Tamara and JJ. The death of his client put Mark over the edge. Mark shared with Austin that he could neither sleep nor eat. Mark said that JJ worked really hard in the session to repair his relationship with Tamara. Like Austin, Mark has observed that Tamara has seemed disengaged and not invested in the sessions Mark has conducted with the two of them; JJ has appeared much more committed. Mark also shared with Austin that during the last session, JJ mentioned that Tamara at times was very angry, but there had been no signs of physical abuse after the domestic violence charge. Mark and Austin have been following local news closely about the police investigation of this incident.

Tamara called Austin this morning and said that she would not continue counseling, because she was moving to Texas for financial reasons. Austin cautioned Tamara that she had not completed court ordered anger management sessions; however,

(Continued)

(Continued)

Tamara said her attorney would take care of the issue. Austin has lingering feelings surrounding Tamara's sudden termination of treatment and consulted with Mark. Austin and Mark concluded that Tamara may have something to do with JJ's death, and she is getting away with it.

Austin and Mark asked Dr. Jones to do something. Dr. Jones asked Austin to complete an incident report, to document a phone conversation with Tamara, and to close her file. Austin became very upset and said to Dr. Jones, "You don't understand. She is getting away with this. We need to call the police." Dr. Jones responded, "There is nothing we can do at this time. Tamara is our client, and that would be a breach of confidentiality. Plus, we don't know for a fact that she did murder her boyfriend. I know I didn't say what you wanted to hear, and you are frustrated with me."

Austin was not pleased with Dr. Jones's response. Austin told Dr. Prentice, the director of the agency, that he questioned Dr. Jones's judgment and action surrounding this case. He also wondered if he had a duty to warn the public that Tamara may be a danger to society. Dr. Prentice suggested that there may be other alternatives; however, she needed more time to process the incident. In the meanwhile, Dr. Prentice said to Austin that she agreed with Dr. Jones's judgment and action. Dr. Prentice felt that she needed to speak with Dr. Jones to follow up on this situation.

Below are questions Dr. Prentice would like to follow up on with Dr. Jones.

1. What is the ethical decision-making model you implemented?

2. What are other possible actions you may have chosen or taken?

3. What are the pros and cons of the decision you have made (to not report to the officials)?

4. Would you make a different decision if you could go back? If so, what would that be?

5. How will you handle your relationship with Austin and other staff counselors?

KEYSTONES

Supervisors play an important role in the professional and personal development of counselors. The purposes of supervision are to promote the counselor's professional competence and to protect the client's welfare. To achieve these purposes, supervisors implement supervision theories and modalities (e.g., developmental models, discrimination model, and psychotherapy-based models) as a guided framework when working with supervisees. In addition to theories and modalities, when working with supervisees, supervisors consider other important areas including the following:

- Supervisory relationship
- Supervision process and task
- Counselor development
- Ethical and legal considerations in supervision

It is important to note that although supervision has various overlapping qualities with other clinical activities, such as counseling and consultation, supervision is uniquely different from those two. The unique characteristics of supervision are the following:

- It is triadic in nature: The supervisor works directly with the supervisee and indirectly with the client. Ultimately, the supervisor is responsible for the counselor's professional performance and the client's well-being.
- It is evaluative in nature: The supervisor performs as a gatekeeper to ensure the counselor's professional competence and the client's welfare.

ADDITIONAL RESOURCES

Readings

Assheim, L. (2012). *Practical clinical supervision for counselors: An experiential guide.* New York, NY: Springer.

Association for Counselor Education and Supervision. (1990). Standards for counseling supervisors. *Journal of Counseling and Development, 69,* 30–32. Retrieved from http://www.acesonline.net/members/supervision/

Bernard, J. M., & Goodyear, R. K. (2009). *Fundamentals of clinical supervision* (4th ed.). Upper Saddle River, NJ: Merrill/Pearson.

Borders, L. D. & Brown, L. L. (2005). *New Handbook of Counseling Supervision.* Mahwah, NJ: Lawrence Erlbaum.

Campbell, J. M. (2000). *Becoming an effective supervisor: A workbook for counselors and psychotherapists.* Ann Arbor, MI: Taylor & Francis.

Powell, D. J. (2004). *Clinical supervision in alcohol and drug abuse counseling: Principles, models, methods.* San Francisco, CA: Jossey-Bass.

Multimedia Materials

Borders, L. D., J. M. Benshoff, L. Armeniox, & K. Coker. (2000). *Learning to think like a supervisor* [DVD]. Alexandria, VA: Association for Counselor Education and Supervision.

Websites

ACES Resources: http://www.acesonline.net/resources/
Approved Clinical Supervisor (ACS) Code of Ethics: http://www.cce-global.org/ACS/Ethics
National Board for Certified Counselors Code of Ethics: http://www.nbcc.org/ServiceCenter/Ethics
National Board for Certified Counselors State Board Directory: http://www.nbcc.org/directory

REFERENCES

American Counseling Association (ACA). (2005). *ACA code of ethics*. Alexandria, VA: Author.

Baltimore, M. L. (1998). Supervision ethics: Counseling the supervisee. *Family Journal, 6*(4), 312–315. doi: 10.1177/1066480798064010

Berger, S., & Buchholz, E. (1993). On becoming a supervisee: Preparation for learning in a supervisory relationship. *Psychotherapy, 30*(1), 86–92. doi: 10.1037/0033–3204.30.1.86.

Bernard, J. M. (1979). Supervisor training: A discrimination model. *Counselor Education & Supervision, 19,* 60–68.

Bernard. J. M. (1987). Ethical and legal considerations for supervisors. In L. D. Borders & G. R. Leddick (Eds.), *Handbook of counseling supervision* (pp. 52–57). Alexandria, VA: American Association for Counseling and Development.

Bernard, J. M., & Goodyear, R. K. (2004). *Fundamentals of clinical supervision* (3rd ed.). Boston, MA: Pearson Education.

Bernard, J. M., & Goodyear, R. K. (2009). *Fundamentals of clinical supervision* (4th ed.). Upper Saddle River, NJ: Merrill/Pearson.

Bomba, J. (2011). Psychotherapy supervision as viewed from a psychodynamic standpoint. *Archives of Psychiatry and Psychotherapy, 4,* 45–49.

Borders, L. D. (1991). Supervision does not equal evaluation. *School Counselor, 38*(4), 253–256. doi: 10.1300/J001v09n02_05

Borders, L. D., & Leddick, G. R. (1987). Handbook of counseling supervision. Alexandria, VA: Association for Counselor Education and Supervision.

Bordin, E. S. (1983). Supervision in counseling: II. Contemporary models of supervision: A working alliance based model of supervision. *The Counseling Psychologist, 11,* 35–42. doi: 10.1177/0011000083111007

Bradley, L. J. & Ladany, N. (2001).*Counselor supervision: Principles, process, and practice* (3rd ed.). Florence, KY: Brunner-Routledge.

Brendel, J. M., Kolbert, J. B., & Foster, V. A. (2002). Promoting student cognitive development. *Journal of Adult Development, 9*(3), 217–227.

Campbell, J. M. (2000). *Becoming an effective supervisor: A workbook for counselors and psychotherapists.* Ann Arbor, MI: Taylor & Francis.

Carifio, M. S., & Hess, A. K. (1987). Who is the ideal supervisor? *Professional Psychology: Research and Practice, 36,* 256–263. doi: 10.1037//0735–7028.18.3.244

Center for Credentialing in Counseling (CCE). (2008). *The approved clinical supervisor code of ethics.* Retrieved from: http://www.cce-global.org/Downloads/Ethics/ACScodeofethics.pdf

Council for Accreditation of Counseling and Related Educational Programs (CACREP). (2009). *2009 Standards.* Retrieved from: http://www.cacrep.org/doc/2009%20Standards%20with%20 cover.pdf

Disney, M. J., & Stephens, A. M. (1994). *ACA Legal Series, Volume 10: Legal issues in clinical supervision.* Alexandria, VA: American Counseling Association.

Fleming, J. (1953). The role of supervision in psychiatric training. *Bulletin of the Menninger Clinic, 17,* 157–159.

Fong, M. L., & Lease, S. H. (1997). Cross-cultural supervision: Issues for the White supervisor. In D. B. Pope-Davis & H. L. L. Coleman (Eds.), *Multicultural counseling competencies: Assessment, education and training, and supervision* (pp. 387–405). Thousand Oaks, CA: Sage.

Freud, S. (1966/1895). Project for a scientific psychology. In J. Strachey (Ed. and Trans.), *The standard edition of the complete psychological works of Sigmund Freud* (vol. I, pp. 281–397). London, UK: Hogarth Press. (Original work published 1895).

Goodyear, R. K. & Bernard, J. M. (1998). Clinical supervision: Lessons from the literature. *Counselor Education & Supervision, 38*(1), 6–22. doi: 10.1002/j.1556–6978.1998.tb00553.x

Hill, W. E., Hatsy, C., & Moore, C. J. (2011). Differentiation of self and the process of forgiveness: A clinical perspective for couple and family therapy. *The Australian & New Zealand Journal of Family Therapy, 32*(1), 43–57. doi: 10.1375/anft.32.1.43

Hogan, R. (1964). Issues and approaches in supervision. *Psychotherapy: Theory, Research, and Practice, 1,* 139–141. doi: 10.1037/h0088589

Holloway, E. L. (1995). *Clinical supervision: A systems approach.* Thousand Oaks, CA: Sage.

Inman, A. G. (2006). Supervisor multicultural competence and its relation to supervisory process and outcome. *Journal of Marital and Family Therapy, 32(1),* 73–85. doi: 10.1111/j.1752–0606.2006.tb01589.x

Jacobsen, C. H. (2007). A qualitative single case study of parallel processes. *Counselling and Psychotherapy Research, 7*(1), 26–33. doi: 10.1080/14733140601140410

Juhnke, G. A. (1996). Solution-focused supervision: Promoting supervisee skills and confidence through successful solutions. *Counselor Education and Supervision, 36,* 48–57. doi: 10.1002/j.1556–6978.1996.tb00235.x

Jung, C. J. (1959). *The archetypes and the collective unconscious* (Trans. R. F. C. Hull). New York, NY: Bollingen Foundation.

Killian, K. D. (2001). Differences making a difference: Cross-cultural interactions in supervisory relationships. *Journal of Feminist Family Therapy, 72,* 61–103.

Ladany, N., Ellis, M. V., & Friedlander, M. L. (1999). The supervisory working alliance, trainee self-efficacy, and satisfaction. *Journal of Counseling & Development, 77,* 447–455. doi: 10.1002/j.1556–6676.1999.tb02472.x

Ladany, N., Walker, J. A., & Melincoff, D. S. (2001). Supervisory style: Its relation to the supervisory working alliance and supervisor self-disclosure. *Counselor Education & Supervision, 40,* 263–275. doi: 10.1002/j.1556–6978.2001.tb01259.x

Lambert, M. J., & Ogles, B. M. (1997). The effectiveness of psychotherapy supervision. In C. E. Watkins, Jr. (Ed.), *Handbook of psychotherapy supervision* (pp. 421–446). New York, NY: Wiley.

Loganbill, C., Hardy, E., & Delworth, U. (1982). Supervision: A conceptual model. *The Counseling Psychologist, 10,* 3–42. doi: 10.1177/0011000082101002

Lopez, S. R. (1997). Cultural competence in psychotherapy: A guide for clinicians and their supervisors. In C. E. Watkins, Jr. (Ed.), Handbook of psychotherapy supervision (pp. 570–588). New York, NY: Wiley.

Magnuson, S., Wilcoxon, S. A., & Norem, K. (2000). A profile of lousy supervision: Experienced counselors' perspectives. *Counselor Education & Supervision, 39*(3), 189-203. doi: 10.1002/j.1556–6978.2000.tb01231.x

Maki, D. R., & Delworth, U. (1995). Clinical supervision: A definition and model for the rehabilitation counseling profession. *Rehabilitation Counseling Bulletin, 38*(4), 282–294.

Morrissey, J., & Tribe, R. (2001). Parallel process in supervision. *Counselling Psychology Quarterly, 14*(2), 103–110. doi: 10.1080/09515070110058567

National Board for Certified Counselors (NBCC). (2005). *Code of ethics.* Retrieved from http://www.nbcc.org/assets/ethics/nbcc-codeofethics.pdf

Neufeldt, S. A., & Nelson, M. L. (1999). When is counseling an appropriate and ethical supervision function? *Clinical Supervisor, 18,* 125–135. doi: 10.1300/J001v18n01_08

O'Hanlon, W. H., & Weiner-Davis, M. (1989). *In search of solutions: A new direction in psychotherapy.* New York, NY: Norton.

Patterson, C. H. (1983). Supervision in counseling: II. Contemporary models of supervision: A client-centered approach to supervision. *Counseling Psychologist, 11*(1), 21–25.

Rogers, C. R. (1975). Empathic: An unappreciated way of being. *The Counseling Psychologist, 5*(2), 2–10.

Ronnestad, M. H., & Skovholt, T. M. (1993). Supervision of beginning and advanced graduate students of counseling and psychotherapy. *Journal of Counseling and Development, 71*(4), 396–405. doi: 10.1002/j.1556–6676.1993.tb02655.x

Ronnestad, M. H., & Skovholt, T. M. (2003). The journey of the counselor and therapist: Research findings and perspectives on professional development. *Journal of Career Development, 30,* 5–44. doi: 10.1177/089484530303000102

Rosenbaum, M., & Ronen, T. (1998). Clinical supervision from the standpoint of cognitive-behavioral therapy. *Psychotherapy: Theory, Research, Practice, Training, 35,* 220–230. doi: 10.1037/h0087705

Schneider, S. (1992). Transference, counter-transference, projective identification and role responsiveness in the supervisory process. *The Clinical Supervisor, 10*(2), 71–84. doi: 10.1300/J001v10n02_05

Stoltenberg, C. (1981). Approaching supervision from a developmental perspective: The counselor-complexity model. *Journal of Counseling Psychologists, 28,* 59–65. doi: 10.1037//0022–0167.28.1.59

Stoltenberg, C. D., McNeill, B. W., & Delworth, U. (1997). Clinical supervision from a developmental perspective: Research and practice. In C. E. Watkins, Jr. (Ed.), *Handbook of psychotherapy supervision* (pp. 184–202). New York, NY: Wiley.

Stoltenberg, C. D., McNeill, B. W., & Delworth, U. (1998). *IDM: An integrated developmental model for supervising counselors and therapists.* San Francisco, CA: Jossey-Bass.

Woods, P. J., & Ellis, A. (1997). Supervision in rational emotive behavior therapy. In C. E. Watkins, Jr. (Ed.), *Handbook of psychotherapy supervision* (pp. 101–113). New York, NY: Wiley.

Worthen, V., & McNeill, B. W. (1996). A phenomenological investigation of "good" supervision events. *Journal of Counseling Psychology, 43,* 25–34. doi: 10.1037/0022–0167.43.1.25

Chapter 8

Ethical and Legal Considerations in Counseling

Cynthia A. Reynolds
Claudia Sadler-Gerhardt

Most people seek to become counselors because of a deep desire to help others; however, clients may have differing opinions and expectations regarding what helping entails and how helpers should behave and perform. Counselors may underestimate the power they possess in the helping relationship and all of the resulting complications. Even within the profession of counseling, counselors may disagree with each other regarding what is appropriate helping behavior on the part of the counselor.

Professional counseling organizations produce ethical codes to promote the professional competence of counselors. Governments enact laws to protect the public safety. At times, counselors may find that a legal requirement appears to not be in the best interest of the client in the helping relationship, or that following a particular ethical code may not be legal. As professional counselors, we rely upon both the ethical codes of our profession and state and legal requirements to guide us in our actions with clients. A greater understanding of both law and ethics will assist you in becoming the most highly competent professional counselor possible, as well as aid you in avoiding lawsuits that could impair your ability to earn a living as a practitioner of counseling.

In this chapter, we describe both legal and ethical requirements in professional counseling. We also present the history of and purpose behind ethical principles. Last, we discuss several ethical decision-making models and how to use them when faced with an ethical dilemma. This chapter serves as the beginning of a process of learning that is necessary to function as a legally and ethically informed counseling professional. This process should continue in every course in your graduate program and extend throughout your professional career. Laws and ethics change over time, and the learning is never finished.

LEARNING OBJECTIVES

After completing the reading and reflection activities provided in this chapter, you will be able to

1. Distinguish between legal requirements and ethical standards,

2. Describe the history of and purpose behind ethical principles,

3. Reference the American Counseling Association (ACA) ethical codes as guidelines for practice as a counselor,

4. Utilize several different ethical decision-making models to resolve an ethical dilemma, and

5. Choose behaviors that will enhance adherence to ethical standards.

DIFFERENCES BETWEEN LAWS AND ETHICS

Ideally, professional counselors are guided in their actions by both the enacted laws of the national, state, and local governments as well as the ethical standards of the profession of counseling. It is important to understand the different purposes of laws and ethics and to be able to distinguish between the two when engaging in decisions regarding what course of action to take in regard to clients. This distinction between laws and ethics is applicable to all professions.

Laws are agreed-upon rules of society designed to protect public safety, health, and welfare. Criminal laws address crime or those behaviors that cause harm to others and set punishment for violations of those laws. Civil laws address personal interest disputes of individuals, groups, organizations, and the government. Laws are written, approved, and then enforced by the level of government at which they were created, whether it is at the federal, state, or local level. Laws may vary among countries, states, or even local governments. Laws carry punishments for violations that may include fines or incarceration. Laws are the minimum standard necessary to keep society functioning smoothly.

Ethical standards for counselors, on the other hand, are guidelines for how we should behave as counseling professionals. Ethics are designed to elevate the standard of competence of professionals and to build values and ideals. Consequences for ethical violations may include professional sanctions such as reprimands, loss of license, or mandated supervision. These penalties are usually determined and administered by peers within the profession.

There are a number of legal considerations that must be addressed by professional counselors. Federal laws apply to counselors in every state. Although all 50 states have counselor licensure, the laws impacting the profession of counseling may differ from state to state. Counselors moving from one state to another cannot assume the laws will be the same; often professional counselors moving into a new state will be required to demonstrate their understanding through additional coursework or through testing results. Finally, individual school districts and counseling agencies have policies and procedures that may be entirely unique to the particular setting. Responsible professional counselors are expected to seek out and abide by all of the laws that apply to them, whether at the federal, state, or local level, and they will be held accountable for their actions legally. The next section addresses some of these important legal considerations.

LEGAL CONSIDERATIONS

There are two important federal laws that have impacted the profession of counseling in the past 50 years: FERPA (Family Education Rights and Privacy Act) and HIPAA (Health Insurance Portability and Accountability Act). In this section, you will learn the importance and implications of FERPA and HIPAA to the practice of professional counselors across settings (e.g., school, clinical mental health).

FERPA was enacted in 1974. It is a set of regulations that applies to those institutions that receive funding from the US Department of Education, such as school districts, preK–12 schools, and postsecondary institutions. FERPA was written specifically for students and their parents and guarantees them the right to inspect and review their education records, the right to seek to amend education records, and the right to have some control over the disclosure of information from those education records.

FERPA requires that schools or systems annually send a notice to parents or guardians regarding their right to review their children's records and file a complaint if they disagree with anything that is kept in the record. The right to consent access to their records transfers to the student from the parent when the student reaches age 18, and FERPA does not specifically limit the rights of students who are 18 and still in high school. Noncustodial parents have the same rights as custodial parents unless there is a court order specifying otherwise, whereas stepparents or grandparents who do not have custody are not granted rights under FERPA, although rights may be granted by a court order. The Protection of Pupil Rights Amendment (PPRA) of 1978, sometimes referred to as the Hatch Amendment, gives parents additional rights, including requiring informed parental consent before the student is subjected to any examination, testing, or program designed to affect the personal values or behavior of the student. For example, if a school psychologist would like to administer an IQ test to students in the second grade, the psychologist would need a written consent from parents of these students. It also gives parents the right to review instructional programs. The No Child Left Behind (NCLB) Act of 2004 continued to increase parental rights.

HIPAA, passed in 1996, primarily protects health insurance coverage for workers and their families when they change or lose their jobs. Title II of HIPAA, known as the administrative simplification (AS) provisions, requires the establishment of national standards for electronic health care transactions and national identifiers for providers, health insurance plans, and employers. The AS provisions also address the security and privacy of health data. The standards were created to improve the efficiency and effectiveness of the nation's health care system by encouraging the widespread use of electronic date interchange in the US health care system. The Privacy Rule specifically excludes any individually identifiable health information that is covered by FERPA. Health records in schools that are governed under FERPA are specifically excluded from HIPAA. Agencies and school systems must develop policies and procedures to address the potential conflicts between FERPA and HIPAA (Erford, 2010).

In addition to federal laws, legislation enacted by each state is binding upon the practice of counseling in the state. Licensing boards (professional counseling, social work, marriage/family therapy, rehabilitation counseling, psychology) review regulations and may develop policies on how to implement a specific law. State departments of education create laws that are binding on the school employees of that particular state. In addition, particular school systems or mental health agencies create policies and procedures that they expect their employees to follow. For example, some states have laws that require parental consent for a child to receive services from a school counselor. Other states have no such law, as school counseling is deemed part of the overall educational program and does not require parental consent. Even without a state law mandating parental consent for school counseling, an individual district may create policy requiring parental consent before a school counselor sees a student. Clearly, it is a challenge for counselors to keep abreast of ethics and federal and state laws and regulations as well as school district and agency policies and procedures. At times school counselors and clinical mental health counselors may feel that they are speaking different languages, as they can be governed by different laws and ethics.

PROFESSIONAL COUNSELING ETHICAL PRACTICE

You have probably heard of incidents where professional counselors are charged with legal or ethical violations regarding their inappropriate behaviors with the clients. When these incidents occur, public confidence in the counseling profession is undermined. Public trust in counseling is critical to the profession, because we want to assure that we deliver high-quality services that promote health and well-being to clients across the lifespan. Our services will not be sought out if we have a reputation for hurting or misusing our clients. The misbehavior of one professional counselor can impact how the public reacts to all members of the profession. We are obligated to behave legally and ethically, not only with our clients, but also to the rest of the profession.

It is an expectation in all professions that members be accountable for their behaviors. A code of ethics provides the necessary framework for a process of accountability. A code of ethics is vital to the process of educating members of the profession, providing counselors with a set of principles to follow when issues or dilemmas arise. Having a national ethical code for the counseling profession helps to provide consistency across states and highlights the areas of knowledge important to understanding and developing an ethical practice. Indeed, having a specific ethical code is one of the criteria in the definition of what a profession is (Vacc & Loesch, 1987). King (2012) studied how ethical codes define counselor professional identity and discovered that counseling shares five core values with the professions of social work, psychology, and marriage and family therapy: general competence and professional conduct, promotion of welfare and avoidance of harm, informed consent and self-determination, privacy and confidentiality, and collaborative professional relationships. Results showed that differences among the professions exist in how these values are promoted; in counseling codes of ethics endorse the values of personal growth, development, and wellness.

Although this is a brief foundation chapter and can cover ethics only in broad terms, the following list may be useful in familiarizing the beginning counselor with the top 10 ethical and legal concepts that will be addressed in later courses.

1. *Confidentiality* refers to the client's expectation that information shared with a counselor remains private and confidential. It is the cornerstone (Erford, 2010) of the counseling profession. Clients have the right to waive confidentiality

and share information with a third party. Confidentiality belongs to the client, not to the counselor. When working with children, parents may have the legal right to know what is being discussed. Therefore the counselor has to balance the child's expectation of privacy with the parent's right to know. Counselors who work with children on a regular basis address confidentiality on a proactive basis, discussing it with both parents and children before counseling begins. There are exceptions to this requirement of confidentiality; it may be breached when there is a risk of harm to self, harm to others, or abuse. Group, couples, and marriage and family therapy counseling have specific interpretations of confidentiality, since the counselor cannot guarantee that confidentiality will not be broken by other parties when there is more than one client in the session. Other limits to confidentiality, according to the ACA code of ethics, exist where there are issues with subordinates, treatment teams, consultation, third party payers, contagious or life-threatening diseases, and court ordered disclosures.

2. *Mandated Reporting* involves the clear directive to mental health practitioners that they must report suspected abuse or neglect of children under 18 years of age within 24 to 72 hours of having "reason to suspect." While there is no liability involved with reporting (without malice) that does not turn out to be verified, there are serious penalties for failure to report. Depending on your state of residence, there may be mandated reporting for elder abuse or abuse of vulnerable populations. Not all states have mandated reporting for domestic violence. It is important to investigate the laws regarding mandated reporting in your state in order to know your exact legal obligations.

3. *Privileged Communication* is the legal term used to describe the privacy of the communication between the counselor and client. Privileged communication exists by statute and applies only to testifying in a court of law.

4. *Informed Consent* is a legal procedure to ensure that a patient, a client, and research participants are aware of all the potential risks and costs involved in a treatment or procedure. The elements of informed consent include informing the client of the nature of the treatment, possible alternative treatments, and the potential risks and benefits of the treatment. In order for informed consent to be considered valid, the client must be competent, and the consent should be given voluntarily.

5. *Duty to Warn* refers to the responsibility of the counselor to break confidentiality in order to warn foreseeable and identifiable victims of potential violence. In situations where there is clear evidence of danger to the client or other persons, the counselor must determine the degree of seriousness of

the threat and notify the person in danger and others who are in a position to protect that person from harm (Herlihy & Sheeley, 1988). For example, if a student tells a school counselor that another student is planning to commit suicide, the counselor is obligated to investigate and should not leave the suicidal student alone until parents or guardians have arrived (Davis & Richie, 1993). The legal precedent of this concept was set in the case of Tarasoff v. Regents of California (1976). According to Davis and Ritchie (1993), this case indicates that "notifying police is not sufficient action to protect the counselor from a lawsuit if the client's threat is carried out" (p. 27). In this case, a young man was being seen at a university health center because a woman (Tarasoff) had spurned his affections. The psychologist, who believed that the young man was dangerous because of his pathological attachment to Tarasoff and his intent to purchase a gun, notified the police verbally and in writing. The police questioned the young man, told him to stay away from Tarasoff, and deemed him rational. Two months later he killed Tarasoff. Her parents sued the university, the health center, and the police, but the court dismissed the case. The Tarasoff family appealed, and in the second ruling, the court released the police from liability and more broadly formulated the duty of therapist, imposing a duty to use reasonable care to protect third parties against dangers posed by patients. The case of *Jablonski by Pahls v. United States* further extended the responsibilities of duty to warn by including the reviews of previous records that might include a history of violent behavior. This ruling originated in a case in which a doctor conducted a risk assessment of a client (Jablonski), but did not review his history of violence. Jablonski's girlfriend was not informed of his history of violent behavior, and when he was released from custody, Jablonski killed her.

6. *Professional Competence* requires counselors to maintain ongoing professional growth and education. Counselors are required to stay up to date on their training and credentials, and to provide only services for which they have be appropriately trained and approved. Counselors do not misrepresent their qualifications.

7. *Scope of Practice* is a term used by national and state licensing boards for professions. It defines the procedures, actions, and processes that are permitted for the licensed individual. The scope of practice limits the counselor's work to those practices in which the counselor demonstrates evidence of specific education, experience, and competency. An example of practicing outside a scope of practice is a counselor who goes to court and testifies in a custody case regarding the fitness of a parent, where the counselor has never met that parent but is testifying based on a request from the other parent,

who is currently a client. The counselor has never taken a course in forensic counseling or custody evaluation. This counselor is acting outside of scope of practice.

8. *Professional Disclosure Statement* informs clients about the counselor's professional background and the limitations of the professional relationship. The state of residence may dictate what must be included in your statement of disclosure. Included are contact information; qualifications, including licenses, certifications, training, and experience; professional association memberships; services offered; theoretical approach; fee structure (broken appointments, collecting debt, cancellation policy); confidentiality and its exceptions; insurance procedures; emergency policies; the specific professional code of ethics followed in the practice; and the address of the specific governing board where the client can file a complaint if needed. The professional disclosure statement is presented during the first meeting with the client, discussed, and then signed by both the client and counselor, with copies kept by both parties.

9. *Minor Consent Laws* refers to the laws permitting certain minors to pursue treatment without parental permission. These laws are based upon federal legislation and cover substance abuse, mental health, and some reproductive health issues. Refer to your particular state for precise information.

10. *A Dual Relationship* occurs when a counselor has any relationship with a client or former client other than that of counseling. Dual relationships are the most frequent complaints filed against counselors and the most frequent reason for professional sanctions. Dual relationships are very difficult to avoid in small rural communities, and there are suggested guidelines for professional counselors who practice in those areas (Campbell & Gordon, 2003). In school settings, school counselors regularly counsel students whom they have taught in classroom guidance sessions or who have been members of groups led by the school counselor. School counselors must learn how to function in the different roles in ways that protect confidentiality and do not harm students and their families.

ETHICAL CONSIDERATIONS

According the Remley and Herlihy (2007), mental health counselors have defined ethics as standards of conduct or actions in relation to others (Levy, 1992), and as acceptable or good practices according to agreed-upon rules or standards of practice established by a profession (Cottone & Tarvydas, 2003). A professional code of ethics attempts to set high standards of competence in the profession, strengthen the relationship among its members, and promote the welfare of the entire community.

The main purposes for a code of ethics (Herlihy & Corey, 1996; Mappes, Robb, & Engles, 1985; Van Hoose & Kottler, 1985) include the following:

1. To protect the public

2. To educate members of the profession

3. To ensure accountability

4. To serve as a catalyst for improving practice

We are all shocked to read of disciplinary actions against members of the counseling profession for boundary violations. When a counselor is charged with legal or ethical violations regarding behaviors with a client, public confidence in the counseling profession is undermined. When a counselor's harm of a client becomes public, the behaviors of all counselors are more carefully scrutinized, so that further abuses do not occur. Public trust in counseling is critical to the profession. Regulatory boards exist to monitor and protect the public, and ethical codes as well as state and national laws are used to make decisions regarding counselors' competence and fitness. Counselors who do harm to clients may face disciplinary actions by the state board that may include suspension or revocation of the license to practice.

A code of ethics is vital to the process of educating members of the profession. By having a set of standards, counselors have a set of principles to follow when issues or dilemmas arise. Having a national ethical code for the counseling profession helps to provide consistency across states and highlights the areas of knowledge important to understanding and developing an ethical practice. Finally, through discussion, review, and revision of the various ethical guidelines, the practice of counseling can be improved. Ultimately, the goal is to provide the best help possible for clients and to minimize any risk of harm to them.

ETHICAL DICHOTOMIES

As beginning-level counselors, we usually want a very clear map of exactly what is expected of us as professionals. The study of ethics may at times be very frustrating, as there is much ambiguity inherent in the history and practice of ethics. Ethical dichotomies that occur frequently include ethical absolutism vs. ethical relativism, utilitarianism vs. deontology, egoism vs. altruism, and principle ethics vs. virtue ethics. We briefly discuss these ethical dichotomies in this section in order to provide for you a context for understanding the complexity involved in ethical issues.

Ethical absolutism is the doctrine that there is only one eternally true and valid moral code that applies to everyone, in all places, and at all times, whether or not people realize it. Historically, ethical absolutism stems from the Judeo–Christian tradition. Morality is seen as issuing from God's commands and not relative to time or circumstance. The idea that life is sacred from the moment of conception and that abortion is absolutely wrong is an example of this doctrine.

Ethical relativism is the view that what is right or wrong is not absolute but varies depending on the person, circumstances, or social situation. This view originated from the works of Protagoras, a leading Greek Sophist of the 5th century BCE. Ethical relativism states that what is really right depends solely upon what the individual or society believes to be right, which will vary with time and place. Therefore, there is no objective way of justifying any principle as valid for all people or all societies. The belief that abortion is justified in cases of rape, incest, or danger to the life of the mother is an example of ethical relativism.

Utilitarianism is an ethical framework that focuses on the outcomes or results of actions. Utilitarianism comes from the Greek work *telos*, which means "end." Acting ethically, according to utilitarianism, means making decisions or taking actions that benefit people by maximizing "good" and minimizing "bad." The ends can justify the means, and theoretically, it is possible for the right thing to be done from the wrong or bad motive.

Deontology is the ethical position that judges the morality of an action based on the action's adherence to a rule or rules. The word *deontology* comes from the Greek words for duty (*deon*) and study (*logos*). Deontological ethics has three important features: First, duty should be done for duty's sake; second, human beings should be treated as beings of intrinsic moral value; third, a moral principle is a categorical imperative that is universalizable.

Ethical egoism is the view that a person should pursue her own self-interest, even at the expense of others. It does not require moral agents to consider the interests and well-being of others when making moral deliberations. What is in an agent's self-interest may be beneficial, detrimental, or neutral in its effect on others.

Ethical altruism is the philosophical doctrine of living for others rather than for oneself. The French philosopher Auguste Comte coined the French word *altruisme* in 1851, and it entered the English language two years later as *altruism*. Ethical altruism holds that moral agents have an obligation to serve and help others.

Principle ethics refers to "What should I do?" Principle ethics is a theory of moral philosophy that promotes morals and responsibility that include rules and consequences. These include respect for autonomy, nonmaleficence, beneficence, justice, fidelity, and veracity. Autonomy means respecting individual decision-making processes and recognizing independence and self-determination. Nonmaleficence is avoiding doing any harm and preventing harmful actions and effects. Beneficence means doing good and promoting well-being and health. Justice promotes fairness and equity in dealings. Fidelity involves being responsible to clients and honoring agreements. Veracity means being truthful and honest with others.

In contrast to principle ethics, virtue ethics refers to "Who should I be?" Virtue ethics is a theory of moral philosophy that puts an emphasis on character rather than rules or consequences. The first systematic description of virtue ethics was written down by Aristotle in the *Nicomachean Ethics*. According to Aristotle, when people acquire good habits of character, they are better able to regulate their emotion and their reason. This, in turn, will assist them in making morally correct decisions when faced with difficult choices. In response to the question, "Who should I be," the counselor acting from a position of virtue ethics believes that she should be a person with integrity, discernment, acceptance of emotion, self-awareness, and interdependence with the community. A person with integrity acts consistently in accordance with the values, beliefs, and principles that she purports to uphold. A virtuous person makes choices using discernment with wisdom and judgment. Acceptance of emotion is an important part of a virtuous person's definition of who she should be. Self-awareness involves the ability to see clearly one's own behaviors, personality, and beliefs in relation to others. Finally virtue ethics emphasizes that an ethical person has an interdependence with the community.

According to Welfel (2012), professional ethics encompass four main dimensions: having sufficient knowledge, skill, and judgment to use efficacious interventions; respecting the human dignity and freedom of the client; using the power inherent in the counselor's role responsibly; and acting in ways that promote the public confidence in the mental health professions. Considering those four dimensions will enable the counselor to wisely use an ethical decision-making model.

Exercise 8.1

After reading the ethical dichotomies, indicate where would you classify the behavior of three major news radio or TV talk show hosts. Do any of them fit more than one classification?

ETHICAL DECISION-MAKING MODELS

You have now learned about the codes of ethics of professional counseling. However, a code of ethics in and of itself does not provide a method to solve ethical dilemmas. Instead, professional counselors rely on ethical decision-making models to help them make informed and appropriate decisions when they face ethical dilemmas. There are numerous ethical decision-making models that have been proposed for counselors to use when faced with an ethical decision (Cottone & Claus, 2000). In this section, we first introduce ethical principles proposed by Kitchener (1984) to help you understand the foundations of ethical concepts pertaining to professional counseling. We then discuss major ethical decision-making models, including the ACA model (2005), Welfel's model (2012), Corey, Corey, and Callanan's model (2011), and a feminist model (Hill, Glaser, & Harden, 1998).

Kitchener's Ethical Principles

An ethical dilemma is a situation that involves conflicting or opposing principles (Urofsky, Engels, & Engebretson, 2008) without an obvious right or wrong answer. It is important to recognize that when there is a need to arrive at an ethical decision, individuals are easily influenced by their own personal values and assumptions and often rely on intuition and emotional factors to guide decisions (Welfel, 2012). Kitchener's (1984) seminal work on ethical decision making indicated that personal value judgments and moral intuition are insufficient for ensuring that ethical choices are made, and value judgments are not equal among all individuals (see also Cottone & Claus, 2000). Cultural norms, political pressures, flawed understanding, and unpredictable intuitions can greatly limit the wisdom of intuition, resulting in unethical decisions (Welfel, 2012).

In order to minimize the potential for harm to clients, professional counselors must be committed to ethical practice that transcends personal opinion and aligns with ethical codes and accepted standards for best practices (Urofsky et al., 2008; Welfel, 2012). Kitchener's critical-evaluative model (1984) supported the need for going beyond intuitive moral reasoning and carefully evaluating ethical issues from a cognitive reasoning approach. When one of the principle ethics of autonomy, nonmaleficence, beneficence, justice, and fairness (Kitchener, 1984) conflicts with another, the counselor must thoughtfully and carefully "weigh, balance, sift, and winnow competing principles" (Urofsky et al., 2008, p. 68) to arrive at a reliable ethical decision.

It will be helpful to briefly define Kitchener's ethical concepts and give an example of each at this point. *Autonomy* is the concept of personal responsibility to make one's own choices and to have freedom to act on one's own behalf. A second aspect of autonomy, according to Kitchener, is to allow others the same choices and freedoms (Kitchener, 1984). An example of exercising autonomy could be an adult who suffers with a terminal illness and decides to refuse additional medical intervention or treatment, against other family members' preferences. *Nonmaleficence* is the principle of "do no harm" (Kitchener, 1984, p. 47), neither by intentionally harming a client nor by practicing in such a manner as to cause harm to the client (Kitchener, 1984). We might all agree that an example of intentional harm would be deliberate physical or sexual abuse of a minor child. A more ambiguous type of harm might be a counselor who utilizes an intervention that she or he is not competent to use, and resultant harm is done to the client's emotional well-being.

Beneficence means to promote the health and well-being of a client, not just avoiding harm. The preamble to the 2005 ACA code of ethics states that "ACA members are dedicated to the enhancement of human development throughout the life span" (p. 3), a professional value that counselors are to aspire to. One important aspect of beneficence is that professional counselors must be competent to practice within their scope of practice, utilizing interventions that are empirically validated and demonstrated to enhance the welfare of the client (e.g., using cognitive behavioral techniques for treating a client with an anxiety disorder, a treatment modality considered to be efficacious for anxiety disorders).

Justice and fidelity are the final two concepts in Kitchener's model. *Justice* broadly means something that is fair, treating clients equally and impartially. An example might be avoiding an unequal sliding scale payment schedule for professional counseling services that would allow certain clients more reductions in rates than other clients. *Fidelity* refers to being faithful to do what we say we will, to be who we claim to be, and to be honest and reliable. An example of lacking fidelity would be a counselor who typically runs late, perhaps allowing prior clients to use more than their allotted time, hence cutting into the starting time of the next client.

It is important to understand how an ethical decision-making model can assist the counselor to critically consider the rationale underlying possible different actions with the goal of providing the safest and most therapeutic care to the client. Additionally, the ACA code of ethics (2005) mandated that counselors are "expected

---

Exercise 8.2

One of the concepts of principle ethics is *autonomy*, which is defined as the right or freedom for a person to determine her own destiny. This appears to be a very Western idea. How might the idea of autonomy conflict with the ideas of clients who come from cultures that are very family or community based? Do you see any other potential multicultural conflicts with the values listed under principle ethics?

to engage in a carefully considered ethical decision-making process" when faced with difficult ethical dilemmas (p. 3). However, often Kitchener's principles appear to be in conflict with one another. People are complex, values can be unreliable or biased, and decisions are not always straightforward. Therefore, understanding how to implement an ethical decision-making model, and for beginning professional counselors, understanding the need for consultation with their supervisors, is an essential part of professional counselor development. There are numerous ethical decision-making models that have been proposed for counselors to use when faced with an ethical decision (Cottone & Claus, 2000). We will continue with discussions about different models for arriving at ethical decisions.

ACA Model for Ethical Decision Making

The American Counseling Association (ACA) in 1996 developed a document to guide ACA members in making difficult ethical decisions (Forester-Miller & Davis, 1996). It is available at www.counseling.org for ACA members. The document includes a summary of the Kitchener moral principles and an ethical decision-making model.

Step one is *identify the problem* in a manner as specifically and objectively as possible, trying to tease apart any innuendos or assumptions. We are encouraged to seek legal counsel if the problem is legal; otherwise, it is important to identify whether the problem is ethical, professional, or clinical in nature. Also we need to ask if the problem is related to our actions or inactions, the client's and/or significant others' actions or inactions, or institution or agency policies. Next, *apply the ACA code of ethics* (ACA, 2005) if there is a specifically applicable standard. If there is not an obvious resolution at this point, Forester-Miller and Davis (1996) claimed that indeed an ethical dilemma must exist, and there are further steps to be taken.

The next step, *determine the nature and dimensions of the dilemma,* includes a consideration of which of the Kitchener principles might apply and which one would assume priority, a review of current professional literature, consultation with colleagues and supervisors, and consulting state or national professional associations. After gathering this information, it is time to *generate potential courses of action* and *consider the potential consequences of all options and determine a course of action.* Creative brainstorming and consultation lead to winnowing of the potential actions with best possible outcomes (Forester-Miller & Davis, 1996).

The sixth step is *evaluate the selected course of action.* One consideration is whether or not the course selected presents any additional ethical dilemmas. Three tests can be applied: For justice, would you treat others in this same manner; for publicity, would you want this action reported in the media; and for universality, would you recommend this action to another counselor in the same situation

(Forester-Miller & Davis, 1996)? Finally, *implement the course of action.* This is not always an easy step to take. Following action, it is then important to assess the effect and consequences of the action taken (Forester-Miller & Davis).

The authors remind counselors that different professionals may arrive at different decisions and complete different actions, since there is not usually just one correct answer to any given dilemma. The important thing is to be able to provide a thoughtful and professional rationale for the decision if asked about it (Forester-Miller & Davis, 1996).

Summary Table of ACA (Forester-Miller & Davis, 1996) Ethical Model

---

Step 1. Problem identification.

Step 2. Apply ACA code of ethics.

Step 3. What is the dilemma?

Step 4. Brainstorm potential actions. Consult.

Step 5. Consider consequences. Decide on action.

Step 6. Implement the planned action.

Step 7. Assess outcome(s).

Welfel's Model for Ethical Decision Making

Welfel (2012) noted that professional ethics encompass four main dimensions: having sufficient knowledge, skill, and judgment to use efficacious interventions; respecting dignity and freedom of the client; using the power inherent in the counselor's role responsibly; and acting in ways that promote the public confidence in the mental health professions. Considering these four dimensions can enable the professional counselor to wisely use an ethical decision-making model to solve ethical dilemmas. To further clarify the application of the ethical decision-making models included in the text, Case Illustration 8.1 provides an example of how the steps of the specific ethical models are used.

Exercise 8.3

Download the ACA ethical standards. Pick at least five ethical concepts, and rate them in accordance to overall importance to the profession of counseling. Be able to defend your rating.

CASE ILLUSTRATION 8.1

A SUICIDAL CLIENT

Barry, a 16-year-old Latino male high school student, is receiving counseling for major depressive disorder from Carol, a recently licensed professional counselor in her state. During his current session, he reported that his girlfriend had dumped him, and consequently he had failed a couple of exams. Barry stated that he questioned his purpose for living without his girlfriend, called himself a failure, and wondered if his family would be better off without him around.

Carol felt quite anxious, but she began thinking through the steps of suicide assessment that she had learned in her classes. She immediately started a suicide assessment and consulted with her supervisor by phone while Barry remained in her office. She asked Barry specifically if he had a plan and any way to implement his plan. She also asked where his parents were, as she had previously identified Barry's parents and siblings as important stakeholders who would be impacted by his actions. She mentally reviewed her knowledge of adolescent development within his Latino culture and the social context of high school.

Carol recognized that two important principle ethical standards were in conflict: autonomy versus beneficence or nonmaleficence. If she allowed Barry to remain autonomous, he might kill himself. If she broke confidentiality and involved his parents, she would adhere to nonmaleficence and beneficence but at possible cost to the therapeutic relationship. Additionally, she had to examine her own values about suicide. Carol knew that the law in her state required breaking confidentiality in a situation where a minor client is suicidal. She and her clinical supervisor together identified the necessary steps to take.

To Carol and her supervisor, the action with the least harm to both the client and his family was to break confidentiality and inform Barry's parents of his suicidality. The risk of death was too great. There would still be a risk of losing him as a client, but that was less harmful than losing him to death. Additionally, Carol would risk losing her license if she did not follow the law in her state. Carol called Barry's parents and stayed with him until they arrived, at which time she and her supervisor talked with all of them. Once Barry had calmed down and worked out a safety plan, his parents stated that they would take him home. Carol made an appointment with him and his parents for the next morning.

Step 1 of Welfel's model (2012) is *becoming sensitive to the moral dimensions of practice*. Client acuity, managed care or third party payer concerns, and large case loads contribute to counselors' lack of sensitivity and recognition of potential ethical issues in clinical practice. Formal education in counselor training, especially in the development of principles and philosophy that align with those of the counseling professions, and assistance in integrating professional values into personal moral belief systems are essential in developing counselors' ethical sensitivity and personal ethical identity (Handelsman, Gottlieb, & Knapp, 2005). Welfel posited that being ethically sensitive goes beyond knowing and following the rules; instead, it is a core aspect of the professional counselor's work and life. Character traits such as personal virtue, altruism, and commitment to social justice are also significant aspects of ethical sensitivity (Jordan & Meara, 1990).

Counselors must have successfully completed all required coursework on ethics in their master's program in order to graduate and become licensed. Additionally, state licensing boards require a specific number of continuing education hours, some of which will be in ethics, to renew licenses. This education will help enhance ethical sensitivity in the professional counselor. Personal attributes such as maturity, thoughtfulness, self-reflection, good self-awareness, and a trusting relationship with the clinical supervisor can also foster ethical discernment and decision making.

Welfel's Step 2 is *identify the relevant facts, sociocultural context, and stake-holders* (2012). This includes fact finding, assessment of the client, and identification of stakeholders (i.e., others potentially impacted by the counselor's actions, such as parents or guardians of a minor). The caution in this step is the recognition that insufficient knowledge of the facts may be misleading and result in erroneous decisions. An important aspect of this and all subsequent steps is the documentation that must occur at each step. In regard to documentation, the counselor should include options identified and considered, outcomes of each step, any and all consultations with supervisors and colleagues, and any other information considered essential as part of the process notes for the client's file.

Step 3 is to *define the central issues in the dilemma and the available options*. This involves a broad classification of the type of ethical dilemma involved and how the context of the client's situation will affect the particular decision. This requires counselors to separate their own cultural and personal values and assumptions from those of their clients so as to not be unduly influenced by personal history. Additionally, it is important to continue brainstorming numerous possible actions as stated in Step 2, without judgment or elimination, while actively looking for reasonable alternatives. An important consideration is the balance of the counselor's own personal moral values and environmental pressure with the potential emotional difficulty a specific alternative might entail.

Step 4 is to *refer to professional ethical standards and relevant laws and regulations*, which involves considering how the standards apply to the particular issue. It is possible that a conflict may be apparent, such as that of protection of client confidentiality versus revealing the risk of suicidal intent to the proper authorities.

Step 5 is *search out the relevant ethics literature*. Consulting the professional literature and the ACA code of ethics (2005) enables the counselor to explore what other professionals have said about the same or similar dilemmas. Other experts' opinions and ideas may illustrate unconsidered points, especially in regard to a multicultural perspective (Handelsman et al., 2005; Welfel, 2012).

Step 6 is *apply fundamental ethical principles and theories to the situation* in an attempt to bring about some sense of order and patterns within the particular dilemma. Autonomy, nonmaleficence, beneficence, justice, and fidelity often are in opposition to each other. The counselor should attempt to abide by all five principles, but often that is not possible. Therefore, the ultimate goal is the prevention of harm to the client by implementing the action resulting in the least amount of harm. Complicating the potential conflict between principles is that certain ones may be more significant than others. According to Kitchener (1984), many have suggested that nonmaleficence is a stronger obligation than beneficence. Also, autonomy does not imply "unlimited freedom" (p. 46) with infringement upon the autonomy or rights of other people. For example, in the case of threatened suicide, the principle of nonmaleficence would trump the principle of autonomy, and a client's right to privacy would be ethically breeched in light of the higher value of not allowing the client to come to harm (death by suicide).

Step 7 is *consult with colleagues about the dilemma*. Ethical dilemmas are potentially overwhelming for counselors and may incur a temptation to become isolated in the face of the distressful situation. Obtaining feedback and advice from colleagues can provide alternative considerations, reduction of moral or emotional isolation, new information, and even comfort. Rather than utilizing consultation as a means to simply guard against malpractice, Welfel endorses consultation with other counselor colleagues at every step along the way of decision making. Also, if a counselor trainee or a licensed counselor under supervision is providing the counseling services, the supervisor must be consulted as soon as possible. Additionally, ACA provides free ethics consultation by phone during standard business hours for ACA members. (Visit www.counseling.org for more details.)

Step 8 is to *deliberate independently and decide which alternative is most ethical and how to implement the decision*. Personal reflection and examination of any competing ethical principles are essential aspects of this step. Ethical choices may coincide with costs to the counselor, such as increased work hours, disapproval from clients or others, or even risk to one's income or job.

Step 9 is *inform appropriate people and implement the decision* by informing supervisors of the choice and the rationale and then actually doing what has been decided. Documentation of the decision with accompanying rationale is a critical part of this step.

Step 10, the final step, is *reflect on the actions taken*. Welfel maintains that reflection and evaluation of the decision making and the actions provide insight for the future. Evaluation can inform future decisions in similar ethical situations. Observation of the outcomes, in consultation with supervisors, and debriefing and processing the counselor's emotional reaction to the experience can be beneficial to both parties.

Summary Table of Welfel's Ethical Model (2012)

Step 1. Become ethically and morally sensitive.
Step 2. Identify facts, context, and stakeholders.
Step 3. Define dilemma and options.
Step 4. Consider professional standards, laws, and regulations.
Step 5. Search relevant ethics literature.
Step 6. Apply ethical principles and theories to dilemma.
Step 7. Consult with colleagues, supervisors, ACA.
Step 8. Deliberate and decide what and how to implement.
Step 9. Inform appropriate people, implement decision.
Step 10. Reflect and evaluate.

Corey, Corey, and Callanan's Model

Another popular ethical decision-making model taught within counselor education programs is the model described by Corey, Corey, and Callanan (2011). The authors suggested examining the answers to two questions: "Which value do I

Exercise 8.4

In a small group, use Welfel's ethical decision-making model to solve an ethical dilemma. Maya is a professor in the counseling department at the local university. She is using the computer lab early one morning and she finds a disk from a local agency with detailed case notes regarding at least 20 clients. Maya realizes that the disk was left by a student doing her internship at that agency. What should Maya do with the computer disk?

rely on and why?" and "How do my values affect my work with clients?" (p. 22). They recommend a careful and intentional consideration of the dilemma and the decision-making process, and state that the process needs to be slowed down in order to allow for "intentional . . . ethical deliberation" (p. 22). The authors also remind us that ethical decisions are not just cognitive, linear processes; we need to recognize that our emotions will be involved. Corey et al. promote the immediate inclusion of the client in the decision-making process.

Step 1 is *identify the problem or dilemma*. It is important to clarify whether the dilemma is truly ethical or possibly a legal, a clinical, a professional, or a moral dilemma. Corey et al. recommend examining the dilemma from multiple perspectives, and consulting with the client and documenting from the very beginning. They also encourage self-reflective action by the counselor to begin this process.

Step 2 is *identify potential issues involved* by listing and describing the critical points. Included in this step is also a consideration of the cultural context, power balance, and acculturation or racial development level of the client. Corey et al. advise adding the construct of veracity to Kitchener's other five principles, prioritizing the principles, and looking for which ones are in conflict.

Step 3 is *review ethical codes*; it encourages professional counselors to look at the ACA code of ethics (2005) or consult with the experts at ACA (as mentioned earlier, a service provided to members during business hours). It is also important for the counselor to *know applicable laws and regulations* of her state and agency's policies (Step 4). It is vital for counselors to remain up to date with changing state or federal laws. The counselor should consider the rules as the starting point, not the end of the process.

Step 5 is to *obtain consultation* with colleagues and supervisors, with legal counsel if necessary, and with the client. The counselor needs to acknowledge that personal biases, needs, and emotional involvement influence the ability to be objective; therefore consultation is essential. The authors suggest applying the "reasonable person" standard: "What would a professional in your community with three years experience have done in your situation?" (Corey et al., 2011, p. 26).

Steps 6 and 7 evaluate the outcomes: *Consider possible and probable courses of action* and *enumerate consequences of various decisions*. Brainstorming a range of possibilities for action may produce the conclusion that no action is required. However, the implications of any action (or no action) must be considered as related to the client, the family or others in relationship to the client, and the counselor. Risks/benefits, psychological or social costs, long- and short-term effects, resource limitations, and necessary time or energy to implement certain actions must be examined.

Step 8, the final step, is to *choose what appears to be the best course of action* with the recognition that the more subtle and ambiguous the dilemma is, the more difficult the decision will be. Once again, the action and any outcomes must be documented. Corey and colleagues admonish counselors not to second-guess themselves for the decisions or actions they arrived at—something that is often difficult for counselors to avoid.

Summary Table of Corey, Corey, & Callanan Model (2011)

Step 1. Identify dilemma.
Step 2. Identify critical issues.
Step 3. Review ethical codes.
Step 4. Consider relevant laws and regulations.
Step 5. Consult colleagues, supervisors, legal counsel, client/s.
Step 6. Consider possible actions.
Step 7. Consider possible consequences.
Step 8. Choose best option.

Feminist Ethical Decision-Making Model

A feminist approach to ethical decision-making is now provided to contrast with Welfel's model; the feminist approach not only utilizes existing ethical codes but also considers the social context of the counselor and the client. There is a greater acknowledgment of the emotional-intuitive responses of the counselor, beyond just the rational cognitive responses. Factors such as race, ethnicity, gender, social class,

---

CASE ILLUSTRATION 8.2

CHANGING FAMILIES GROUP

Carole is an elementary school counselor who works in a K–6 building. She has begun a series of "Changing Family" groups for fourth through sixth graders who are experiencing difficulties with the divorce of their parents. She obtains signed permission from parents to allow the participation of the children. Midway through the group sessions, she receives a phone call from an attorney representing the father of one of the group members. The attorney is demanding all of Carole's records of the group sessions to use in the divorce trial. What should Carole do? What are the major ethical issues she needs to face in this situation?

affectional preferences, and spirituality of both client and counselor are important. The power differential between the client and the counselor is minimized as much as possible and when appropriate, and the client is intentionally included in the decision-making process (Hill, Glaser, & Harden, 1998). However, inclusion of the client in decision making is not unique to a feminist model. Others have reported the engagement of clients as beneficial in linking professional concepts within the framework of the client (Corey et al., 2011; Cottone & Claus, 2000; Garcia, Cartwright, Winston, & Borzuchowska, 2004) and based on the values of cooperation and inclusion of all parties involved in the dilemma (see Davis, 1997).

As described by Kitchener (1984), the intuitive level of moral reasoning is based on beliefs, assumptions, and knowledge of ethical codes, and is that initial response to a situation that includes a sense of what to do. The concern feminist approaches raise is that intuitive thinking is value-permeated and often marginalizes women and other undervalued groups. There is also a risk that intuition can promote moral relativism that may reduce the likelihood of sound ethical decisions (Hill et al., 1998). Another consideration is the recognition that the counselor's position in her own social context and culture will affect any definition of the five basic ethical principles and will influence the prioritization of ethical guidelines in the consideration of the decision. As an example, in terms of nonmaleficence, feminist counselors believe that women historically have been harmed by counselors practicing from theoretical orientations that defined problems and solutions in a manner that blamed victims (e.g., encouraging battered women to return to abusive intimate partners). Similarly, when counselors view heterosexual relationships as normative, clients with different affectional preferences may be at risk of harm (Hill et al., 1998).

In feminist therapy, the person of the counselor is considered an important factor in ethical decision making. It is not possible to separate the person of the counselor from the decisions she makes (Hill et al., 1998). Urofsky and colleagues (2008) described "Who am I?" as virtue ethics, and "What should I do?" as principle ethics (p. 71). Some attributes that would be important in the person of a feminist counselor would include the following: sensitivity to the counselor's own degree of acculturation, acknowledgment of the power differential inherent in the counseling relationship, possible self-disclosure of values or biases, and empowerment of the client to make informed choices about treatment strategies. Decision making would be shared with the client in a collaborative manner as one consideration of what to do. Feminist ethics adds the recognition of a power differential and the inclusion of the person of the counselor to the rational evaluative models most common in the literature (Hill et al., 1998).

The Feminist Therapy Group was established in 1983 to provide education, training, and support for counselors, and their code of ethics states five areas of importance: cultural diversity and oppression, power differentials, overlapping relationships, counselor's accountability, and social change (Evans, Kincade, & Seem, 2011). Cultural diversities and oppressions include the awareness of ethnic and cultural backgrounds, flexible provision of counseling services, recognition of the dominant culture's impact on individuals, advocacy for oppressed persons, and constant self-monitoring of the counselor's own biases or attitudes. Power differentials include acknowledgment of power, disclosure of information beneficial to the client, mutual decision making, and psychoeducation of clients about power relationships in their lives. Overlapping relationships are more frequent, because the feminist counselor would be likely to be actively involved in the community and would be responsible for monitoring potential risks in those multiple relationships. Sexual relationships with clients are prohibited (Evans et al., 2011). Accountability includes the counselors' obligation to be responsible to clients, colleagues, and especially to themselves. Additionally, counselors practice within their limits of competence; utilize self-evaluation and monitoring, peer consultation, or supervision as needed; and must be proactive in self-care measures. In regard to social change, feminist counselors attempt to create change by advocating for clients and societal issues within professional organizations and within the community. Finally, feminist counselors recognize that "the political is personal in a world where social change is a constant" (Evans et al., 2011, p. 38).

CASE ILLUSTRATION 8.3

THE USE OF THE FEMINIST MODEL

Susan is a licensed professional counselor in her state and a national certified counselor who practices from a feminist theoretical model. Anna is a new client who was recently laid off from her job of 25 years. She told Susan that she was interested in exploring other career options, perhaps even returning to school for a different degree. As a feminist counselor, Susan was very careful to use a collaborative approach with Anna, involving her in making decisions about what the counseling sessions would look like and what types of actions Anna wanted to begin with.

After a couple of sessions, Anna mentioned that she was joining a fitness center that happened to be the same center Susan attended. Susan's dilemma was whether or not to drop her membership there and join a different one, which would be further away, or to continue to attend her workouts as usual. She recognized that dual relationships are frequently the cause of professional complaints against counselors, but she also knew that from a feminist model there often would be overlapping relationships. After thinking through the steps of ethical decision making, she concluded that it would be good to discuss this with Anna and involve her in the decision.

Anna and Susan jointly arrived at the decision that Susan would continue at the same center, but that they would not enroll in the same exercise class, and they would plan different exercise schedules as much as possible. They agreed that if they happened to be there at the same time, Anna would determine whether or not she would speak to Susan, and Susan would not approach Anna.

Summary Table of Feminist Ethical Model (Evans, Kincade, & Seem, 2011; Hill, Glaser, & Harden, 1998)

Step 1. Consider the person of the counselor.

Step 2. Minimize power differentials. Decision making is collaborative with client(s).

Step 3. Be aware of cultural differences. Consider dominant cultural influences.

Step 4. Monitor risks of multiple relationships.

Step 5. Advocate for social change and justice.

Step 6. Seek peer consultation.

Step 7. Recognize the "personal is political."

ETHICAL CONCERNS IN THE USE OF TECHNOLOGY

Today's professional counselors live and work in a world that is based on technology. We live in a digital instant world with ready access to information at super speed, and the ability to communicate with others in digital and electronic formats. These technologies, including the World Wide Web, have altered the ethical landscape in which counselors practice. Not only are there concerns about sharing private medical or behavioral health information to third-party payers electronically (as addressed by the HIPAA Act of 1996, discussed earlier in this chapter), but additional concerns target e-mail, web-camera virtual conversations such as with Skype or FaceTime, and social media communication such as on Facebook or Twitter. With the demise of telephone landlines, most of our clients and many counselors rely on cell phone usage for communication. Clients in underserved areas, where in-person counseling may be unavailable, may request counseling services via the Internet. The concern is how secure any form of electronic conversation or submission of data really is. The responsibility for avoiding any breach of client confidentiality (e.g., use of encryption measures) is solely the counselor's (Welfel, 2012). Depending on the particular state where the client and the counselor live, according to the ACA code of ethics, Internet counseling is considered legal (ACA, 2005, Standard A.12.e); the question is whether or not it is done in an ethical manner and whether all measures to maintain confidentiality and client welfare are ensured. As a topic of current concern, we will now consider one particular aspect of digital communication: Facebook.

Social Media and Counseling

Facebook is one of the most well-known social media sites, and many of our clients will be accustomed to sharing all sorts of personal information via social networking with their Facebook contacts, called friends. Potential ethical dilemmas with Facebook and counseling concern the areas of dual relationships, privacy, and confidentiality. Dual relationships are addressed in the ACA code of ethics, standards A.5.c. and A.5.d. (2005). Dual relationships in themselves are not always unethical (Herlihy & Corey, 1996), but we are admonished to obtain client consent, provide a rationale that the dual relationship is beneficial to the client, and carefully document it (ACA, 2005).

Becoming a Facebook friend with a client also jeopardizes the privacy and confidentiality of both the client and the counselor. If a client were to view the personal pages of the counselor, potentially with pictures or personal information including home and relationships, the professional therapeutic relationship between the two would be altered and possibly damaged (Brown, Byrnes, & Fleenor, 2012). Under the ACA code of ethics (2005), self-disclosure by the counselor is limited to information that is of benefit to the client's well-being (Standard A.2.b.), so the question of beneficence or nonmaleficence would arise. Additionally, a counselor could potentially invade the privacy of a client by learning information from Facebook that has no bearing on the therapeutic goals or that has not been divulged in counseling sessions (ACA, 2005, Standard B.1.b, B.1.c.), which could also be very damaging (see also Welfel, 2012).

CASE ILLUSTRATION 8.4

FACEBOOK

Joe is a 22-year-old college student who is obtaining counseling from Edward at the local university counseling center. Joe and Edward have similar interests in technology and computers and have discussed Joe's use of Facebook as part of their treatment goals of obtaining social supports for Joe. One morning before work, Edward opens his Facebook account and finds a friend request from Joe. Discuss what you think Edward should do.

Edward is curious about Joe, as he has learned enough to realize that they have some common interests. He decides to try to look at Joe's Facebook wall and see what else he might be able to learn without having to directly ask Joe. Discuss whether you think this violates any ethical code and why.

Edward is engaged in using the instant message feature of Facebook and he realizes that a friend of his also is a Facebook friend with Joe. How do you think Edward should handle this? Should he tell his friend that he knows Joe? Why or why not?

KEYSTONES

This chapter has presented a foundation in professional counseling ethics, including some distinctions between laws that govern practice and ethics that relate to professional competence and fitness. We have discussed the ambiguity and complexity inherent in ethical dilemmas that occur with clients, and we have acknowledged the importance of the person of the counselor in arriving at ethical decisions. Additionally, we have described the critical nature of supervision and consultation and the essential need for documentation throughout the process.

The topics that were covered included the following:

- Differences between laws and ethics
- Laws related to professional counseling
- Ethical practice in professional counseling
- Ethical dichotomies
- Kitchener's model of ethics
- Ethical decision-making models, including those of the ACA, Corey et al., and Welfel as well as a feminist model
- Ethical concerns with use of technology

Exercise 8.5

Read the ethical fitness test for practitioners. What do you believe was the author's reason for including each of the eleven items? Are there items that you would like to drop from the list? What items would you add?

Ethical Fitness and Readiness for Counselors

1. I understand the need for ethical codes and guidelines.

2. I have read the ethical codes and guidelines of my profession.

3. I have read the state-revised code as it applies to my profession.

4. I keep relevant copies of the ethical and legal codes and practice guidelines of my profession handy in case I need to refer to them in a hurry.

5. I have a trusted colleague or peer who I can consult with when needed regarding ethical issues.

6. I engage in self-care and assess my professional fitness so that I am able to make quality ethical decisions or get help if impaired.

7. I can recognize at least one ethical issue per day on the job.

8. I have a limited scope of practice and follow the guidelines of my profession.

9. I belong to my professional organization(s) and its listservs, and I keep my license/certificate up-to-date with the appropriate CEUs.

10. I have a high tolerance for ambiguity and appreciate the complexity of ethical dilemmas.

11. I know how to use and apply at least one ethical decision-making model.

ADDITIONAL RESOURCES

Feminist Theory Code of Ethics: http://www.chrysaliscounseling.org/Feminist_Therapy.html
American Counseling Association: http://www.counseling.org
American Psychological Association: http://www.apa.org/ethics/code/index.aspx
American School Counselor Organization: http://schoolcounselor.org
National Association of Social Workers: http://www.socialworkers.org/pubs/code/code.asp
National Board for Certified Counselors: http://www.nbcc.org
US DHHS Office of Civil Rights Information on HIPAA: http://hhs.iv/ocr/hipaa/

REFERENCES

American Counseling Association (ACA). (2005). *ACA code of ethics*. Alexandria, VA: Author.

Brown, K. M., Byrnes, E., & Fleenor, K. G. (2012). Maintaining the counselor-client relationship: Ethical decision-making in online counseling and social networking. *VISTAS Online, Article 90*. Retrieved from http://www.counseling.org/resources/library/vistas_2012_article_90pdf

Campbell, C. D., & Gordon, M. C. (2003). Acknowledging the inevitable: Understanding multiple relationships in rural communities. *Professional Practice and Research in Psychology, 34*(4), 430–434.

Corey, G., Corey, M., & Callanan, P. (2011). *Issues and ethics in the helping professions* (8th ed.). Pacific Grove, CA: Brooks/Cole.

Cottone, R. R., & Claus, R. E. (2000). Ethical decision-making models: A review of the literature. *Journal of Counseling & Development, 78*, 275–282.

Cottone, R. R., & Tarvydas, V. M. (2003). *Ethical and professional issues in counseling.* Upper Saddle River, NJ: Merrill Prentice-Hall.

Davis, A. H. (1997). The ethics of caring: A collaborative approach to resolving ethical dilemmas. *Journal of Applied Rehabilitation Counseling, 28,* 36–41.

Davis, T., & Ritchie, M. (1993). Confidentiality and the school counselor. A challenge for the 1990s. *The School Counselor, 41,* 23–30.

Erford, B. T. (2010). *Orientation to the counseling profession: Advocacy, ethics, and essential professional foundations.* Upper Saddle River, NJ: Merrill.

Evans, K. M., Kincade, E. A., & Seem, S.R. (2011). *Introduction to feminist therapy: Strategies for social and individual change.* Thousand Oaks, CA: Sage.

Fischer, L., & Sorenson, G. P. (1996). School law for counselors, psychologists, and social workers (3rd ed.). White Plains, NY: Longman.

Forester-Miller, H., & Davis T. (1996). *A practitioner's guide to ethical decision making.* American Counseling Association. Retrieved from http://www.counseling.org

Garcia, J. G., Cartwright, B., Winston, S. M., & Borzuchowska, B. (2004). A transcultural integrative model for ethical decision making in counseling. *Journal of Counseling & Development, 81,* 268–277.

Handelsman, M. M., Gottlieb, M. C., & Knapp, S. (2005). Training ethical psychologists: An acculturation model. *Professional Psychology: Research and Practice, 36,* 59–65.

Herlihy, B., & Corey, G. (1996). *An ethical standards casebook* (5th ed.). Alexandria, VA: American Counseling Association.

Herlihy, B., & Sheeley, V. L. (1988). Counselor liability and the duty to warn: Selected cases, statutory trends, and implications for practice. *Counselor Education and Supervision, 27,* 203–215.

Hill, M., Glaser, K., & Harden, J. (1998). A feminist model for ethical decision making. *Women & Therapy, 21,* 101–121.

Jordan, A. E., & Meara, N. M. (1990). Ethics and the professional practice of psychologists: The role of virtues and principles. *Professional Psychology: Research and Practice, 21,* 107–114.

King, J. H. (2012). *How ethical codes define counselor professional identity.* Doctoral dissertation, Capella University. ProQuest Dissertations & Theses Database, 3505737.

Kitchener, K. S. (1984). Intuition, critical evaluation and ethical principles: The foundation for ethical decisions in counseling psychology. *The Counseling Psychologist, 12,* 43–55.

Levy, C. (1992). The context of social work ethics. *Social Work, 17*(2), 95–107.

Mappes, D. C., Robb, G. P., & Engles, D. W. (1985). Conflicts between law and ethics in counseling & psychotherapy. *Journal of Counseling & Development, 64*(4), 246–252.

Remley, T. P., & Herlihy, B. (2007). *Ethical, legal and professional issues in counseling* (2nd ed.). Upper Saddle River, NJ: Pearson Merrill/Prentice-Hall.

Urofsky, R. I, Engels, D. W, & Engebretson, K. (2008). Kitchener's principle ethics: Implications for counseling practice and research. *Counseling & Values, 53,* 67–78.

Vacc, N. A., & Loesch, L. (1987). *Counseling as a profession.* Muncie, IN: Accelerated Development.

Van Hoose, W. H., & Kottler, J. A. (1985). *Ethical and legal issues in counseling and psychotherapy* (2nd ed.). San Francisco, CA: Jossey-Bass.

Welfel, E. R. (2012). *Ethics in counseling and psychotherapy: Standards, research, and emerging issues* (5th ed.). Pacific Grove, CA: Brooks/Cole Cengage.

Chapter 9

Wellness and Self-Care for Professional Counselors

A. Stephen Lenz
Varunee Faii Sangganjanavanich

Personal wellness and professional performance are closely related in the field of counseling. Often, individuals may have only a vague or underdeveloped concept about what personal wellness is, how it is promoted, and what constitutes individuals' well-being. As a consequence, many helping professionals, including counselors, do not discover the powerful and positive influences of routine wellness education, self-monitoring, planning, and evaluation. You may have heard a story about incompetent counselors or counselors who are burned out due to inadequate self-care. These counselors may also fail to understand how these practices affect their professional and personal quality of life until they experience events that illustrate the potential emotional, spiritual, and psychological vulnerabilities of working with clients. Rollo May (1953), a prominent existential theorist, stated, "Those who are concerned with making the world more healthy had best start with themselves. . . . The center of strength that we find in ourselves is in the long run the best contribution we can make to our fellow men" (pp. 68–69). Subsequent literature in counselor burnout addresses the importance of counselor self-care and wellness. Wellness and holistic developmental practices have gained momentum and prominence in the counseling profession.

In this chapter, we provide an overview of wellness in relation to counseling practice with special emphases on prevention, recognizing the signs of burn-out, compassion fatigue, and vicarious trauma as well as a number of self-care approaches that are helpful for professional counselors. You will have an opportunity to use the activities and resources provided in this chapter to facilitate your learning and implementation of the wellness concepts in the counseling profession.

LEARNING OBJECTIVES

After completing the reading and reflection activities provided in this chapter, you will be able to

1. Describe the importance of wellness concepts significant to counseling students and professionals;

2. Identify the differences among burnout, compassion fatigue, and vicarious trauma; and

3. Describe strategies that counseling students and professionals can use for self-care and burnout prevention.

WELLNESS OF COUNSELORS: AN IMPORTANT CONCEPT IN THE 21ST CENTURY

The pursuit of wellness and optimum functioning is not a new endeavor within our profession. Accounts of wellness and holistic development that have influenced counseling practices are noted in Greek mythology, the writings of Aristotle, Eastern medicine traditions, and contemporary public policy. Evidence of a culture that is actively monitoring and promoting awareness about the activities associated with longevity and happiness is evident in print and television media as well as in advertising practices. In the current society, individuals have more access to information, curricula, and research outcomes that provide a road map for pursuing positive, growth-oriented lifestyle choices than previous generations had. What has been revealed to individuals is paradoxically intricate, yet easy to implement, and has substantial implications for the counseling profession and professional counselors.

Definitions

You may find that early definitions of wellness were rooted in the absence of disease; however, more modern conceptualizations regarding optimal functioning have moved toward examining the combination of myriad domains that promote personal functioning (Granello, 2012; Myers & Sweeney, 2005a). The National

Wellness Institute (n.d.) has defined wellness as a conscious, self-directed process leading toward fulfilling one's unique potential that is holistic and multidimensional. This definition exemplifies the subjective and self-directed nature of personal wellness; however, the World Health Organization has provided a more descriptive definition that includes specific details:

> Wellness is the optimal state of health of individuals and groups. There are two focal concerns: the realization of the fullest potential of an individual physically, psychologically, socially, spiritually, and economically, and the fulfillment of one's role expectations in the family, community, place of worship, workplace and other settings (Smith, Tang, & Nutbeam, 2006, p. 344).

Concerning the counseling profession, Myers, Sweeney, and Witmer (2000) defined wellness as the activities and attitudes reflected in all individuals' propensity toward living a full and robust experience that integrates mind, body, and spirit in a manner that promotes harmony within the human and natural communities. This is representative of 20th-century views by individuals such as Dunn (1957), who was critical of health care professionals' predisposition to parcel out the biological, spiritual, and sociopsychological aspects of the individual and treat each aspect as if they were not interrelated. Later, Hettler (1984) proposed an expanded model of personal wellness that encompassed six aspects of the self that were integrated and complementary in persons demonstrating high levels of wellness and thriving: occupational, emotional, social, intellectual, physical, and spiritual. Similar to Dunn, Hettler suggested that the physical individuals that helping professionals see is the manifestation of their status within these six dimensions of functioning.

In the 21st century, the investigation of how personal wellness influences the counseling profession has become less anecdotally based on practice and increasingly supported by empirical evidence. For example, Jane Myers and colleagues (e.g., Lawson & Myers, 2011; Myers, Luecht, & Sweeney, 2004; Myers, Mobley, & Booth, 2003; Myers & Sweeney, 2005a; Spurgeon & Myers, 2004) have continued to develop support for the indivisible self model of wellness (Myers & Sweeney, 2005b), which has emerged as the result of statistical analyses to organize the actions and attitudes that contribute to a positive lifestyle in a meaningful way. The product of these analyses revealed that an individual's total wellness is contingent upon the level of functioning within five distinctive second-order aspects of oneself, each with a unique contribution to personal well-being.

The indivisible self model of wellness comprises five domains, including the coping self, creative self, essential self, physical self, and social self. First, the coping self is represented by elements that help us adjust to and transcend life circumstances through realistic beliefs, stress management, self-worth, and leisure.

Second, the creative self is composed of the qualities that make each of us unique in our interpretations of and interactions with the environment; these include thinking, emotions, control, work, and positive humor. Third, the essential self is made up of those elements that help us make meaning of the world and include spirituality, gender identity, cultural identity, and self-care. Fourth, the physical self is represented by the biological and physiological components that contribute to development and functioning, including exercise and nutrition. Finally, the social self is composed of those meaningful associations with others that provide us support and give us meaning; these include love and friendship. All of these personal factors are influenced by the local, institutional, and global systems within which we live throughout the lifespan (Myers & Sweeney, 2005a, 2005b).

Conceptualizations of wellness range from simple to complex with three underlying characteristics: holism, synergy, and balance. Holism is the notion that each of us represents the totality of all our component features and that any separation is artificial (May, 1953; Myers & Sweeney, 2005a). Adopting the concept of holism, counselors are not just mental health professionals when they are meeting with their clients; what they bring into the session with them is the total sum of their character, including their cultural identity, affective orientation, creative interests, and family history. Likewise, you as a professional counselor must learn to not view the client as someone experiencing the symptoms of a mental illness; instead you must view the entire constellation of the presenting issue. The concept of synergy assumes that each of our component parts interacts with the others to have an effect on our lives that is greater than the sum of each alone. Based on this supposition, proponents of wellness-oriented counseling suggest that a change in one area of the individual's life influences the overall well-being. For instance, some graduate students report that as they put more energy into their schoolwork and professional development, other aspects of their lives, such as coping with stress or leisure time, are neglected. It is worth pointing out that finding this balance can be particularly challenging when demands are mounting. Therefore, it is important you, as a counseling student and future professional counselor, discover the balance between professional activities and personal maintenance that promotes a healthy, high functioning lifestyle. In addition, you must develop a personal definition of wellness to guide you in finding this balance.

The complexity of one's unique definition of personal wellness is not nearly as important as whether it is meaningful, represents personal values, and contributes to longevity and healthy well-being. For example, for one individual it may be sufficient to conceptualize personal wellness as being a balance of mind, body, and spirit; for another, it may be imperative to focus on the many subcategories. In either case, what is important is that your personal definition of wellness resonates with you and serves as a meaningful basis for self-understanding, growth, and maintenance. Furthermore, having an established perspective about what constitutes high functioning will be an asset in identifying where you are along the wellness–impairment continuum throughout your career. We have identified some commonly accepted theories of what wellness is, but you are certainly encouraged to view these models as a consumer and decide what is relevant to you and your values. What is certain is that adopting a wellness-oriented perspective about human development will be a great asset to you throughout your professional career, and the cost of not doing so may have some negative implications for your work with clients. In the next section, you will learn how counselors' personal wellness influences their work with clients.

Link Between Counselor Wellness and Work With Clients

Caring for the mental health needs of others can be a physically, psychologically, and emotionally exhausting endeavor. In particular, it can be more draining when paired with high demands for productivity, challenging client populations, restrictions from funding sources, mandates for short-term interventions, and/or personal life stressors. Despite efforts to educate and monitor counseling students and professionals about the risks associated with mismanagement of personal wellness, there is considerable evidence indicating that the majority of mental health professionals will be challenged at some point in their professional careers to maintain and promote their optimal level of functioning (Clark, Murdock, & Koetting, 2009; Lawson, 2007; Lawson & Myers, 2011; Lee, Cho, Kissinger, & Ogle; 2010; Osborn, 2004; Smith, Robinson, & Young, 2007).

All individuals have a certain amount of stamina and resources for enduring and adapting to challenges; however, when this personal threshold for being empathic,

---

Exercise 9.1

DEVELOPING A PERSONAL DEFINITION OF WELLNESS

Directions: Reflect on the theories of wellness that were discussed in this chapter. Write down a personal definition of wellness that identifies what activities and attitudes are present in a person demonstrating a high level of wellness. Is your definition similar to those that were illustrated? Is your definition simple or complex? Ask someone you are close to what her definition of wellness is, and compare and contrast your perspectives.

compassionate, and satisfied in our work is surpassed, our effectiveness as professionals and our personal wellness may be compromised. There is a consensus that counselors with higher levels of wellness are more helpful to their clients than those experiencing marked distress and impairment (Lawson & Myers, 2011; Lawson, Venart, Hazler, & Kottler, 2007; Meyer & Ponton, 2006). Fortunately, counselors can regain their professional vitality and their ability to be effective healers through concerted efforts as well as available supports and resources. The road to preventing burnout, compassion fatigue, and vicarious trauma begins with recognition of the symptoms associated with these phenomena and is followed by a conscious decision to take action—developing and maintaining personal wellness.

HOW DO YOU KNOW IF YOU ARE EXPERIENCING BURNOUT?

Self-reflection and self-monitoring are two of the most significant aspects of becoming a professional counselor. You as a professional counselor are required not only to monitor your personal well-being and professional performance but also to provide quality service to clients. To do so, it is important for you, who are entering the counseling profession, to recognize signs and symptoms of burnout and related syndromes that emerge from your function as a professional counselor.

Definitions

Occupational burnout represents a marked depletion of physical, emotional, cognitive, and spiritual resources that can have longstanding deleterious effects on one's quality of life across several domains (Shapiro, Brown, & Biegel, 2007). One commonly accepted definition of burnout among helping professionals describes a condition characterized by emotional exhaustion, depersonalization, and a diminished sense of personal accomplishment (Maslach, 1982, 2003; Maslach & Leiter, 2008). Maslach and Leiter (2008) noted that emotional exhaustion occurs as individuals become less energetic about the activities that once provided a source of enthusiasm and self-efficacy related to their professional activities. Depersonalization occurs as a response to emotional exhaustion, as individuals attempt to create emotional and psychological distance between themselves and aspects of their job associated with emotional strain. A diminished sense of personal accomplishment results as a function of the exhaustion and depersonalization and represents a state in which individuals begin to demonstrate deficits in their overall vocational effectiveness. In other words, burnout is the opposite of optimal functioning; it is at the opposite end of the professional wellness continuum. It is important to note that the presence of burnout symptoms does not automatically indicate a chronic condition; however, if counselors do not make an effort to assuage burnout symptoms, they may eventually find themselves far from a state of personal and professional well-being.

In general, any combination of variables related to the work environment, psychological factors, or lifestyle can contribute to the development of burnout. When individuals work in environments in which it is unclear how to succeed, success is perceived as nearly unattainable, fear of failure is constant and chronic, and they are more prone to negative reactions to their professional responsibilities. Furthermore, work environments in which the majority of a counselor's time is allocated to high-stress, high-demand activities, and in which there is little down time to process or recover, can also promote burnout, especially in the absence of sufficient accolades or acknowledgment for initiative, effort, and accomplishment. In addition to these characteristics of the work environment that contribute to burnout, individual personality dispositions may also contribute to exhaustion and chronic distress. For instance, individuals who are perfectionists, have a pessimistic take on their work with clients, or have a naturally high stress response may be more susceptible to experiencing burnout symptoms. Finally, individual choices in lifestyle, such as a lack of balance between work and restorative activities, minimal use of social supports and other resources, having few hobbies, sleeping too little, or not taking time off from responsibilities, can contribute to burnout. However, it is important to note that professional counselors can, at some point in their career, experience burnout simply due to the demands of the profession (e.g., caring for clients, high number of cases in caseload).

Exercise 9.2

PEOPLE WHO ARE EXPERIENCING BURNOUT

Directions: Think about people around you or recall the stories you have heard about people who become burned out. Then, answer these following questions:

1. How do you describe their personal (e.g., family relationship, friendship) and professional (e.g., job performance, career satisfaction) characteristics?

2. What do you observe or hear about their mental health (e.g., depression, anxiety, substance use)?

3. What could have prevented them from becoming burned out?

Next, take some time to chat with your classmates or study partners to exchange stories and answers.

Impacts of Burnout

When a sufficient number of these conditions are present, the compounding effects can result in some harmful outcomes for you as a counselor and for your clients. For professional counselors, the physical reactions to burnout are closely associated with those reported by individuals experiencing prolonged stress exposure, including increased risk for somatic complaints such as a depleted immune system, gastrointestinal problems, headaches, fatigue, and physical discomfort (Appels, Falger, & Schouten, 1993; Lee et al., 2010; Melamed, Shirom, Toker, Berliner, & Shapira, 2006). Emotionally, as burnout becomes pronounced, counselors can become apathetic, anxious, depressed, and resistant to client needs for empathy, and they can experience decreased self-esteem (Lee et al., 2010; Osborn, 2004). When these physical and emotional reactions reach a critical level, counselors may report distinct changes in their effectiveness when working with clients, confidence that they chose the right profession, and satisfaction with peer relationships in the workplace. Consequently, counselors experiencing burnout are more likely to underserve clients, provide services that are ineffective, leave their jobs or the profession, and suffer losses of personal satisfaction.

Although burnout is detrimental to the professional development of counselors and the welfare of the clients, in most cases, early burnout symptoms and signs can be detected by counselors themselves or by colleagues surrounding them. Moreover, counselors who experience burnout can take action to promote positive growth. Critical to early detection and remediation of symptoms that contribute to burnout is the understanding of how vicarious trauma and compassion fatigue contribute to the development of this syndrome.

Differences Among Vicarious Trauma, Compassion Fatigue, and Burnout

The counselor–client relationship is inherently characterized by mutuality and shared experience. When clients experience an empowering breakthrough, they begin to live more authentic lifestyles and adapt to changes in a positive way. In many cases, these are the successes that remind professional counselors why they have chosen the profession so closely associated with the core of the human condition. However, when these breakthroughs do not occur, not only may clients experience frustration with counseling, but counselors also may experience feelings of hopelessness and worthlessness as a result of not being able to help clients. It is possible that in the event of nonproductive or discouraging treatment outcomes that counselors begin to experience compassion fatigue, vicarious trauma, or burnout; we conceptualize these phenomena as representing a hierarchy of impairment leading away from counselor wellness, optimal functioning, and the conditions necessary to live a satisfactory lifestyle.

Compassion fatigue can be conceptualized as the adverse emotional, spiritual, cognitive, and physical reactions associated with providing care to clients that are not transient, supersede our interpersonal stamina, and are associated with undesired changes in functioning (Figley, 2002a, 2002b). As exposure to stressors and traumas mount, counselors developing compassion fatigue may demonstrate a lessening of empathic ability, concern for client issues, therapeutic attachment, sense of satisfaction, and personal responsibility for ethical practices. A distinguishing characteristic between compassion fatigue and burnout is that counselors experiencing compassion fatigue are not as distressed and are still able to rebound from their difficulties using available resources and supports (Figley, 2002, 2002b). Typically, when counselors are relentlessly exposed to significantly affecting material in the absence of sufficient restorative activities and supports, they may begin to develop compassion fatigue over time.

Vicarious traumas are transient stressors that we are able to mitigate through our usual restorative coping and processing practices. Kadambi and Truscott (2004) described vicarious trauma as "changes in how therapists think, feel, and behave in relation to others and themselves as a result of their exposure to and empathic bonding with their clients' traumatic material" (p. 261). In this manner, counselors are vulnerable to negative effects of working with clients who have backgrounds associated with traumatic experiences such as abuse, violence, neglect, war, or bearing witness to assault or death. While counselors provide support and guidance to clients along their road to recovery, they are inadvertently exposed to emotional bumps and bruises. The effects of these encounters may be minimal and leave counselors feeling "off" after session or on the way home; in more noteworthy cases, counselors may experience subjective discomfort, night terrors, or re-experiencing the clients telling of the trauma and the emotional reactions they felt.

In the absence of a proactive approach to developing and maintaining their personal wellness through self-care activities, counselors are at risk for vicarious traumas that may develop into compassion fatigue and ultimately a state of burnout. Although precipitating factors can be disrupting and challenge the popular public persona that counselors are always well-adjusted and living a full and rich life that is impervious to emotional exhaustion, awareness of these symptoms and their negative effects can be transformative. By making an individual commitment to monitoring and maintaining personal wellness throughout training and supervision, professional counselors can facilitate resiliency from within themselves and with others while providing services to clients. It is often said that wellness is a journey, not a destination; with

CASE ILLUSTRATION 9.1

MADDIE

Maddie is a licensed professional counselor (LPC) working for a community-based counseling agency treating adults that have been diagnosed with major depression, bipolar disorder, schizophrenia, and post-traumatic stress disorder (PTSD). Maddie supported herself during graduate school as a case manager at this agency and was fortunate to attain hours toward her licensure after graduation when she received a promotion to work in a unit where she conducted eligibility screenings and intake assessments. After graduation Maddie was thrilled to start making an impact on her local community by providing mental health counseling services; Maddie volunteered on work-service committees to facilitate community outreach initiatives, employee enrichment, and holiday celebrations.

Maddie loved her job doing screenings and intake. These activities helped her to develop her skills for interviewing, conducting nonstandardized and standardized assessments, differential diagnosis, and crisis intervention. Due to the nature of agency counseling, client volume is high and the associated demand for productivity and billing hours is too. As a consequence, Maddie often found herself staying late at the office or coming in early to complete documentation and committee work. During this time she heard recurrent client narratives and was able to develop the skill for identifying those who were eligible for services, but she was also exposed to individuals attempting to manipulate the health system to obtain welfare benefits.

During this experience, Maddie began to regard herself as someone who could see through a client's story and get to the bottom of what was really going on using clinical objectivity and distancing herself emotionally from the client's circumstances. During her first-year performance review, her boss commended her on this skill; however, in her personal life, friends had noticed a new cynicism about people's circumstances when they reached out to her for support, and her partner had mentioned that she was not as warm and compassionate as she once had been. When addressing this with her friends and partner, she cited that she had been "super busy at work," "distracted," and "tired from long weekends destressing" and that she had not been exercising the way she used to.

As an LPC, Maddie maintains a manageable caseload of 30 clients to whom she provides services two or three times a month based on their level of functioning and the severity of their problems. She describes her work as meaningful, but she cites that her clinical perspective has grown keener and is helpful to protect her from the affective experiences associated with the graphic descriptions of abuse, manipulation, and difficulty coping presented by many of her clients with PTSD. Maddie finds herself begrudging appointments with clients that require her to help them manage panic attacks, especially the parts where triggers to traumatic events are described. She particularly feels an overidentification with her clients who are women and who are similar to her in age. When leaving these sessions, she often feels keyed up and replays the stories her clients tell her; she has even began displacing anger toward her clients' perpetrators onto her partner, who is becoming increasing dissatisfied with the quality of their relationship. She does not discuss these reactions in her weekly supervision.

Maddie frequently asks colleagues to cover for her with these "lovely, but troubled" clients, and if she cannot get someone to help her, she has begun not showing up for appointments, and in some cases she has even submitted progress notes indicating that a client was not home when, in fact, she had simply skipped the appointment. The stress of this unethical client abandonment and not meeting her minimum billing requirements is mounting; Maddie is increasingly irritable, has difficulty sleeping, has gained a noticeable amount of weight, has started smoking again, and has started questioning whether she made the right choice getting into the counseling profession.

In her most recent performance review, she received several average and low scores, which her boss described as uncharacteristic. Her boss mentioned that several coworkers have expressed concern about her irritability around the office and wants to know what is going on with her once-star employee.

this assumption in mind, you can begin your professional journey through active approaches to self-awareness—an examination and a reflection of your own approach to wellness (Lenz & Roscoe, 2011; Lenz, Sangganjanavanich, Balkin, Oliver, & Smith, 2012; Lenz & Smith, 2010).

Questions to Ask Yourself

These questions may help you begin or continue to raise self-awareness in relation to your vulnerabilities to vicarious trauma, compassion fatigue, and burnout:

1. Do I place my own sense of well-being at the forefront among my many academic or professional responsibilities?

2. Is my lifestyle one that values restorative practices, including getting enough sleep, eating well, engaging in meaningful social activities, and pursuing hobbies?

3. Do I have a support system in place (e.g., peers, supervisors, friends, family) that actively acknowledges and appreciates my achievements and efforts?

4. Would someone close to me describe me as a person who is committed to self care?

5. Do I have a formal wellness plan that I routinely reference and modify?

If the answers to a majority of these questions are no, learning about and becoming involved in practices that prevent and overcome burnout and related syndromes among counselors may be beneficial.

You, by now, may recognize that for a counseling student and emerging professional counselor, the complexities of professional development can be both exhilarating and overwhelming. Often, the decision to become a helping professional will surely be characterized by moments of actualization in which you perceive that you fit with the community of learners in your courses and those in the clinics, schools, and agencies that you will occupy. We caution you that, generally speaking, graduate students across many fields of study are often individuals striving for high levels of academic and professional achievement. During your quest for personal and professional development, you may find yourself neglecting to treat yourself kindly spiritually, emotionally, and physically. There are plenty of opportunities to dedicate yourself to school and work and neglect the other domains of your life that promote balance, vitality, and wholeness. To some extent, this is a natural reaction; however, we submit to you that the consequences can be dire. In the next section we will introduce you to some fundamental concepts related to counselor burnout and some strategies that others have found helpful to prevent or overcome this condition.

Exercise 9.3

ASSESSING YOUR CURRENT LEVEL OF LIFE STRESS

Directions: Use the Internet to navigate to www.compassionfatigue.org/pages/selftest .html and complete the Life Stress Self-Test. When you have totaled your score, use the interpretation rubric to identify your present susceptibility to stress-related illness.

PREVENTING AND OVERCOMING BURNOUT

All helping professionals are vulnerable to the experiences of vicarious trauma, compassion fatigue, and burnout by virtue of repeated exposure to the vulnerabilities and distress associated with the human condition that clients bring into sessions. Conversely, you as a professional counselor have the education, disposition, and skills to prevent or remediate the onset of burnout. With these assumptions noted, each helping professional and counselor education program has a stake in the identification of risk factors and the development of proactive wellness interventions and routine monitoring to promote optimal functioning. There has been some emerging evidence that wellness interventions are effective mediators of stress-related factors during counseling training, practice, and supervision (Lenz at al., 2012; Schure, J. Christopher, & S. Christopher, 2008; Shapiro et al., 2007).

Burnout Prevention

Burnout prevention starts with knowledge about the characteristics of optimal functioning, self-awareness, and action. Earlier in this chapter we noted that the concepts of holism, synergy, and balance are consistent across theories of wellness. It is imperative that, as a professional counselor, you find a balance among the many demands of your schedule and implement activities that promote your personal well-being. On a physical level, this may include routine moderate exercise, getting sufficient sleep, eating nutritious meals, and recognizing the signals that your body sends you to let you know that you are becoming tired or even exhausted. Without sufficient rest and nourishment, individuals are more prone to develop fatigue in the workplace and at home. Cognitively, it is important to have realistic beliefs about what you can accomplish given the resources available, and to develop boundaries that allow you to mentally separate from work. With realistic goals about work priorities and effective time management skills, you will be more able to pursue interests in other areas of life that promote happiness and resiliency to stress. Monitoring your emotions and being aware of your experiences, including those that do not seem apparent, is also a useful prevention activity. As a professional counselor, you are regularly called to be involved in the affective experiences of others; however, it is important to ensure that you are capable of living within the entire spectrum of emotionality when relating to your life.

Managing Burnout

Whereas preventing burnout often entails maintaining a sense of balance while responding to the challenges of being a counseling professional, managing burnout requires regaining a sense of stability. There are many resources available for professional counselors to regain control of their lives; successful approaches to burnout management are usually intentional approaches that involve making gradual but lasting changes over time. Scholars in the field of counselor education (e.g., Lenz & Smith, 2010; Lenz et al., 2012; Myers et al., 2000) have demonstrated how the four step process of education, assessment, planning, and evaluation can be helpful for restoring a sense of balance and heartiness with counseling professionals. Developing an understanding of causes, symptoms, and helpful strategies through self-guided education is a great place to start to manage symptoms when experiencing burnout. Although this chapter provides some introductory information, there are several web-based and academic resources that can promote understanding and normalize this reaction.

Next, we recommend completing an informal self-assessment or receiving a formal evaluation from a medical or mental health professional. These holistic appraisals can be helpful in identifying the onset, duration, severity, and biopsychosocial effects of the presenting circumstances; such appraisals generally provide both qualitative and quantitative information that is easy to understand and nonthreatening. With a developed understanding of burnout and the results of a comprehensive assessment, counselors can put together a formal developmental plan to promote change. Developmental plans should include specific information, such as the domains in which you need to change, your current level of satisfaction, how changes in each domain may positively affect your level of functioning, behavioral descriptions of the strategies that you will engage in, and a description of how you will know when progress has been made (see Figure 9.1). Finally, routine evaluation of developmental plans can be a helpful way to determine whether goals are practical and to track progress through burnout into restoration and renewed levels of functioning. By reviewing goals and progress regularly (e.g., weekly, biweekly, monthly), counselors experiencing burnout have an opportunity to revise their goals, acknowledge personal gains, and celebrate their successes.

Many resources are available to help you recognize and remediate the causes and symptoms associated with vicarious trauma, compassion fatigue, and burnout; however, some of the most accessible resources are those already in place, but you may need to use them in new ways. Counselors often have a great awareness of the resources available in their community but can neglect acknowledging those in a more immediate proximity. Counselors in many settings have several social supports, including peers, mentors, and supervisors in the workplace, who may be willing to partner in their growth experience. Outside of the workplace, most individuals have friends or family members who are willing to provide some degree of supportive assistance. Finally, many companies such as schools, mental health agencies, and hospitals provide employee assistance programs that cover the cost of short-term support from professionals, including counselors, accountants, and legal advisors. When working with people in the process of transcending the effects of burnout, authentic engagement in such a relationship is necessary to promote long-term growth.

JAIME

Jaime is a Mexican American counseling student working full time as a rehabilitative case manager for a local community mental health agency. Since he came of working age, Jaime has always been gainfully employed, but after spending two years as a case manager, he became motivated to develop his helping skill set, challenge himself to grow personally, and increase his eligibility for promotion by enrolling in graduate studies at a local university. Jaime's father was a manual laborer most of his life and supported his mother while she completed law school and became licensed to practice. Jaime is the father of a young son, Esteban, for whom he and the mother share joint custody. Despite encouragement from his family about hard work and completing graduate school, the family was conflicted about providing care for Esteban while Jaime worked full time during the days and completed courses in the evenings. The family made a number of accommodations and commitments to assure that Esteban and Jamie would both be successful at meeting academic and developmental milestones during this time.

Jaime was a standout student from the start of his graduate coursework. He was prepared for and active in his courses, became involved in Chi Sigma Iota early on, and even got one of his term papers printed in the state counseling association newsletter. In the workplace Jaime was able to apply the knowledge he was acquiring in his coursework and make a marked difference in the lives of his clients in ways that were mutually validating. During this preparation, Jaime was able to maintain several friendships and stay in touch with his family, although much familial support was directed to the care of his son.

As Jaime transitioned from coursework to his applied practicum and internships, the stress of taking on another work-related responsibility requiring 10 to 30 hours a week proved to be taxing on his overall well-being. As the demands of school and work became greater and greater, Jaime slept less and less and began eating lots of fast food, drinking coffee and energy drinks regularly, and experiencing considerable amounts of subjective anxiety. The situation was further complicated by a waning support base. After two years of late-night babysitting, pick-ups from school, and last-minute cancellations, his backing from family and friends was beginning to wear thin. Most challenging for Jaime was confronting the fact that he was very tired after a day at work and internship and found it difficult to maintain focus when helping Esteban with homework or reading to him.

When his site supervisor noted a difference in energy and mood, Jaime commented that "I am beginning to feel out of touch with those around me, and sometimes I just miss having nothing to do. Even when I have days off or am spending time with my son, I am not in the moment, not really there I guess. Something is missing, or exhausted, or blurred." When questioned by his supervisor about how this was affecting his work at the clinic, Jaime remarked, "Sometimes I really resent coming in. When I get here and am working with the clients, it's fantastic and I am motivated, but even in session I find my mind wandering or that I am just spacing out, because the client's dialogue has cued me to consider some of my own limitations. What's worse is I just don't feel well. But I have to finish strong, I have to make my hours, and I just keep telling myself it's only another semester and a half."

Jaime and his site supervisor developed an individual wellness plan for him to take action toward regaining his subjective sense of well-being. Jaime was educated about theories of personal wellness and the relationship between graduate students and wellness, he completed and interpreted a wellness inventory, and he developed a written plan to be reviewed each week during the check-in portion of supervision. Jaime's personal wellness plan (see Figure 9.1) addressed the domain of self-care and included several attainable goals developed by him with the support of his supervisor.

Integration of Wellness Concepts

Both preventing and managing burnout are enhanced by understanding the interconnected and synergistic nature of wellness in daily attitudes and activities. Furthermore, when you begin to view your own experience holistically, this will also extend to your work with clients. It is often the case that when wellness and self-care become integral parts of personal and professional activities, longevity and happiness follow.

Integration of wellness concepts into your professional and personal life can occur in many forms. Some may choose to focus on physical wellness (e.g., exercise, nutrition) at first, while others may focus on psychological aspects of wellness (e.g., social support, stress reduction). It is important to note that a path to wellness is individualized, and each person is responsible for her own wellness plan in approaching and developing self-care strategies. In the next section, you will learn basic self-care strategies for counselors that can be utilized both during your program of study as a counseling student or counselor in training and when you become a professional counselor.

SELF-CARE STRATEGIES FOR COUNSELORS IN TRAINING

The regular practice of total self-care can promote positive adjustment to the stresses associated with life. Frequent comments made by counselors and counselors in training include, "I don't have time to take care of myself," "I am too tired to get to be active / cook healthy meals / have hobbies / meet with friends," or "I have so much work to do that I cannot take any time to myself to do the things that I enjoy." Sound familiar? If so, this is normal. These comments are misconceptions; that is, it is a misconception that taking care of oneself requires a lot of time and energy and takes away from one's professional performance. In fact, an unbalanced lifestyle is the cornerstone of and represents the path to burnout, illness, and even disease. Fortunately, individuals can make choices for themselves to determine who they want to be and how they want to live their lives.

Taking action to reclaim happiness, energy, and one's fullest sense of identity begins with a choice to engage in regular and meaningful self-care practices. As we have mentioned, when counselors and counseling students adopt an active approach to self-care, they are more likely to report attitudes about themselves and their work with clients that reflects positive adjustment and coping with work-related demands (Lawson, 2007; Lawson & Myers, 2011; Schure et al., 2008; Shapiro et al., 2007). For helping professionals at risk of burnout, we recommend easing into self-care practices and approaching self-care as a journey toward well-being rather than a destination.

Additionally, counselors need to be realistic regarding their expectations and consistent in their commitment. Too often, high-achieving individuals (such as those who enroll in graduate coursework) set standards for change and success that may be difficult to execute and/or accomplish. After resolving to take action, we recommend that you ask yourself the following questions: What is realistically doable given my schedule, obligations, and available resources? How can I promote accountability and consistency with my commitment? and What are some ways that I can reward myself for following through? Once you have honestly answered these questions, you may be prepared with some of the information that you need to put together a manageable formal wellness plan or even begin establishing informal goals for yourself.

Exercise 9.4

EXPLORING YOUR PERSONAL WELLNESS

Directions: Using the Internet, navigate to www.hettler.com and explore the information provided about Hettler's (1984) six domains of occupational, social, intellectual, spiritual, physical, and emotional wellness. Next, complete the LiveWell Wellness Appraisal located toward the bottom of the site's homepage, and review your results. Finally, use this information and your knowledge of self-care practices to develop your own developmental wellness plan using Figure 9.1 as a guide.

(Continued)

(Continued)

Figure 9.1 Example of a Wellness Plan for Managing Burnout

1.) Domain: *Self-Care:* Taking care of myself self through preventative behaviors and getting adequate rest.
2.) Satisfaction with: Self-care

1	2	3	X	5	6	7	8	9	10

3.) Change in this domain may affect self and work with my clients in the following ways:

(a.) Greater sense of relief when considering how I manage stress from school and work

(b.) Increased awareness of the areas of my life that are stressful

(c.) Increased awareness of activities that do and do not work for moderating my mood and energy level

(d.) Greater ability to connect with my clients

4.) Intervention:
Objective: *Increase amount of self-care activities that I do every week.*
Strategies:

(a.) Take two 10-minute breaks at work: one where I take a brief walk, one where I complete a brief breathing exercise

(b.) Do no homework on Saturdays! Instead, spend the day with Esteban

(c.) Journal every day before going to bed about what my emotional experience was throughout the day and how I hope that this will inform my approach to living a full life tomorrow

(d.) Pack my lunch every day to assure that I am eating nutritious meals in the middle of the day

(e.) Call people I care for on the way to work to say hello and let them know they are appreciated.

5.) I will know when I have made some progress when:

(a.) My rating has increased on satisfaction scale from a 4 to at least a 6.

(b.) I have completed at least three of my strategy tasks regularly for two weeks.

(c.) I perceive a greater sense of well-being.

(d.) I can describe two ways that these new activities have been helpful.

We have provided below a number of activities associated with the six domains of wellness that we believe are specific to counselors. Remember that because individuals are finite energy systems, changes in one domain of our lives will affect the overall self. Therefore, by regularly making a few of these activities a part of your self-care regimen, your overall level of wellness will be promoted.

Career Aspects

- Leave work at work. Happiness is about embracing a full range of experiences across domains of wellness; sure, work pays the rent, but you are entitled to visit with family, laugh with friends, and have down time.
- Keep your case load manageable.
- Staff cases routinely with peers and supervisors. Regular collaboration can increase the support you receive from others in your workplace.

- Take regular breaks to clear your head, get your blood moving, or just to relax before moving on.

Social Aspects

- Accept invitations to get-togethers with friends and family that have potential to be rejuvenating and to help you recharge your sense of self.
- Engage in encouraging exchanges with people in your life.
- Take some time to know what you want from relationships, and pursue those qualities.
- Do new things with people who are important to you, and keep your relational connection in the forefront.
- Communicate your love. Letting loved ones know how you think and feel about them can create space for reciprocal communications.

Cognitive Aspects

- Read nonfiction or something you enjoy for leisure.
- Set realistic expectations for yourself. By being aware of your abilities and limitations, you can establish boundaries that promote a sense of self-efficacy.
- Break problems down into manageable pieces. When goals are clearly defined into short-, medium-, and long-term goals, the stress of having to complete abstract tasks is decreased.
- Do something that promotes cognitive flexibility, like painting, hobbies, or performing arts.
- Journal. Whether you have dreams, personal reflections, or contemplations about daily activities, journaling can help connect the meaning to events and activities in our lives.

Spiritual Aspects

- Become active within a spiritual community.
- Embrace mindfulness activities that focus your attention on the here and now of your life. These activities may include meditation, focused breathing, or progressive relaxation.
- Reflect on what is important in your life, and pay attention to the physical, cognitive, and affective associations.

Physical Aspects

- Eat regular, balanced meals. Consider food as the fuel that is taking you off-roading all day long—quality fuel will keep your engine running longer and more smoothly.

- Drink plenty of water. Although coffee, tea, and sodas have water in them, they are diuretics and promote dehydration over time.
- Get a healthy amount of activity most days of the week. All exercise programs should be within your physical limits, but regular exercise reduces stress and promotes optimal body functioning.
- Stretch and treat yourself to massages. Both of these activities promote circulation of the blood and restoration of muscle tissue.
- Get some sleep! The roles of student and professional can encourage us to have a lifestyle characterized by little sleep, but the body and mind need sleep to complete several critical activities.

Emotional Aspects

- Practice emotional awareness. We have a full range of emotions for a reason; it is just as important to be aware of feelings that we often experience as it is to be aware of those we rarely feel.
- See a counselor. Everyone could benefit from visiting with a counselor from time to time.
- Be authentic. Often counselors are expected to hide their emotions; when interacting with friends and family, use your feeling words and acknowledge your experience of being.
- Do things that positively impact others. Doing things characterized by social interest can be a great way to develop a positive sense of self-esteem.

Exercise 9.5

STRESS REDUCTION ACTIVITIES

Direction: You can assess your stress level by visiting www.harvestenterprises-sra .com/The%20Holmes-Rahe%20Scale.htm and completing an online version of the Holmes-Rahe Life Stress Inventory. Once you've completing the inventory, you will have an idea of the stress level (e.g., mild, moderate, severe) that you may be experiencing. It is common, however, that graduate students, like yourself, experience a higher level of stress during their program of study due to the demanding nature of graduate training. Particularly, counseling students experience emotional stress caused by being exposed to various clients' situations and conditions (e.g., child abuse, chronic mental illness), which at times can be emotionally challenging and consuming.

It is never too late to start managing your stress. If you find yourself becoming stressed, regardless of the reasons, you can engage in some of these stress reduction exercises to help you relieve some stress and to refresh your mind:

- Practicing deep breathing—taking long deep breaths and finding yourself relaxed
- Taking a time-out—stepping outside of a stressful environment in order to gather and process your thoughts, feelings, and actions
- Engaging in activities you enjoy—getting back to things that bring enjoyment and relaxation to your emotional and physical self (e.g., listening to music, watching movies, gardening, exercising)
- Showing yourself compassion—acknowledging your positive qualities, growth, and accomplishments

As noted by May (1953) one of the greatest contributions that counselors can make to their clientele is taking care of themselves to ensure that the individual who sits down with them is prepared to work collaboratively and is not in a state of burnout. As mentioned throughout this chapter, wellness is a journey, not a destination, so we encourage you not to be discouraged by any setbacks along the way, but instead to celebrate and acknowledge all of your successes, whether minor or substantial. Furthermore, because self-care activities are related to habitual patterns of behavior, if you commit to your personal wellness during your counseling program, you will be more likely to carry these health- and happiness-promoting activities into your professional career as a counselor.

KEYSTONES

Wellness is an integral part of the professional development of counselors. Wellness not only serves to prevent against burnout, compassion fatigue, and vicarious trauma but also allows professional counselors to engage in self-care strategies that help enhance their personal and professional development. In this chapter, the importance of wellness and self-care for counseling professionals was discussed. Key concepts noted in this chapter include the following:

- Counselors benefit from viewing self and others through a holistic lens that conceptualizes an individual as being at a dynamic position along the wellness–impairment continuum at any given point in time. Adopting a wellness initiative entails forming a personal definition of wellness and allowing that conceptualization to change as your knowledge about theories of wellness continues to grow.

- Through good times and bad, counselors are all sensitive to the affective, cognitive, and behavioral experiences of the clients they work with. If counselors do not monitor their experiences and are not proactive toward mediating vicarious traumas and compassion fatigue, they may experience the unpleasant effects of burnout syndrome.
- However, through regular education, assessment, planning, and evaluation of personal wellness, including self-care, counselors can promote happiness and longevity in their personal and professional endeavors.

ADDITIONAL RESOURCES

Books and Publications

American Counseling Association (ACA). (2005). *Code of ethics.* Alexandria, VA: Author.

Granello, P. F. (2012). *Wellness counseling.* Upper Saddle River, NJ: Merrill.

Lawson, G., & Venart, B. (2008). Preventing counselor impairment: Vulnerability, wellness, and resilience. *VISTAS 2008.* Retrieved from www.counseling.org/resources/library/vistas/vistas05/Vistas05.art53.pdf

Lenz, A. S., & Smith, R. L. (2010). Integrating wellness concepts within a clinical supervision model. *The Clinical Supervisor, 29,* 228–245. doi: 10.1080/07325223.2010.518511

Myers, J. E., & Sweeney, T. J. (2005). *Counseling for wellness: Theory, research, and practice.* Alexandria, VA: American Counseling Association.

Myers, J. E., & Sweeney, T. J. (2006). *The five factor wellness and habit change workbook.* Menlo Park, CA: Mindgarden.

Websites

Bill Hettler's homepage: www.hettler.com

Compassion Fatigue Awareness Project: www.compassionfatigue.org

Green Cross Academy of Traumatology: www.greencross.org

National Institutes of Health: www.nih.gov

REFERENCES

Appels, A., Falger, P. R. J., & Schouten, E. G. W. (1993). Vital exhaustion as risk indicator for myocardial infarction in women. *Journal of Psychosomatic Research, 37,* 881–890.

Clark, H. K., Murdock, N. L., & Koetting, K. (2009). Predicting burnout and career choice satisfaction in counseling psychology graduate students. *The Counseling Psychologist, 37,* 580–606. doi: 10.1177/001100008319985

Dunn, H. L. (1957). Points of attack for raising the levels of wellness. *Journal of the National Medical Association, 49,* 225–235.

Figley, C. R. (2002a). Compassion fatigue: Psychotherapists' chronic lack of self-care. *JCLP/In Session: Psychotherapy in Practice, 58,* 1433–1441. doi: 10.1002/jclp.10090

Figley, C. R. (2002b). *Treating compassion fatigue.* New York, NY: Routledge.

Granello, P. F. (2012). *Wellness counseling.* Upper Saddle River, NJ: Pearson.

Hettler, W. (1984). Wellness: Encouraging a lifetime pursuit of excellence. *Health Values: Achieving High Level Wellness, 8,* 13–17.

Kadambi, M. A., & Truscott, D. (2004). Vicarious trauma among therapists working with sexual violence, cancer, and general practice. *Canadian Journal of Counselling, 38,* 260–276.

Lawson, G. (2007). Counselor wellness and impairment: A national survey. *Journal of Humanistic Counseling, Education and Development, 46,* 20–34.

Lawson, G., & Myers, J. E. (2011). Wellness, professional quality of life, and career-sustaining behaviors: What keeps us well? *Journal of Counseling and Development, 89,* 163–171.

Lawson, G., Venart, E., Hazler, R., & Kottler, J. (2007). Toward a culture of counselor wellness. *Journal of Humanistic Counseling, Education, and Development, 46,* 5–19.

Lee, S. M., Cho, S. H., Kissinger, D., & Ogle, N. T. (2010). A typology of burnout. *Journal of Counseling and Development, 88,* 131–138.

Lenz, A. S., & Roscoe, L. (2011). Personal wellness card sort: A strategy for promoting relational healing. *Journal of Creativity in Mental Health, 6,* 69–83. doi: 10.1080/15401383.2011.562755

Lenz, A. S., Sangganjanavanich, V. F., Balkin, R., Oliver, M., & Smith, R. L. (2012). Wellness model of supervision: A comparative analysis. *Counselor Education and Supervision, 51,* 207–221.

Lenz, A. S., & Smith, R. L. (2010). Integrating wellness concepts within a clinical supervision model. *The Clinical Supervisor, 29,* 228–245. doi: 10.1080/07325223.2010.518511

Maslach, C. (1982). *Burnout: The cost of caring.* Englewood Cliffs, NJ: Prentice-Hall.

Maslach, C. (2003). Job burnout: New directions in research and intervention. *Current Directions in Psychological Science, 12,* 189–192.

Maslach, C., & Leiter, M. P. (2008). Early predictors of job burnout and engagement. *Journal of Applied Psychology, 93,* 498–512. doi: 10.1037/0021–9010.93.3.498

May, R. (1953). *Man's search for himself.* New York, NY: W.W. Norton.

Melamed, S., Shirom, A., Toker, S., Berliner, S., & Shapira, I. (2006). Burnout and risk of cardiovascular disease: Evidence, possible causal paths, and promising research directions. *Psychological Bulletin, 132,* 327–353. doi: 10.1037/0033–2909.132.3.327

Meyer, D., & Ponton, R. (2006). The healthy tree: A metaphorical perspective of counselor well-being. *Journal of Mental Health Counseling, 28,* 189–201.

Myers, J. E., Luecht, R. M., & Sweeney, T. J. (2004). The factor structure of wellness: Reexamining theoretical and empirical models underlying the wellness evaluation of lifestyle (WEL) and the five-factor WEL. *Measurement and Evaluation in Counseling and Development, 36,* 194–208.

Myers, J. E., Mobley, A. K., & Booth, C. S. (2003). Wellness of counseling students: Practicing what we preach. *Counselor Education and Supervision, 42,* 264–274.

Myers, J. E., & Sweeney, T. J. (2005a). *Counseling for wellness: Theory, research, and practice.* Alexandria, VA: American Counseling Association.

Myers, J. E., & Sweeney, T. J. (2005b). The indivisible self: An evidence-based model of wellness. *The Journal of Individual Psychology, 61,* 269–279.

Myers, J. E., Sweeney, T. J., & Witmer, J. M. (2000). The wheel of wellness: A holistic model for treatment planning. *Journal of Counseling and Development, 78,* 251–266.

National Wellness Institute. (n.d.). *Defining wellness.* Retrieved from http://www.nationalwellness .org/index.php?id_tier=2 & id_c=26

Osborn, C. J. (2004). Seven salutary suggestions for counselor stamina. *Journal of Counseling & Development, 82,* 319–328.

Schure, M., Christopher, J., & Christopher, S. (2008). Mind–body medicine and the art of self-care: Teaching mindfulness to counseling students through yoga, meditation, and qigong. *Journal of Counseling & Development, 86,* 47–56.

Shapiro, S. L., Brown, K. W., & Biegel, G. M. (2007). Teaching self-care to caregivers: Effects of mindfulness-based stress reduction on the mental health of therapists in training. *Training and Education in Professional Psychology, 1,* 105–115. doi: 10.1037/1931–3918.1.2.105

Smith, B. J., Tang, K. C., & Nutbeam, D. (2006). WHO health promotion glossary: New terms. *Health Promotion International, 21,* 340–345. doi: 10.1093/heapro/da1033

Smith, H. L., Robinson, E. H., III, & Young, M. E. (2007). The relationship among wellness, psychological distress, and social desirability of entering master's level counselor trainees. *Counselor Education and Supervision, 47,* 96–109.

Spurgeon, S. L., & Myers, L. E. (2004). Relationships among racial identity, college type, and wellness. *Journal of Black Studies, 1,* 1–17. doi: 10.1177/0021934708315153

Chapter 10

Professional Organizations and Membership

RObert C. Schwartz

In general, professional organizations reflect the values of their members and the direction of the field they represent, including future directions of the profession espoused by organizational leaders in collaboration with and on behalf of the membership. Similar to other professions, the counseling profession consists of various organizations that have unique histories and specific missions to serve the members and counseling profession at large. Understanding counseling professional organizations and membership can be confusing due to the large number of organizations available. Therefore, understanding how counseling professional organizations relate to the field as a whole may clarify linkages among these various groups and which ones are important to participate in depending on one's professional aspirations.

In the previous chapters, you learned the historical perspectives and current trends of the counseling profession (Chapter 2). You also learned about different specialty areas of counseling and the professional functions of professional counselors in each specialty area (Chapter 4). In this chapter, you will be introduced to major counseling organizations. You will also learn about the missions, activities, and membership benefits of each professional counseling organization. Reflection exercises and case illustrations will enhance your learning about the professional counseling organizations and how becoming a member of professional counseling associations can benefit you as a professional counselor.

LEARNING OBJECTIVES

After reading information and engaging in reflection exercises provided in this chapter, you will be able to:

1. Identify major organizations in professional counseling;

2. Describe the roles and functions of professional counseling organizations; and

3. Describe ways to build professional identity through membership.

AMERICAN COUNSELING ASSOCIATION AND ITS DIVISIONS

The counseling profession has evolved from many professional organizations of various sizes and at various levels of influence. The American Counseling Association (ACA) is a not-for-profit, professional and educational organization that has a mission of enhancing the quality of life in society by promoting the development of professional counselors and promoting respect for human dignity and diversity through counseling. In this regard, ACA is dedicated to the growth of the counseling profession. In addition, ACA has a long history and has advanced since the 1950s into the large and interdisciplinary organization it is today.

As Aubrey (1977) explained, "If one decade in history had to be singled out for the most profound impact on counselors, it would be the 1950s" (p. 292). Founded in 1952, the American Personnel and Guidance Association (APGA) grew out of a loose array of counseling-related organizations "concerned with educational and vocational guidance" and related personnel issues (Harold, 1985, p. 4). Therefore, APGA was originally more of a professional interest network focused on bringing disparate counseling-related groups together to promote and improve school guidance and per-sonnel counseling. Related to this, the original four organizations that became part of APGA were the American College Personnel Association, the National Association of Guidance Supervisors and Counselor Trainers, the Student Personnel Association for Teacher Education, and the National Vocational Guidance Association.

In 1961, APGA published the first "sound code of ethics for counselors" (Nugent, 1981, p. 28), and both professionalism and membership increased sub-stantially. During the 1970s, APGA became a more formalized national organiza-tion for counseling professionals, coinciding with the formation of new helping skills programs and the beginnings of state licensure for counselors. In the 1970s, APGA built its headquarters in Alexandria, Virginia (where it remains today), added several counseling specialty divisions (e.g., Association for Counselor Educators and Supervisors in 1973), and began questioning its role and professional identity, because the organization was growing beyond guidance and personnel issues.

In the 1980s, counselor licensure began to grow rapidly nationwide, and therefore the number of counseling graduate programs increased dramatically. In 1981, the Council for the Accreditation of Counseling and Related Educational Programs (CACREP) was formed by APGA as an affiliate organization to help refine and standardize counselor education programs. Given these fundamental and widespread changes in the evolution of counseling, inside APGA there was a growing awareness that the focus on guidance and personnel was too limiting to encompass APGA membership and interested potential members. In 1983, APGA officially changed its name to American Association for Counseling and Development (AACD) to "reflect the changing demographics of its membership and the settings in which they worked" (Herr, 1985, p. 395). This change, along with external factors such as new legislation and employment opportunities for counselors, led to a rapid increase in AACD divisions (e.g., specialty organizations focused on group counseling, multicultural concerns, offender populations, religious and value issues, and others). In 1992, to develop a simpler and more easily recognizable name, to reflect a change in membership and mission of the organization, and to align with similar organizational names of related professions (e.g., American Psychological Association, American Psychiatric Association), AACD changed its name to American Counseling Association (ACA) (Gladding & Newsome, 2010).

You may be surprised to learn that, today, ACA is the world's largest association exclusively representing professional counselors in a wide range of practice settings by providing training, publications, continuing education opportunities, and advocacy to its members (ACA, 2011a). ACA can be considered the umbrella counseling professional organization within which are various state-level branches, regional organizations, and specialty divisions. Membership in state-level branches, regional, and divisional organizations is voluntary, in addition to, and separate from ACA membership, usually requiring additional dues but also providing additional and more focused benefits. ACA regional organizations separate membership areas of the United States into four sections, each composed of several states (i.e., Midwest, North Atlantic, Southern, and Western regions). ACA state branches separate membership areas into states within the United States and international areas such as Europe. ACA regions and branches were created in order to provide additional and tailored membership services to those in certain parts of the country and abroad to meet their unique needs. For example, each state has a state-level counseling branch or organization that focuses on supporting, promoting, and educating counselors within that state (e.g., Ohio Counseling Association, Florida Counseling Association, North Carolina Counseling Association). State-level counseling branches usually hold an annual conference for members that is similar to the ACA Annual Conference and Exhibition and includes keynote speakers, presentations, business meetings, and exhibitions with publishers and counseling products. In addition, state-level branches lobby for changes or additions to counselor licensure in that state.

ACA specialty divisions provide leadership, resources, and information unique to specialization areas and/or types of counseling, rather than physical locations (which are the focus of regional organizations and state-level branches). Divisions chartered by ACA elect division officers who govern their divisions' activities independently and also participate in national ACA governance, so ACA has representation from professionals with a variety of specialty interests and skills. There are 19 ACA divisions, each having its own unique purpose and mission (ACA, 2011b). Table 10.1 provides a summary of the purposes and missions of all ACA divisions.

Membership in ACA can be attained through payment of annual dues after meeting minimum criteria for a specific membership type: student, professional, retiree, and

Table 10.1 ACA Divisions

Association for Assessment in Counseling and Education (AACE)	The purpose of AACE is to promote the effective use of assessment in the counseling profession.
Association for Adult Development and Aging (AADA)	AADA serves as a focal point for information sharing, professional development, and advocacy related to adult development and aging issues; it addresses counseling concerns across the lifespan.
Association for Creativity in Counseling (ACC)	The ACC is a forum for counselors, counselor educators, creative arts therapists, and counselors in training to explore unique and diverse approaches to counseling. ACC's goal is to promote greater awareness, advocacy, and understanding of diverse and creative approaches to counseling.
American College Counseling Association (ACCA)	The focus of ACCA is to foster student development in colleges, universities, and community colleges.
Association for Counselors and Educators in Government (ACEG)	ACEG is dedicated to counseling clients and their families in local, state, and federal government or in military-related agencies.
Association for Counselor Education and Supervision (ACES)	ACES emphasizes the need for quality education and supervision of counselors for all work settings.
The Association for Humanistic Counseling (AHC)	AHC provides a forum for the exchange of information about humanistic-oriented counseling practices and promotes changes that reflect the growing body of knowledge about humanistic principles applied to human development and potential.

Table 10.1   (Continued)

Association for Lesbian, Gay, Bisexual and Transgender Issues in Counseling (ALGBTIC)	ALGBTIC educates counselors about the unique needs of client identity development and provides a nonthreatening counseling environment by aiding in the reduction of stereotypical thinking and homoprejudice.
Association for Multicultural Counseling and Development (AMCD)	AMCD strives to improve cultural, ethnic, and racial empathy and understanding by programs to advance and sustain personal growth.
American Mental Health Counselors Association (AMHCA)	AMHCA represents mental health counselors, advocating for client-access to quality services within the health care industry.
American Rehabilitation Counseling Association (ARCA)	ARCA is an organization of rehabilitation counseling practitioners, educators, and students who are concerned with enhancing the development of people with disabilities throughout their life span and in promoting excellence in the rehabilitation counseling profession's practice, research, consultation, and professional development.
American School Counselor Association (ASCA)	ASCA promotes school counseling professionals and interest in activities that affect the personal, educational, and career development of students. ASCA members also work with parents, educators, and community members to provide a positive learning environment.
Association for Spiritual, Ethical, and Religious Values in Counseling (ASERVIC)	ASERVIC is devoted to professionals who believe that spiritual, ethical, religious, and other human values are essential to the full development of the person and to the discipline of counseling.
Association for Specialists in Group Work (ASGW)	ASGW provides professional leadership in the field of group work, establishes standards for professional training, and supports research and the dissemination of knowledge.
Counselors for Social Justice (CSJ)	CSJ is a community of counselors, counselor educators, graduate students, and school and community leaders who seek equity and an end to oppression and injustice affecting clients, students, counselors, families, communities, schools, workplaces, governments, and other social and institutional systems.
International Association of Addictions and Offender Counselors (IAAOC)	Members of IAAOC advocate the development of effective counseling and rehabilitation programs for people with substance abuse problems or other addictions as well as both adult and juvenile public offenders.
International Association of Marriage and Family Counselors (IAMFC)	IAMFC members help develop healthy family systems through prevention, education, and therapy.

(Continued)

Table 10.1 (Continued)

National Career Development Association (NCDA)	NCDA inspires and empowers the achievement of career and life goals by providing professional development, resources, standards, scientific research, and advocacy.
National Employment Counseling Association (NECA)	The commitment of NECA is to offer professional leadership to people who counsel in employment and/or career development settings.

regular. Student members must be enrolled at least half time in a college or university counseling program. Professional membership criteria include holding a master's degree or higher in counseling or a closely related field from a college or university that was accredited when the degree was awarded. Retiree membership criteria relate to current members who are retired from the counseling profession and have been active ACA members for the past five consecutive years. Regular membership is for individuals whose interests are consistent with those of ACA but who are not qualified for professional membership. Each membership category has a different annual fee structure.

With such diversity of interests among counseling membership possibilities, it is useful for readers to begin considering the direction a counseling career may take. Exercise 10.1 is offered to stimulate the beginning of that process.

Membership Benefits

There are a wide a range of direct benefits to members of ACA, the largest counseling professional organization, currently comprising approximately 55,000 members. These benefits help members become more successful throughout their careers as counselors. A plethora of direct benefits are available through ACA, most of which can be accessed through its website, www.counseling.org. Some of these many direct benefits include the following:

Exercise 10.1

IN-DEPTH LOOK AT THE DIVISIONS OF ACA

Directions: Reflect on the 19 unique American Counseling Association divisions. Select five that you believe may fit your career aspirations. Review each of their websites to learn about their unique missions, membership benefits, and costs. Finally, rank order the five organizations you reviewed from most likely to the least likely you would choose to join.

A List of ACA Divisions and Websites

Association for Assessment in Counseling and Education:
  www.theaaceonline.com
Association for Creativity in Counseling:
  www.creativecounselor.org
American College Counseling Association:
  www.collegecounseling.org
American Mental Health Counselors Association:
  www.amhca.org
American Rehabilitation Counseling Association:
  www.arcaweb.org
American School Counselor Association:
  www.schoolcounselor.org
Association for Counselors and Educators in Government:
  no website currently available
Association for Counselor Education and Supervision:
  www.acesonline.net
Association for Humanistic Counseling:
  afhc.camp9.org
Association for Lesbian, Gay, Bisexual and Transgender Issues in Counseling:
  www.algbtic.org
Association for Multicultural Counseling and Development:
  www.multiculturalcounseling.org
Association for Spiritual, Ethical, and Religious Values in Counseling:
  www.aservic.org
Association for Specialists in Group Work:
  www.asgw.org
Counselors for Social Justice:
  counselorsforsocialjustice.com
International Association of Addictions and Offender Counselors:
  www.iaaoc.org
International Association of Marriage and Family Counselors:
  www.iamfconline.com
National Career Development Association:
  www.ncda.org
National Employment Counseling Association:
  www.employmentcounseling.org

Bolstering one's resume

Including membership in counseling organizations on one's resume helps to show one's support for the profession and increases one's reputability.

Networking opportunities

Joining a formal network of colleagues helps build an invaluable brotherhood and sisterhood of similar professionals who advocate for one another, are available for support and guidance when needed, and steer each other toward opportunities that could advance one's career (e.g., employment openings, awards). In addition to many face-to-face networking opportunities, ACA also offers members free access to student and professional listservs, a counseling blog, and a counselor directory called CounselorFind.

Counseling-related publications

The nationally renowned *Journal of Counseling and Development,* which provides up-to-date research and practice-related knowledge, is available online and through mailings, free for all ACA members. Similarly, *Counseling Today,* a monthly counseling magazine providing news updates, job postings, commentaries, opinions, and professional articles, is available online and through mailings, free for all ACA members. Also, counseling-related books published by ACA are made available to all members at reduced cost. In addition, free articles summarizing counseling conference presentations (for those unable to attend in person) are made available to members through the publication *VISTAS Online.* An online library and podcast series involving specialty topics of interest are also available free to members.

Conferences

Professional conferences, such as the ACA Annual Conference and Exhibition, allow members to attend a vast array of presentations and learn from experts in the field, collect the continuing education units (CEUs) required for licensure renewal, attend meetings that deliver updated information about the profession, reconnect with peers and former educators, and—through publishers and other providers—review up-to-date resources (e.g., book, technology, and university-related information) available for practitioners. Professional conferences also provide much-needed opportunities to network with leaders in the counseling profession, counselor educators (e.g., if you are interested in applying for doctoral programs), publishers (e.g., if you are interested in publishing books or journal articles), and potential employers both in the United States and abroad.

JOINING A PROFESSIONAL ORGANIZATION— PROFESSIONAL NETWORKING AT CONFERENCES

Bob was a doctoral student in counselor education and supervision at a large northeastern university. During the first year of his doctoral program, his faculty advisor encouraged Bob to attend the annual ACA national conference. Bob looked into the possibility and found that although the conference seemed interesting, it also seemed expensive, and he was nervous about attending such a large conference with so many leaders in the profession. Essentially Bob realized that in order to attend such a conference, he would need to both save funds and get over his fears of intimidation and of not fitting in or being good enough to contribute to the profession. Bob therefore put off the decision.

During Bob's second year in the doctoral program, several other faculty members shared that he could be giving up an important opportunity if he did not attend the next year's ACA national conference. They explained that it was both a unique chance for professional development (through presentations, poster sessions, keynote speakers, and more), and also a rare chance to meet future mentors, colleagues, and employers. Being somewhat hesitant, Bob did further investigate conference attendance through self-reflection, speaking to peers in the doctoral program, and seeking information about where, when, and how the conference was to be held the following year. However, Bob ended up convincing himself that it was not the right time and that he should focus on his courses, on being an officer in the university's Chi Sigma Iota chapter (for which he was recently elected), and on joining a research team with his faculty advisor.

During Bob's third year in the doctoral program, he was approached by two peers who asked him to join a team applying to present a workshop at the next ACA national conference. The topic was one Bob felt he had some competence in, and he trusted his peers after working with them on course-related projects during their first two years in the doctoral program. So Bob agreed to join the team, knowing that if their presentation application was accepted, he would be committed to attending the next conference. To Bob's surprise, he and his peers received a congratulatory acceptance e-mail soon after, and he was both excited and nervous about the future. When the time came, Bob flew to the conference with one of his presentation teammates, they roomed together at a hotel near the conference center, and after settling in at the hotel, they checked in at the conference registration desk.

Over the next three days, Bob was amazed at how inaccurate his preconceptions of the conference had been and at how energized he became. First, Bob reconnected with several friends from his former master's program who were staying at the same hotel. They had dinner together, talked about their families and careers, and learned about the conference together while planning to attend similar workshops. Bob was also congratulated on acceptance of his own conference presentation, an honor that impressed his friends and inspired them to apply for presentations at the following national conference.

Next, Bob attended workshops by the authors of books he used in his doctoral coursework. He was thrilled to see these authors in person and developed a renewed appreciation for his doctoral coursework. He also gained knowledge that went beyond his textbooks, leading him to become a more well-rounded student. In addition, many leaders in the field were pointed out to Bob by his friends, such as the president of Chi Sigma Iota, the current president and past presidents of the American Counseling Association, the editor of the *Journal of Counseling and Development,* and many more.

Then, at the exhibition hall, Bob met several well-known counselor educators who spoke about future tenure-track faculty job openings coming available. After discussing his clinical specialty areas, his current doctoral program progress, and his upcoming conference presentation, Bob was encouraged by several counselor educators to apply for their soon-to-be-posted faculty positions. They even provided their business cards and offered additional information and assistance in the future.

Finally, Bob was overjoyed that he and his teammates completed a very successful presentation on the final day of the conference. Attendance was higher than expected, the presentation ran smoothly, and many people from the audience congratulated him on his work after the presentation was completed. On the flight back from the conference, Bob felt on top of the world. He learned more than he had imagined he would about the counseling profession, built his sense of self-confidence, met important and accepting professionals from around the country, and reconnected with old friends. He realized that his faculty mentors were right all along and that the only thing he had to fear was fear itself. His only regret was waiting so long to gain this positive experience, wishing that he had attended the conference earlier in his doctoral career.

Grants and other funding

Funding for students, professionals, and other organizations is available to members, usually focused on specific goals or outcomes. For example, ACA hosts an annual ethics-related scholarship competition for counseling students with a grand prize of $1,000 and publication of the winner's ethics essay in *Counseling Today.*

Leadership opportunities

All counseling professional organizations are overseen and often staffed by elected members holding officer positions in the organization (e.g., president, treasurer, secretary). Most organizations also develop a wide range of committees related to important professional topics (e.g., ethics or advocacy) or governance (e.g., officer elections or conference development). Joining an organization can help you learn leadership skills, build your resume, and contribute in different and important ways to the organization itself.

Awards and other recognition

Most counseling professional organizations at the state and national levels offer annual awards to outstanding members, and often recognition of member contributions in newsletters and other publications. For example, ACA distributes annual awards for member contributions in research, human rights, professional development, legislation, clinical practice, multiculturalism, mentoring, graduate student work, and other areas. Awards not only bolster your resume and lead to other professional opportunities, they can enhance your professional self-efficacy.

Ethics and legal consultation

ACA not only publishes the ACA *Code of Ethics* (2005), which governs professional conduct among counselors, it also provides free confidential assistance with ethical questions or concerns through consultation five days each week during normal business hours. Given the increasingly litigious nature of consumers and other professionals, this service is invaluable for clarifying ethical dilemmas and minimizing professional risk.

Professional liability insurance

Due to the array of complex ethical codes and laws governing counseling practice, maintaining comprehensive professional liability insurance is a vital part of one's professional life. Although it is not required, it is always a good practice for you as a professional counselor to hold professional liability insurance when engaging in counseling practice. Through its advocacy efforts, ACA has secured reduced member premiums for professional liability insurance through the Healthcare Providers Service Organization (HPSO). Student members of ACA receive free or discount liability insurance from HPSO throughout their graduate careers. Many counselor education programs require students to have professional liability insurance during practicum and internship.

CASE 10.2

WHEN SUPPORT IS NEEDED

Jane was a recent graduate of a counseling master's program. Jane received her licensed professional counselor credential soon after being granted her degree and passing a state licensure examination. Throughout Jane's counseling internship experience, she consulted with peers and her instructor (during group supervision), and with her site supervisor (during individual supervision). Jane enjoyed the aspect of consultation involving ethical decision making with these individuals in order to both reinforce her learning of ACA ethical guidelines and limit her personal liability and harm to her clientele. Jane witnessed many peers share ethical dilemmas during the internship experience, and although these issues were often complex and confusing, they were resolved through objective and collegial feedback from others.

However, now that she is licensed and working at a local mental health agency, Jane has found that the same level of support is not available. Work-related pressures have increased, and she does not get the same degree of objective feedback. In addition, she has felt less safe disclosing ethical dilemmas to work supervisors and colleagues because of fears that it could damage her reputation or future workplace evaluations.

Jane then remembered that, as an ACA member, she could access both ethics-related resources and consultation for free. When the next ethical dilemma occurred, she followed the steps outlined in Section H (Resolving Ethical Issues) of the ACA Code of Ethics. She also used *A Practitioner's Guide to Ethical Decision Making* and other online resources offered by ACA. Finally, Jane contacted the ACA ethics and professional standards department for confidential guidance related to her ethical decision making. Jane soon realized that gaining this type of important support when needed was one of the many benefits of joining ACA, and she was relieved that her membership remained active.

CHI SIGMA IOTA

Founded in 1985, Chi Sigma Iota (CSI) is an international counseling honor society that promotes academic and professional excellence through a strong counselor identity among counseling students and professionals who contribute to a healthy society by fostering wellness and human dignity. This mission is accomplished by promoting scholarship, research, professionalism, leadership, advocacy, and excellence in counseling. CSI has a long history of promoting counseling as a unique profession with its own goals, identity, philosophy, and services to consumers. These goals are achieved both through CSI leadership (i.e., headquarters staff, officers, and committees) and through the activities of local university campus-based chapters (CSI, 2011). You can find more information about the CSI chapter of your graduate program in counseling by talking with your advisor, instructors, and fellow students.

The founding president and first life member of CSI was Thomas Sweeney. He and his partner, Jane Meyers (the second CSI president), have worked tirelessly since 1985 to promote CSI as a networking and advocacy organization, which also serves as an honor society, specifically for counselor trainees, professionals, and educators. CSI presidents have included many leaders in the profession, such as six presidents of ACA (i.e., Sweeney, Cooper, Myers, Lee, Herr, and Gladding), eighteen ACA divisional presidents, three ACA regional branch chairs, five division regional presidents, four chairs and one executive director of CACREP, and one chair of the National Board of Certified Counselors. Thus, CSI leadership is synonymous with counseling leadership (CSI, 2011).

CSI has 79,000 members and over 277 chapters in the United States and around the world, all affiliated with campus-based organizations within counselor education programs. Membership in CSI is voluntary, and because it is an honor society, the application process includes enrollment in or graduation from a counseling degree program with a GPA of 3.5 or higher, as well as the endorsement of a local chapter affiliated with a counseling degree program and membership dues (approximately $50 annually) (CSI, 2011).

The many benefits of joining CSI include, but are not limited to, the following:

- Listing an honor society on one's resume
- Networking with national leaders in the profession and local colleagues and faculty
- Local (e.g., chapter officer) and national (committee and executive council) leadership opportunities
- Mentorship opportunities, such as the CSI Academy of Leaders for Excellence
- Receipt of CSI publications, such as the *CSI Exemplar* and *CSI E-News* updates
- The possibility of receiving CSI-sponsored research grants and grants for CSI chapters at different counseling programs
- The possibility of being recognized through annual CSI-sponsored awards (e.g., Outstanding Entry-Level Student Award, Outstanding Doctoral Student Award, Outstanding Research Award)
- Attending CSI-specific business meetings, trainings, and ceremonies held annually at the ACA Conference
- The opportunity to present CSI-sponsored presentations and poster sessions at state and national conferences

Membership Benefits

Similar to other counseling professional organizations, CSI has general member benefits that include voting in officer elections; communicating with a broad network of counseling professionals; opportunities to develop leadership skills through the potential to hold chapter offices; opportunities to receive grants and

---

CASE 10.3

PROFESSIONAL RECOGNITION

Stan was a third-year doctoral student in counselor education and supervision. He had spent his first two years learning teaching, supervision, and research-related knowledge and skills. Stan's career goal was to become a counselor educator, preferably at a research-oriented university with a counseling department offering doctoral degrees. However, he was aware of how competitive these positions were nationwide. He therefore engaged in independent research and writing throughout the first two years of his doctoral program with the guidance of a faculty mentor. After completing a research study as principle investigator toward the beginning of his third year in the doctoral program, Stan was encouraged to promote his fine work through applying for a Chi Sigma Iota award.

Stan researched the Chi Sigma Iota awards websites and discovered that applications for a national Outstanding Research Award were being sought later that year. During the next six months, Stan devoted himself to writing a manuscript related to his recently completed research study. He received feedback from his faculty mentor and submitted the manuscript to his local Chi Sigma Iota chapter for consideration as their representative for the national Outstanding Research Award. He received accolades from his peers and the chapter faculty advisor and was nominated for the national award. To Stan's surprise, he did win the national Outstanding Research Award, which included a plaque, recognition at the American Counseling Association National Conference, encouragement from national leaders in the counseling profession, and the addition of this prestigious award to his resume. Perhaps most important, Stan also gained much needed confidence in his abilities as a researcher and future counselor educator, confidence that led him to publish his award-winning manuscript in a national counseling journal and pursue additional professional writing during his doctoral program.

accolades through fellowships, internships, and awards; and member-only access to web-based resources such as the organization's newsletter (i.e., *CSI Exemplar*), JobLinks, and the Counselor's Bookshelf (CSI, 2011). Membership benefits for counseling students include those outlined above and additional growth-producing yet less tangible rewards.

Because all CSI chapters must be affiliated with a university department housing at least one counseling program, you as a student member of CSI can become more involved in your graduate program. For example, CSI participation can often lead to overlooked benefits of connecting with and learning from more senior students. This type of connection can result in valuable feedback about strategies for academic success, avoiding unnecessary academic hurdles, and other forms of peer mentoring. These relationships can also lead to longer-term friendships that may carry over into your future career, resulting in client referrals, employment opportunities, linkages with other professionals in your geographic area, or simply trusted colleagues to consult with or rely on when challenging professional experiences arise.

In addition, CSI involvement during your graduate career yields the opportunity to build new skills related to developing and coordinating professional activities, such as CSI-sponsored meetings, workshops and trainings, social events, and recognition events. Learning organizational skills such as these early on helps promote abilities that will generalize into longer term expertise in areas such as counseling supervision, administration, and outreach.

Finally, all of the important student development opportunities described above can enhance your sense of professional confidence and self-efficacy, leading to greater comfort with and competence in the counseling profession, thereby opening up yet additional avenues for professional growth. Exercise 10.2 will help you become more familiar with the benefits of becoming an active CSI member.

Exercise 10.2

CHI SIGMA IOTA—PLANNING FOR THE FUTURE

Directions: Locate the Chi Sigma Iota (CSI) web address from this chapter. On the website, find the criteria for outstanding individual awards. Review the purposes and criteria for these awards. With intentionality and a future-oriented perspective, consider which award(s) you might be eligible for and why. What could you do in the near future to increase your chance of attaining one of these coveted awards, and what would the next step be in that process?

COUNCIL FOR ACCREDITATION OF COUNSELING AND RELATED EDUCATIONAL PROGRAMS

Counseling professionals and training programs can be certified, licensed, or accredited, each of which is a different type of endorsement by a specific organization, each for a different purpose.

Certifications are granted to individual counseling professionals and usually focus on specific knowledge or skills (e.g., specialty areas) gained through community (e.g., local, state, or national workshops) or academic (e.g., university) training completed. Certifications allow others (i.e., consumers, employers) to know about expertise in specialty areas that has been acquired by the counseling professional. However, in and of themselves, certifications are usually not sufficient to allow a professional to practice counseling. In general, certifications add to your practice areas after you become licensed.

State boards grant licenses and oversee and govern professional counseling. Professional counseling licenses are offered state by state (i.e., there is currently no national-level counselor license), and each state has its own unique educational and supervised training requirements. Licenses allow a professional to legally use a specific title (e.g., licensed professional counselor) and practice counseling in that state according to specific scope of practice guidelines.

Accreditation is essentially the endorsement of an academic program that has been deemed by a separate, objective organization to have met minimum quality standards for training in a specific profession. Accreditation for graduate programs is increasingly important, not only for stature and enrollment purposes, but also and most important in order to ensure the competence of students graduating from each program. The national accreditation body for counseling programs is the Council for Accreditation of Counseling and Related Educational Program's (CACREP). Founded in 1985, CACREP's mission is to promote the professional competence of counselors through the development of preparation standards, the encouragement of excellence in program development, and the accreditation of professional preparation programs.

Essentially, through a board composed of counselor educators and profes-sional counselors, along with feedback from counselors across the United States, CACREP establishes guidelines that must be followed by accredited counseling programs. Among many others, these guidelines include requirements related to faculty-to-student ratios, minimum semester credit, course content, and knowledge/skill requirements for specific counseling degrees; minimum clinical competency standards; and administrative (e.g., faculty, academic environment) guidelines (CACREP, 2011a). Program accreditation through CACREP is voluntary, deter-mined by each program's faculty/university or state, and is granted after stringent reviews of curriculum, site visits and interviews, and payment of accreditation fees. Exercise 10.3 invites you to review the latest CACREP standards. While doing so, consider the benefits and overall value of attending a CACREP accredited program.

Accreditation Benefits

CACREP accreditation provides recognition that the content and quality of a counseling program has been evaluated and meets national standards set by the profession. You, as a consumer of graduate-level training, can be assured that appropriate knowledge and skill areas are included and that the program is stable both professionally and financially (CACREP, 2011a). One part of the accreditation process is a self-assessment by program faculty. The self-assessment entails an evaluation of the program's resources, objectives, strengths, and limitations with the purpose of improving the program effectiveness. The self-assessment process helps ensure plans are made and goals are set for the program, that the program is measured, and that the program meets professional standards. Accreditation also involves site visits from respected counselor educators from around the United States. These site visits include in-depth reviews of program-related functions, course-work, facilities, and student-faculty interactions. The combined self-assessment and site visitation process helps ensure a well-rounded quality education for graduates of accredited programs.

Increasingly, prospective counseling students are seeking CACREP accredited programs in order to ensure a minimum quality of education, and faculty members are committed to maintaining accreditation for reputability and marketability purposes. Although some programs (maybe your counseling program is one of them) may require coursework beyond the minimum CACREP accreditation standards (e.g., due to state licensure board requirements), graduating from a CACREP accredited program may help you avoid discovering that you lack needed course-work or training demanded by employers, supervisors, or credentialing bodies.

Exercise 10.3

CACREP ACCREDITATION STANDARDS—GUIDING TRAINING

Directions: Locate the CACREP web address in this chapter. On the website, find the link for the most recent accreditation standards. Finally, determine how many different types of counseling programs can be accredited by CACREP and what the primary differences are.

Entering a CACREP accredited program for a master's or doctoral degree in counseling also provides a level of comfort should an unanticipated change in program or university be needed for personal or professional reasons. For example, you have been admitted to a CACREP accredited master's program in clinical mental health counseling (CMHC); however, you must move to another location for personal reasons during the program, and therefore transfer to another CMHC master's program. In this scenario, you can rest assured that you have completed some of the coursework from a CACREP accredited program and are likely to be able to transfer your core CMHC coursework to the new institution, so your study is not greatly affected by relocation.

In addition, for quality assurance purposes, state counselor licensure boards are increasingly requiring that students graduate from CACREP accredited programs before licensure applications will be approved. Many state licensure boards already require a CACREP accredited degree before professional counselor licensure applications will be considered. Additional state licensure boards across the United States are considering changing state laws to include this requirement. This movement is also taken by some state licensure boards and counseling organizations as aligning professional counselor laws with those for social work and psychology, most of which require accredited graduate degrees in order to obtain independent licensure for social workers or psychologists. CACREP is a specialized national accrediting body recognized by the Council for higher education accreditation. In that regard, CACREP grants accredited status to master's programs in addictions counseling; career counseling; clinical mental health counseling; marriage, couple, and family counseling; school counseling; and student affairs and college counseling as well as a doctoral program in counselor education and supervision (CACREP, 2011b). Therefore, it is important that you review licensure requirements in your state. The information located in the next chapter (Chapter 11) of this textbook can help you navigate licensure requirements for professional counselors.

PROFESSIONAL COUNSELING: A UNIFIED PROFESSION

Among many other missions, counseling professional organizations advocate for important causes related to members and those they serve; promote the profession at local, state, national, and international levels (e.g., funding, legitimacy, reputability, and access to employment); and offer resources to their membership, often in the form of journals and conferences (i.e., learning opportunities), continuing education (i.e., licensure renewal units), ethical and legal support, networking opportunities, and more. The counseling profession is diverse. In fact, there has been much debate over the past decade regarding whether counseling reflects one unified and comprehensive profession, or multiple distinct professions with a common core and history (Kaplan & Gladding, 2011). This debate may seem trivial or superfluous to some; however the outcome can have significant implications for the field, such as counselors' professional identity (e.g., sense of self from a professional standpoint) and state licensure (e.g., common nationwide requirements allowing for easy state-to-state portability of one's license versus a complicated network of unique licensure requirements governed by each state independently). It will also help public understanding of who counselors are and what they do (e.g., easy identification of counselors' knowledge, skills, and professional competencies versus confusion between different types of counselors and how they are similar to or different from other mental health professionals).

In addition, this debate has had significant implications for counseling-related organizations and will affect whether they will become more unified or instead more competitive for membership, their own identities, and human and financial resources. Recently a group of 31 counseling-related organizations with an interest in the profession banded together to seek solutions to this dilemma and promote the needs of all counselors. For example, these organizations have set out to identify the most pressing needs of the counseling profession, including how the profession as a whole can unify and advocate with one voice. This group is called 20/20—A Vision for the Future of Counseling. In "A Vision for the Future of Counseling: The 20/20 Principles for Unifying and Strengthening the Profession," Kaplan and Gladding (2011) explained the importance of this issue and provide several guiding principles developed by counseling organizations across the United States. In the following sections, we present overviews of two such principles, both of which greatly impact professional organizations' missions and membership.

Presenting counseling as one unified profession

The counseling profession should create a common counselor identification that would also allow for additional designations of special interests and specialties. While being unified, the counseling profession should respect counseling specialties.

Strengthening a common counselor identity

The counseling profession should develop a paradigm that identifies the core commonalities of the profession and a body of core knowledge and skills shared by all counselors. The counseling profession should reinforce for students that we are a single profession composed of counselors with specialized areas of training, and accreditation of counseling programs should reflect one identity. Ultimately, based on the principles described above and others developed by 20/20—A Vision for the Future of Counseling, a new consensus definition of counseling has been promoted: Counseling is a professional relationship that empowers diverse individuals, families, and groups to accomplish mental health, wellness, education, and career goals (ACA, 2010). As described in this broad definition, counselors do many things and serve many types of people in many settings. Thus, there are many counseling-related organizations, most of which work together to promote the profession and assist their members in achieving success while effectively serving consumers.

Building Your Professional Identity Through Membership

You as a member of a counseling professional organization not only receive direct benefits, but also have an opportunity to support and promote the profession through increased status and financial resources. Non-counseling-related professional organizations (e.g., American Psychological Association, National Association of Social Workers) accrue status and financial support through membership, and these organizations often compete for employment opportunities and third-party (i.e., insurance) reimbursement for their members, legitimacy, and governmental recognition by virtue of how many members they represent and the financial resources at their disposal. For example, the larger an organization's membership, the more likely it is that its leaders can influence state and national legislators. This, in turn, impacts laws that prescribe what professionals are able to do, where they are able to work, and how much they are able to earn. The greater an organization's financial resources (which are largely garnered through membership dues), the more funding is available for hiring lobbyists and advertisements marketing the profession to lawmakers and consumers (i.e., voters). Given increasingly limited funding for mental health services, different types of mental health professionals

Exercise 10.4

UNIFIED COUNSELING PROFESSION—FUTURE DIRECTIONS

Directions: Locate web-based information about the purposes and goals of 20/20—A Vision for the Future of Counseling. Reflect critically on the pros and cons of the 20/20 vision and on whether counseling is one unified profession with specialty areas or a group of unique professions guided by a set of common principles. Finally, determine how you believe counseling should evolve to both honor a diverse array of professionals and strengthen its identity.

are simultaneously challenged to compete for similar employment opportunities. Counseling professional organizations are a primary means of advocating for the unique and valuable contributions of counselors within local communities, states, and nationwide. It is, therefore, important that you, as a graduate student in counseling and future professional counselor, join both state and national counseling professional organizations, in addition to local and regional organizations, if available, to promote your ongoing professional identity.

KEYSTONES

In this chapter, counseling professional organizations and membership were discussed. Counselors may choose to join a wide diversity of organizations, some focused on providing tailored benefits to and advocating for counselors within specific geographic areas (e.g., states or regions). Other organizations focus on counseling specialty areas in order to provide members with information, networking opportunities, and other benefits when working with a specific consumer population or work setting. Still others, such as CSI or CACREP, function as counseling-related honor societies or educational accreditation bodies. To summarize the information in this chapter, it is important for you to remember the following:

Counseling professional organizations have evolved toward promoting a unified profession for public marketing and interdisciplinary reputability purposes while also celebrating intraprofessional uniqueness among the many licenses, educational programs, and work roles shared by counselors.

Membership in the professional organizations has several benefits, although it comes with costs. Membership dues usually depend on type of membership (e.g., student, professional) and scope of the organization (i.e., regional, state, or national).

Although this fact is sometimes underrecognized by members, organizational dues are well worth the cost, because financial support from members is a primary means by which organizations fulfill their missions.

Some organizations have more direct benefits available to members than others.

ADDITIONAL RESOURCES

Books

Corey, G. (2010). *Creating your professional path: Lessons from my journey.* Alexandria, VA: American Counseling Association.

Gladding, S. Y. (2009). *Becoming a counselor: The light, the bright, and the serious* (2nd ed.). Alexandria, VA: American Counseling Association.

Hazler, R. J., & Kottler, J. A. (2005). *The emerging professional counselor.* Alexandria, VA: American Counseling Association.

DVD

American Counseling Association (Producer). (2010). *The counselor as person and professional* [DVD]. United States: American Counseling Association.

Websites

American Counseling Association: www.counseling.org
Chi Sigma Iota: www.csi-net.org
Council for Accreditation of Counseling and Related Educational Programs: www.cacrep.org

REFERENCES

American Counseling Association (ACA). (2005). *ACA code of ethics.* Alexandria, VA: Author.
American Counseling Association (ACA). (2010). *20/20—A vision for the future of counseling.* Retrieved from http://counseling.org/20–20/definition.aspx
American Counseling Association (ACA). (2011a). *About us.* Retrieved from http://www.counseling.org/AboutUs/
American Counseling Association (ACA). (2011b). *ACA divisions.* Retrieved from http://www.counseling.org/AboutUs/DivisionsBranchesAndRegions/TP/Divisions/CT2.aspx
Aubrey, R. F. (1977). Historical development of guidance and counseling and implications for the future. *Personnel and Guidance Journal, 55,* 288–295.
Chi Sigma Iota (CSI). (2011). *What is CSI?* Retrieved from http://www.csi-net.org/displaycommon.cfm?an=1 & subarticlenbr=679
Council for Accreditation of Counseling and Related Educational Programs (CACREP). (2011a). *Vision, mission and core values.* Retrieved from http://www.cacrep.org/template/page.cfm?id=40
Council for Accreditation of Counseling and Related Educational Programs (CACREP). (2011b). *Scope of accreditation.* Retrieved from http://67.199.126.156/template/page.cfm?id=52
Gladding, S. T., & Newsome, D. W. (2010). *Clinical mental health counseling in community and agency settings.* New York, NY: Merrill.
Harold, M. (1985). Council's history examined after 50 years. *Guidepost, 27,* 4.
Herr, E. L. (1985). AACD: An association committed to unity through diversity. *Journal of Counseling and Development, 63,* 395–404.
Kaplan, D. M., & Gladding, S. T. (2011). A vision for the future of counseling: The 20/20 principles for unifying and strengthening the profession. *Journal of Counseling and Development, 89,* 367–372.
Nugent, F. A. (1981). *An introduction to the profession of counseling* (4th ed.). Upper Saddle River, NJ: Merrill.

Chapter 11

Professional Credentialing

Matthew J. Paylo
Jake J. Protivnak
Victoria E. Kress

For neophyte professional counselors, the process of counselor credentialing can be exciting; however, at the same time, it can be elusive and even confusing. Counselor licensure is ultimately governed by state counseling boards; therefore, expectations and requirements for licensure are not uniform across the United States. Generally, in order to grant a counseling license, state governments require counselors to complete specific coursework, complete a supervised residency (a time spent practicing under supervision), and successfully pass various standardized examinations. It is important to note that state counselor licensure requirements are continually evolving due to new legislation and lobbying endeavors. Therefore, from state to state, there is significant variability in terms of the requirements necessary to become a licensed professional counselor.

Counselor credentialing serves to increase the professional legitimacy of counselors by ensuring that these individuals have met ascribed training standards related to their education, knowledge, and experience. *Credentialing* is a broad term that covers many areas (e.g., state licensure, counseling program accreditation, specialization, and national certifications). Essentially, credentialing is the grouping and identifying of professionals into occupational groups by registration, certification, or licensure (Sweeney, 1995). Some credentials are essential and are required to practice as a professional counselor, while other credentials are clinically helpful, and some others are even of questionable value in establishing professional credibility (Remley & Herlihy, 2007). In this chapter, you will be introduced to different types of counselor credentials, program accreditations, counseling specializations, and portability. You will learn a great deal about the different types of counseling credentialing, the role and functions of state licensure, the differences among national certifications, and issues of portability of licenses. Reflection exercises and case illustrations included in this chapter will facilitate your understanding of professional counselor credentialing. To help you become more informed as a future counselor and to aid you in navigating the upcoming credentialing opportunities, practical resources are included at the end of this chapter.

LEARNING OBJECTIVES

After completing the reading and reflection activities provided in this chapter, you will be able to

1. Identify different types of counselor credentialing;

2. Describe the roles and functions of state licensure, program accreditation, and counseling specializations and national certifications; and

3. Describe considerations related to state license portability.

TYPES OF COUNSELOR CREDENTIALING

As you enter the field of professional counseling, you will want to make sure you are able to practice what you have been trained to do, and related to this, be appropriately compensated for your services. The type of credentialing you have and the licenses you hold are critically important in ensuring you are able to practice as a counselor. This section will summarize how licensure at the state level is governed and how graduate education, supervised clinical experience, and counseling examination pave the way for you to practice as a professional counselor.

State Licensure

In the United States, every state has counselor licensure laws that dictate the practice of professional counselors in that jurisdiction. The Commonwealth of Virginia was the first state to implement a practice act, which permitted professional counselors to be licensed under the state laws in 1976, and in 2009, California became the 50th state to develop professional counselor licensure laws. A state's counselor practice law—or practice act—dictates the scope of practice of a professional counselor and determines the processes for garnering and maintaining a license to practice in that state. The development of licensure laws involves extensive political negotiations with professional associations and with stakeholders who have an interest in the law. It also involves an extensive review process, which involves members of both the house and senate reviewing the law and making modifications where they believe they are needed and in response to feedback from their constituents. Consequently, the process of enacting or revising counselor licensure law is complicated, and it can take years to decades of time-intensive efforts and negations before a practice act is fully adopted. For example, in California on October 11, 2009, California Governor Arnold Schwarzenegger signed Senate Bill 788 into law. This bill established licensure requirements for professional counselors, making the State of California the final state to create such requirements for counselors. This action was the fulfillment of years of professional advocacy by many national organizations (e.g., American Counseling Association) and by the California Coalition for Counselor Licensure (CCCL).

Professional counseling licensure is established through an act of the state legislature, and licensed professional counselors are required to abide by the laws detailed in the practice act. Professional counselors are expected to abide by federal and state laws and rules, and failure to do so can result in professional sanctions and/or legal actions. For instance, if a professional counselor engaged in a sexual relationship with a client within less than two years of terminating the counselor–client relationship, most states would pursue suspending the counselor's license, and many states would revoke the counselor's license if it is found that the counselor violated the state statutes relative to such relationships.

CASE ILLUSTRATION 11.1

A CASE OF FORGOTTEN STATE STATUTES

Stan had always wanted to be a professional counselor. He was thoughtful and empathetic, and overall he received high marks in his graduate program and later from his supervisor. He was licensed in the State of Washington as a professional mental health counselor and practiced in a small agency that specialized in trauma work. After about three years of practice, he started working with a married female client whose chief complaint was she wanted to examine issues arising from her current relationship. The female client made it clear on three occasions that she was interested in Stan and wished to pursue having a personal relationship with Stan. The client invited Stan on outings and even called him at home on one occasion. At this time Stan did not act on the advances, but sought counsel in supervision, disclosing that he felt he could no longer work with the female client. Shortly after this turn of events, Stan decided to contact the female client and began dating her. He married the client two months later. This violated the state statute at the time that a counselor must allow two years to pass after terminating a counseling relationship before beginning a personal relationship with a former client. Stan's license was suspended, and he was terminated from his place of employment.

Reflection Questions:

1. What did Stan do that was appropriate?

2. What options did Stan have that may have aided him in keeping his license and employment? What else could he have done in this situation?

3. Take a moment to consider how difficult it would be to be sexually interested in and attracted to a client. How would you have dealt with this desire/scenario?

Proponents of the promotion of state licensure laws (e.g., American Counseling Association) highlight that regulating counseling licensure laws increases the public's protection by increasing the accountability that standards of professional practice require of counselors, while also increasing accessibility of mental health services (G. Corey, M. Corey, & Callanan, 2011). Third-party reimbursement (e.g., from Medicare, Medicaid, insurance companies) is an additional benefit of a licensure law, as counselors who hold licensure are eligible for reimbursement for their services. While most would agree with these mentioned benefits, others within the counseling field have highlighted that state licensure creates a culture of competition instead of collaboration among counseling specialists (i.e., psychologists, counselors, social workers, marriage and family therapists). However, counselors have an ethical obligation to the public to convey and promote a professional identity that is based on the professions' areas of competency, and historically this has been done in all health professions through the utilization of licensure and certifications.

There are a variety of licensure titles used by professional counselors in different states. Those include licensed professional counselor (LPC), licensed professional clinical counselor (LPCC), licensed mental health counselor (LMHC), licensed clinical professional counselor (LCPC), licensed professional counselor of mental health (LPCMH), and licensed clinical mental health counselor (LCMHC). However, LPC is the most common designation for counselors in the United States. Additionally, some U.S. states have a tiered licensing system by which a counselor can initially earn an entry-level license (e.g., LPC), and after several years of supervised practice, have the opportunity to earn the higher tiered license (e.g., LPCC). This higher tiered license generally allows the licensees the ability to practice more independently than was possible with the lower tiered license. Licensure is typically required in order to practice as a counselor in a given state, and it is required to receive reimbursements from third party payers (e.g., insurance companies, Medicaid). As more states move toward using consistent counselor titles and develop similar scopes of practice, counselors' visibility and reputation will be enhanced among other professionals, third-party payers, and consumers.

Although there is significant variability in what a state might require for licensure, some similarities do exist. Currently, all states require applicants for counselor licensure to have a combination of educational experiences and supervised counseling experience and to successfully pass an examination that assesses a prospective counselor's knowledge and/or decision-making ability to practice as a professional counselor. Each of the aforementioned expectations is discussed below: education, supervised experience, and examinations.

Education

Although there is wide variability on educational expectations for licensure, some similarities do exist. Most state boards require an individual to complete a master's degree in counseling from an accredited institution. Although the minimal amount of required semester credit hours historically has been 48, most states have moved toward adopting 60 semester hours of required graduate study for licensure consideration (Watson, Erford, Tasch, Kaplan, & Eliason, 2010). Core competency areas in which students are required to take courses may include counseling theories and techniques, life-span development, the diagnosing and treatment of mental illness, assessment, career development, group counseling, and often ethics. Additionally, some states have moved toward requiring specific coursework that aligns with the Council for Accreditation of Counseling and Related Educational Programs (CACREP) educational standards and expectations. The alignment with one national program accreditation body is consistent with other professions' standards and may help decrease any confusion related to counselors' professional identity stemming from differing standards and expectations.

It is important for you to understand that educational requirements for professional counseling licensure may vary from one state to another. In other words, you may meet the requirements for licensure in one state, but in another state you may be required to take additional educational coursework or even complete an additional supervised experience. For example, in the State of Florida, counselors are expected to have an educational background (e.g., completed coursework) in human sexuality theories for state licensure (Florida Department of Health, 2009).

Therefore, it is your responsibility to seek to understand the differences in the state professional counseling licensure requirements so that you can be prepared to fully meet the expectations of your specific state.

Supervised experience

In addition to educational requirements, most U.S. states require professional counselors to complete a residency or supervised clinical experience postgraduation. Like the residency model used in the medical profession, this process involves prospective licensees or licensed professional counselors documenting supervised counseling experience. In many U.S. states (e.g., Commonwealth of Virginia), the site and the specific supervisor of record will need to be approved by the licensure board prior to the accumulation of hours. Usually, state requirements concerning the amount of experience needed vary significantly from 2,500 to 4,500 hours of postgraduate supervised clinical experience (Watson et al., 2010). The practical residency requirements often align with CACREP's internship requirements, which require that at least 40% of a student's internship time be spent in direct service of clients (e.g., individual counseling, group counseling). The remainder of the supervised time usually consists of supervision, record keeping, staff meetings, and other counseling-related activities. In many states, the state licensure boards require proof that a counselor-in-training has had experience in diagnosis and treatment of mental illnesses in a client population during the residency experience (e.g., State of Ohio).

Additionally, some states (e.g., Texas and Ohio) have a supervisor designation that can be added to a license; this indicates that a licensed professional counselor has met standards to supervise counselors-in-training. Generally, supervisors or counselors with a supervision designation are required to have completed educational coursework (e.g., graduate coursework, workshops, continuing education) in the area of supervision and a supervised experience (i.e., supervised supervision) for a predetermined amount of time. Often, these supervised clinical experiences require direct supervision from a professional counselor with a supervisor's designation, with some states allowing for supervision to come from other related professions' licensed practitioners (e.g., licensed clinical psychologist, licensed clinical social worker, licensed marriage and family therapist).

Examinations

Every state requires an applicant for licensure to pass a comprehensive examination. These examinations assess the prospective licensee's knowledge and/or application of the practice of counseling. The National Board for Certified Counselors (NBCC) prepares and manages all of the examinations that are used by state regulatory boards. The two most utilized NBCC examinations for state licensure are the National Counselor Examination (NCE) and the National Clinical Mental Health Counseling Examination (NCMHCE). The structure and specifics of each examination follow.

The NCE evaluates general counseling knowledge, skills, and abilities. Prospective licensees have four hours to complete the 200 multiple-choice questions assessing areas such as counseling theories, assessment, research, professional ethics, multiculturalism, personality theories, group counseling, career counseling, and the diagnosing and treatment of mental disorders. This nationally administered examination is also administered to those who want to receive national credentialing endorsement as a national certified counselor (NCC).

The NCMHCE is an examination used to assess a prospective licensee's ability to diagnose and treat a range of clinical issues. This examination consists of 10 simulated clinical mental health cases that a counselor is likely to see in general clinical practice. The NCMHCE evaluates a prospective licensee's ability to evaluate and assess a clinical case, to diagnose and treat clinical issues, and to address clinical practice issues along the way. This nationally administered examination is also utilized for those applying for a national credentialing endorsement as a certified mental health counselor (CMHC).

Specific State Licensure

Addictions counseling

Some states also regulate counselors' ability to deliver addictions counseling services. Individuals may receive a specialized state licensure in addictions counseling to demonstrate they possess advanced training and expertise in the addictions counseling field. Each state individually regulates minimum standards and requirements. Often, addictions counselors will need to provide some evidence of specific education/training in the theories of addictions counseling and the treatment of addictions, along with a supervised experience with this specific clinical population. Prospective licensees are advised to review the education, training, and supervised experience requirements for their states. In addition to these requirements varying from state to state, the titles of these kinds of counselors may also vary from state to state. For example, the designations include licensed addictions counselor (North Dakota), certified substance abuse counselor (Virginia), licensed clinical addictions counselor (Indiana), and licensed substance abuse technician (Arizona). However, some states, such as Ohio, have a four-tier credential system; their credentials include those of chemical dependency counselor assistant, licensed chemical dependency counselor II and III, and licensed independent chemical dependency counselor. If you are interested in becoming an addictions counselor, you should consult their state licensing board for specific requirements and expectations outlined by each state.

School counseling

School counselors are licensed, certified, or endorsed to practice school counseling in all 50 states, the District of Columbia, Guam, Puerto Rico, and the Virgin Islands. Some states provide a school counseling license (e.g., Tennessee, Virginia), while other states provide only a certification/certificate (e.g., South Carolina, Washington) to practice as a school counselor. Each state has differing requirements for licensure (e.g., master's degree, specific number of credit hours, internship, previous experience, Praxis examination, background check). For example, four states still require an individual to have a teaching license or certificate in order to obtain a school counseling credential (ACA, 2011). Some states provide one K–12 school counseling licensure (e.g., Ohio), while others may divide the licensure between the elementary and secondary level (e.g., Pennsylvania). Additionally, individuals may receive a temporary or provisional credential as a school counselor through their school districts until education/experience requirements can be met. This practice varies from state to state. Individuals should review specific state requirements for licensure in their specific states.

Examples

The ACA publication *Licensure Requirements for Professional Counselors* (2010) provides information about each state board's licensure law requirements. For example, in Ohio, an individual is required to complete a 60-hour counseling degree from a CACREP accredited program that is also regionally accredited, pass the NCE, and accumulate 700 hours of practicum and internship experience in order to obtain an LPC. To earn an LPCC in Ohio (i.e., to practice independently) the LPC must complete 3,000 hours of clinical counseling experience with at least 50% of the time spent diagnosing and treating under the supervision of an LPCC-S, and the applicant must pass the NCMHCE.

In the Commonwealth of Virginia, a prospective LPC is required to complete a 60-hour counseling degree from a regionally accredited college or university. Graduate courses from a program accredited by CACREP or by the Council on Rehabilitation Education (CORE) are recognized as meeting the definition of an approved graduate degree program; other programs/courses need to be approved on a case-by-case basis. After graduation, a prospective licensee must complete a preapproved 4,000-hour supervised residency with 2,000 of those hours coming from direct contact with clients. Additionally, 200 hours of supervision by a preapproved supervisor must occur during those 4,000 hours. Supervision must come from an LPC who is at least two years post licensure and who has the appropriate supervision training according to the board's standards. After completion of the residency, a prospective licensee must then pass the NCMHCE to receive the designation of LPC. Since licensure requirements for education, supervision, and examination vary from state to state, it is important to thoroughly research the education, supervision, and examination requirements (see Table 11.1).

Licensure Portability

Because we live in an increasingly mobile society, licensure portability is important to many counselors. Licensure portability is the ability of a licensee to transfer her state counseling license to another state (Gerig, 2007). The means that an individual licensed in Virginia could apply to obtain a counseling license in Ohio based upon her holding of a license in Virginia. As discussed previously, due to state variability concerning required education, supervised experience, and examinations, some states will have more—or less—portability and reciprocity with other states. Reciprocity is the agreement that is made between states (i.e., licensing boards) to fully accept license transfers from another state. These agreements are rare and often still require a completed application for consideration. Historically, LPCs desiring to move and practice in another state would need to apply for the entry-level license at the new state. Currently, some states with similar standards and requirements have begun to allow full reciprocity with other states due to similar standards and expectations. Groups such as the American Association of State Counseling Boards (AASCB) have encouraged reciprocity. Since licensure and certifications may vary from state to state, it is important that you thoroughly research the education, supervision, and examinations requirements of the state in which you would like to pursue professional counseling licensure (see Table 11.1).

CASE ILLUSTRATION 11.2

SEEKING STATE LICENSURE

Monica graduated from a clinical mental health counseling program. When searching for a graduate program to enroll in, she considered only those schools whose programs met the requirements of the state licensure board. Before entering the program, she contacted the state licensing board to confirm that the curriculum and degree offered by her program met the state licensure requirement. Monica completed the licensure application, passed a criminal background check, and took the NCE in order to proceed to the next step—collecting direct and indirect clinical hours. After two years collecting her clinical hours, Monica became an LPC.

Three year later, Monica is thinking about relocating to a different state. Because she knows that each state has different educational requirements (e.g., varying requirements for credit hours), exams (e.g., NCE vs. NCMHCE), and clinical experience requirements (e.g., 2,000 to 3,000 clinical hours) for various levels of licensure (e.g., LPC, LPCC), she decides to research the possibilities in several states where she would like to reside. Monica understands that seeking licensure outside of her state requires a greater level of effort on her part than in-state certification.

Monica learns that some states require her to take additional coursework to receive a licensure, while others require more clinical hours. Monica then thinks back to what her professor, Dr. Tang, said during an Introduction to Counseling course lecture: Most common problems that applicants encounter occur when pursuing counseling licensure in different states. Dr. Tang stated, "First, it is important to understand that just because you are licensed in your home state does not mean you will get licensed in another state. Since every state has different laws and rules, I recommend that you start investigating these rules and laws at least six months prior to moving. Next, your degree will need to have the word *counseling* in it in some states. For example, there are some states, that will deny a license to a graduate who has a master's in education degree, even though it is a counseling degree and acknowledged as such by the licensure board in that state. Also, many students attend CACREP accredited programs and assume this accreditation will automatically provide them licensure. However, many states have additional coursework or training requirements that are needed to garner a license."

Monica also recalled Dr. Tang mentioning, "It is also helpful to be aware that some states have endorsement policies that may help you become licensed in that state. Endorsement occurs when a state allows you to get license based on your having been licensed in another state for a set period of time (e.g., in Ohio, you must have been licensed in another state for five years). In summary, it is critical for counseling students and professionals to be well informed and plan ahead for the state in which they would like to obtain counseling licensure."

Monica knows she will need to jump through many hoops before she can be licensed in the state to which she wants to relocate. However, it becomes obvious that the proactive approach that she is implementing facilitates her transition. Monica is very thankful that her graduate program prepared her to be aware of this information prior to graduation and planning to relocate. Monica believes that knowing these realities may enable future counselors to plan and prepare and ultimately have a more successful career and personal experience.

PROFESSIONAL ACCREDITING ORGANIZATIONS FOR COUNSELING PROGRAMS

As individuals seek counselor licensure as a means of establishing professional legitimacy, counseling programs at colleges and universities seek to establish external rigor and prestige when they undergo voluntary review by an external education accrediting body. These accreditation bodies ensure standards are met and reasonable oversight has been maintained. An accreditation process provides professional education programs with legitimacy. The two accreditation bodies associated with counseling degrees are CACREP and CORE.

Council for Accreditation of Counseling and Related Educational Programs (CACREP)

CACREP is the national body that specializes in accrediting programs in the field of counseling. CACREP develops standards for the training of graduate level counselors and accredits master's level programs in counseling in the following areas: addictions counseling; career counseling; clinical mental health counseling; marriage, couple, and family counseling; school counseling; and student affairs and college counseling. The core competencies of a CACREP accredited program consist of the following eight areas as outlined by CACREP (2009): professional orientation and ethical practice, social and cultural diversity, human growth and development, career development, helping relationship, group work, assessment, and research and program evaluation. Additionally, CACREP accredits doctoral programs in counselor education and supervision. Graduation from a CACREP program can have a significant impact on one's ability to become credentialed, and in some states (e.g., New Jersey, Ohio) to be licensed.

Council on Rehabilitation Education (CORE)

CORE is the national body that specializes in accrediting programs in the field of rehabilitation counseling. CORE accredits programs that provide the academic preparation for work in professional rehabilitation counseling. CORE seeks to provide graduates with the necessary knowledge and skills to work with individuals with physical, mental, and/or emotional disabilities. CORE and CACREP have worked together over the years, and there have been ongoing discussions regarding a possible CORE/CACREP merger. In 2013, CACREP and CORE entered into an agreement whereby CORE is a corporate affiliate of CACREP, and together the two organizations have developed policy and accreditation standards for the clinical rehabilitation counseling specialty—the seventh specialty (in addition to the six counseling specialties listed above).

Exercise 11.1

COUNSELING ACCREDITATION ORGANIZATIONS

Directions: In this chapter, locate the websites for CACREP and CORE. At each agency's website, locate its accreditation standards. Briefly summarize each set of standards. Next, compare and contrast the accreditation principles for each accreditation agency. Answer the following questions:

- What is the central aim of each accreditation body? How well does that aim align with that of other professional counseling organizations (e.g., ACA, NBCC)?
- How similar are the standards and core principles of the two accreditation bodies? In what ways do the two bodies differ in focus/structure?
- What types of guidelines/requirements do the accreditation bodies place on curriculum requirements, student supervision, and on students' practicum/ internship experiences?

PROFESSIONAL COUNSELING CERTIFICATION

In contrast to licenses, certifications generally are not legally necessary to practice. However, certification suggests to consumers and employers that a counselor has met a set of national standards in a given specialization/area. Again, while there are government regulations, which require counselors to be licensed to practice in each of the 50 states, a counselor does not need to hold any certification to practice counseling in any state. Thus, certification serves—in part—to assert a consistent professional identity (Sweeney, 1995). The two primary national certification agencies in the counseling profession are the National Board of Certified Counselors (NBCC), which certifies over 80,000 counselors (NBCC, n.d.) and the Commission on Rehabilitation Counselor Certification (CRCC), which certifies over 35,000 rehabilitation counselors (CRCC, n.d.). The Center for Credentialing and Education (CCE), a subsidiary under NBCC, will also be discussed, as they provide two additional professional counseling certifications.

National Board of Certified Counselors (NBCC)

The NBCC was created in 1982 as a national agency to certify counselors who met prescribed minimum requirements to practice counseling. It provides counselors with an opportunity to earn the NCC credential (NBCC, n.d.). In order to become an NCC, applicants must meet certain educational and counseling experience requirements and pass the NCE for licensure and certification. The NBCC provides various examinations, and all states require candidates to pass one or more of NBCC's examinations to garner different counseling licenses.

The NBCC has three additional certifications: the certified clinical mental health counselor (CCMHC); the national certified school counselor (NCSC); and the master addictions counselor (MAC). All of these certifications require an individual to already possess an NCC credential. In addition to initially meeting the minimum criteria for certification, individuals must maintain their certifications through the accumulation of continuing education credits. These three certifications will be discussed further (e.g., including specific educational, examination, and practice requirements) in the next section (i.e., Credentials for Counseling Specializations).

The NBCC's certifications (i.e., NCC, CCMHC, NCSC, and MAC) provide counselors with proof of professional competency and punctuate their identification with the counseling profession. This increase in identification not only enhances a counselor's sense of professional identity but also provides the public with proof of professional legitimacy, which is evidenced by the rigor involved in the certification process. Additionally, NBCC's specialty certifications (CCMHC, NCSC, and MAC) can aid counselors in carving out an identified specialty niche within the counseling profession. While some argue that states should license counselors as specialists (e.g., Cottone, 1985), others (Remley, 1995; Sweeney, 1995) have argued that states should continue to license counselors generically, and agencies like NBCC should identify and define specialty areas, which counselors can voluntary select. Once a counselor is licensed, she has the opportunity to carve out a personal scope of practice based upon her state laws and unique training, experience, and choice of certifications.

Commission on Rehabilitation Counselor Certification (CRCC)

Another accreditation body that certifies counselors nationally is CRCC. The CRCC was created in 1974 as a national agency to set the standard for quality rehabilitation counseling standards and practices. The commission designates individuals as certified rehabilitation counselors (CRCs) once they have demonstrated good moral character, fulfilled educational requirements, completed work experiences, and successfully passed the CRC exam (CRCC, n.d.). Additionally, individuals desiring to maintain the CRC designation must either pass the CRC examination again or meet ongoing continuing education requirements every five years.

Center for Credentialing and Education (CCE)

The CCE, an affiliate of the NBCC, is an agency that provides professional organizations and professionals with numerous different professional credentials as well as continuing education opportunities. Assessment and examinations are a major component of the CCE mission and identity. Additionally, CCE has two credentials relevant to counselors. They are the approved clinical supervisor (ACS) and the distance credentialed counselor (DCC). Each certification will be discussed (e.g., including specific educational, examination, and practice requirements) in the next section (i.e., Credentials for Counseling Specializations).

These three agencies—the NBCC, CRCC, and CCE—have established numerous professional counseling certifications. These certifications are not an exhaustive list of all the certifications available, and some others have been added to the following section to provide a fuller perspective of professional counseling certifications. Certifications aid not only the profession of counseling and its consumers but also counselors themselves. A counselor with a professional counseling certification has evidence of her professional competency due to the rigor inherent in each certification process, and she can more readily identify with a specialization within the counseling profession. In the next section, each certification will be fully discussed, including its specific educational, examination, and practice requirements, within the correlating specialization of counseling (i.e., mental health, rehabilitation, addictions, school counseling, and career counseling).

CREDENTIALS FOR COUNSELING SPECIALIZATIONS

Early on in this chapter, you learned that professional counseling certifications serve two primary roles: (a) to confirm that an individual has met minimum educational and training requirements in a given specialization within counseling outlined by an external credentialing body, and (b) to assert a consistent professional identity among those professionals (Sweeney, 1995). Logistically, the professional counseling certifications in this chapter have been grouped according to specific counseling specialization (i.e., mental health, rehabilitation, addictions, school counseling, and career counseling) for increased usability. In this section, you will learn how you can obtain these certifications/credentials in each specialty area and the perceived benefits of having these certifications/credentials.

Clinical Mental Health Counseling

The primary generalist certification for clinical mental health counselors is the national clinical counselor (NCC), which is regulated by NBCC. The primary benefit of this certification is to confirm a minimal knowledge, skill, and ability to practice, because a counselor has met the educational, examination, and experience requirements. The requirements for an NCC certification are (a) satisfactory performance on the NCE (i.e., 70% correct), (b) graduation from either a CACREP

Exercise 11.2

PROFESSIONAL COUNSELORS AND COUNSELING SPECIALIZATION CREDENTIALING

Directions: Find one of your classmates or study partners, and discuss the following questions:

1. Why does the counseling profession offer different credentials based on the areas of specialization?

2. Do different credentials benefit professional counselors? If so, how? If not, why not?

3. How interested are you in seeking different credentials based on the area in which you would like to specialize (e.g., school counseling, addictions counseling, career counseling)?

---

accredited counseling program or from a master's-level program in counseling, and (c) 3,000 hours of post-master's counseling experience (with 100 hours of supervision) within a 24-month period. Alternatively, a candidate may be NCC certified if she graduates from a master's program in counseling and holds a current and active state license as a professional counselor.

Individuals with advanced training, supervision, and experience in clinical mental health counseling can apply for certified clinical mental health counselor (CCHMC) credentials through the NBCC. The CCHMC exam—as previously described—assesses applicants' knowledge of clinical counseling. This advanced designation requires the NCC as a prerequisite and has additional experience and education requirements as well. To earn the CCHMC, applicants must (a) document 60 semester hours of graduate-level academic credit in counseling *or* document participation in equivalent clinical workshops (for workshop documentation, 15 clock hours are considered equal to 1 academic credit hour), (b) complete 3,000 hours of client contact with 100 hours of supervision *or* hold a current and active state license as a professional counselor, (c) submit a taped clinical session to the NBCC, and, finally (d) receive a passing score (i.e., 70%) on the NCMHCE.

The CCE, which is closely associated with the NBCC, also provides two credentials for clinical mental health counselors. The approved clinical supervisor (ACS) credential certifies competence in clinical supervision. Initially, the ACS was offered only by NBCC. With the move to CCE, professional counselors in all related disciplines could seek the certification without possessing an NCC credential. The requirements for the ACS are (a) a master's degree in a mental health field, (b) current status as an NCC *or* licensed/certified mental health provider *or* licensed/certified clinical supervisor, (c) graduate training in supervision *or* a total of 30 clock hours of workshop training in clinical supervision, (d) three years post-masters' experience in mental health, including 1,500 hours of direct services with clients, (e) 100 hours of supervision of the applicant as supervisor, by either a certified or licensed supervisor, and (f) a self-assessment and professional disclosure statement. Alternative entry to the ACS certification may be considered by the CCE board concerning clinical and supervision experience; therefore an applicant should consult the requirements and the board to consider her specific qualifications.

The distance credentialed counselor (DCC) is another CCE certification aimed at the delivery of technology-assisted counseling services. This designation attempts to provide the public with assurance that the counselor has met a minimal requirement of knowledge concerning distance counseling, including knowledge of technology needed to be an effective distance counselor, best practices in distance counseling, techniques to build relationships via distance methods, and awareness of the legal and ethical issues involved in distance counseling. The DCC requires (a) a master's degree in counseling or a related field and a current/active state license *or* certification as an NCC and (b) proof of successful completion of the two-day (15 hours) training for the DCC designation.

There are a large number of theory-based specialization certifications promoted by a variety of organizations and associations. A few examples of these include the board certified behavioral analyst (BCBA), eye movement desensitization and reprocessing (EMDR) certification, choice theory or reality therapy certification (CT/RTC), and registered play therapist (RPT). More examples of theory-based certifications exist, but these four designations were selected to highlight four distinctly different certifications and the requirement for these designations.

Counselors who hold a BCBA certification conduct behavioral analyses and functional analyses, and they provide behavioral interpretations of those analyses for clients with a range of mental health concerns. The requirements for certification as a BCBA are (a) possession of bachelor's and master's degrees in behavioral analysis *or* other related field and (b) 225 classroom hours of graduate instruction in behavioral analysis with experience *or* completion of one academic year (full time) teaching appointment in behavioral analysis with experience *or* a completed doctorate in behavioral analysis (or related field) with 10 years of experience in behavioral analysis.

Another theory-based certification is available in EMDR, a treatment approach based on an individual's information processing. EMDR has been most associated with the treatment of clients who have experienced trauma (e.g., PTSD, sexual abuse, physical abuse, neglect, domestic violence). The requirements for a certification in EMDR are (a) a combination of supervised practice and two weekend trainings totaling 40 hours of continuing education credits (i.e., 20 hours didactic and 20 hours supervised practice), (b) reading the EMDR textbook (Shapiro, 2001), and (c) 10 hours of case consultation with an EMDR-approved consultant.

CT/RTC is another example of a theory-based certification. The CT/RTC is an 18-month educational/experiential process aimed at training individuals in reality therapy as developed by William Glasser. The certification includes five discrete steps: (a) basic intensive training, (b) basic practicum, (c) advanced intensive training, (d) advanced practicum, and (e) a 4½-day certification training. Upon completion of these five steps, the CT/RTC is awarded.

RPT and the related RPT-S (registered play therapist-supervisor) are certifications/credentials for mental health professionals desiring specialized training and experiences in play therapy. The requirements for an RTP certification are as follows: (a) hold a current and active state license to engage in either independent or supervised mental health practice, (b) hold a master's- or higher-level mental health degree from an institution of higher education, (c) complete at least two years and 2,000 hours of supervised clinical experience, (d) complete at least 150 hours of play therapy instruction, and (e) complete at least 500 hours of supervised play therapy experience and 50 hours of concurrent play therapy–specific supervision.

Certification as a RPT-S requires two additional components: (a) an additional 500 hours of play therapy (additional supervision not required) and (b) state licensure in supervision *or* be in a state that does not require a supervision designation to supervise. To maintain certification, an individual must maintain an active state license and complete 36 hours of continuing education every three years. An RPT-S must have 2 of the 36 hours of continuing education in supervision training.

Through advanced training and supervised practice, professional counselors can develop a variety of specializations focused on theory (e.g., cognitive–behavioral therapy), client population (e.g., adolescents), clinical disorder (e.g., eating disorders), and/or typical life issues (e.g., grief and loss). For additional information on these certifications, visit the following websites:

- NCC and CCMHC certifications: www.nbcc.org/OurCertifications
- ACS and DCC certifications: www.cce-global.org/Prof/Credentials
- BCBA certification: www.bacb.com/
- EMDR certification: www.emdr.com/
- CT/RTC certification: www.wglasser.com/
- RPT and RPT-S certifications: www.a4pt.org/

Rehabilitation Counseling

Rehabilitation counselors assist individuals with disabilities on issues related to employability and independence. The Commission on Rehabilitation Counselor Certification (CCRC) manages the certified rehabilitation counselor (CRC) credential. The requirements for the CRC designation are (a) a master's in rehabilitation counseling (i.e., accredited by CORE) with an internship supervised by a CRC and (b) a passing score on the CRC examination. Alternative eligibility requirements exist, and the *CRC Certification Guide* (CCRC, n.d.) or the board should be consulted. The CRC designation indicates that individuals have specific training in the principles of rehabilitation counseling. The CCRC also maintains the certified vocational evaluation specialist (CVE), certified work adjustment specialist (CWA), and certified career assessment associate (CCAA) credentials. These credentials are helpful for counselors who work as career assessment professionals and demonstrate that counselors have met national standards of knowledge and training in the areas of career assessment, vocational evaluation, and work adjustment, respectively. Counselors interested in these designations should consult the CRCC board or the CRCC website (www.crccertification.com/) for further clarification of the requirements for and benefits of these designations. For additional information about these certifications, visit the following websites:

- CRC certification: www.crccertification.com/
- CRC Certification Guide: www.crccertification.com/filebin/pdf/ CRCCertificationGuide.pdf

Addictions Counseling

Addictions counseling focuses on substance (i.e., drug and alcohol) abuse as well as the process addictions (e.g., sex, gambling, shopping addictions). The National Association of Alcoholism and Drug Abuse Counselors (NAADAC) and the Association for Addiction Professionals, in conjunction with the National Certification Commission, maintain two certifications for addictions counselors: the national certified addictions counselor, levels I and II (NCAC I and NCAC II). The NCAC I requirements are (a) current state certification/licensure as an alcoholism and/or drug abuse counselor, (b) three years full time (i.e., 6,000 hours) of supervised experience, (c) documentation of 270 contact hours of education and training in the field, (d) reading and signing the NAADAC code of ethics, and (e) passing the level I examination. The NCAC II requirements are (a) a bachelor's degree, (b) current state licensure/certification, (c) five years (i.e., 10,000 hours) of supervised experience, (d) documentation of 450 contact hours of education and training in alcoholism and/or drug abuse, (e) reading, and signing the NAADAC code of ethics, and (f) passing the level II examination.

In conjunction with NAADAC, NBCC provides the master addictions counselor (MAC) credential. The requirements for a MAC designation are (a) hold an NCC credential, (b) documentation of 12 semester hours in the area of addictions, which may include coursework in group and/or marriage and family counseling, (c) three years supervised experience in an addiction setting, and (d) a passing score on the Examination for Master Addictions Counselor (EMAC). This credential demonstrates a minimal level of training, knowledge, and experience in addictions counseling.

The American Academy of Health Care Providers in Addictive Disorders provides a certified addiction specialist (CAS) credential, which demonstrates competency in working with alcohol, drug, eating, sex, and gambling addictions. The requirements for the designation of CAS include (a) a master's or doctoral degree in mental health and (b) three years (i.e., 6,000 hours) of supervised experience in providing direct health services to those identified with an addictive disorder. Alternative eligibility requirements exist, and the American Academy of Health Care Providers in Addictive Disorders should be consulted to address specific considerations.

For additional information about these certifications, visit the following websites:

- NCAC I and II certifications: www.naadac.org/
- MAC certification: www.nbcc.org/OurCertifications
- CAS certification: www.americanacademy.org/

School Counseling

While most school counseling licensure and credentialing is regulated at the state level, credentialing at the national level is another means to regulate the school counseling profession by creating minimal standards of education, experience, and examination that are consistent across the United States. Individuals with advanced training, supervision, and experience in school counseling can apply for the national certified school counselor (NCSC) credential through the NBCC. The requirements of NCSC are (a) have a graduate degree with a major study in counseling, (b) hold the designation of NCC, (c) have three semesters post-master's degree of school counseling experience with ongoing supervision from an individual with either an NCC designation or state certification as a school counselor, and (d) pass the National Certified School Counselor Examination (NCSCE). Two applications exist for the NCSC, one for applicants who hold a state-level certification for school counseling and another for those who do not hold a state certification. Individuals should consult NBCC directly to address specific considerations.

For additional information, visit the following websites:

- State School Counselor Certification: www.schoolcounselor.org/content. asp?contentid=242
- NCSC certification: www.nbcc.org/OurCertifications

Career Counseling

Counselors in a variety of settings frequently provide career counseling. As with clinical mental health counseling, state professional counseling licensure and/or national certifications in career counseling provide assurance that a counselor has achieved a minimum level of career counseling knowledge. The CCE, in association with the NBCC, provides credentials for career counselors. The global career development facilitator (GCDF) is a certification for individuals who have advanced training in career development and seek to provide career guidance in a variety of settings. Requirements for a GCDF consist of 120 hours of training designated by CCE. The distanced credentialed facilitator (DCF) is a certification for individuals who provide career and life planning through online technology. To become a DCF, one must already be a GCDF, hold a master's degree in the helping profession, and be able to document 2,000 hours of career development or related experience. Individuals who would like to provide vocational guidance services on an international level can apply for the educational and vocational guidance practitioner (EVGP) credential. Requirements for the EVGP designation vary significantly according to education (i.e., high school only, some college, bachelor's degree, or graduate degree), experience (ranging from 1,000 to 4,000 hours), and training (e.g., in assessment, career development, or information management). Individuals interested in this designation should contact the CCE for specific requirements of this designation.

There are also specialization certifications based on career theories that can be earned by professional counselors and other mental health professionals. These specialization certificates include the Myers-Briggs Type Indicator (MBTI) master practitioner credential, Strong Interest Inventory certification, and certification for the Self-Directed Search. While having the certifications is not mandatory for professional counselors to utilize these career instruments, obtaining these certifications demonstrates that the professional counselor has met a standard of competence in the administration and interpretation of these specific career assessments. Finally, the National Career Development Association maintains special membership designations (e.g., master career counselor, MCC; master career development professional, MCDP) for career counselors with professional experience and education.

For additional information about these certifications, visit these websites:

- GCDF, DCF, and EVGP certifications: www.cce-global.org/Prof/Credentials
- MBTI master practitioner credential: www.mbtimasterpractitioner.org/
- MCC and MCDP designations: http://associationdatabase.com/aws/NCDA/pt/sp/membership_categories_special

Exercise 11.3

COUNSELING SPECIALIZATION AND CREDENTIALING

Directions: Locate one of the certifications under any of the counseling specializations (i.e., clinical mental health, rehabilitation, addiction, school, and career) and the associated website from this chapter.

- First explore the educational, experience, and examination requirements to become certified in that specialized area.
- Considering what you have already done educationally and professionally, what specifically do you need to do to meet the requirements for this certification?
- What privileges and opportunities are afforded because of this certification?
- In what ways can you imagine that this certification would strengthen your professional identity?
- What may this certification say about you and your ability to practice with certain clients in certain situations? How would this be advantageous for your current and/or future clients?
- Finally, what would you need to do to maintain this certification over time?

- Strong Interest Inventory certification: www.cpp.com/contents/qual_strong .aspx
- Self-Directed Search certification: www.thecareermaze.com/workshops/ workshop-nzcer

CONTINUING EDUCATION AND ADDITIONAL TRAINING OPPORTUNITIES

Professional counseling certifications confirm that an individual has met minimum requirements in a given specialization and aid in maintaining a consistent professional identity among those professionals (Sweeney, 1995), while state licensures address the individual's minimum qualifications to practice counseling under the state laws. Regardless of the specialization (i.e., clinical mental health, rehabilitation, addictions, school, or career), professional counseling certifications and licensures provide another means to regulate the counseling profession in creating minimal standards of education, experience, and examination.

Obtaining certifications and licensures is not the end of your professional journey. In fact, there is more to do after that. This typically includes participating in professional development (e.g., advanced trainings) to develop clinical competencies according to one's specialty area, and receiving continuing education units (CEUs) or continuing education credits (CECs) to maintain one's professional licensure. Professional development opportunities are offered through workshops and trainings by the providers/institutions (e.g., a trained expert) or at professional conferences (e.g., state and national annual conferences). These opportunities can be recognized as CEUs if those providers are qualified and approved by the state licensing boards and/or the organizations governing certifications (e.g., NBCC). Licensed and certified counselors, regardless of their specialty areas of practice, are required to provide evidence of completion of continuing education requirements mandated by the licensing boards and/or certification bodies. This is because the field of counseling is always changing in terms of professional knowledge (e.g., evidence of new treatment modalities) and current issues (e.g., ethical and multicultural issues) that professional counselors should utilize in their professional practice to enhance their quality of client care. It is important to note that licenses or certifications can be revoked and/or suspended in the event that licensed or certified counselors fail to comply with the CEU requirements set by the licensing boards or certification bodies. Therefore, you should pay close attention to CEU requirements once you become licensed or certified in order to maintain your professional license or certification.

KEYSTONES

In this chapter, types of professional counselor credentialing were discussed. As mentioned, professional counselors seek credentials, including state licensures and national certifications, in order to show individual competency, support professional legitimacy, and promote professional identity. State licensures and national certifications are two different things: Licensure represents the ability to practice as a professional counselor in a certain jurisdiction (i.e., a certain U.S. state), while certifications reflect the meeting of minimum criteria in a given specialization within counseling or within a counseling specialty.

Concepts highlighted in this chapter include the following:

- Credentialing is a broad term that covers many areas (e.g., state licensure, program accreditation, specialization, and national certifications).
- Currently, all U.S. states require applicants for counselor licensure to have some combination of educational experiences and supervised counseling experience, and to have successfully passed an examination that assesses their knowledge and/or decision-making ability to practice as a professional counselor.

- Just as counselors seek licensure as a means of establishing professional legitimacy, the programs that prepare them also establish legitimacy by undergoing voluntary reviews by an external accrediting body such as CACREP or CORE to prove the programs have meet consistent standards and expectations.
- In contrast to licensure, national and specialization certifications, while not legally necessary to practice, suggest that a counselor has met a set of national standards in a given specialization or area.
- Licensure portability is the ability of licensed counselors to transfer their state licenses to other states (Gerig, 2007).
- It is important that you, as a future professional counselor, adequately research the specific requirements to practice counseling in your state. Consider utilizing a professional counseling credential to promote your professional identity and to allow others to see that you have met minimal criteria in specific specializations within the counseling profession.

Exercise 11.4

END OF CHAPTER EXERCISES AND REFLECTIONS

Directions: Answer the questions in parts I, II, and III. Utilize Table 11.1 (provided below) to help you answer those questions.

Table 11.1   US State Licensure Boards—Websites

ALABAMA (www.abec.alabama.gov)
ALASKA (www.commerce.state.ak.us/occ/ppco.htm)
ARIZONA (http://azbbhe.us)
ARKANSAS (www.arkansas.gov/abec)
CALIFORNIA (www.bbs.ca.gov/)
COLORADO (www.dora.state.co.us/mental-health)
CONNECTICUT (www.ct.gov/dph/)
DELAWARE (www.dpr.delaware.gov/)
DISTRICT OF COLUMBIA (www.hpla.doh.dc.gov/hpla/site/default.asp)
FLORIDA (www.doh.state.fl.us/mqa/491)
GEORGIA (www.sos.georgia.gov/plb/counselors/)
HAWAII (www.hawaii.gov/dcca/areas/pvl/programs/mental/)
IDAHO (www.ibol.idaho.gov/)

(Continued)

Table 11.1 (Continued)

ILLINOIS (www.idfpr.com/dpr/who/prfcns.asp)

INDIANA (www.in.gov/pla/social.htm)

IOWA (www.idph.state.ia.us/licensure/)

KANSAS (www.ksbsrb.org/)

LOUISIANA (www.lpcboard.org)

MAINE (www.maine.gov/pfr/professionallicensing)

MARYLAND (www.dhmh.maryland.gov/bopc)

MASSACHUSETTS (www.mass.gov/dpl/boards/mh)

MICHIGAN (www.michigan.gov/healthlicense)

MINNESOTA (www.bbht.state.mn.us)

MISSISSIPPI (www.lpc.state.ms.us)

MISSOURI (www.pr.mo.gov/counselors.asp)

MONTANA (www.bsd.dli.mt.gov/license/bsd_boards/swp_board/board_page.asp)

NEBRASKA (www.dhhs.ne.gov/crl/mhcs/mental/mentalindex.htm)

NEVADA (www.marriage.state.nv.us/)

NEW HAMPSHIRE (www.nh.gov/mhpb)

NEW JERSEY (www.njconsumeraffairs.gov/proc)

NEW MEXICO (www.rld.state.nm.us/counseling)

NEW YORK (www.op.nysed.gov/prof/mhp/mhclic.htm)

NORTH CAROLINA (www.ncblpc.org)

NORTH DAKOTA (www.ndbce.org)

OHIO (www.cswmft.ohio.gov)

OKLAHOMA (www.pcl.health.ok.gov)

OREGON (www.oregon.gov/oblpct)

PENNSYLVANIA (www.dos.state.pa.us/social)

PUERTO RICO (www.salud.gov.pr)

RHODE ISLAND (www.health.ri.gov/hsr/professions/mf_counsel.php)

SOUTH CAROLINA (www.llr.state.sc.us/pol/counselors)

SOUTH DAKOTA (www.dhs.sd.gov/brd/counselor)

TENNESSEE (www.health.state.tn.us/boards/PC_MFT&CPT/)

TEXAS (www.dshs.state.tx.us/counselor)

UTAH (www.dopl.utah.gov/licensing/professional_counseling.html)

VERMONT (www.vtprofessionals.org)

VIRGINIA (www.dhp.virginia.gov/counseling)

WASHINGTON (www.doh.wa.gov/licensing/)

WEST VIRGINIA (www.wvbec.org)

WISCONSIN (www.drl.wi.gov/board_detail.asp?boardid=32&locid=0)

WYOMING (www.plboards.state.wy.us/mentalhealth/index.asp)

Part I

1. What state do you live in? Utilize Table 11.1 from this chapter to locate your state's counseling licensure website. Based on the information at your state's website, answer the next three questions.

2. What are the education requirements for licensure in your state?

3. What are the supervision requirements for licensure in your state?

4. What are the examination requirements for licensure in your state?

Part II

Now, consider that you are recently licensed in your home state, but a wonderful opportunity in [insert desired state] becomes available.

1. How easily would your license transfer? Utilize Table 11.1 from this chapter, and locate your desired state's counseling licensure website. Based on the information at your desired state's website, answer the next four questions.

2. What are the education requirements for licensure in this new state?

3. What are the supervision requirements for licensure in this new state?

4. What are the examination requirements for licensure in this new state?

5. Do any provisions exist for total reciprocity in this new state?

Part III

1. Consider what population and counseling area you would like to specialize in.

2. What certifications would you like to pursue to demonstrate competency in that area?

3. Using the websites in this chapter, what are the requirements needed to obtain and maintain this type of credentialing?

ADDITIONAL RESOURCES

American Association of State Counselor Licensure Boards: www.aascb.org/aws/AASCB/pt/sp/home_page
American Counseling Association: www.counseling.org
American Counseling Association Divisions: www.counseling.org/AboutUs/DivisionsBranchesAnd Regions/TP/Divisions/CT2.aspx
Commission on Accreditation for Marriage and Family Therapy Education: www.aamft.org/imis15/content/coamfte/coamfte.aspx
Commission on Rehabilitation Counselor Certification: www.crccertification.com

Council for Accreditation of Counseling and Related Educational Programs: www.cacrep.org
Council on Rehabilitation Education: www.core-rehab.org
National Board of Certified Counselors: www.nbcc.org

REFERENCES

American Counseling Association (ACA). (2010). *Licensure requirements for professional counselors.* Retrieved from http://www.counseling.org/counselors/LicensureAndCert.aspx

American Counseling Association (ACA). (2011). *A guide to state laws and regulations on professional school counseling.* Alexandria, VA: Author.

Commission on Rehabilitation Counselor Certification (CRCC). (n.d.) *About CRCC.* Retrieved from http://www.crccertification.com/pages/aboutcertification/46.php

Commission on Rehabilitation Counselor Certification (CRCC). (n.d.) *CRC certification guide.* Retrieved from http://www.crccertification.com/filebin/pdf/CRCCertificationGuide.pdf

Corey, G., Corey, M. S., & Callanan, P. (2011). *Issues and ethics in the helping profession* (8th ed.). Belmont, CA: Brooks/Cole.

Cottone, R. (1985). The need for counselor licensure: A rehabilitation counseling perspective. *Journal of Counseling and Development, 63,* 625–629. doi: 10.1002/j.1556- 6676.1985.tb00647.x

Council for Accreditation of Counseling and Related Educational Program (CACREP). (2009). *Standards.* Retrieved from http://www.cacrep.org/doc/2009%20Standards%20with%20cover.pdf

Florida Department of Health (2009). *Board of clinical social work, marriage and family therapy and mental health counseling: Application for Licensure.* Retrieved from http://www.doh.state.fl.us/mqa/491/ap_applicationpacket.pdf

Gerig, M. S. (2007). *Foundations for mental health and community counseling: An introduction to the profession.* Ventura, CA: Academic Internet Publishers.

National Board of Certified Counselors (NBCC). (n.d.). *Understanding NBCC's national certifications.* Retrieved at http://www.nbcc.org/OurCertifications

Remley, T. P., Jr. (1995). A proposed alternative to the licensing of specialties in counseling. *Journal of Counseling and Development, 74,* 126–129. doi: 10.1002/j.1556–6676.1995.tb01835.x

Remley, T. P., Jr., & Herlihy, B. (2007). *Ethical, legal and professional issues in counseling* (2nd ed., Rev.). Columbus, OH: Pearson Merrill Prentice-Hall.

Shapiro, F. (2001). *Eye movement desensitization and reprocessing: Basic principles, protocols, and procedures* (2nd ed.). New York, NY: Guilford Press.

Sweeney, T. J. (1995). Accreditation, credentialing, professionalization: The role of specialties. *Journal of Counseling & Development, 74,* 117–125. doi: 10.1002/j.1556–6676.1995.tb0184.x

Watson, J., Erford, B. T., Tasch, K., Kaplan, D., & Eliason, G. T. (2010). Professional counseling associations, licensure, certification and accreditation. In B. T. Erford (Ed.), *Orientation to the counseling profession* (pp. 24–54). Columbus, OH: Pearson Merrill Prentice-Hall.

Chapter 12

Advocacy for Professional Counseling

Cynthia T. Walley
Stuart F. Chen-Hayes

When you hear the word *advocacy,* what images first come to mind? You may imagine the act of standing up for something you believe in, such as free tuition for students in public universities and no more budget cuts to K–12 public schools. You may also visualize speaking up for someone or something to create a change, such as starting a mental health awareness week in your agency or school to do outreach to support persons with mental health issues. Advocacy refers to "the act or process of supporting a cause or proposal" ("Advocacy," n.d.). Advocacy efforts, however, are not confined to the micro level, in which a counselor supports or is actively involved in the welfare of one client or student. Advocacy is comprehensive and multidimensional (Trusty & Brown, 2005), and it includes advocating for the profession of counseling. Other defining characteristics of advocacy in helping professions involve addressing external barriers that interfere with human development (Gibson, 2010); promoting and safeguarding the well-being and interests of service recipients (Vaartio, Leino-Kilpi, Salantera, & Suominen, 2006); and persuading others on behalf of another (Wiener, 1948). But advocacy in professional counseling practice involves larger systems to strengthen and make progressive changes to the counseling profession (Chibbaro, 2009). Advocacy efforts range from collaborating and supporting individuals (micro level) as well as system, school, or community initiatives (meso level) to addressing legislative decision and policy making (macro level) to creating sociopolitical changes that challenge multiple types of oppression (Chen-Hayes, 2009; Ratts, DeKruyf, & Chen-Hayes, 2007; Toporek, Lewis, & Crethar, 2009).

Advocacy is a part of your professional service and responsibility as a member of the counseling profession. Previously, in Chapter 6, you were introduced to the importance of advocacy and how professional counselors can advocate for clients, communities, and other stakeholders. In this chapter, you will learn ways to advocate for the counseling profession. First, expanding on the information in Chapter 2, you will learn more about historical development and advocacy efforts of the counseling profession and the seven major specialty practice areas in the United States: addictions counseling; career counseling; clinical mental health counseling; marriage, couple, and family counseling; rehabilitation; school counseling; and student affairs counseling (Council for Accreditation of Counseling and Related Educational Programs [CACREP], 2009). Second, you will become aware of ongoing efforts to unify the counseling profession by members of many professional organizations. We outline various advocacy methods you can implement to maintain and support the counseling profession. Reflection exercises and activities, including case studies, will help you develop an advocacy plan to enhance your professional identity and strengthen the counseling profession.

LEARNING OBJECTIVES

After reading the information and engaging in the reflection exercises provided in this chapter, you will be able to

- Assess your level of advocacy competency in professional counseling;
- Describe the history of advocacy in professional counseling and the seven specialty areas of practice; and
- Identify specific advocacy strategies to help shape and promote professional counseling.

Exercise 12.1

AMERICAN COUNSELING ASSOCIATION ADVOCACY COMPETENCIES

Before you begin, it is important to assess your professional advocacy skills by reviewing the ACA advocacy competencies (ACA, 2010). Write down your strengths, and list areas of improvement in which you would like to increase your awareness, knowledge, and skills in advocating for the profession of counseling.

PROFESSIONAL COUNSELING AND ADVOCACY

In the United States, the counseling profession has been affected by and responded to historical and political forces. A focus on professional advocacy is found in U.S.–based counseling association codes of ethics and standards of practice from several professional organizations: American Counseling Association (ACA, 2005), American Mental Health Counceling Association (AMHCA, 2011), American School Counselor Association (ASCA, 2010), and the National Board for Certified Counselors (NBCC, 2005). There are basic principles fundamental to advocacy across all professions: beneficence, autonomy, nonmaleficence, justice, and fidelity are key ethical elements of advocacy, and each may be involved in action required to make changes on behalf of clients or students (March, 1999). For example, as the U.S. population diversifies, through social and professional advocacy, professional counselors have responded to issues of individual and systemic oppressions (Chen-Hayes, 2007, 2009; Hof, Scofield, & Dinsmore, 2006).

Social advocacy is one way professional counselors have made changes in response to historical forces for individuals, groups, and the profession to meet the holistic needs of diverse client populations (Chang, Hays, & Milliken, 2009), such as ensuring that war veterans receive timely and adequate mental health services, ensuring that school counselors help close achievement, opportunity, and attainment gaps with their K–12 school counseling programs (ASCA, 2010; Holcomb-McCoy & Chen-Hayes, 2011), and ensuring that counselors and graduate students adhere to counseling professional standards in providing services to any marginalized or oppressed group (Student Press Law Center, 2012). Although some see social advocacy as a "fifth force" within the counseling profession (Ratts, 2009), others contended that social advocacy is cyclical and not a contemporary issue (Smith, Reynolds, & Rovnak, 2009). In addition, Myers, Sweeney, and White (2002) suggested effectively advocating for clients involved in advocating for the profession. For example, in 2012, the American Counseling Association launched an aggressive media campaign to address the Veterans Administration's failure to hire licensed mental health counselors (Rudow, 2012). With multiple U.S. war involvements in the early 2000s, the unique mental health needs of veterans were unmet, when they could have been filled if the administration had hired licensed mental health counselors; thus, this policy contributed toward lack of access to mental health services for war veterans (Barstow & Terrazas, 2012) and substantiated the need for professional advocacy efforts.

Professional advocacy is working with or on behalf of one's profession (Hof, Dinsmore, Barber, Suhr, & Scofield, 2009). In other words, professional advocacy involves specific course and fieldwork requirements in counselor education (e.g., requiring advocacy projects in class and at practicum and internship sites), intraprofessional relations (e.g., presenting advocacy projects at local, state, and national counseling organization conferences), marketplace recognition (e.g., developing counseling brochures and websites for public use), interprofessional issues (e.g., collaboration between K–16 schools and local agencies related to drug prevention and intervention and raising student achievement), research (e.g., establishing evidence-based practice for counselor efficacy), and prevention and wellness (e.g., counselor education students developing wellness outreach activities in schools and agencies affected by violence or terror such as mass shootings or accidents) (Chi Sigma Iota [CSI], n.d.). Thus, the importance of professional counselors advocating on behalf of their profession is well documented.

Advocacy in counseling, however, has historically suffered from disagreement among counselors and from multiple counseling definitions that traditionally focused on counseling individual clients or students and groups, families, and couples over time. Nevertheless, with the ACA advocacy competencies (Lewis, Arnold, House, & Toporek, 2002), the counseling profession expanded focus to systemic change and advocacy in six key areas: empowerment of clients and students, advocacy for clients and students, community (and school) collaboration, systems advocacy, public information, and social/political advocacy. The shift was toward public information, systemic change, and sociopolitical advocacy moving the profession away from only an individual, group, couple/family, or client/student focus to a profession focused on external systems needing change. You will see that this chapter honors the spirit of the ACA advocacy competencies (Lewis et al., 2002) and applies a systemic change, public information, and sociopolitical lens toward promoting counseling as one profession with multiple voices and interpretations. Therefore, it is important for you to examine the components of advocacy for professional counseling as one profession with seven current specialty areas of practice.

CASE ILLUSTRATION 12.1

KRISTOPHER'S DILEMMA

Kristopher is a master's student in a school counseling program. His internship experience is in a high school setting. One day, Tonya, a junior on his caseload, confides in him that she is pregnant. Kristopher listens, empathizes, and supports Tonya in the session. However after the session, Kristopher feels extremely anxious regarding what should be his next course of action. Kristopher feels that his first obligation is to Tonya, his client. Tonya reported, and it was confirmed by Tonya's teachers, that she is missing classes or having to be excused from class due to feeling ill often, which has contributed to decreased grades in four of her seven classes. Tonya states she has not told her parents, as they would not understand and would kick her out of the house, since they are religious conservatives. Since Kristopher and Tonya live in a state that grants minors access to health care and contraception without parental consent, Kristopher is unsure if confidentiality should be broken. Kristopher would like to make general statements to the teachers about excusing Tonya's illness and suggesting to Tonya's parents that she might need a physical.

Courts have consistently ruled that graduate students must follow the professional counseling codes of ethics; counselors cannot ethically pick and choose whom they choose to work with based on their beliefs. What professional advocacy role do codes of ethics play versus laws for professional counseling in this situation? ACA, NBCC, ASCA, and AMHCA all have separate codes of ethics, and all 50 states have unique laws and regulations. As a graduate student, you are responsible for knowing your state laws and the codes of ethics specific to the entire profession (ACA) and your specialty area (ASCA, AMHCA).

Although advocacy has been a theme throughout the history of the counseling profession, it has only been within the last two decades that it has gained greater systemic attention. Eriksen's (1997) publication on advocacy was the first book devoted to uniting and promoting the profession through the use of advocacy. The author discussed a model for organizing and managing an advocacy campaign for professional counseling and suggested a seven-step process of advocacy. The steps included professional identification, problem identification, resource assessment, strategic planning, advocacy training, taking action, and evaluating outcomes (Eriksen, 1999). Yet, even with this publication, some professional counselors disagreed with focusing on advocacy for the profession, because it could be perceived as "selfish," and "reducing resources from the client" (McClure & Russo, 1996, p. 162). However, this view has not been proven, and the 2009 CACREP standards required that advocacy be taught in every professional specialty area (CACREP, 2009). McClure and Russo's assertions were unfounded.

In the 21st century, professional counseling organizations (e.g., ACA, CACREP, CSI, and NBCC) support professional advocacy, as it promotes an environmental transformation creating meaningful impact addressing client and community needs (ACA, 2010; Chang et al., 2009). Thus, advocacy is a necessary skill for professional counselors of all specialties to strengthen their role and promote the entire profession. In the next section, you will learn about the evolutionary path of advocacy in the profession of counseling.

COUNSELING: AN EVOLVING PROFESSION

As stated in Chapter 2, advocacy for the counseling profession has developed during times of great economic, societal, and political change in the United States and worldwide. As the Great Depression caused suffering for many U.S. citizens in the 1930s (Zinn, 2010), career and employment services were the only types of counseling offered early in the profession's history, but they were not the only counseling resources needed. After World War II and the subsequent boom in postwar education and career development needs, disparate counseling organizations united to better advocate for and promote the entire profession. Historically, the Cold War raged during the 1950s between the U.S. and the former Soviet Union. It was a conservative, repressive time in the United States, with Wisconsin Senator Joseph McCarthy's anticommunism hearings and the postwar economic boom (Zinn, 2010). In 1952, the American Personnel and Guidance Association (APGA), forerunner to the ACA, was formed as an umbrella professional counseling organization by the collaboration of four initial divisions: the National Career Development Association (NCDA), formerly known as the National Vocational Guidance Association (NVGA); the Association for Counselor Education and Supervision (ACES), formerly known as the National Association of Guidance Supervisors and Counselor Trainers (NAGSCT); College Student Educators International, formerly known as the American College Personnel Association (ACPA); and the Student Personnel Association for Teacher Education (SPATE) (Kaplan, 2002). By joining forces, APGA collaboratively advocated for larger issues and expanded shared resources for mutual needs and professional challenges.

Unifying these groups under one professional identity provided a larger professional voice and strengthened the profession by supporting the similar interests of professional counselors in diverse specialty practice areas. Members of the fledgling ACA echoed the need to work as a collective in advocating for the profession to influence national and state legislation, increase employment opportunities, and develop shared professional competencies and standards (Stiller, 1972). Thus, by advocating collaboratively as a unified profession, professional counselors also advocated for their clients to improve counseling services and delivery systems. With a unified counseling professional identity, they maintained unique specialty practice areas.

In the 1960s, a decade after the founding of ACA, major societal changes occurred that involved professional advocacy. For example, there was expanded funding for counselor education graduate programs in schools of education in many U.S. land-grant universities. At the same time, multiple human rights movements rocked the country—antiwar demonstrations about an unjust and deadly war in Vietnam, Cambodia, and Laos; and civil rights demonstrations for

---

Exercise 12.2

COUNSELING ORGANIZATIONS

Think about current local, state, and national issues impacting your various systems (body, relationships/friendships, family, school, community, state, country, hemisphere, planet). How can counselors and counseling organizations advocate to address academic, career, and social/emotional issues affecting the multiple systems you inhabit?

---

people of color (African Americans, Latinos and Latinas, Asian Americans, Native Americans, and biracial groups); women; lesbians and gays; and poor and working class people (Zinn, 2010). These progressive movements challenged a conservative profession that reflected the traditional cultures and biases of the dominant American culture and provided a platform for social advocacy. Counselors of color banded together to create what is now the Association for Multicultural Counseling and Development (founded in 1972 as the Association of Non-White Concerns) as a response to a profession that was largely White and unresponsive to the needs of counselors and clients of color. The atmosphere of the 1960s exuded advocacy, both in the funding that became available for counselor education program expansion in universities across the United States, and in the demonstration of social justice interests by students and clients, who advocated for multiple human rights issues and multicultural competencies and who challenged diverse oppressions in schools and communities.

EVOLUTION OF ACA BRANCHES AND REGIONS

The growth of the counseling profession is evidenced by the many divisions, branches, and regions of ACA that focus on the professional needs of members, clients, students, and the community as well as on legislative issues at the local, state, and regional levels. Divisions, branches, and regions provide specific advocacy efforts (leadership, resources, and information) distinct to specialized areas of practice and populations. With a shared commitment to human development, additional divisions emerged in ACA from the original four founding divisions. The APGA changed its name to the American Association for Counseling and Development (AACD) in 1984 to better represent the settings where most members could be found in a range of specialty areas of practice (Herr, 1985). New counseling specialty divisions that followed included counselor education, career counseling, and student affairs counseling. After 1952, new divisions included school counseling with the ASCA in 1953, mental health counseling with the AMHCA in 1978, addictions counseling with the International Association of Addictions and Offender Counselors (IAAOC) in 1972, and a host of specialty groups, including the Association for Multicultural Counseling and Development (AMCD) and the Association for Specialists in Group Work (ASGW). In 1992, AACD changed its name to the American Counseling Association (ACA) to reflect the common bond among association members, reinforcing counseling as the primary professional identity. An additional practice specialty division developed in the mid-1990s, the American College Counseling Association (ACCA), after ACPA disaffiliated from ACA. Other ACA divisions emerged in the late 1990s and 2000s, including the Association for Lesbian, Gay, Bisexual, and Transgender Issues in Counseling (ALGBTIC) in 1997; Counselors for Social Justice (CSJ) in 2002; and the Association for Creativity in Counseling (ACC) in 2004. As stated in Chapter 10, today, there are 19 divisions in the ACA, increasing professional identity for specific practice and interest areas (ACA, 2010). Through these divisions, counselors provide advocacy for diverse needs and populations within the counseling community.

To address the diverse professional needs of counselors and to provide leadership, four ACA regions were established: Midwest, North Atlantic, Southern, and Western (Herr, 1985). Each region provides advocacy efforts supporting members in their jurisdiction. For example, a region leadership team may provide support, outreach, and information regarding a state policy to enhance licensure for mental health professionals or national school counselor certification bonuses for school counselors. Within each jurisdiction are state/commonwealth branches; there are 56 chartered branches in the United States, Europe, and Latin America. ACA branches address specific needs and goals of counselors in varied work settings in their state or country by enhancing communication and aligning state and national agendas and policies into statements and practices; many professional issues are state related, such as licensure and certification (Herr, 1985).

Within a few divisions there are regional associations; for instance, the Association for Counselor Education and Supervision (ACES, found online at www.acesonline.net) has five regions:

- North Atlantic Region (NARACES)
- North Central Region (NCACES)
- Rocky Mountain Region (RMACES)
- Southern Region (SACES)
- Western Region (WACES)

These five regions and state counselor education branches in most states combine to offer regional professional development, essential for professional advocacy, for counselor educators and supervisors through annual conferences and electronic and in-person forums. Advocacy activities include networking, sharing research, and publication in ACES and regional journals. For example, the Counselor Education and Supervision Network (CESNET) is an online listserv for counselor educators, supervisors, and graduate students interested in counselor education and supervision.

Counseling divisions, branches, and regions formed to provide additional venues for professional counselors to increase advocacy efforts, such as supporting members' efforts, keeping them informed, and increasing public visibility. Besides the branches, divisions, and regional associations that support and represent members of the counseling profession, there are seven core specialty areas of practice that distinguish the profession.

SEVEN CORE SPECIALTY AREAS OF PROFESSIONAL PRACTICE

You learned from previous chapters (Chapter 4 and 11) that each different counseling specialty area is unique but represents the unified counseling profession. Each core specialty area has a history of defining the specialty, and sometimes there have been differences between the parts and the whole. The reason for disagreement is that specialties define themselves by purpose and function relative to the overall profession. In addition, some specialties are multidisciplinary; for example, couple, marriage, and family counseling has commonalities with marriage and family therapy; student affairs counseling also can include higher education administration and student affairs specialty organizations in residence life, admissions, international student advising, academic advising, and student activities. Thus, it has sometimes been a challenge to describe a unique professional counseling identity within a multidisciplinary context. In this section, we further expand information regarding the seven core counseling specialty areas first described in Chapter 4 and highlight this information in the context of professional counseling advocacy.

Addictions Counseling

The International Association of Addictions and Offender Counselors (IAAOC) is a multidisciplinary organization of professionals who work with individuals, groups, and families with varied addiction behaviors (e.g., alcohol and other substance abuse/dependence, compulsive gambling, compulsive sexual behaviors) and/or with adult and juvenile offenders (IAAOC, n.d.). Thus, defining addictions counseling depends upon the setting, since IAAOC members work in varied settings such as mental health agencies, correctional facilities, higher education, and public and private offender and addiction treatment programs. This diversity of fields has contributed to a small membership pool for IAAOC, which has no branches. Without effective leadership and active members, chapters cannot develop or thrive. To counteract this dilemma, professional advocacy endeavors to increase IAAOC membership and professional activities have been proposed (Lambert, 2010) to increase viability and recognition of IAAOC at the branch level, such as the following: provide a new organizational structure to meet the needs of members; increase technology use to provide member services and governance more efficiently and to collaborate with other agencies; and cosponsor professional development workshops with other organizations. Another leading advocacy and research group of interest to addictions counseling professionals is the federal government's Substance Abuse and Mental Health Services Administration (SAMHSA). In 2009, CACREP included addictions counseling as one of the professional practice specialty areas in counseling (CACREP, 2009).

Exercise 12.3

CONFLICT IN ADDICTIONS COUNSELING

There has always been conflict in addictions counseling over the training and credentialing of counselors, who may have master's level or bachelor's level training or even be nondegreed persons who are in recovery, and these are compared with those who are not in recovery. As a graduate student, what are some ways you can share the value of your training with clients and other professionals who still believe only recovering persons know best? How can you appreciate their depth of experience and at the same time share that the field has moved toward research and evidence-based treatment in addictions counseling? How can you demonstrate that the best addictions counselors use research in their counseling, not only personal experience? You might want to mention that having a master's degree in counseling gives professional addictions counselors skills and training to do the work successfully, regardless of whether or not they are recovering from addictions themselves. As a student, what additional information can you provide to clients, community, and other professionals about your training and skills that will help recovering clients and colleagues accept your presence?

Including addictions counseling in the CACREP standards signifies the importance and impact of addictions in every area of counselors' work (Hagedorn, 2007). Many professional advocacy efforts; such as shows of support from IAAOC members, counseling students, and other auxiliary interested parties; were utilized to promote this inclusion.

Career Counseling

There are two divisions in the ACA that focus on career and employment counseling. The National Career Development Association's (NCDA) mission is to inspire and empower the achievement of career and life goals by providing professional development, resources, standards, research, and advocacy (NCDA, n.d.), while the National Employment Counseling Association's (NECA) purpose is providing professional development, resources, professional advocacy, and support to maintain and support employability (NECA, n.d.).

The lack of public policies addressing career development, lack of competency standardization, and lack of innovative training programs are a few factors that have influenced career development practice and preparation (Niles, 2009). Thus, this has caused the career development field to be overwhelmed with persons not trained in career counseling doing career development, because career counseling is neither licensed nor certified as a profession at the state level; anyone with any degree or background may call herself a career counselor. To survive and thrive, career counselors need to explain their unique training and background and show the evidence and research behind their successful interventions and outcomes.

To improve the preparation of professional career counselors, several advocacy efforts are warranted. Essential advocacy steps include, for instance, development of career development policies and regulations that focus on employment and career development; development of clear comprehensive standards that are systemic and inclusive for practice and preparation; and provision of specific training in counseling courses, where students have more practical experience through collaboration and technology (Niles, 2009). Thus, engaging in advocacy should not be limited to the individual and must include influencing and making changes at the professional level to strengthen the profession.

Marriage, Couple, and Family Counseling

Several associations are focused on marriage, couple, and family relationships. The International Association of Marriage and Family Counselors (IAMFC) is an ACA division. The largest organization of marriage and family therapists, however, is the American Association for Marriage and Family Therapy (AAMFT), and they have several professional advocacy efforts at the state and federal levels. For instance, AAMFT seeks recognition for marriage and family therapists (MFTs) to be hired by the Veterans Administration and advocates for MFTs to be recognized as viable mental health practitioners. At the state level, AAMFT members advocate recognition of MFTs by state-licensed insurance companies and state Medicaid plans. As a result of their efforts, 38 states now allow MFT reimbursement and recognition from Medicaid for services rendered (AAMFT, n.d.). For more initiatives at the state and federal levels, see www.aamft.org.

In addition to AAMFT, other collaborative forces have been instrumental in strengthening the voice of marriage and family counselors. The National Council on Family Relations (NCFR, 2012) is a multidisciplinary organization that conducts research on families. IAMFC promotes the use of resources, including professional development for marriage, couple, and family counseling, among ACA members (IAMFC, n.d.). NCFR is a multidisciplinary forum for researchers, educators, and practitioners; it promotes learning about families and family systems. Like AAMFT, NCFR is open to members from multiple disciplines and focuses on research, theory development, and education for professionals from multiple professional backgrounds (i.e., social work, psychology, counseling, family studies) who identify with marriage and family therapy (AAMFT, n.d.). Although CACREP maintains a specific set of marriage, couple, and family counseling specialty accreditation standards (CACREP, 2009), AAMFT endorses the Commission on Accreditation for Marriage and Family Therapy Education (COAMFTE), which accredits master's degree, doctoral degree, and postgraduate degree clinical training programs in marriage and family therapy throughout the United States and Canada. Graduates of both CACREP- and COAMFTE-accredited marriage, couple, and family counseling/therapy programs are able to be licensed as MFTs around the U.S.

Clinical Mental Health Counseling

In 1972, the Virginia Supreme Court ruled that counseling was a distinct profession. This led to creation of the American Mental Health Counselors Association, chartered in 1978, to promote the growth of community mental health counseling within ACA (AMHCA, n.d.). To demonstrate a distinction from psychology, Seiler and Messina (1976) contended mental health counseling was an "interdisciplinary, multifaceted, holistic process of the (1) promotion of healthy life-styles, (2) identification of individual stressors and personal levels of functioning, and (3) preservation or restoration of mental health" (p. 6). According to AMHCA standards of practice, a more inclusive description reads as follows:

Clinical mental health counseling is the provision of professional counseling services involving the application of principles of psychotherapy, human development, learning theory, group dynamics, and the etiology of mental illness and dysfunctional behavior to individuals, couples, families and groups, for the purpose of promoting optimal mental health, dealing with normal problems of living and treating psychopathology. The practice of clinical mental health counseling includes, but is not limited to, diagnosis and treatment of mental and emotional disorders, psycho-educational technique(s) aimed at the prevention of mental and emotional disorders, consultations to individuals, couples, families, groups, organizations and communities, and clinical research into more effective psychotherapeutic treatment modalities (AMHCA, 2011).

Although mental health counseling is seen by some as multidisciplinary, AMHCA and CACREP (2009) define mental health counseling as a unique specialty practice area in the counseling profession. Two additional professional advocacy groups for mental health counseling professional advocacy and research are the National Alliance on Mental Illness (NAMI), and the federal government's National Institute of Mental Health (NIMH). In the late 1990s, AMHCA voted to keep a professional division connection with ACA and became financially and administratively separate. This enabled AMHCA to collect membership dues and hire a separate executive director and professional staff. By maintaining its connection with ACA, AMHCA focused collaboratively on the common needs of professional counselors and constituents (Colangelo, 2009) to advance the profession. Similar to MFTs, mental health counselors are advocates for license portability and for professional inclusion in Medicare and TRICARE mandates.

Clinical Rehabilitation Counseling

The field of rehabilitation counseling began in the early 20th century. The purpose of early rehabilitation counseling was to provide services to veterans with disabilities and assist them in achieving their independent living and vocational goals (Sporner, 2012). In addition, the holistic practice of rehabilitation counseling (sometimes called vocational rehabilitation) assists individuals with cognitive, mental, developmental, physical, and emotional disabilities to attain their individual, occupational, and self-determined living goals (Leahy & Szymanski, 1995). Rehabilitation counselors provide comprehensive counseling services in a range of counseling settings (Berens, 2009) such as private rehabilitation companies, community and private mental health counseling practices, substance abuse programs, and educational institutions (high school and college/university).

In addition to the American Rehabilitation Counselors Association (ARCA), there are several other organizations advocating for the profession of rehabilitation counseling; they are the Commission on Rehabilitation Counselor Certification (CRCC), which focuses on quality rehabilitation counseling services to individuals with disabilities through the certification of rehabilitation counselors and the promotion of leadership in advocating for the rehabilitation counseling profession (CRCC, 2013); the National Rehabilitation Association (NRA), which provides advocacy, awareness, and career advancement for professionals in the field of rehabilitation (NRA, 2009); the National Council on Rehabilitation Education (NCRE), which is a professional organization of educators dedicated to competence services for persons with disabilities through education and research—NCRE advocates for education and training and the maintenance of professional standards in the field of rehabilitation (NCRE, 2013); and the National Rehabilitation Counseling Association (NRCA), which represents rehabilitation counselors practicing in a variety of work settings (NRCA, 2013). In recent years, there has been collaboration among various rehabilitation counseling organizations in an effort to promote the profession of rehabilitation counseling. However, with membership declining in many rehabilitation organizations (ARCA, 2013), there have been some discussions at the national level regarding the development of a single organization, because separate organizations ultimately dilute the voice of rehabilitation counselors and the profession.

CASE ILLUSTRATION 12.2

LEGISLATIVE ADVOCACY

You are a member of a counseling association, and your president has appointed you to the advocacy committee. Your first action is to gauge your membership regarding issues and concerns locally and in the state. From the needs assessment, it is determined that many members are concerned about the scope of practice for mental health counselors. In addition, you notice that mental health interns are increasingly denied practice in mental health agencies. In your state, licensed mental health counselors are not able to diagnose and treat mental illness, which has implications for students in mental health counseling programs and their employment options. Legislation has sometimes minimized counselors' ability to practice in other states. For example, in Indiana, for years legislation did not allow counselors to use psychological testing, and counselors had to fight for the right to use it. Also, you are unsure whether your focus should be on the mental health specialty area or whether you should advocate for the counseling profession in general.

What are some pros and cons for advocacy for a specialty area versus the counseling profession as a whole? Does legislative advocacy for a specialty area impact the counseling profession? What can you do in terms of legislative advocacy for counseling as a profession at the state and national levels?

School Counseling

School counseling originated in the 20th century in vocational guidance and career development. School counseling often focused on sorting and selecting which students would go to college or trade schools and which would not (Hart & Jacobi, 1992). After the American School Counselor Association (ASCA) formed in 1953, school counseling added an equal focus on academic issues and personal/social issues to its existing career focus. A focus on postsecondary planning, including college admission, was also developed in high schools. School counselors' roles have often involved advocacy and leadership to provide equitable services to all students, although the focus on all students was not the case until much later in the profession's history (ASCA, 2010; Chen-Hayes, 2007). With the release of *The ASCA National Model: A Framework for School Counseling Programs* (ASCA, 2012; Hatch & Bowers, 2002), advocacy became a key role for professional school counselors based on the work of the National Center for Transforming School Counseling (NCTSC), which had a new vision for the role of school counseling and a definition of the field that focused on advocacy, leadership, teaming and collaboration, technology, culturally competent counseling and coordination, and equity assessment using data (Chen-Hayes, 2007). In addition, the ASCA model demonstrated how to implement school counseling programs for all students' success (ASCA, 2012; Hatch & Bowers, 2002) through the use of advocacy activities in building a comprehensive, data-driven school counseling program focused on foundation, delivery, management, and accountability elements. The ASCA model, along with the NCTSC new vision for school counseling, clarified professional school counselors' roles and responsibilities—at the secondary, middle, and elementary levels—and gave the profession recognition, strength, and substance.

ASCA engages in several advocacy efforts, such as putting on an annual conference at the national level, disseminating the ASCA ethical code for school counselors, and issuing numerous publications, including the journal *Professional School Counseling.* In addition, every February, ASCA celebrates school counselors and provides ways for them to advocate for the profession through National School Counseling Week. The week increases recognition of the unique contributions of professional school counselors within U.S. school systems. For the school counseling profession to thrive, it is essential that professional advocacy efforts be made at all levels in conjunction with other organizations.

There are five additional organizations advocating for the profession of school counseling: The Center for Excellence in School Counseling and Leadership (CESCAL), founded and directed by school counselor educator Dr. Trish Hatch; The Center for School Counseling Outcome Research and Evaluation (CSCORE), founded and directed by school counselor educators Drs. Jay Carey and Carey Dimmitt; The National Office for School Counselor Advocacy at the College Board (NOSCA), founded and directed by Ms. Pat Martin and school counselor educator Dr. Vivian Lee; the National Center for Transforming School Counseling (NCTSC), founded and directed originally by Pat Martin and school counselor educator Dr. Reese House, and currently directed by school counselor educator Dr. Peggy Hines; and the National Association for College Admission Counseling (NACAC). Like AMHCA, in the early 2000s, ASCA voted to stay an ACA division to focus on common goals but became financially independent, collecting membership

Exercise 12.4

SCHOOL COUNSELORS' ROLES

District and building leaders, teachers, and parents are sometimes confused over school counselor roles and skills in academic, career, college access, and personal/social competency development for every K–12 student. As a graduate student, in practicum and internship indirect hours, you can create a school counseling program bulletin board (including traditional and digital formats), a school counseling brochure to explain school counselor roles and programs, and a school counseling program website that advocates for all students at your site and for future students as well. What are additional ways that you can advocate for the school counseling profession, since we are the ones who usually educate others about appropriate school counselor roles and the changes in the field from a service-based delivery model to a program-based model focused on data, accountability, and closing achievement and opportunity gaps for every student?

dues and hiring an executive director and professional staff to ensure support and advocacy for the unique needs of K–12 school counselors.

Student Affairs Counseling

Student affairs counseling involves varied functions and roles for students at the college and university level, including administration and counseling in academic advising, admissions, career centers, counseling centers, international student offices, multicultural and diversity offices, residence life, orientation, student activities, financial aid and scholarships, and Greek life. There are three main associations: the American College Counseling Association (ACCA, n.d.), an ACA division; the American College Personnel Association: College Student Educators International (ACPA), a founding division of ACA that disaffiliated and became a separate entity in the early 1990s due to a philosophical differ-ence in focus on higher education administration more than counseling; and the National Association of Student Personnel Administrators: Student Affairs Administrators in Higher Education (NASPA, n.d.). The mission of ACCA is working in higher education settings for practitioners with a professional identity in counseling to foster college student development. ACPA emphasizes policy, practice, and programming related to college student learning. NASPA culti-vates student learning through student affairs administrators in higher education (NASPA, n.d.).

In 2011, a task force made up of representatives from NASPA and ACPA mem-bership concluded a multiyear study on unification of the two associations with a vote that fell 3 percentage points short of unification. Unification failed for varied reasons: a loss of autonomy, a cumbersome process, disenfranchisement of impor-tant constituencies, and financial strain (NASPA, 2010; Ruffins, 2011). However, because these two organizations have maintained separate identities, the field's voice is splintered rather than united, competitive rather than shared, and similar rather than efficient (NASPA, 2010). Thus, with as many as 15 additional smaller student affairs specialty groups, it is a challenge to maintain a consistent profes-sional student affairs counseling identity.

Although the counseling specialty practice areas differ by practice, mission, and values, they share a common core of preservice coursework and internship (CACREP, 2009) and their commonality as professional counselors. The advocacy efforts for all of the counseling specialties are essential to strengthening the pro-fession and increasing the visibility of professional counselors at the local, state, and federal level. Contributing to the challenges and strengths of a professional counseling identity has been the shifting definition of counseling in the profession over time.

Exercise 12.5

ADVOCATING FOR THE SPECIALTY AREA

Consider the seven specialties practices in professional counseling (addictions; career; marriage, couple, and family; mental health; rehabilitation, school; student affairs), and discuss how you could advocate for each one. What challenges might you face at the local, state, and federal level to advocate for your specialty area? What tools will you use to overcome these obstacles?

EVOLVING DEFINITION OF PROFESSIONAL COUNSELING

The evolving definition of counseling over the years has complicated the understanding of a professional counselor identity. The defining attributes of a counselor have led to confusion and conflict within the profession and for the public (Mellin, Hunt, & Nichols, 2011). For instance, there are two other major helping/mental health professions: social work (with three foci—administrative, public policy, and clinical social work), and psychology (with multiple specializations, including counseling, clinical, and school) that utilize counseling theories and techniques to address individual, group, and/or family needs in school and community settings. Thus, members of the public easily confuse the professions, since they appear to perform overlapping functions.

Since *counseling* means to provide a type of human service (National Organization for Human Services, 2009), it has been used broadly by other professional associations not connected to ACA and its divisions. Additional professions that use the term interchangeably include college admission counseling (National Association for College Admission Counseling), financial counseling, sexuality counseling (American Association for Sex Education, Counseling and Therapy), credit counseling (National Foundation for Credit Counseling), and pastoral counseling (American Association of Pastoral Counselors).

As APGA became AACD and then ACA, the definition of counseling also changed, and the organization's professional advocacy efforts represented collective diverse needs, including changing practice settings for professional counselors. Counseling was defined in the 1980s as "a mutual exchange of opinion, ideas, advice, and information for the purpose of instruction, such as warning, exhorting, and advising persons to seeking assistance in some matter" (Cole & Sarnoff, 1980, pp. 146–147). This definition reflected the multidisciplinary nature of the profession when the counseling profession was not distinct from other helping professions. With the influence of Carl Rogers (Farson, 1974; Lopez, 1987) and the emergence of the humanistic perspective and the therapeutic relationship's importance, counseling was defined as a way "to assist a client through the counseling relationship, using a combination of mental health and human development principles, method and techniques, to achieve mental, emotional, physical, social, moral, educational, spiritual and/or career development and adjustment through the lifespan" (Bloom, 1990, p. 513). As managed care became the primary agent mediating payment for behavioral health care during the late 1990s, challenges developed for mental health counselors. For instance, requirements such as the number of sessions allowed had to be met, which negatively affected the quality of mental health services (Murphy, DeBernardo, & Shoemaker, 1998) and affected the whole counseling profession. Consequently, counseling was "defined as a relatively short-term, interpersonal, theory-based process of helping persons who are basically the psychologically healthy resolve developmental and situational problems" (ACA, 2007). As the profession evolved and formalized itself through professional standards, practice, and mission within the sociopolitical environment, a unified mission was needed. ASCA and ACPA maintained their own definitions of school counseling and student affairs that differed from ACA's definition of counseling.

Concerning advocacy efforts to unify professional counseling, rehabilitation counseling is one of the recent examples reflecting a success of such efforts. For decades, rehabilitation counseling has been a counseling specialty practice area recognized by the American Rehabilitation Counseling Association (ARCA, 2013) but not recognized by CACREP. Rehabilitation counseling program accreditation is based upon standards set forth by the Council on Rehabilitation Education (CORE), which was formed in 1971 and incorporated in 1972. CORE accredits only rehabilitation counseling undergraduate and graduate programs (CORE, 2013).

CORE is similar to CACREP in many ways. They have similar counselor preparation standards: For accreditation, both require study in the eight common core curricular areas, a minimum number of semester hours (48 or 60 for CACREP and 48 for CORE), 100 hours of supervised counseling practicum, and 600 hours of internship experience. Despite these similarities in accreditation standards, attempts in the early 2000s to merge CORE and CACREP were not successful, because many rehabilitation counseling educators are psychologists who feared their professional identity would be compromised (CACREP, 2007a). But pursuant to significant events within the counseling profession in the past decade (e.g., the ACA's 20/20 vision, licensure portability, TRICARE/Medicare reimbursement issues, and passage of PL 109–461, which addressed contracting opportunities for small businesses owned by veterans with disabilities), CORE determined that "the existence of multiple accrediting bodies within the counseling profession fractionalizes the profession and impedes the recognition of qualified counselors for hiring, third-party reimbursement, and other practice related issues" (CORE, 2013, para. 1). Therefore, as of 2013, CACREP and CORE entered into an agreement whereby CORE is a corporate affiliate of CACREP, and together they have developed policy and accreditation standards for the clinical rehabilitation counseling specialty.

The current ACA definition of counseling was developed by focus groups and approved by most members of the ACA governing council in 2010. Differentiating between counseling and other professions was crucial in order to represent counselors at the federal level (e.g., TRICARE, Medicare). Being included in eligibility for reimbursement of fees at the federal level was seen as having a domino effect, with mental health counselors being better recognized for jobs at the state and local levels. To have a unified voice, a basic definition was developed, allowing participating divisions to amend the statement by specialty or interest group (ACA, 2010). As stated in previous chapters, the current ACA definition of counseling is "a professional relationship that empowers diverse individuals, families, and groups to accomplish mental health, wellness, education, and career goals" (ACA, 2010). This definition was derived from 31 delegates representing various ACA counseling divisions, regions, and affiliates convening between 2005 and 2010 to discuss issues to be addressed to advance the profession of counseling. Although many professional counselors adopt this definition, others, such as many ASCA and ACPA members, contend that there are unique counseling profession specialty needs that are not served well with a singular definition of professional counseling.

In trying to position counseling as a unified profession with a history of divergent specialty practice areas and interest groups, controversies have always emerged. The mission of ACA is to enhance the quality of life in society by promoting the development of professional counselors, advancing the counseling profession, and using the profession and practice of counseling to promote respect for human diversity (ACA, 2010). This broad mission reflects the shared training, ethics, and practice standards of members of the profession; however, attempts to be inclusive in defining professional counseling have caused disputes, because the agreed-upon process and outcome were not perceived as a best fit with all specialty practice areas.

IDENTITY OF THE COUNSELING PROFESSION

You have learned about the concept and importance of a professional counseling identity in previous chapters. Although we, as professional counselors, refer to the identity of professional counseling as part of a larger picture of professional advocacy, there are many components of professional identity. Brott and Myers (1999) contended that professional counseling behavior, such as meeting ethical standards, determines professional identity; while Wester and Lewis (2005) believed a core aspect of professional identity was membership in appropriately identified professional organizations. For instance, Chi Sigma Iota (n.d.) is an honor society that supports and encourages the educational and scholarly achievement of professional counselors, counselor educators, and students in counseling by promoting a strong professional identity through its members. Thus, a professional identity represents integration of professional training and personal characteristics influenced by intrapersonal and interpersonal experiences (Gibson, Dollarhide, & Moss, 2010).

There are four beliefs that distinguish the counseling profession from other professions (Remley & Herlihy, 2009). First, counseling uses a *wellness model,* a strengths-based approach to mental health care, instead of a *medical (illness) model,* which treats a person's deficits and pathology. The wellness model integrates mind, body, and spirit to treat the whole person, not just the symptom(s) (Myers, Sweeney, & Witmer, 2000) and views mental health on a continuum (Remley & Herlihy, 2009). Another defining feature of the counseling profession is the belief that personal and emotional issues are developmental. This perspective recognizes that many challenges people face are transitory and part of a regular progression of the human experience (Cook-Greuter & Soulen, 2007). Third, counselors use prevention and early intervention methods to address issues such as psychoeducational activities (parenting training); that is, they see a client early, at the beginning stages of a crisis or problem, to prevent the development of further problems (Remley & Herlihy, 2009). Last, empowering clients is the fourth assumption that differentiates counseling from other professions. Empowerment means that clients are capable of solving their problems by themselves (Lewis, 2011).

According to a study by Mellin et al. (2011), counselors in their sample embraced an identity that reflected a unified profession rather than their specialization; participants' identity was linked to licensure/certification, adhering to the ACA ethical code, and training in a CACREP-accredited program. Future studies with ASCA, AMHCA, or ACPA members who are not ACA members might yield interesting contrasts. Regardless of the attributes, a professional counselor identity is essential in distinguishing counselors from other professions. To advocate, counselors need to understand and convey specific professional skills, credentials, preparation, outcomes, and identity to the general public. Counselor preparation is a significant method for transmitting a professional counselor identity. Thus, a defining feature for large numbers of professional counselors in the field and a majority of current graduate students in counselor education master's and doctoral programs is preparation rooted in the evolving accreditation standards of CACREP.

Accreditation: CACREP Advocating Best for Counselor Preparation Practices

The purpose of establishing CACREP was to advance the counseling profession through professional advocacy, also known as accreditation. CACREP standards ensure a counselor identity is developed from minimum practice standards for students in master's and doctoral programs. By developing standards for preparation for students' preservice counseling programs at the graduate level (CACREP, 2009), accreditation lays the foundation to master the core professional counseling knowledge and skills to effectively practice in master's level specialty settings and doctoral programs. A definition of accreditation follows. As you read it, think about how it relates to professional advocacy:

> Accreditation is a voluntary process of peer review and self-regulation. The standards of each accrediting agency are slightly different but, generally, each agency ensures that its members meet basic standards in their administrative procedures, physical facilities, and the quality of their academic programs. (College Board, 2006, p. 8).

There are two types of accreditation in the United States. The first one is an *institutional accreditation* granted by regional and national accrediting commissions (CACREP, 2007b). In evaluating quality, the accrediting agency looks at the entire institutional unit, such as state universities or private institutions. Accreditation is awarded based on overall compliance with the criteria. A college or university may have institutional accreditation without seeking accreditation from any of the specialized accrediting agencies. The second one, *specialized accreditation,* is awarded to professional programs within institutions or to occupational schools offering specific training, skills, and knowledge. Specialized accrediting agencies define standards of excellence in educational preparation programs for recognized professions (CACREP, 2009). Accreditation has many advocacy components. Accreditation promotes the profession by setting standards that are recognized by states and federal agencies. In addition, accreditation ensures that the members meet certain professional standards that protect the public. Also, accreditation provides programs with support and representation within higher education institutions that allow many programs to improve their graduate education practices and often includes expansion of faculty and facilities.

CASE ILLUSTRATION 12.3

MARIA'S CONFUSION

Maria has been working as a mental health counselor for three years now and recently has been licensed in her state as a licensed professional counselor. Maria's husband is in the army, and they will need to relocate, since he is being stationed in another state. Maria, being proactive, contacted the new state's licensing board and was told that she was not eligible to be licensed in the new state. She was confused because she had been told by her current state licensure board that transferring her license would be an easy process; thus, she submitted all the required paperwork and completed the necessary hours for licensure in her home state, and went ahead with applying for licensure in the new state.

When Maria inquired about her application in the new state, she was told that her educational qualifications were not sufficient. As she did her research, Maria noticed that the educational requirements for licensure in her home state were different from those of the new state. Her master's program was not accredited by CACREP, which was acceptable in her home state, but not in the state she was moving to. Maria remembered that her program of study was 36 credit hours and did not require a practicum, only an internship. She was not sure what the difference was between accredited and nonaccredited programs. Maria stated that she selected her master's program because it required a relatively small time commitment and would enable her to be in the field sooner than other programs. Now she feels like she is stuck and really unsure what she should do next.

What is the difference between accredited and nonaccredited counseling programs? How would knowledge about the importance of graduation from a CACREP-accredited master's program have assisted Maria in her decision to graduate from a nonaccredited program? How can Maria advocate for herself and the profession to support universal educational standards, so that other licensed professional counselors are not in the same situation?

ADVOCACY STRATEGIES TO STRENGTHEN PROFESSIONAL COUNSELING

Throughout this chapter, you have learned about several professional advocacy efforts implemented to support the profession of counseling. Advocacy requires that counselors, regardless of the specialty area, are proactive and intentional when seeking reform for the profession. For professional advocacy efforts to be successful, activities need to be collaborative, systemic, and focused at the micro, meso, and macro levels. You are an important part of professional counseling advocacy. The strategies provided below are things you can do to advocate for the counseling profession.

Collaborating With Other Helping Professions

In reality, professional counselors, regardless of their practice settings or specialty areas, must work collaboratively with other helping professions within counseling (e.g., a mental health counselor must connect with a school counselor on behalf of a student) and outside of counseling (e.g., consultation with a psychiatrist about medication). All counseling specialties benefit from collaboration and effective interaction with other helping professions, and each makes an important contribution to client and student welfare. For example, as a counseling student, you can join Chi Sigma Iota and promote the various specialties. Or you can work with various helping professionals as a team by partnering with another organization, such as a women's center, to advocate against intimate partner violence (Sikes, Walley, & Hays, 2012) during a Take Back the Night rally.

Professional counselors have potential allies (and sometimes legislative foes) in each of the following professions: marriage and family therapy (American Association of Marriage and Family Therapy, AAMFT), social work (National Association of Social Workers, NASW), psychology (American Psychological Association, APA), and psychiatry (American Psychiatric Association, APA). Thus, professional counselors must maintain their identity while working collaboratively with other mental health professionals for the well-being of clients/students, yet remain vigilant so they are aware of any challenges to counselors' scope of practice or attempts to eliminate counselor jobs in favor of jobs for other professions. Strategies to use include advertising their educational degrees (MSEd, PhD), certifications (NCC, NCSC, CCMHC), and licenses (LPC) on their letterhead, business cards, brochures, professional websites, and social networking sites; sharing counseling articles and literature to support evidence- and research-based interventions and prevention strategies; and—most important—sharing effective outcomes with clients, students, colleagues, and the general public. In addition, sharing the professional counseling perspectives of developmental theory, wellness, and career development highlights the uniqueness of counseling.

It is essential for professional counselors, as leaders and advocates, to be involved with local, state, and national associations, to take an active role in promoting the profession wherever possible, and to work to create allies in other professions to help them see us not as a threat but as highly skilled professionals with specific skills ready to help clients and students effectively and collaboratively.

Professional counselors rarely work in a vacuum; even counselors in private practice have to constantly refer to and interact with other mental health professionals. School and college counselors work daily with teams of professionals that often include school social workers and school psychologists. Mental health; marriage, couple and family; and addictions counselors work in agencies on multidisciplinary teams that often include psychiatrists, psychologists, and social workers. Lee and Rodgers (2009) contend that collaboration should be based on shared commitment, common goals, and shared responsibility for positive outcomes. Thus, it is essential that counselors work collaboratively with other professionals and balance advocacy for counseling as a profession with mutual respect for and understanding of the unique contributions and educational backgrounds of other professionals in assisting clients and students while using evidence-based interventions.

Encouraging the Use of Data, Research, and Evidence-Based Practice

Today's counseling practice is fueled by accountability. There is a growing movement within the counseling profession toward *evidenced-based practice,* which means following practice (techniques or approaches) based upon research. Thus, one of the most powerful tools for promoting the profession is the ability of counselors to show the effectiveness of their interventions by reporting results and outcomes and relying on data-based decision making (ASCA, 2012) and on research and evidence-based practices. Utilizing evidence-based practice educates the public and legislators about who counselors are as well as their effectiveness (Bradley, Sexton, & Smith, 2005). Having a thorough, vigorous research base that demonstrates practicing counselors' data-based decision making and effective outcomes allows professional counselors to compete effectively in demonstrating accountability, use of research-based practices, and use of managed care (Bradley et al., 2005) in mental health as well as in helping to close achievement, opportunity, and attainment gaps in school counseling programs (ASCA, 2010, 2012; Holcomb-McCoy & Chen-Hayes, 2011).

Managed care companies expect mental health; marriage, couple, and family; and addictions counselors to use evidence-based practices. K–12 school and college counselors are also expected to use data and show their results and outcome effectiveness with students, particularly in closing achievement, opportunity, and attainment gaps (ASCA, 2010, 2012; Hatch & Bowers, 2002; Holcomb-McCoy & Chen-Hayes, 2011). There are several sources that school counselors can refer to to learn about research-based practices, including the What Works Clearinghouse (www.whatworks.ed.gov) and the Center for School Counseling Outcome Research and Evaluation (CSCORE, www.umass.edu/schoolcounseling/). To determine if interventions work, Carey and Dimmitt (2008) suggested the following model for school counselors: (1) Use data to define the problem, (2) locate interventions that have successfully addressed the problem in other settings, and choose one, (3) implement the chosen intervention, and (4) evaluate the intervention. As a result, counselors are advocating for best practices for clients and students while promoting the effectiveness and visibility of the profession.

Engaging in Public Relations in the Digital Age

Counselors need to promote the profession as often as possible using both traditional and digital media. Milsom and Bryant (2006) contended technology is a method that should be used for professional advocacy. There are many ways counselors engage in public relations utilizing technology. For instance, counselors in each of the seven specialty areas have created blogs, developed electronic newsletters, created digital brochures, and developed counseling websites (Milsom & Bryant, 2006) that help educate potential students and clients by defining the counseling profession and the uniqueness of the specialty areas that counselors practice in. For instance, ASCA provides information to parents and the public about the roles of school counselors (see http://schoolcounselor.org). Developing a blog sponsored by NCDA regarding career assessments and career options can be useful for career counselors, since the Internet is now the primary place where people seek employment. Developing an electronic newsletter can be extremely effective for a comprehensive school counseling program. The newsletter can provide information about activities, school counseling core curriculum lessons, group and individual counseling, and individual planning for every student offered by school counselors (ASCA, 2012); share outcome data regarding interventions; provide college and career access and readiness calendars and tips for teachers, parents, and students; and provide information about the role of the school counselor and the school counseling program. Creating a digital brochure to advertise workshops and services for every specialty is effective in an age where millions of people in the United States and billions globally use the Internet daily. Working with community groups and providing professional workshops are also critical to assisting persons in understanding the training and skills of professional counselors.

Participating in Legislative Action

To protect clients and students, the profession of counseling has developed codes of ethics; however, ethics are not as powerful as laws in shaping the future of the profession (Remley & Herlihy, 2009). Professional counselors need to work in both state and national counseling associations to influence public policy to help shape the profession, protect the public and all current and future clients and students, ensure funding for counseling positions, and keep legislators updated on the role and focus of counselors in the specialty practice areas. Every counselor, graduate student, and counselor educator needs to be skilled in calling, e-mailing, texting, and visiting local, state, and national representatives about core key counseling issues as often as possible. Two strategies are effective in lobbying efforts: have a united front and speak with one clear voice on the issue(s), and use data with conviction and evidence as a strong rationale for change (Lee & Rodgers, 2009). Legislators respond to constituents who contact them regularly and who present data on counseling's effectiveness and the need for legislative action in favor of counselors and the specialty practice areas.

Conducting Needs Assessments

One of the easiest and most important steps for you to implement is a needs assessment with all stakeholders to learn what is working well, what needs to be improved, and what clients/students/stakeholders want from professional counselors. School counselors can use the ASCA Model Program Assessment (ASCA, 2012; Hatch & Bowers, 2002) or The ACCESS Questionnaire (Chen-Hayes, 2007) as a needs assessment specific to school counseling program components. To build relationships and ensure a strong professional identity for what counselors can provide to clients/students, counselors specializing in rehabilitation; mental health; marriage, couples, and families; addictions; careers; and student affairs can create checklists of needs their specialties can address and distribute these to learn what stakeholders need/want from a counselor.

Joining Professional Associations

One of the best ways you can advocate for professional counseling and the seven specialty areas of practice is by developing a large professional network starting in graduate school. At the national level, joining ACA and the national counseling association division in a specialty area of practice is essential (AMHCA, ARCA, ASCA, NCDA/NECA, IAAOC, IAMFC, and ACCA). In addition, family counselors may also join AAMFT, school counselors may also join NACAC, and college counselors may also join ACPA or NASPA. At the state level, joining respective state and specialty-area counseling associations is equally important for visibility, support, educational opportunities, conferences, and shared professional advocacy, including work with legislators about the specialty areas. Attending and presenting at conferences, sharing your results/effectiveness/outcomes with stakeholders, and connecting through social media are key ways to network. Many, if not all, associations (e.g., ACA, NARACES, AMHCA) have graduate student resources in addition to graduate student representatives on their boards from whom the voices of master's- and doctoral-level students are heard, and through whom students advocate for training, awards/scholarships, and recognition.

Promoting an Outcomes Focus

Tight budgets and challenges in funding have been part of the counseling profession since the early 1970s. After the golden era of expansion of counselor education programs and school and community mental health counseling in the 1960s, funding has been a challenge since, in most states and nationally. The long-term economic malaise during and after the Great Recession of 2008–2009 was particularly difficult for counselors and counselor education programs. One way to challenge the budget cuts and funding difficulties in K–12 schools, agencies, and practices is to show the effectiveness of one's interventions on outcomes for students and clients. In school counseling, CSCORE has been a leader in promoting effective outcomes, and its website (www.umass.edu/schoolcounseling/) contains summaries of all major research studies in school counseling, including information about outcome effectiveness and the program evaluation tools each study used. A focus on closing achievement, opportunity, and attainment gaps in public schools around the country (ASCA, 2012; Holcomb-McCoy & Chen-Hayes, 2011) has been reflected in school counselors' needs to show how they help close the gaps, such as using small group, school counseling core curriculum, and closing-the-gap action plans, results reports, and program assessments (ASCA, 2012; Hatch & Bowers, 2002). In mental health counseling, managed care environments have changed the landscape in the last two decades; there is now a strong focus on evidence-based practices and an expectation of outcome effectiveness; counselors are expected to provide cost-effective and quality services for clients. Similarly, budget cuts and difficulty in funding have pushed couple/marriage/family counselors, addictions counselors, student affairs counselors, and career counselors to show their outcomes and effectiveness to ensure not only client/student success but the viability of their jobs in challenging funding environments in K–16 schools and agencies.

Although there are many micro-, macro-, and meso-level activities for counselor involvement, there must be sustained action at multiple levels, involving multiple advocacy groups and stakeholders, to make a difference in the profession of counseling. Advocacy is the cornerstone of the counseling profession. Through advocacy efforts, the profession has grown and strengthened its voice while supporting and advocating within the seven specialty areas.

KEYSTONES

The future of professional counseling is in all of our hands. It calls for commitment, compromise, and a shared belief in the profession of counseling. It depends on the skills of current and future practitioners, counselor educators and supervisors, graduate students, and future graduate students who are emerging as the next generation of professionals supporting a unified counseling profession with seven specialty areas of practice. Key points to remember include the following:

- *Advocacy* refers to supporting a cause or a proposal at a micro, macro, or meso level to create change. *Professional advocacy* is working with or on behalf of one's profession, while *social advocacy* is making changes in response to historical forces.

- The counseling profession has evolved from professional advocacy efforts united as one professional identity to strengthen the profession by supporting similarities and diverse specialty practice areas.
- The evolution of ACA branches and regions stems from the need for advocacy efforts for specific counseling issues and professional development in state and local jurisdictions.
- The profession of counseling is divided into seven core specialty areas: addictions counseling; career counseling; marriage, couple, and family counseling; mental health counseling; rehabilitation counseling; school counseling; and student affairs counseling. Each specialty has a collaborative relationship with other organizations at the state and national levels that advocate on behalf of the specialty area.
- The professional identity of the counseling profession involves a wellness model and developmental, prevention and intervention, and empowerment perspectives. CACREP ensures that counselor identity is developed from minimum practice standards for students in master's and doctoral programs and is an example of professional advocacy.
- Professional identity is also shaped by other professional behavior, such as licensure and/or certification standards and ongoing professional development expectations.
- Reciprocity and portability pertain to recognition of one's certification or license to practice across state lines. Challenges to both involve lack of standardization of training, titles, and postgraduate supervision hours.
- Advocacy strategies to strengthen professional counseling consist of collaborating with other helping professions; encouraging the use of data, research, and evidence-based practice; engaging in public relations utilizing digital means; participating in legislative action; conducting needs assessments; joining professional associations; and promoting an outcomes focus.
- There are many strategies that professional counselors can use to advocate for the profession as a whole and the specialties using traditional and digital means.

ADDITIONAL RESOURCES

Books

Eriksen, K. (1999). *Making an impact: A handbook on counselor advocacy.* New York, NY: Taylor & Francis.
Ratts, M. J., Toporek, R. L., & Lewis, J. A. (2010). *ACA advocacy competencies: A social justice framework for counselors.* Alexandria, VA: American Counseling Association.

Websites

American College Personnel Association (ACPA): www2.myacpa.org/

American Counseling Association (ACA): www.counseling.org

American School Counselor Association (ASCA): www.schoolcounselor.org/

Association for Counselor Education and Supervision (ACES): http://www.acesonline.net/

Chi Sigma Iota: www.csi-net.org/

Council for Accreditation of Counseling & Related Educational Programs (CACREP): www.cacrep.org/template/index.cfm

International Association of Addictions and Offender Counselors (IAAOC): www.iaaoc.org/

International Association of Marriage and Family Counselors (IAMFC): www.iamfconline.org/

National Association of Student Personnel Administrators (NASPA): www.naspa.org/

National Board for Certified Counselors (NBCC): www.nbcc.org/

National Career Development Association (NCDA): http://associationdatabase.com/aws/ncda/pt/sp/home_page

National Office for School Counselor Advocacy (NOSCA): http://nosca.collegeboard.org/

State clinical mental health and marriage and family counseling licensure board listings: www.counseling.org/counselors/licensureandcert/tp/staterequirements/ct2.aspx

State school counseling certification board listings: www.schoolcounserg/content.asp?contentid=242

REFERENCES

Advocacy. (n.d.). In *Merriam-Webster Online*. Retrieved from http://www.merriam-webster.com/dictionary/advocacy

American Association of Marriage and Family Therapy (AAMFT). (n.d.). *About AAMFT.* Retrieved from http://www.aamft.org/imis15/content/about_aamft/AAMFT.aspx

American College Counseling Association (ACCA). (n.d.) *Mission statement.* Retrieved from http://collegecounseling.org/about/mission-statement

American Counseling Association (ACA). (2005). *ACA code of ethics.* Alexandria, VA: Author. Retrieved from http://www.counseling.org/Resources/CodeOfEthics/TP/Home/CT2.aspx.

American Counseling Association (ACA). (2007). *Counseling fact sheets: Definition of counseling.* Retrieved from http://www.counseling.org/Resources/ConsumersMedia.aspx?AGuid=97592202–75c2–4079-b854–2cd22c47be3f

American Counseling Association (ACA). (2010). *Licensure and certification: Licensure requirements for professional counselors.* Retrieved from http://counseling.org/Counselors/LicensureAndCert.aspx

American Mental Health Counseling Association (AMHCA). (2011). *Standards for the practice of clinical mental health counseling.* Retrieved from http://www.amhca.org/assets/content/AMHCA_Standards_1–26–2012.pdf

American Rehabilitation Counseling Association (ARCA). (2013). *ARCA E-Newsletter – Spring 2013.* Retrieved http://www.arcaweb.org/wp-content/uploads/ARCANewsletter-Spring2013.pdf

American School Counselor Association (ASCA). (2010). *Ethical standards for school counselors.* Alexandria, VA: Author. Retrieved from http://www.schoolcounselor.org/content.asp?contentid=173

American School Counselor Association (ASCA). (2012). *The ASCA national model: A framework for school counseling programs* (3rd. ed.). Alexandria, VA: Author.

Barstow, S., & Terrazas, A. (2012). *Pressure increases on VA to improve mental health treatment. Counseling Today.* Retrieved from http://ct.counseling.org/2012/06/pressure-increases-on-va-to-improve-mental-health-treatment.

Berens, D. E. (2009). Rehabilitation counseling. In B. T. Erford (Ed.), *The ACA encyclopedia of counseling* (pp. 446–448). Alexandria, VA: American Counseling Association.

Bloom, J. (1990). Model legislation for licensed professional counselors. *Journal of Counseling & Development, 68,* 511–522. doi: 10.1002/j.1556-6676.1990.tb01402.x

Bradley, L. J., Sexton, T. L., & Smith, H. B. (2005). The American Counseling Association practice research network (ACA-PRN): A new research tool. *Journal of Counseling & Development, 83,* 488–491. doi:10.1002/j.1556–6678.2005.tb00370.x

Brott, P. E., & Myers, J. E. (1999). Development of professional school counselor identity: A grounded theory. *Professional School Counseling, 2,* 339–334.

Carey, J., & Dimmitt, C. (2008). A model for evidence-based elementary school counseling: Using school data, research, and evaluation to enhance practice. *The Elementary School Journal, 108,* 422–430. doi: 10.1086/589471

Chang, C. Y., Hays, D. G., & Milliken, T. F. (2009). Addressing social justice issues in supervision: A call for client and professional advocacy. *The Clinical Supervisor, 28,* 20–35. doi: 10.1080/07325220902855144

Chen-Hayes, S. F. (2007). The ACCESS questionnaire: Assessing K–12 school counseling programs and interventions to ensure equity and success for every student. *Counseling and Human Development, 39,* 1–10. Retrieved from http://www.highbeam.com/doc/1G1–167932892.html

Chen-Hayes, S. F. (2009). Types of oppression. In American Counseling Association (Ed.), *American Counseling Association encyclopedia of counseling* (pp. 383–384). Alexandria, VA: Author.

Chibbaro, J. S. (2009). Advocacy counseling. In *The ACA encyclopedia of counseling* (pp. 10–11). Alexandria, VA: American Counseling Association.

Chi Sigma Iota (CSI). (n.d.). *Promoting excellence in the profession of counseling.* Retrieved from http://www.csi-net.org/

Colangelo, J. J. (2009). The American Mental Health Counselors Association: Reflection on 30 historic years. *Journal of Counseling & Development, 87,* 234–240. doi: 10.1002/j.1556–6678.2009.tb00572.x

Cole, H. P., & Sarnoff, D. (1980). Creativity and counseling. *Personnel and Guidance Journal, 59,* 140–146. doi: 10.1002/j.2164–4918.1980.tb00518.x

College Board. (2006). *The college counseling sourcebook: Advice and strategies from experienced school counselors* (2nd ed.). Washington, DC: Author.

Commission on Rehabilitation Counselor Certification (CRCC). (2013). *Welcome.* Retrieved from http://www.crccertification.com/

Cook-Greuter, S. R., & Soulen, J. (2007). The developmental perspective in integral counseling. *Counseling & Values, 51,* 180–192. doi: 10.1002/j.2161–007X.2007.tb00077.x

Council for Accreditation of Counseling and Related Educational Programs (CACREP). (2007a). *The CACREP connection: CACREP/CORE merger fails.* Retrieved from http://www.cacrep.org/doc/Connection%20Fall%202007.pdf

Council for Accreditation of Counseling and Related Educational Programs (CACREP). (2007b) *Types of accreditation.* Retrieved from http://www.cacrep.org/typesofacc.html

Council for Accreditation of Counseling and Related Educational Programs (CACREP). (2009). *2009 CACREP standards.* Alexandria, VA: Author. Retrieved from http://www.cacrep.org/template/index.cfm

Council on Rehabilitation Education (CORE). (2013). *CACREP/CORE correspondence: CACREP Ltr to Frank Lane 12-3-12.* Retrieved from http://www.core-rehab.org/Files/Doc/PDF/WhatsNewPDFs/CACREP%20Ltr%20to%20Frank%20Lane%2012-2012.pdf

Eriksen, K. (1997). *Making an impact: A handbook on counselor advocacy.* Washington, DC: Taylor & Francis/Accelerated Development.

Eriksen, K. (1999). Counselor advocacy: A qualitative analysis of leaders' perceptions, organizational activities, and advocacy documents. *Journal of Mental Health Counseling, 21,* 33–40. Retrieved from http://www.eric.ed.gov/ERICWebPortal/search/detailmini.jsp?_nfpb=true_ERICExtSearch_SearchValue_0=EJ592724&ERICExtSearch_SearchType_0=no&accno=EJ592724

Farson, R. (1974). Carl Rogers: Quiet revolutionary. *Education, 95,* 197. Retrieved from http://www .eric.ed.gov/ERICWebPortal/search/detailmini.jsp?_nfpb=true_ERICExtSearch_SearchValue_0 =EJ111851&ERICExtSearch_SearchType_0=no&accno=EJ111851

Gibson, D. M. (2010). Advocacy counseling: Being an effective agent of change for clients. In B. T. Erford (Ed.), *Orientation to the counseling profession: Advocacy, ethics, and essential professional foundations* (pp. 340–358). Upper Saddle River, NJ: Pearson.

Gibson, D. M., Dollarhide, C. T., & Moss, J. M. (2010). Professional identity development: Grounded theory of transformational tasks of new counselors. *Counselor Education and Supervision, 50,* 21–38. doi: 10.1002/j.1556-6978.2010.tb00106.x

Hagedorn, W. (2007). Accredited addiction counseling programs: The future is upon us. *Journal of Addictions & Offender Counseling, 28,* 2–3. doi: 10.1002/j.2161-1874.2007.tb00027.x

Hart, P. J., & Jacobi, M. (1992). *From gatekeeper to advocate: Transforming the role of the school counselor.* New York, NY: College Entrance Examination Board.

Hatch, T., & Bowers, J. (2002). *The ASCA national model: A framework for school counseling programs* (1st ed.). Alexandria, VA: American School Counselor Association.

Herr, E. L. (1985). AACD: An association committed to unity through diversity. *Journal of Counseling & Development, 63,* 395–404. doi: 10.1002/j.1556–6676.1985.tb02819.x

Hof, D. D., Dinsmore, J. A., Barber, S., Suhr, R., & Scofield, T. R. (2009). Advocacy: The T.R.A.I.N.E.R. model. *Journal for Social Action in Counseling & Psychology, 2,* 15–25. Retrieved from http://www.psysr.org/jsacp/hof-v2n1–09_15–28.pdf?q=advocacythe

Hof, D. D., Scofield, T. R., & Dinsmore, J. A. (2006). *Social advocacy: Assessing the impact of training on the development and implementation of advocacy plans.* Retrieved from http:// counselingoutfitters.com/vistas/vistas06/vistas06.47.pdf

Holcomb-McCoy, C., & Chen-Hayes, S. F. (2011). Culturally competent school counselors: Affirming diversity by challenging oppression. In B. T. Erford (Ed.), *Transforming the school counseling profession* (3rd ed.) (pp. 90–109). Boston, MA: Pearson.

International Association of Addictions and Offender Counselors (IAAOC). (n.d.). *About IAAOC.* Retrieved from http://www.iaaoc.org/about.html.

International Association of Marriage and Family Counselors (IAMFC). (n.d.). *2000–2002 strategic plan.* Retrieved from http://www.iamfconline.com/index.php?option=com_content&view=artic le&id=64&Itemid=84

Kaplan, D. M. (2002). Celebrating 50 years of excellence! *Journal of Counseling & Development, 80,* 261. doi: 10.1002/j.1556–6678.2002.tb00189.x

Lambert, S. F. (2010). Supporting IAAOC members: Potential localized services. *Journal of Addictions & Offender Counseling, 31,* 4–9. doi: 10.1002/j.2161-1874.2010.tb00062.x

Leahy, M. J., & Szymanski, E. (1995). Rehabilitation counseling: Evolution and current status. *Journal of Counseling & Development, 74*(2), 163–166. doi: 10.1002/j.1556-6676.1995. tb01843.x

Lee, C. C., & Rodgers, R. A. (2009). Counselor advocacy: Affecting systemic change in the public arena. *Journal of Counseling & Development, 87,* 284–287. doi: 10.1002/j.1556–6678.2009. tb00108.x

Lewis, J. A. (2011). Operationalizing social justice counseling: Paradigm to practice. *Journal of Humanistic Counseling, 50,* 183–191. doi: 10.1002/j.2161-1939.2011.tb00117.

Lewis, J. A., Arnold, M. S., House, R. M., & Toporek, R. (2002). *The American Counseling Association advocacy competencies.* Alexandria, VA: American Counseling Association.

Lopez, F. G. (1987). Erikson and Rogers: The differences do make a difference. *Journal of Counseling & Development, 65,* 241. doi: 10.1002/j.1556-6676.1987.tb01274.x

March, P. A. (1999). Ethical responses to media depictions of mental illness: An advocacy approach. *Journal of Humanistic Counseling, Education, & Development, 38,* 70–79. doi: 10.1002/j.2164– 490X.1999.tb00065.x

McClure, B. A., & Russo, T. R. (1996). The politics of counseling: Looking back and forward. *Counseling & Values, 40,* 162. doi: 10.1002/j.2161- 007X.1996.tb00849.x

Mellin, E. A., Hunt, B., & Nichols, L. M. (2011). Counselor professional identity: Findings and implications for counseling and interprofessional collaboration. *Journal of Counseling & Development, 89,* 140–147. doi: 10.1002/j.1556-6678.2011.tb00071.x

Milsom, A., & Bryant, J. (2006). School counseling departmental web sites: What message do we send? *Professional School Counseling, 10,* 210–216. Retrieved from http://www.biomedsearch.com/article/School-counseling-departmental-web-sites/157032934.html

Murphy, M. J., DeBernardo, C. R., & Shoemaker, W. E. (1998). Impact of managed care on independent practice and professional ethics: A survey of independent practitioners. *Professional Psychology: Research and Practice, 29,* 43–51. doi: 10.1037/0735–7028.29.1.43

Myers, J. E., Sweeney, T. J., & White, V. E. (2002). Advocacy for counseling and counselors: A professional imperative. *Journal of Counseling & Development, 80,* 394–402. doi: 10.1002/j.1556–6678.2002.tb00205.x

Myers, J. E., Sweeney, T. J., & Witmer, J. M. (2000). The wheel of wellness counseling: A holistic model for treatment planning. *Journal of Counseling & Development, 78,* 251–266. doi: 10.1002/j.1556–6676.2000.tb01906.x

NASPA—Student Affairs Administrators in Higher Education (NASPA). (n.d.) *About us.* Retrieved from http://naspa.org/about/default.cfm.

NASPA—Student Affairs Administrators in Higher Education (NASPA). (2010). *Proposal for the consolidation of ACPA & NASPA.* Retrieved from http:/www.naspa.org.proxy.wexler.hunter.cuny.edu/unification/prop.pdf.

National Board for Certified Counselors (NBCC). (2005). *Code of ethics.* Retrieved from http://www.nbcc.org/Assets/Ethics/nbcc-codeofethics.pdf.

National Career Development Association (NCDA). (n.d.). *About NCDA.* Retrieved from http://www.ncda.org/aws/NCDA/pt/sp/about

National Council on Family Relations (NCFR). (2012). *About us.* Retrieved March 26, 2012 from http://www.ncfr.org/about.

National Council on Rehabilitation Education (NCRE). (2013). *About NCRE.* Retrieved from http://www.ncre.org/about.html#overview

National Employment Counseling Association (NECA). (n.d.). *About NECA.* Retrieved from http://www.employmentcounseling.org/

National Organization for Human Services (NOHS). (2009). *What is human services?* Retrieved from http://www.nationalhumanservices.org/index.php?option=com_content&view=article&catid=19%3Asite-content&id=88%3Awhat-is-human- services%3F&Itemid=85

National Rehabilitation Association (NRA). (2009). *About the National Rehabilitation Association.* Retrieved from http://www.nationalrehab.org/cwt/external/wcpages/About/Our_Mission.aspx

National Rehabilitation Counseling Association (NRCA). (2013). *Welcome.* Retrieved from http://nrca-net.org/

Niles, S. (2009). Training career practitioners. *Career Development Quarterly, 57,* 358. doi: 10.1002/j.2161–0045.2009.tb00122.x

Ratts, M. J. (2009). Social justice counseling: Toward the development of a fifth force among counseling paradigms. *The Journal of Humanistic Counseling, Education and Development, 48,* 160–172. doi: 10.1002/j.2161–1939.2009.tb00076.x

Ratts, M., DeKruyf, L., & Chen-Hayes, S. F. (2007). The ACA advocacy competencies: A social justice advocacy framework for professional school counselors. *Professional School Counseling, 11,* 90–97. Retrieved from http://www.eric.cd.gov/ERICWebPortal/search/detailmini.jsp?_nfpb=true&ERICExtSearch_SearchValue_0=EJ817454&ERICExtSearch_SearchType_0=no&accno=EJ817454

Remley, T. P., & Herlihy, B. (2009). *Ethical, legal, and professional issues in counseling* (3rd ed.). Upper Saddle River, NJ: Pearson.

Rudow, H. (2012). ACA speaks out to media regarding need to hire counselors within VA. *Counseling Today.* Retrieved from http://ct.counseling.org/2012/05/aca-speaks-out-to-media-regarding-need-to-hire-counselors-within-va/

Ruffins, P. (2011). NASPA/ACPA merger facing opposition from within. *Diverse Issues in Higher Education, 27,* 8–9. Retrieved from http://www.questia.com/library/1P3–2247608031/naspa-acpa-merger-facing-opposition-from-within

Seiler, G., & Messina, J. J. (1976). Toward professional identity: The dimensions of mental health counseling in perspective. *Journal of Mental Health Counseling, 1,* 3–7. Retrieved from http://coping.us/images/Seiler-Messina_1979_MHC- Identity.pdf

Sikes, A, Walley, C., & Hays, D. G. (2012). A qualitative examination of ethical and legal considerations regarding dating violence. *Journal of Interpersonal Violence, 27,* 1474–1488. doi: 10.1177/0886260511425791

Smith, S. D., Reynolds, C. A., & Rovnak, A. (2009). A critical analysis of the social advocacy movement in counseling. *Journal of Counseling & Development, 87,* 483–491. doi: 10.1002/j.1556–6678.2009.tb00133.x

Sporner, M. L. (2012). Service members and veterans with disabilities: Addressing unique needs through professional rehabilitation counseling. *Journal of Rehabilitation Research & Development, 49*(8), xiii–xvii. doi: 10.1682/JRRD.2012.07.0131

Stiller, A. (1972). Three R's for APGA: Responsive, responsible, restructured. *Personnel & Guidance Journal, 50,* 486–490. doi: 10.1002/j.2164–4918.1972.tb03917.x

Student Press Law Center (2012). *Jennifer Keeton v. Mary Jane Anderson-Wiley.* Retrieved from http://www.splc.org/pdf/Keeton.

Toporek, R. L., Lewis, J. A., & Crethar, H. C. (2009). Promoting systemic change through the ACA advocacy competencies. *Journal of Counseling & Development, 87,* 260–268. doi: 10.1002/j.1556–6678.2009.tb00105.x

Trusty, J., & Brown, D. (2005). Advocacy competencies for professional school counselors. *Professional School Counseling, 8,* 259–265. Retrieved from http://www.eric.ed.gov/ERICWebPortal/search/detailmini.jsp?_nfpb=true_ERICExtSearch_SearchValue_0=EJ710408&ERICExtSearch_SearchType_0=no&accno=EJ710408

Vaartio, H., Leino-Kilpi, H., Salantera, S., & Suominen, T. (2006). Nursing advocacy: How is it defined by patients and nurses, what does it involve and how is it experienced? *Scandinavian Journal of Caring Sciences, 20,* 282–292. doi: 10.1111/j.1471–6712.2006.00406.x

Wester, K., & Lewis, T. F. (2005). *Chi Sigma Iota, it's not just another line on your resume. . . .* Retrieved from http://www.csi-net.org/associations/2151/files/Wester-Lewis%20Paper.pdf

Wiener, F. B. (1948). Oral advocacy. *Harvard Law Review,* 6256–6275. Retrieved from http://www.jstor.org/discover/10.2307/1336399?uid=3739256&uid=2&uid=4&sid=21101430169957

Zinn, H. (2010). *A people's history of the United States.* New York: Harper Perennial.

From the Editors' Chair

Writing a text book is part research—part experience—but mostly the articulation of the author's unique perspective on practice and profession. Each author has made personal decisions on how to organize the book and on what, from the mass of information available, should be included. These decisions reflect the author's bias—personal interest—values and professional identity. We, as editors of the series, have invited each author to respond to the following questions as a way of providing the reader a glimpse into the "person" and not just the product of the author. In the case of this edited work, we are asking the editors to respond as a reflection of their experience producing this work.

It is our hope that these brief reflections will provide a little more insight into our view of our profession—and ourselves as professionals.

RP/NZ

Question: There is certainly an abundance of insightful points found within this text. But if you were asked to identify a single point or theme from all that is presented that you would hope would stand out and stick with the reader, what would that point or theme be?

Professional counseling is a comprehensive profession that has evolved over a century. It is safe to say that professional counseling will continue to evolve and will require professional counselors to stay current with the contextual changes in order to promote quality service to clients. Each professional counselor, including you, directly and indirectly contributes to and is affected by this professional evolution. Therefore, it is vital that you stay active in and involved with the counseling profession to witness and be part of this thriving profession.

Question: In the text there is a great deal of research cited—theories presented. Could you share from your own experience how the information presented within the text may actually look—or take form—in practice?

In the process of developing this textbook, we, the contributing authors and coeditors, focused not only on highlighting the theoretical concepts and empirical evidence but also, drawing from our experiences, on providing practical aspects of professional counseling to facilitate readers' understanding of the profession. You will find that the information and examples provided in this textbook are easy to understand and help you visualize how the information is manifested in real-life professional counseling practice. In addition, you will find that reflection exercises and case illustrations present an opportunity for you to apply those concepts and information you learn in each chapter. These mechanisms are designed to prepare you to function as a professional counselor in various counseling practices and settings.

Question: As editors of this text—what might this book reveal about your own professional identity?

This textbook is a remarkable reflection of our strong professional counseling identity. As you will see in this text, all the contributing authors and editors communicate a clear sense of their professional counseling identity through a strong presentation of the awareness, knowledge, and skills used in professional counseling. You will sense that we are proud and feel privileged to be professional counselors. We hope the information in this text will inspire you to start examining and developing your professional identity.

Question: What final prescription—direction—might you offer your readers as they continue in their journey toward becoming professional counselors?

It is important that you as a future professional counselor continue to promote and strengthen your own professional identity. Ultimately, you, along with other professional counselors, are responsible to represent, promote, strengthen, and advocate for professional counseling. Your professional identity and continued advocacy will help move the counseling profession in a positive direction, resulting in better quality of service for clients.

Appendix

Navigating a Graduate Program in Counseling

Varunee Faii Sangganjanavanich
Cynthia A. Reynolds

The decision to pursue a master's degree in the field of counseling requires a significant investment of resources such as time and financial commitment. You may have already moved away from home and loved ones or given up a high-paying job to be in school. You and your loved ones may have already made some sacrifices in order for you to be able to enroll in a graduate program, and to complete your graduate work may have become one of your most important life priorities. Although you have made many sacrifices and have planned to finish the program and to assume your role as a professional counselor, it is important that you maximize your educational experience while pursuing a counseling degree.

In this appendix, we offer ways that you can navigate through the many steps of your graduate program, including developing your program plan, progressing through the program, and preparing yourself to enter the counseling profession. The information offered here is general information about a graduate program in counseling that may apply to the structure of your graduate program. We review strategies and resources that can enhance your academic success. Reflection exercises and case illustrations will facilitate your academic and professional planning during your graduate study.

Exercise A.1

EXPLORING YOUR SACRIFICES

Directions: Needless to say, you have made many sacrifices to pursue a graduate program in counseling. First, list all the personal and professional sacrifices you have made to date. Second, list all the personal and professional sacrifices your loved ones (e.g., family members, friends) have made for you to date. Next, identify similarities and differences between your sacrifices and those of your loved ones. Be sure that you take a close look, cognitively and emotionally, at this comparison. Finally, spend at least 20 minutes to discuss the information you identified and discovered with at least one person who is important to you. Questions during this discussion may include, but are not limited to, the following:

1. How did you feel when you first learned that I entered a graduate program in counseling?

2. How come you have made this (these) sacrifice(s) for me?

3. What do you expect from me (e.g., shared time, financial contribution) during my study?

4. I realize that you have made many sacrifices for me, and I am wondering how I can make this process fair to you as much as possible.

5. What are three most effective ways that we can ask for each other's support?

PLANNING THE ROAD MAP: ENTERING A GRADUATE PROGRAM IN COUNSELING

When traveling with a destination in mind, it is important for you to have a road map to ensure that you understand the routes and arrive at the destination in a timely manner or according to the plan you have developed. A similar concept is applied to your road map for the graduate program. Many aspects of your graduate program are essential and require you to map out your educational plan and goals. To develop the road map during your journey in your graduate program in counseling, important documents can help facilitate your academic, professional, and personal success. Those documents include the graduate bulletin and program handbook.

Graduate Bulletin

Your university has a graduate bulletin that contains information regarding all graduate programs, relevant departments, schools, colleges, and lists of graduate program requirements and courses, as well as institutional policies, rules, and regulations. As when you are traveling, before you visit a new country, it is always wise to read about that country to learn about its culture, language, climate, laws, and people in order to avoid potential difficulties you might encounter during travel or when you arrive at the destination. Think of your university's graduate bulletin as the travelogue for your journey in higher education. It may be available as a paper copy or as an electronic file that you can easily access. As you immerse yourself in a new culture, in this case a graduate program, you may find that ignorance of the facts of the program could place your academic and professional successes at significant risk. It is important that you recognize that it is your responsibility, as a new resident in a graduate school, department, and program, to be aware of the essential information and to follow the rules, regulations, and policies of your institution.

Exercise A.2

OBTAINING THE GRADUATE BULLETIN

Directions: First, obtain and review the graduate bulletin of your institution. Most schools now post the graduate bulletin in an electronic format, which can be downloaded through your institution's graduate school website. Second, make a list of the five most important facts you discovered about your institution and counseling program that you did not know before reviewing the bulletin. Next, discuss with a classmate, and identify five facts that your classmate has discovered. Then, compare the facts you discovered with those of your classmate: Are they similar or different? Questions you may use during the discussion could include the following:

1. What surprises you the most about your discoveries and your classmate's discoveries?

2. How will these discoveries impact your personal, professional, and academic plans and goals while you are in the graduate program?

3. Within your graduate department or school, who would be a person that you can talk with when you have any questions about these discoveries (e.g., policy related concerns)?

Program Handbook

Whereas the graduate bulletin helps you understand general information about your institutional requirements, the program handbook, often referred to as student handbook or program student handbook, provides you with detailed information about your department and program, including their organizational structures (e.g., departmental/program faculty, divisions/parts), program requirements (e.g., number of credit hours), and rules/policies (e.g., student grievance policy). It is important that you secure and review these specific requirements as soon as you begin your graduate program, because this information can be helpful for you as an informed consumer. The Council for Accreditation of Counseling and Related Educational Programs (CACREP, 2009) requires that counseling and counselor education programs provide a program handbook to all students and allows them to utilize this handbook as a part of the program orientation. That means it is your right as a graduate student in a counseling program to obtain and review the program handbook. When you have questions about statements in the program handbook or discover discrepancies between the program handbook and information you receive from other sources (e.g., other students, program's web page), it is important that you contact your faculty adviser in order to clarify these statements and requirements.

Exercise A.3

MEETING WITH YOUR FACULTY ADVISER

Directions: To achieve your academic goals, it is important that you meet with your graduate faculty adviser early on in your program. This exercise offers steps you can take to facilitate your meeting with your adviser. Here are the steps:

- Find out who your assigned graduate faculty adviser is,
- Make an appointment with your adviser to complete your program plan,
- Obtain and review your student program handbook to understand program requirements,
- Outline questions and concerns that you would like to discuss with your adviser,
- Meet with your adviser and ask questions that you have, and
- Thank your adviser for meeting with you.

Approximately half of graduate-level counseling programs across the United States are accredited by CACREP. The curriculum of each counseling program must meet the CACREP requirements and is further determined by the licensure requirements of the state where the program is located. As a result, the number of semester credit hours of these programs varies—generally ranging from 48 to 60 semester credit hours—and may further vary depending on the counseling specialty for which you are preparing. For example, school counseling programs typically require fewer semester credit hours than clinical mental health counseling programs due to the difference in professional practices.

Typically, in the program handbook, your institution provides a sequence of all coursework you will be required to take during your graduate program. An example of a course sequence can assist you in the process of determining your plan of study. At most universities, a plan of study is a document that is signed by the student and adviser and that serves as a contract between you and your institution. This document indicates that if you fulfill all of the program requirements, you will be eligible for a degree from the university in the specific program area outlined in your plan. In addition to signing the document, it is important to discover the time limit that your university places on your degree. You may have a six-year period in which you will need to complete all coursework and program-related requirements in order to obtain your degree. You may find that transferring credits for previous coursework can significantly reduce your six-year timeline for completion. Because many programs or institutions have exceptions to this timeline, you should also investigate whether it is ever possible to petition for an extension of time for degree completion. Although you probably cannot imagine that you would ever take more than six years or whatever time period your university allots, unpredictable life events can occur that may end up being detours on your particular journey. Knowing the parameters can assist you if you ever are faced with making such a decision.

PROGRAM ORIENTATION

Most counseling programs will host an orientation for new students. This is your opportunity to meet and greet program and department faculty, meet the department chair, connect with other new students, set up an appointment to meet individually with your specific faculty adviser, and learn more about the functioning of the department, college, and university. Many times, this is also an opportunity for you to learn about your institution's resources, such as its library, writing center, career services, and health care clinic.

Orientations are designed to help students learn important information relative to their success in their specific program. During the orientation, you may hear other students ask questions that you had never even thought of yourself and find that the answers are helpful and informative. If your program does not have a face-to-face orientation, make sure that you download the video or other information from the department or program website.

In addition to the program orientation, your university may have other orientations available to students. You may need to use student services offices (e.g., graduate school, registrar office, writing center, library) during your time of study. Knowing your way around the campus may increase your comfort level and your confidence in the program and institution.

Exercise A.4

GETTING INFORMATION ABOUT THE PROGRAM ORIENTATION

Directions: It is common for counseling programs to provide a student/program orientation. You need to get information about the student/program orientation that is available to you. Your department or program may require you to sign up for the orientation. Therefore, it is important that you search for information about the orientation (e.g., when, where) once you have been accepted to the program.

Exercise A.5

STUDENT SERVICES OFFICES ON YOUR CAMPUS

Directions: Your institution (e.g., college, university) generally provides many educational services that help enhance your graduate study. These educational services may include career services, a counseling center, a writing center, an office of accessibility services, and an office of international studies. You are entitled to these resources, as your institution charges you for these resources through your student fees. Once you enter your counseling program, you should inquire for information about student service offices on your campus and review services provided by each office in order to be knowledgeable of and to utilize these services when needed.

THE TRAVEL GUIDE: YOUR FACULTY ADVISER

Shortly after your admission to graduate school, you are generally assigned a faculty adviser. Depending on your institution, you are usually expected to meet with your adviser to design your program of graduate study. It is wise to schedule that appointment in a timely fashion. It is helpful if you can determine which method of communication your adviser prefers—e-mail, phone calls, face-to-face visit, or Skype. You can also find the times that the faculty member has posted as office hours. It is essential to check in with your adviser, especially when you get conflicting information from other sources (e.g., announcements, fellow students).

Some of the factors that you may consider discussing with your adviser include, but are not limited to, the following: previous relevant graduate coursework, full-time or part-time study, summer attendance, financial aid and scholarships, ability to commit to practicum and internship, personal and professional goals, and electives or additional certifications. You may also prepare questions that are relevant to your program, college, or university to discuss with your adviser in order to have a better understanding about their functions that may affect your study. Other advising issues may address taking comprehensive exams, registering for a practicum and internship, licensure exams, licensure/certification processes, and graduation clearance.

Developing a positive relationship with your adviser is important, because she not only serves as your travel guide, but also mentors you as you progress along your journey in the counseling program, and, in many cases, after you graduate. For example, you may need to ask your adviser to write a letter of recommendation on your behalf for an internship or employment application. There are some informal rules of etiquette that might assist you in that process. First, give the recommendation writer warning about what you are asking her to do and ample time to do it. Second, let her know specifically whether you are looking for a blanket reference for a portfolio or if you are looking for a recommendation for a specific job. If the recommendation needs to be sent to a particular person, provide an accurate name, title, and address as well as a copy of the job posting so that the writer can tailor the letter to better highlight your strengths for that position. Finally, it is only good manners to thank the writer and to inform her if you ended up getting the job.

As noted in this section, your graduate faculty adviser can be a helpful resource who can facilitate your academic success in your graduate program. There are many benefits of meeting with your graduate faculty adviser and discussing questions or concerns that you have throughout your graduate study. Not only can your faculty adviser provide suggestions or advice related to academia, but also she can help mentor you to develop a pathway to professional success. Therefore, it is critical to develop a positive relationship with your graduate faculty adviser in order to pave the road for your academic and professional success.

CASE ILLUSTRATION A.1

FACULTY ADVISER CAN HELP

Sally is a first-year graduate student in counseling program at a small university. Sally is entering her second semester of her graduate study, and she finds herself getting a little lost. Sally relocated for her graduate study after staying home with her parents throughout her undergraduate years. During her first semester in the program, Sally made some friends in the program and was able to work on course projects with them. Sally believed having friends helped her with adjustment issues (e.g., loneliness). Things were going well with Sally until she entered the second semester.

This semester, Sally is having trouble concentrating in class and is unable to complete her class assignments on time. Sally told her friends that she finds current courses challenging, because they require her to improve her note-taking, reading, and writing skills. With a strong determination to pursue and complete graduate school, Sally still continues coming to classes, although she feels behind in all courses. Last week, one of her course instructors approached her and asked, "How are things going with you?" Sally answered, "Everything is fine." However, the instructor said, "I am concerned about your tardiness and written exam grades. It is important that you come to class on time, and when you are in class, you need to pay full attention to the material being presented. You also need to study for the exams."

After the conversation with the course instructor, Sally felt very discouraged and was ready to quit her graduate program. When she voiced this concern to her friends, they suggested that she discuss this matter with her adviser, whom Sally never met. Sally decided to meet with her adviser, Dr. Stanley, and express her concerns to him.

Sally told Dr. Stanley she had nowhere and no one to turn to for advice on dealing with the stress of graduate study. She said she did not understand the difference between undergraduate and graduate studies. She could not accept the feelings of failure in graduate school after being a long-time honor student during her undergraduate study. Dr. Stanley listened and helped normalize the situations that Sally has experienced. Dr. Stanley also described to Sally the difference between undergraduate and graduate study. For example, Dr. Stanley mentioned, "Unlike undergraduate courses, graduate courses have a smaller class size, which facilitates in-depth discussion about particular topics. This requires students to critically think about the topic and actively participate in the discussion." In addition to giving his support to Sally, Dr. Stanley discussed other resources offered on campus (e.g., counseling center, writing center) that may help Sally cope with her concerns.

By talking with Dr. Stanley, her graduate faculty adviser, Sally felt more empowered and supported to continue her graduate study and to pursue her career as a professional counselor.

BROADENING YOUR HORIZON THROUGH NETWORKING

Making connections with your adviser is just one part of your journey in graduate school. There are other connections that can contribute to your academic and professional successes. Through networking, you establish personal and professional contacts and relationships that potentially facilitate your growth and development. Those contacts and relationships include reaching out to fellow students; joining professional groups, chapters, and organizations; and volunteering at agencies in your community.

Forming connections with other students will help to provide you with companionship and peer support as well as plant seeds for networking in the future. One of the unique aspects of being a graduate student is that no one will completely understand the experience except the other students who are working on their master's degrees as well. You can cultivate relationships with fellow students to provide notes, materials, and information for each other when one of you is unable to attend class or misses an event because of illness. You may also form lifelong friendships that will continue to delight you for years to come. You may also build relationships with faculty and eventually serve as an internship site supervisor for other students from your alma mater.

Joining national, state, regional, and/or local professional chapters, groups, and organizations can promote your professional development (e.g., obtaining information about licensures and certifications) and your identity development (e.g., learning about roles and functions of professional counselors). Many graduate students benefit from an opportunity to acculturate themselves to the counseling profession by becoming members of the counseling chapters, groups, and organizations. More information about professional counseling organizations can be found in Chapter 10 of this textbook.

Last, you may want to consider engaging in volunteer experience in the area of your interest. Not only can a volunteer experience be rewarding, it also can be helpful for you in terms of gathering necessary career information from professional counselors working in the field, and gaining knowledge and skills as you immerse yourself in a specific setting or environment. This opportunity also gives you an opportunity to engage with local professional counselors in your field of interest and may promote your chances of obtaining a practicum and/or internship.

RECORDING YOUR JOURNEY

Travelers' diaries are notes that document the journey. As a graduate student, it is essential to find a way to record and store the important aspects of your time in graduate school. Because you do not know what the future will bring, documentation can one day come in handy. For your own protection, you need to begin by making sure you have copies of all documents you have signed in relation to your study, such as items documenting your program course of study, grades, and financial aid or assistantship. In addition to these legal documents, there are other important documents that you may consider keeping, including a syllabus from each course, course materials (e.g., books, notes), and acknowledgment or recognition of your achievements (e.g., award, portfolio) during your graduate program. These documents can be helpful as you move further along in the program and enter the counseling profession.

Keeping copies of all syllabi for classes you have taken helps you keep track of your study and also helps you if you ever move to another state or are trying to seek a different licensure (e.g., licensed professional counselor vs. marriage and family therapist). The licensing board may require proof that a certain course you took covered specific objectives in order for your application for the different license to be approved. Having that kind of evidence could save you time and financial resources.

Course materials are also important to keep for your immediate and future reference. After you complete your coursework, you will be engaging in other academic and professional activities, such as preparing for a master's comprehensive examination and state licensure or for a national certification examination. Therefore, it is critical that you keep track of textbooks, course materials, and other artifacts of your work needed for study or documentation.

Exercise A.6

DEVELOPING A SYSTEM TO KEEP YOUR DOCUMENTS

Directions: It is important that you collect all documents related to your academic and professional performance throughout your graduate study. For this exercise, you are to do the following:

- Locate a specific area in your residence (e.g., home, apartment) to store your documents
- Select materials and equipment to organize your documents (e.g., cabinet, binder)

- Create an organizational system with different categories (e.g., course syllabi, grades, evaluations, accomplishments)
- Place each document in the category to which it pertains
- Review your documents regularly and keep them up to date

This system of keeping and managing your educational and professional records will not only help you stay organized throughout your graduate study but also assist you in your professional career once you complete your counseling degree.

As you plan your roadmap during your graduate study journey, it is important to recognize that things may not go according to plan. There are many variables, both personal and professional, that may alter your goals or may force you to readjust your goals (e.g., obtaining new positions, unexpected academic performance, financial constraints, having newborns during your graduate program). In the next section, you will have a glance at situations that may present challenges to your graduate study and ways to cope with them.

CHALLENGES ALONG THE WAY

Challenges may emerge from plan changes, lack of resources, and unforeseen roadblocks. At times, travelers may face frustration, disappointment, and hopelessness. However, challenges can also be viewed as opportunities. Many challenges introduce new avenues for personal and professional growth that facilitates your outlook and/or coping skills. For example, you may find yourself getting frustrated when you learn that you did not do well on your comprehensive examination. But the results of your comprehensive examination provide an opportunity for you to study harder and longer in order to prepare for the national or state licensure examination.

Challenges can also make you aware that your progress is being assessed during the journey. During your graduate program, your progress in the program will be assessed. How this is done will vary from institution to institution. Classroom performance may be measured through outcome-based assessment of your performance at certain checkpoints along the way. Depending on your university, a certain grade point average (such as a 3.0) must be maintained in order to be active in the program. A passing score on a comprehensive exam or portfolio assessment may determine whether or not you graduate. Faculty may meet and do a fitness assessment on each master's student. Your readiness to enter a practicum or internship will be evaluated based on how you perform in the prerequisite classes.

How you behave in classes is monitored, as well as how you get along with other students, staff, and faculty. Counseling programs attempt to advocate for and balance the needs of each individual student while also functioning as gatekeepers to the profession, so they can protect the public from counselors who are impaired, unethical, or incompetent. It is important to read the program handbook to determine exactly what the parameters of evaluation are for students.

Assessing Your Progress and Managing Challenges

Students typically monitor their academic progress by reviewing grades on their assignments and coursework, talking to course instructors, and meeting with graduate faculty advisers. These resources not only help you assess your improvements and any setbacks you may encounter, but they also provide an early opportunity for you to determine your direction or course of action during your graduate study. For instance, it is a good idea to meet with your graduate adviser regularly (once a semester) in order to review your coursework grades and to discuss your experience as a graduate student.

In addition to the aforementioned resources, you may seek professional support. Most universities have counseling centers that have full-time licensed mental health professionals who are available to provide assistance for students experiencing emotional or behavioral concerns. Generally, this would not be the same facility your department uses to train students in practica, as confidentiality would be difficult to maintain, and dual relationships could put you at risk as a student in your program or as a client. In addition to individual counseling, group counseling services on a variety of topics might be available.

Your instructor or adviser might suggest that you pursue counseling for yourself if you are struggling in the academic or personal/social areas. In fact, many professional counselors have received personal counseling themselves. As you progress through your counseling program, life events could happen that impact your ability to be fully present with clients or attend to your coursework in a focused manner. You can demonstrate self-care by seeking help for yourself and experience the benefits of counseling firsthand.

Your student handbook or course syllabi may have statements of expectations of student behavior, so that students know what the standards of behavior are in the classroom. Not taking responsibility to read these standards does not give you the right to claim ignorance of them. If you find yourself in a situation where you think that you have been unfairly judged or your rights have been violated, there are policies and procedures for filing a grievance. A first step might be to try to resolve the issue informally with faculty, your adviser, or your department administrator.

It is important that you maximize use of resources that are available to you in order to enrich your educational experience during your graduate study. The earlier you can access and utilize these resources, the better you can promote your academic performance during your graduate study. Although challenges may be presented at some point in time during your graduate program, it is critical to remember that they can become an opportunity for you to learn about yourself and your environment as well as to grow personally and professionally.

CASE ILLUSTRATION A.2

WHEN A CHALLENGE PRESENTS ITSELF

John is now in practicum after completing a year of counseling coursework. Before entering practicum, John perceived his counseling skills as superior to those of other students. He felt that he did better than other students in role-plays and mock counseling sessions. Many students also complimented John on his nonverbal counseling skills—that is, he seemed very empathetic toward others. However, his perceptions have shifted since the beginning of the third week in practicum.

John has a difficult time receiving feedback from his supervisor and classmates. Feedback he received indicated that he should avoid giving advice, listen to the clients more, be open to the clients' cultural backgrounds, and end the session on time. John tried to improve in those areas; however, being open to the client's cultural background presented challenges to John.

John believes a higher power does not exist, and individuals should rely on themselves as resources rather than on a higher power. One of John's clients was turned off by John's comment about her spiritual belief. The client asked God for forgiveness after having multiple affairs. Because she couldn't forgive herself, she sought counseling as another source of support. However, John told the client, "God can't forgive you. Nobody can. You have to forgive yourself. Everything is up to you." After learning of this incident, John's supervisor told him that his comment was inappropriate, and he should respect the client's belief. John argued that the goal of counseling is for the client to be an agent of change, and his comment was meant to help the client meet that goal.

While John believed he had done nothing wrong, his supervisor and instructor believed that John should be more open-minded with respect to the client's experiences and backgrounds, and they told John that he would need to do more "work" to foster his own personal and professional growth and development. Although John disagreed, he had no choice but to proceed with the supervisor's and instructor's requests. First, John sought counseling to resolve issues of being rigid and insensitive to other's beliefs that were different from his. Second, John met with his faculty adviser to obtain different perspectives on providing culturally appropriate counseling services to diverse populations. Last, John spent time with other students whose cultural backgrounds were different from his own.

After two months of engaging in this process to foster self-growth, John reported to his supervisor that he had gained more confidence to serve people who are different from him.

REACHING THE FINISH LINE

As you grow closer to achieving your goal of a graduate degree in counseling, you will need to make a decision as to whether you will walk through the graduation ceremony or simply have your diploma mailed to you. Depending on when your graduation is scheduled, you may receive only a blank diploma until grades are posted and calculated. Although objections to the costs of attending graduation are legitimate, there can be great joy in taking time to celebrate your incredible achievement. Graduation is sometimes known as commencement, which implies not only the completion of a degree but also the commencing of a professional career. The graduation ceremony can be viewed as a rite of passage, where you can be appropriately honored by friends, family, peers, and the faculty who have come along with you on this journey. It can be quite rewarding to take the time to stop and celebrate what you have achieved through your persistence and hard work. You are now ready to step out into your professional career and put into practice all that you have learned.

Your final steps will include fulfilling any additional licensure requirements and submitting your material to the counselor licensing board. Generally, there are two major components for licensure: educational requirements and clinical requirements. The educational requirement refers to standard academic coursework that provides minimum knowledge for professional counselors to serve clients. The clinical requirement refers to standard clinical coursework that enables counselors in training to develop the clinical counseling competencies necessary to work with clients. To be licensed, you will need to fulfill both requirements and other requirements indicated by the licensing board, such as passing the licensure examination.

Some licensure boards allow students who are enrolled in an internship or are in the last semester of their program to take the state or national licensure examination. That means you can take the examination before graduation. After you pass the examination, you can begin collecting direct and indirect clinical/service hours toward your professional counselor license. Once you complete collecting clinical/service hours, you are another step closer to being licensed as a professional counselor. While, in some states, you can be licensed right away after passing the state examination (e.g., National Counselor Examination) and completing clinical/service hours, others may require you to take another licensure exam (e.g., National Clinical Mental Health Counselor Examination). Therefore, it is important that you review and understand the professional counselor licensure guidelines in your state in order to plan ahead of time and feel prepared to start your professional journey.

KEYSTONES

Generally, individuals enter a graduate program with little knowledge of what graduate study entails. Graduate study can be time- and labor-intensive for many individuals, and it requires individuals to utilize both internal resources (e.g., motivation, determination) and external resources (e.g., graduate faculty adviser, student service offices) in order to achieve academic excellence.

It is important that you

- Review the information in your program handbook;
- Understand the policies, rules, and regulations of your academic institution;
- Meet with your academic/faculty adviser in order to discuss questions and/or concerns you may have throughout your graduate study;
- Develop a plan that serves as a road map to guide you through your graduate program; and
- Network with fellow students in order to promote your career opportunities and professional connections.

ADDITIONAL RESOURCES

Capuzzi, D., & Gross, D. R. (2009). Introduction to the counseling profession (5th ed.). Boston, MA: Pearson.

Council for Accreditation of Counseling and Related Educational Programs (CACREP). (2009). *2009 CACREP standards.* Alexandria, VA: Author. Retrieved from www.cacrep.org/template/index.cfm

Erford, B. T. (2010). *Orientation to the counseling profession: Advocacy, ethics, and essential professional foundations.* Boston, MA: Pearson.

Gerig, M. (2007). *Foundations for mental health and community counseling: An introduction to the profession.* Upper Saddle River, NJ: Pearson.

Hackney, H., & Cormier, S. (2004). *The professional counselor: A guide to helping* (4th ed.). Boston, MA: Allyn & Bacon.

Hazler, R. J., & Kottler, J. A. (2005). *The emerging professional counselor: Student dreams to professional realities* (2nd ed.). Alexandria, VA: American Counseling Association.

About the Contributors

Stuart F. Chen-Hayes, PhD, is an associate professor and program coordinator in the Counselor Education/School Counseling Program at City University of New York Lehman College in New York City, New York. He has worked in addictions, college student affairs, couple and family, school, and sexuality counseling settings. He is a past president of Counselors for Social Justice and the North Atlantic Region Association of Counselor Educators and Supervisors. He has written 50 refereed publications and delivered over 200 presentations focused on transforming school and college access counseling, LBGTQ issues, and multicultural and social justice issues. (Chapter 12)

Elysia Clemens, PhD, is an associate professor of counselor education and supervision at the University of Northern Colorado in Greeley, Colorado. She serves as the coordinator of UNC's CACREP-accredited master's degree programs in school counseling; clinical mental health counseling; and couples, marriage, and family counseling/therapy. (Chapter 5)

Stephen V. Flynn, PhD, is an assistant professor of counselor education and supervision at Plymouth State University in Plymouth, New Hampshire. He is a licensed professional counselor with supervision endorsement in the states of Colorado and South Dakota. He is a licensed marriage and family therapist in the states of Colorado and New Hampshire. He has authored and coauthored publications in the fields of professional counseling and counselor education and supervision. (Chapter 3)

Tara Hill, PhD, is an assistant professor of counseling at Old Dominion University in Norfolk, Virginia. She is a licensed professional clinical counselor with supervisory endorsement in the states of Ohio and Virginia. She has worked as a counselor in community mental health for 10 years. (Chapter 5)

Victoria E. Kress, PhD, is a professor in the counseling program at Youngstown State University in Youngstown, Ohio. She is a licensed professional clinical counselor and has over 20 years of clinical experience working in various settings, such as community mental health centers, hospitals, residential treatment facilities, private practice, and college counseling centers. She has coedited a book on the DSM and has over 70 peer-reviewed publications, and she has made over 100 presentations. (Chapter 11)

A. Stephen Lenz, PhD, is an assistant professor in the Department of Counseling, Educational Psychology and Research at the University of Memphis in Memphis, Tennessee. He is a licensed professional counselor in the state of Texas and a licensed professional counselor–mental health service provider in the state of Tennessee. His scholarly interests include holistic approaches to counselor preparation and counseling outcome research. (Chapter 9)

Melissa Odegard-Koester, PhD, is an assistant professor of counseling at Southeast Missouri State University in Cape Girardeau, Missouri. She is also a licensed professional counselor in Missouri. She offers services for clients with a variety of mental health concerns. She has authored or coauthored numerous publications, presentations, and workshops in the field of counseling and counselor education. (Chapter 7)

Matthew J. Paylo, PhD, is an assistant professor and director of the student affairs and the college-counseling program at Youngstown State University in Youngstown, Ohio. He has over 10 years of clinical experience in various settings, including community mental health centers, prisons, hospitals, residential treatment facilities, and college counseling centers. He has authored or coauthored numerous publications and presentations in the field of counseling and counselor education. (Chapter 11)

Mark Pope, EdD, is a professor in and chair of the Department of Counseling and Family Therapy at the University of Missouri–Saint Louis in Saint Louis, Missouri. He has been president of the American Counseling Association; National Career Development Association; Association for Lesbian, Gay, Bisexual, and Transgender Issues in Counseling; and Society for the Psychological Study of Lesbian, Gay, Bisexual, and Transgender Issues (Division 44). He is an author of numerous books, book chapters, and professional journal articles; has given presentations at international, national, regional, state, and local conferences; and was the editor of *The Career Development Quarterly*. He has written extensively on various aspects of counseling, including the career development of ethnic, racial, and sexual minorities; violence in the schools; teaching career counseling; psychological testing; international issues in counseling; and the history of and public policy issues in counseling. (Chapter 2)

Verl T. Pope, EdD, is a professor of counseling and chair of the Department of Counseling, Social Work and Leadership at Northern Kentucky University in Highland Heights, Kentucky. He is a licensed professional counselor in the state of Missouri and the Commonwealth of Kentucky. He is nationally certified as a counselor, a mental health counselor, and a clinical supervisor. He has served or currently serves on a number of state and national committees, including seven years on the Missouri State Committee for Professional Counselors. He maintains a number of professional memberships, has published in professional venues, and has given many presentations at local, state, national, and international meetings. (Chapter 7)

Jake J. Protivnak, PhD, is an associate professor and chair of the Department of Counseling, Special Education, and School Psychology at Youngstown State University in Youngstown, Ohio. He is a licensed professional clinical counselor with supervisor endorsement in the state of Ohio. He is past-president of the Ohio Counseling Association. He has authored or coauthored numerous counseling publications and made numerous presentations. He is a past-president of the Ohio Counseling Association. (Chapter 11)

Manivong J. Ratts, PhD, is an associate professor in the Department of Counseling and School Psychology at Seattle University in Seattle, Washington. He is past-president of Counselors for Social Justice, a division of the American Counseling Association, and founder of Seattle University Counselors for Social Justice, an advocacy organization that addresses issues of equity impacting individuals, communities, and schools. His writing and research is in the area of social justice and social justice advocacy. His teaching, scholarship, and service promote social justice in the counseling profession and encourage mental health professionals to consider the place of social justice in counseling. (Chapter 6)

Cynthia A. Reynolds, PhD, is a professor, school counseling coordinator, and assistant chair in the department of counseling at The University of Akron in Akron, Ohio. She is a licensed professional clinical counselor with supervisor endorsement and certified school counselor in the state of Ohio. She is credited with numerous presentations and publications in the field of counseling and counselor education. (Chapters 8 and Appendix)

Claudia Sadler-Gerhardt, PhD, is an associate professor of counseling at Ashland Seminary/University in Ashland, Ohio. She is a licensed professional clinical counselor in the state of Ohio. She has authored articles and presented at professional counseling conferences in the areas of ethics, grief, compassion fatigue, and breast cancer survivorship. She is a past president of Ohio Association for Spiritual, Ethical, and Religious Values in Counseling (ASERVIC). She currently serves as a board member of ASERVIC. (Chapter 8)

Varunee Faii Sangganjanavanich, PhD, is an assistant professor of counseling at The University of Akron in Akron, Ohio. She is a licensed professional clinical counselor with supervisor endorsement in the state of Ohio and a licensed professional counselor in the state of Colorado. She has held many leadership positions in state and national counseling organizations. She has authored or coauthored numerous publications and presentations in the field of counseling and counselor education. (Chapters 1, 3, 7, 9, and Appendix)

Christopher Schmidt, PhD, is an assistant professor of counseling at Villanova University in Pennsylvania. He is a licensed professional counselor and licensed marriage and family therapist in both Virginia and Pennsylvania. He has been working in the fields of education and counseling for over 15 years and has particular research and teaching interests focused on counselor development. (Chapter 4)

Robert C. Schwartz, PhD, is a professor of counseling at The University of Akron in Akron, Ohio. He is a licensed professional clinical counselor with supervisor endorsement in the state of Ohio. He has authored or coauthored over 50 publications and given more than 40 presentations in the mental health field, ranging from mental illness diagnosis and treatment to countertransference and mindfulness. (Chapter 10)

Adria Shipp, PhD, is a licensed professional counselor and licensed school counselor in North Carolina. She is currently developing school-based and school-linked programs for a federally qualified community health center based in Carrboro, North Carolina. She regularly teaches at the University of Northern Colorado and the University of North Carolina at Greensboro. (Chapter 5)

Cynthia T. Walley, PhD, is an assistant professor of counseling as well as the school counseling coordinator at Hunter College of the City University of New York. She is a licensed professional counselor as well as a nationally certified counselor. She is actively involved in professional advocacy by holding positions in regional and state counseling organizations. She has authored or coauthored publications and presentations on school counseling, mental health, and counselor preparation. (Chapter 12)

Alexa Wayman is a graduate student in counseling at Seattle University in Seattle, Washington. Her clinical experience involves working in an alternative education K–8 school and with children and families in a low-income neighborhood in Seattle. She is actively pursuing ways to engage in research and practice to respond to the needs of marginalized communities, including ELL student dropout and retention rates and causal factors. (Chapter 6)

Index

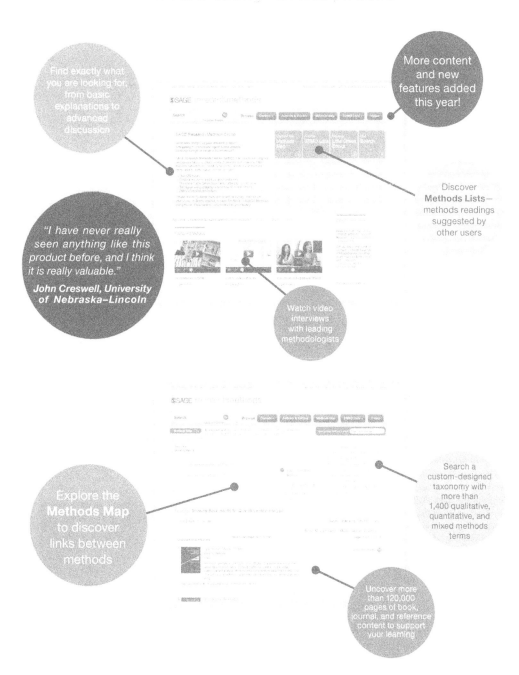

SAGE researchmethods

The essential online tool for researchers from the world's leading methods publisher

Find exactly what you are looking for, from basic explanations to advanced discussion

More content and new features added this year!

Discover **Methods Lists**—methods readings suggested by other users

"I have never really seen anything like this product before, and I think it is really valuable."

John Creswell, University of Nebraska–Lincoln

Watch video interviews with leading methodologists

Explore the **Methods Map** to discover links between methods

Search a custom-designed taxonomy with more than 1,400 qualitative, quantitative, and mixed methods terms

Uncover more than 120,000 pages of book, journal, and reference content to support your learning

Find out more at
www.sageresearchmethods.com

CPSIA information can be obtained
at www.ICGtesting.com
Printed in the USA
JSHW030944210920
8073JS00001BA/3

9 781452 240701